Outlook 2000 VBA Programmer's Reference

Dwayne Gifford

Wrox Press Ltd. ®

Outlook 2000 VBA Programmer's Reference

Published by Wrox Press Ltd. Arden House, 1102 Warwick Road, Acocks Green, Birmingham, B27 6BH.

Printed in USA

ISBN 1-861002-53-X

Trademark Acknowledgements

Wrox has endeavored to provide trademark information about all the companies and products mentioned in this book by the appropriate use of capitals. However, Wrox cannot guarantee the accuracy of this information.

Credits

Author
Dwayne Gifford

Additional Material
Joe Sutphin

Development Editor
Dominic Shakeshaft

Editors
Susan Holmes
Julian Skinner
Craig Berry

Technical Reviewers
Mark Bell
Robert Chang
Chris Devrill
Robin Dewson
Jon Laughery
Rich Lindauer
Erick Nelson
David Rowlands
Elizabeth Seifert
Mike Sussman
Richard Ward

Cover
Andrew Guillaume
Image by Rita Ruban

Design/Layout
Mark Burdett
Frances Olesch

Index
Martin Brooks

DEDICATION

With Love and gratitude to my parents:

For giving me the most valuable support a loving parent can ever provide.

For nourishing the days of my childhood with unforgettable happiness, confidence, compliments, and lasting values.

For teaching me to reach out for my dreams, and to strive always after the highest goal.

For showing me the magnificent way of love, of giving, and of understanding…

For allowing me to become involved in unique activities, which lead to bring out the essence of my soul, my spirit, and my body.

Dad, Mom, thank you for your enduring love, strength, and encouragement that have shaped me into the person I am. Thank you for being my first teachers, and unquestionably the most important ones in my early days…

Happy Anniversary!

Acknowledgements

I would like to express my appreciation and recognition to many special people who have contributed to the successful completion of this book:

To Dominic Shakeshaft, for challenging me to execute this unique and exciting project, which I have thoroughly enjoyed. Furthermore I like to thank him for his valuable comments and support, which significantly contour and enhance the nature of this book.

Special thanks are also due to the dedicated efforts of my editors Susan Holmes, Julian Skinner and Craig Berry for their extraordinary patience and assistance throughout the writing of this book.

I would like to also express appreciation to very special relatives, friends and business associates: Gonzalo Barrientos, Hernan Barrientos, Marco Peredo, William Rojas, Javier Revuelta, Tito Urquieta, Rosario Quiroga de Urquieta, Juan Carlos Roman L. Kim Spilker, Bruce Gillispie, Eric Borrows, Robert Atlinger, Lance Lindburg, Aaron Carta, Kwing Ng, John Wells, Jack Gillispie, Tom Buser, Jonathan Laughery, Mike Murphy, Dr. Delio Montano Z. and Dra. Bertha Anaya de Montano.

Additional special thanks to Tom Eaves a wise man, President of Star software Inc. for his unconditional support, and outstanding performance managing the company.

I'm very much indebted to Steve Straiger for his vast support throughout my writing career.

To my dear friend Brian McDowell, for the great basketball games, which gave me the needed break while writing this exciting book. I wish you the best and keep up the terrific job.

To my lovely sister's in-law: Mirnita, Jimenita and Silvita, and to my sister Sandy, for the wonderful sharing, laughter and joy we had while growing up.

To the beautiful memory of the greatest man I have ever met: "Dr. Hernan Barrientos Urquieta".

To Mamita, an extraordinary human being with awe-inspiring virtues… the supreme example of kindness and thoughtfulness every soul wishes to have. A guardian angel that spreads happiness, love and joy around others, an exceptional women with strength, perseverance and courage.

To my precious children, for bringing peace, joy and gentle love to my heart, for making my days glow and shine even brighter. May our love assure your tender hearts that "you are the most beautiful miracles that came in to Mommy's and Daddy's lives", Kevin, Monica Michelle and Jason "we are very proud of you".

To my best friend "my wife", for being the dazzling fountain at which my soul nourishes with delightful inspiration. For exhilarating me to so much happiness and splendor, plenty of beauty and love. Irisita you make my life so beautiful, magnificent, and worth to cherish every single second.

ABOUT THE AUTHOR

Dwayne R. Gifford is a senior Engineer with remarkable database knowledge. His current position is Information Engineer Manager for Star Software Systems. He has been involved in designing, developing and architecting a number of very successful applications. His range of expertise includes MS Access, Visual Basic, MS SQL Server and Visual C++ to name a few. Computers have been a hobby that he has enjoyed since he was eleven years old. He began his professional career in Canada, where he worked for Labatt Breweries. Subsequently he consulted for Microsoft as a Lead Analyst for its Volume Licensing Operation. In addition, he is the author and co-author of several books on Microsoft Access, Visual Basic, Microsoft SQL Server and Microsoft Office. Throughout his career, he has delivered a number of seminars, workshops and training courses to industry professionals worldwide.

Foreword

When end users look at Outlook, they appreciate the feature set that enables them to store contact information, manage email and tasks and manage their schedules. When developers look at Outlook, they recognize the tremendous opportunity to build solutions which automate and customize Outlook to build collaborative workgroup solutions, contact management systems, automated email solutions, etc. With Outlook 2000, developers can now take advantage of Outlook more so than ever before. The Outlook team was hard at work for this release of Microsoft Outlook –for end user features and especially for exposing the functionality of Outlook to developers. No less than 30 new programmatic "events" have been added to provide greater access to the application functionality and for customizing the Outlook application. In addition, the wait for VBA in Outlook is over. Over 3 Million developers out there already know how to program using the Visual Basic language and now they can leverage that skill set with Microsoft Outlook.

In fact, Office 2000 is the most programmable version of Office to date, with VBA now in FrontPage and Outlook in addition to Word, Excel, PowerPoint and Access. We've even created a version of Office specifically for the millions of developers out there building solutions with Office –Office 2000 Developer (see, we made it easy to figure out which version you should get!)

OK, so you may already know that Office is a great platform for building solutions and that VBA is one of the premiere programming environments. But what you might not know is how to best take advantage of all of this functionality currently on the desktop. Dwayne Gifford's "Outlook 2000 VBA Programmer's Reference" is the guide for helping you explore the power and capabilities of Outlook 2000.

I first met the Dwayne Gifford, the author of this book 4 years ago while working on a project at Microsoft. We were building one of the first global, web based intranet applications for Microsoft. It was still relatively early in the "web" revolution and so there were more unanswered questions than certainties. Dwayne was the guy on the project that you relied on to "make it work". There were many times when Dwayne would be up all night, making sure things worked as expected. No matter how exhausted he was from the previous 24 hours, Dwayne would patiently explain what he had done, how he had done it and actually improved performance, reliability and stability. That's not the incredible part of the story. The incredible part of the story is that I later found out that Dwayne wasn't even working on my project –he was involved in another, entirely unrelated effort but managed to make time to help us, simply because he was interested and we needed his help.

So what does that mean to you? It means that if you're reading this book, you too will benefit from the intelligence, style and knowledge of Dwayne Gifford. And perhaps the best part (at least for him) is that he doesn't have to stay awake all night helping you out –he's already done this putting together a compendium of tips, tricks, and just good, solid code for you to be successful. So congratulations on recognizing the tremendous power and benefits that come from building solutions with Microsoft Office, and congratulations on choosing a great resource for helping you get results quickly with Office 2000.

Neil Charney

Microsoft VBA Team

Table of Contents

Introduction

This book provides a concise guide for programmers to the kinds of applications you can build using Outlook 2000. It demonstrates the use of Outlook through two example applications written in Visual Basic for Applications and Visual Basic. It also includes a full reference section for quick reference on all the events, properties and methods that are available with Outlook.

What is Outlook?

So, what is Outlook? Well, in Office 97 Microsoft released the first version of Outlook. It was an application designed to give you Scheduling/Meeting capability and Email all under one hood. At the same time it gave you a way to manage Tasks, Notes, Contacts and Journal Entries.

What Is This Book About?

This book is about Outlook 2000 and how to use Outlook in your applications in order to handle all your email, appointments and tasks more efficiently. It shows you how to make use of mail items, contacts, appointments, meetings, tasks, journal items, notes and posts. As we encounter each of these items we will cover all their associated objects including their properties, methods and events.

So by interfacing into Outlook, we can exploit all of Outlook's functionality that would take a long time for us to write ourselves. This book will first help you learn how to make use of this functionality and second it will become a handy reference for later when you have a quick question that you just cannot remember the answer to.

This book offers you the reader an easy-to-follow tutorial and reference to Outlook 2000, by splitting the whole topic into neat and intuitive segments. This also makes it easier to find specific information later when you need it, i.e. when you're coding real-world applications. To aid you in finding this information as quickly as possible a comprehensive quick reference section is included. The reference section lists all of the properties, methods and events of each of the Outlook 2000 objects.

This book falls into three main parts.

❑ The first part provides a rapid introduction to Outlook and its object model, to Visual Basic for Applications and demonstrates the potential of Outlook by building two complete applications.

❑ The middle part supplies an exhaustive and detailed walk through the object model, explaining the methods, properties and events of each object, complete with many and varied code examples demonstrating their use.

❑ Finally, there is a quick reference section which gives you a description of all the members of all Outlook objects at a glance.

There are two ways to get hold of Outlook 2000. Firstly by purchasing Outlook 2000 itself or secondly as part of the Microsoft Office package. Most likely you will get Outlook installed with your Office 2000 installation. One thing to be aware of is that if you install Outlook you must have an Outlook License for your machine.

The source code for the major samples in this book can be found on our web site at http://www.wrox.com.

Who Is This Book For?

The book is a reference guide for Outlook programmers, and is primarily designed to explain and demonstrate the features of Outlook 2000. As such, this is not a beginner's guide – though if you have programmed in any language that can interface with other COM objects, then you can easily use and understand this book.

In particular, the book is aimed at programmers who use Outlook for daily tasks and can see benefits in using Outlook in their own applications. This could be anything from just sending automated email responses to building entire collaborative workgroup solutions.

There is virtually no limit to the uses that you can put Outlook to. If you can think it up, then I bet you can use Outlook in some way to help you achieve your goal.

Conventions

We have used a number of different styles of text and layout in the book to help differentiate between the different kinds of information. Here are examples of the styles we use, and an explanation of what they mean:

Advice, hints, and background information comes in this type of font.

> Important pieces of information come in boxes like this.

Important Words are in a bold type font.

Words that appear on the screen in menus, like <u>F</u>ile or <u>W</u>indow, are in a similar font to the one that you see on screen.

Code comes in a number of different styles. If it's something we're talking about in the text — when we're discussing a `For...Next` loop, for example — it's in a fixed-width font. If it's a block of code from a program, then it's also in a gray box:

```
<SCRIPT>
    ' Some VBScript...
</SCRIPT>
```

The syntax for methods, properties and events appears in a similar font, but without the gray background:

```
Set Object = MailItem.Parent
```

The words in italics represent instances of the objects in question, and should be replaced by the name of the variable which refers to the object. For properties which can be both read and updated, two lines of code are given to indicate this:

```
MailItem.Body = String
String = MailItem.Body
```

These formats are designed to make sure that you know exactly what you're looking at. We hope they make life easier.

Tell Us What You Think

We've worked hard on this book to make it enjoyable and useful. Our best reward would be to hear from you that you liked it and that it was worth the money you paid for it. We've done our best to try to understand and match your expectations.

Please let us know what you think about it. Tell us what you liked best and what we could have done better. If you think this is just a marketing gimmick, then test us out — drop us a line! We'll answer, and we'll take whatever you say on board for future editions. The easiest way is to use e-mail:

feedback@wrox.com

You can also find more details about Wrox Press on our web site. There you'll find the code from our latest books, sneak previews of forthcoming titles, and information about the authors and the editors. You can order Wrox titles directly from the site, or find out where your nearest local bookstore with Wrox titles is located. The address of our site is:

http://www.wrox.com

Customer Support

If you find a mistake in the book, your first port of call should be the errata page on our web site.

If you can't find an answer there, send e-mail to support@wrox.com telling us about the problem. We'll do everything we can to answer promptly. Please remember to let us know the book your query relates to, and if possible the page number as well. This will help us to get a reply to you more quickly.

The World of Outlook

Outlook 2000 helps organize the information needed to communicate effectively with your clients and co-workers. It is a collaboration and messaging tool that goes beyond simple email. For example Outlook 2000 provides the tools to track your contacts, schedule appointments, and organize tasks. This chapter will outline each of the tools provided by Outlook 2000 and explain how each one is used to help you increase your effectiveness through better organization.

Those tools include:

- ❑ Outlook Today – your day at a glance
- ❑ Calendar – your appointment book
- ❑ Contacts – your address book
- ❑ Inbox –your incoming email
- ❑ Journal – your personal diary
- ❑ Notes – instead of scraps of paper on your desk
- ❑ Tasks – your list of "Things To Do"

Outlook Today

Outlook 2000 uses a folders analogy with Outlook Today being the filing cabinet and Calendar, Contacts, Inbox, Journal, Notes and Tasks being file folders within that cabinet. Outlook Today provides a snapshot view of the day ahead. At a glance you can see what appointments you have for that day. It displays your tasks in a checklist format for easy viewing including the due date. The number of incoming email messages you have, how many draft emails you have to complete and the number of outgoing messages that need to be sent are all listed in the Outlook Today view.

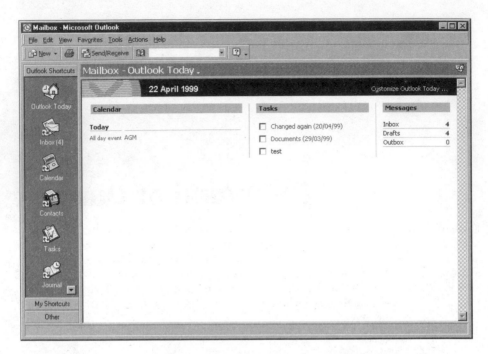

Outlook Today provides the best overview of everything you have planned - the meetings you need to attend and the communication with clients and co-workers that you need to deal with.

Next, we will take a look at what each of these components has to offer and how you might benefit from the features that are built into each of them.

Calendar

The Calendar folder is used to manage your appointments and meetings.

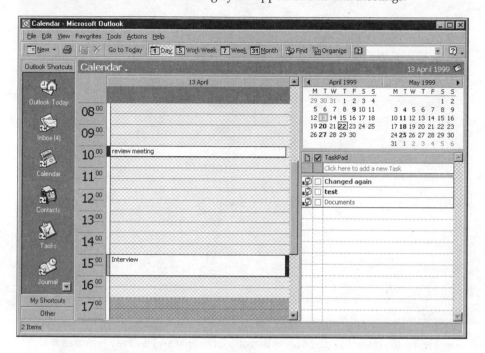

Appointments are activities that you schedule in your Calendar folder that do not involve a group of people and which do not require resources such as a conference room to be reserved. Outlook 2000 provides a means to set reminders for your appointments. You have the option to show others who may view your Calendar whether at the scheduled time for an appointment you are **busy, free, tentative** or **out of office.**

You can view your appointments by day, week, or month and when you select the start and end times for an appointment, you can take advantage of **Autodate** feature. This means that you only need to type text such as "next Monday" or "noon" and the proper date will be selected automatically. This feature relieves you from having to type in the exact date and time.

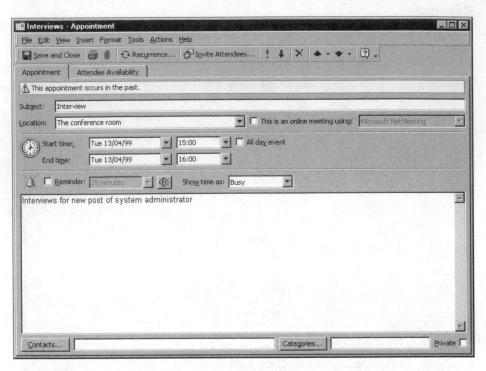

A meeting, on the other hand, involves a group of people and usually requires that resources such as a conference room or site be reserved. You can create and send meeting requests and reserve resources for meetings in person or for online meetings using the Microsoft NetMeeting application.

When scheduling a meeting you identify the people involved, the resources needed and you assign a meeting time. Responses to your meeting request appear in your Inbox. You can track responses by opening a meeting and then click Show attendee status on the Attendee Availability tab in the Meeting dialog box. You can add people to an existing meeting or reschedule a meeting.

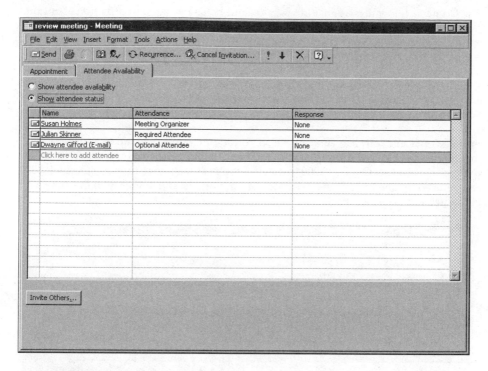

Contacts

The Contacts folder is used to manage your personal and professional contacts.

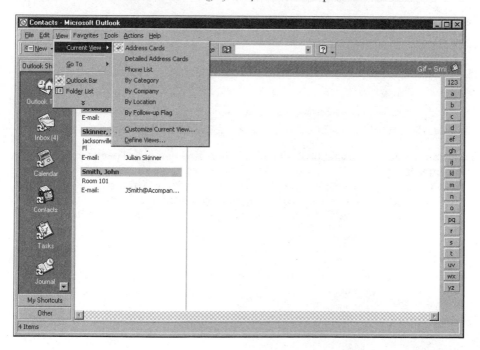

The Contacts folder acts as an address book and holds pertinent information about the personal and professional contacts you communicate with. The Contacts folder can store e-mail addresses, street addresses, telephone numbers and other information that is specific to each contact, such as their birthday or anniversary date.

When you enter a name or address for a contact, Outlook 2000 manages the name and address as individual parts and stores each part in a separate field. This means that you can sort, group or filter contacts by any part of the name or address.

From a contact in your list, you can click a button or menu command to address a meeting request, e-mail message, or task request to that person or business. With a modem, you can set Outlook 2000 to dial the contact's telephone number. Outlook 2000 can be used to time the call and keep a record in your Journal folder with the notes you take during the conversation.

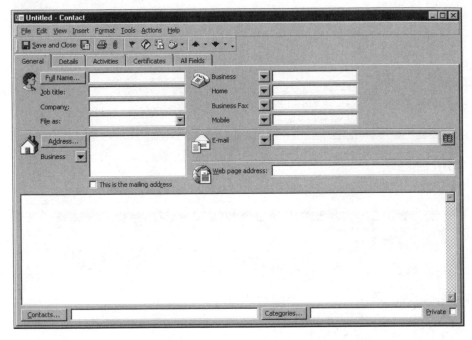

You can file contact information under a last name, first name, company name, nickname, or any word that helps you find the contact. Outlook 2000 gives you several choices to file the contact name under, or you can enter your own choice. You can enter up to three addresses for each contact, designate one address as the mailing address and use it for mailing labels, envelopes, or creating mail merge letters in Microsoft Word 2000.

Inbox

The Inbox folder is used to manage your communication with clients and co-workers.

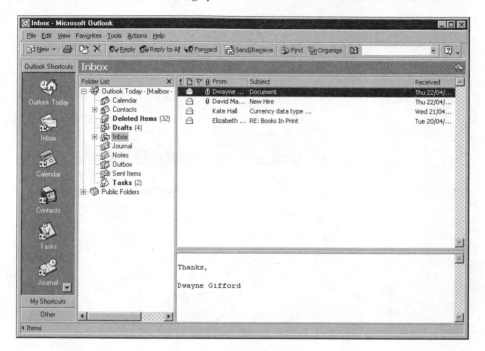

The Inbox folder is the basis for more than just e-mail. This feature is the backbone of the collaboration functionality built into Outlook 2000. Every feature of Outlook 2000 relies on the ability to send and receive messages. These messages take the form of requests, reminders, notifications, and replies. Armed with the functionality of the Inbox it is possible to manage information among a company workgroup, which could span the globe.

Journal

The Journal folder is used to manage your activities within Outlook 2000.

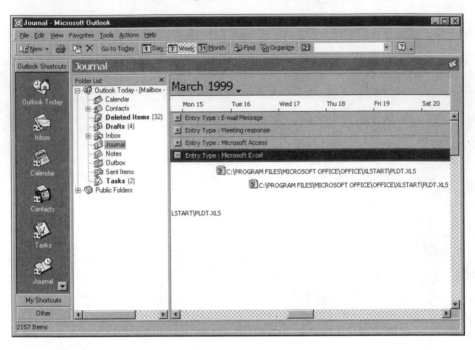

The Journal folder is a unique application capable of recording activities performed by Outlook 2000 automatically, such as those in the following list:

- ❑ E-mail messages
- ❑ Meeting request / response / cancellation
- ❑ Task request / response

The Journal is capable of recording the documents created in the following list of Office applications:

- ❑ Microsoft Access
- ❑ Microsoft Excel
- ❑ Microsoft Office Binder
- ❑ Microsoft PowerPoint
- ❑ Microsoft Word
- ❑ Other programs that are part of the Microsoft Office Compatible program

You can now search through the Journal entries that are categorized to find a specific e-mail message or response to a task request without having to search through every entry.

Notes

The Notes folder is used to manage your activities within Outlook 2000.

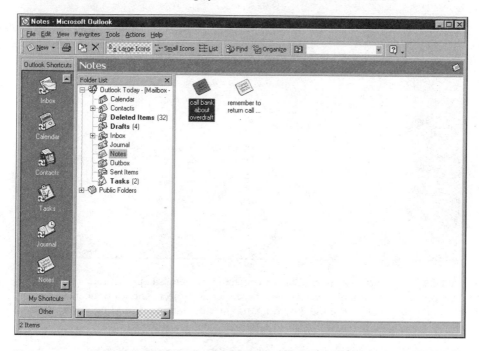

Notes is one of those features that seemed right to have in an application like Outlook 2000. Its only function is to provide a simple reminder to do something that typically has no need to be managed or collaborated upon. Basically, it gives you a means of creating a quick note to yourself electronically instead of on a piece of paper.

Tasks

The Tasks folder is used to manage your "To-Do" list within Outlook 2000.

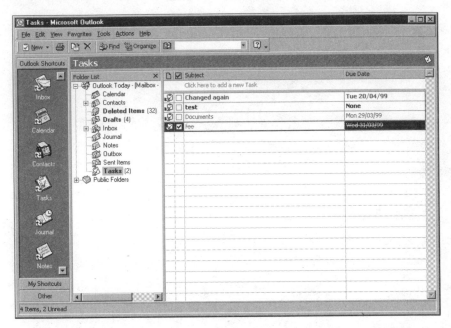

The Tasks folder very closely emulates a project management application. You input the various items pertinent to your everyday tasks or projects and then the Tasks folder will help you manage them by tracking the due dates and sending you a reminder message when a particular task has not been completed.

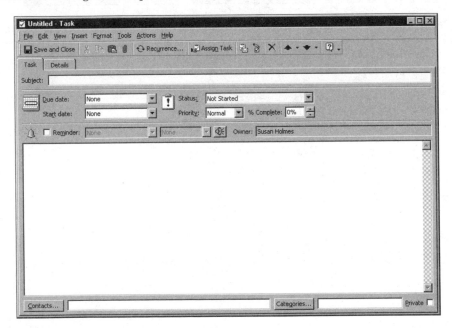

Although you cannot manage and assign resources or create reports and charts for large projects like you can in Microsoft Project 98, you do have some nice features available. You can record your time spent on a particular task or how many miles you traveled to and from a client site. Also, you have the ability to track the status of tasks, prioritize tasks and show a percentage of the task completed.

Also, you can use the Task folder to request someone else to perform a task for you. This allows you to manage the tasks you delegate to co-workers. Again, it's not a full-blown project management application but it does have some powerful features.

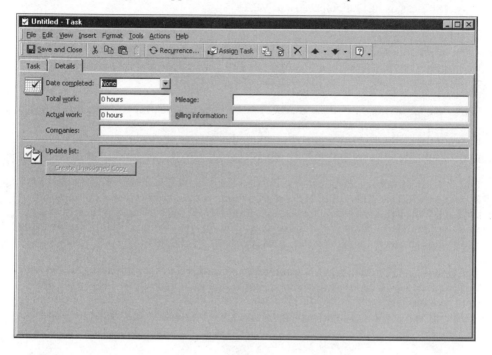

Customizing Outlook 2000

Since Outlook 2000 is so powerful, incorporating all the functionality and features that have been mentioned, you may be wondering why you would want to customize Outlook 2000. Even with the power Outlook 2000 provides "out of the box" you can easily add your own specific applications using the Visual Basic for Applications (VBA) programming environment that is integrated into all Office 2000 products.

Typically, every company is slightly different from the next. Therefore, the flexibility to customize Outlook 2000 is provided through VBA. Outlook 2000 provides the messaging and collaboration capabilities that other Office 2000 applications lack.

Enterprise wide issues such as document management, process approval routings and project management are ideal candidates for solutions using Outlook 2000 integrated with other Office 2000 applications.

Document management, for example, may be implemented using Outlook 2000 as the front-end-user interface application. Then, using Microsoft Word 2000 for creating documents and reports, and a Microsoft Access database to store information about our documents such as who created it and when, you can create a complete application that suits your specific criteria.

Project management, as mentioned in the section on the Tasks folder, can be more fully implemented by using a true project management application such as Microsoft Project 98 and creating the messaging and collaboration capabilities that Microsoft Project 98 lacks using Outlook 2000 and VBA.

There is any number of possibilities for your own applications that you can create using applications such as Office 2000 that are ActiveX Automation VBA enabled. Having this feature has added to your flexibility and options to create the exact application and user interface that you desire.

Before we move into the body of this book, which details the properties, methods and events exposed by each of the Outlook objects, we are going to take a brief walk through the Outlook object model describing the different types of object and how they fit into the Outlook that you are already familiar with.

I'll then provide a brief introduction to Visual Basic for Applications or VBA and the Visual Basic Editor. This editor is the place where most of your code for automating Outlook will be placed. If you are already familiar with VBA you can probably skip this chapter. It is, of course, possible to access Outlook from other applications and this is reflected in one of the two applications given in the chapter 4.

The first is actually written in VBA in the Visual Basic Editor provided by Outlook. It is designed to search for tasks that are overdue and automatically sets up an email to request a meeting with the people associated with that task. The second application is written from outside Outlook in Visual Basic 6 and provides mail merge functionality.

2

The Object Model

As with all Microsoft Office applications, the Outlook object model defines a unique and distinct hierarchy for all the objects which Outlook exposes. This hierarchy defines the relationship between the objects and the order in which they must be instantiated or created.

The diagram overleaf gives a schematic representation of the entire Outlook object model.

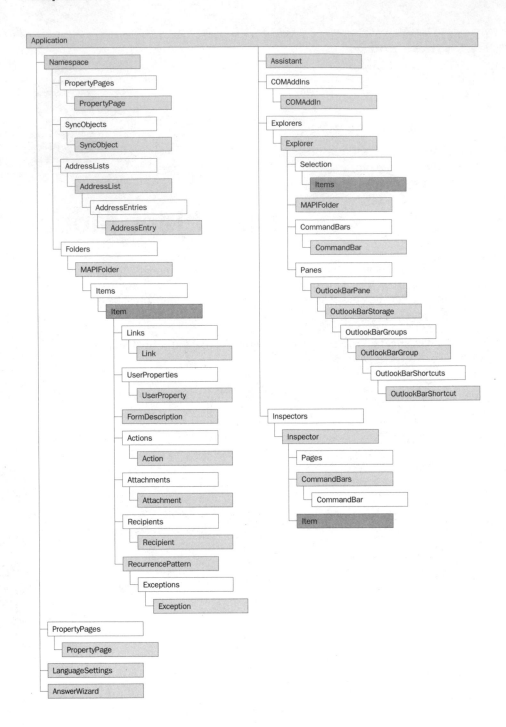

Collections and Objects

The Outlook object model distinguishes between two types of object: collections and individual objects, such as Outlook items. In the above diagram, the unshaded boxes represent collections and the lightly shaded boxes non-collection objects. The more heavily shaded boxes represent an Outlook item; this can be any one of a number of closely related objects.

Collections can only contain objects of a certain type: for example, an `Attachments` collection can contain only `Attachment` objects. They have a number of common properties and methods, for example to return the number of objects in the collection, to add objects to or remove them from the collection, and to return a specific member of the collection by its position. Note that Outlook collections are one-based, so the first object in them has an index of 1, not 0.

In contrast, objects that are not collections can often contain more than one type of child object. For example, a `MAPIFolder` object can contain Outlook items or other `MAPIFolder` objects. Whenever an object can hold more than one child object, these children are grouped together in a single collection. So the `MAPIFolder` objects and Outlook items which are children of a given `MAPIFolder` are grouped together into a `Folders` collection and an `Items` collection respectively.

Instantiating the Object Model

The only way to instantiate the Outlook object model is through the `Application` object. This is the only object that is exposed as publicly creatable. The other objects are creatable, but not publicly; that is, they can only be created from within a specific instance of the application. The `Application` object is therefore the ancestor of all Outlook objects.

Since the Outlook object model is multiple levels deep, I have broken it down into individual levels in an attempt to make it easier to follow and to learn how to use the model.

Application

The `Application` object represents an individual instance of the Outlook program. Only one instance of this object may be open at any one time, so the `Application` object always represents the current instance of Outlook. It exposes us to the life of Outlook, and it is only through this object that we are able to access the other objects exposed to us by Outlook.

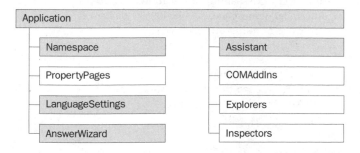

The `Application` object exposes to us the `NameSpace` object, which contains all the data available to a user; the `Inspectors` collection, which contains the objects used to display items; the `Explorers` collection, which contains the objects that allow us to navigate through the different data items available to the user; and the `PropertyPages` collection, which allows us to add custom pages to the Tools I Options... tag or to the Properties tag of an Outlook folder. It also provides access to a number of objects which belong to Office rather than to Outlook: the `AnswerWizard` object, which can be used to manage help files; the `Assistant` object, which represents the Office Assistant (the animated help that you either love or loathe); the `COMAddIns` collection, which contains the add-ins currently loaded into Outlook; and the `LanguageSettings` object, which contains information about the language settings of the current Outlook application.

The `Application` object exposes to us methods to retrieve the active explorer or inspector, to quit Outlook, to get a namespace, and to create new items. Even though these methods are exposed to us through the `Application` object, nothing meaningful can be done without first signing into a `NameSpace` object. For example, it is possible to create a new mail item, but it cannot be sent until you are logged into a namespace. Fortunately, Outlook logs us into the correct namespace automatically when we open the application, or, if accessing Outlook from another Office product or from Visual Basic, when the reference to the `Application` object is set.

NameSpace

The `NameSpace` object represents all the data sources available to Outlook; that is, the profiles which have been set up for each individual user and which contain the settings and the items for that user. This object exposes methods to log into and to log out of the data sources. Once you have a reference to a data source and have logged in, you now have access to all the data elements that the user has available to them.

This object gives us methods to retrieve different data objects that are available in Outlook. It also gives you the ability to open other users' profiles if you have the requisite permissions. Presently, the only way to retrieve a `NameSpace` object is through the `GetNamespace` method exposed by the `Application` object.

```
Dim onNameSpace As NameSpace
...
Set onNameSpace = Application.GetNamespace("MAPI")
```

Presently there is only one namespace available for Outlook — the MAPI (Messaging Application Programming Interface) namespace. This is the industry-standard programming interface for email

The `PropertyPages` collection and the `PropertyPage` object exposed here are the same objects as those exposed by the `Application` object.

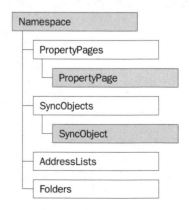

SyncObjects and SyncObject

The SyncObjects collection is, unsurprisingly, a collection of SyncObject objects. These objects contain the settings used by Outlook to make a user's mailbox available offline, so the items in it can be accessed even if the user does not have access to the Internet or network. Each SyncObject represents a single synchronization profile, specifying which folders will be synchronized (that is, made available offline) when that SyncObject is executed. These objects are only available if Outlook has been set up to make the data in a profile available offline. These objects are read-only and can only be built from the GUI — they cannot be created through code. They can only be viewed, or their execution started or stopped. Examining the SyncObject does not even reveal where Outlook gets the information to execute the synchronization of a folder.

AddressLists

The AddressLists collection is a collection of AddressList objects. This collection gives you a way to access the different AddressList objects available to this user. An AddressList is a list of email addresses, and can be thought of as a phone book holding email addresses instead of phone numbers. To continue this metaphor, the AddressLists collection can be thought of as the desk draw that holds your phone books.

An individual email address is represented by an AddressEntry object, and this can be compared to an individual entry or phone number in the phone book. All the AddressEntry objects in the AddressList belong to an AddressEntries collection (our analogy falls down a bit here). Note that each AddressList must hold only one AddressEntries collection.

Folders

The `Folders` collection consists of `MAPIFolder` objects; that is, folders which contain objects in the MAPI Namespace.

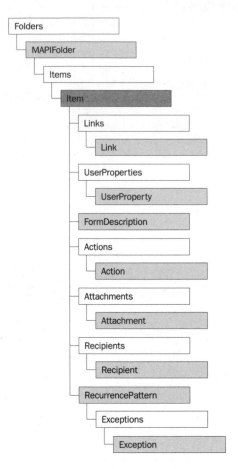

The `MAPIFolder` object represents a folder in which the Outlook items we saw in Chapter 1 are stored. We can think of a `MAPIFolder` as the Outlook equivalent of a folder in Windows Explorer; examples are the Inbox, Outbox, etc. We use these `MAPIFolder` objects to organize and navigate through Outlook items and other `MAPIFolder` objects.

Items

The `Items` collection contains all the Outlook items that reside in a specific `MAPIFolder`. For example, the `Items` collection of the Inbox contains all the mails that you have received (unless they have been moved to other folders). Outlook items can actually be any of a number of objects exposed by Outlook, each of which represents a specific message type: `AppointmentItem`, `ContactItem`, `DistListItem`, `DocumentItem`, `JournalItem`, `MailItem`, `MeetingItem`, `NoteItem`, `PostItem`, `RemoteItem`, `ReportItem`, `TaskItem`, `TaskRequestAcceptItem`, `TaskRequestDeclineItem`, `TaskRequestItem`, or `TaskRequestUpdateItem`. These objects are generally considered to be the heart and soul of Outlook, since these represent the actual messages with which the user deals.

Links and Link

The `Links` collection is a grouping of `Link` objects for a specific item. These allow us to group related Outlook items by specific contacts. Each `Link` object represents a specific contact item, so we can use items' `Links` collections to group Outlook items together by shared contacts. However, note that the `Link` object only represents a contact; the items are not linked by the contact items themselves.

UserProperties and UserProperty

The `UserProperties` is a collection of custom properties that you can define for a given item and which are stored in `UserProperty` objects. These `UserProperty` objects can be assigned a name and a data type. To set or retrieve the value for these `UserProperty` objects, you must use the `Value` property exposed by the `UserProperty` object.

```
Dim ocContact As ContactItem
...
ocContact.UserProperties("Relationship").Value = "Friend"
```

In the sample above, we assign a value of `"Friend"` to the custom property `"Relationship"` of a contact item. There is nothing particularly special about this, but it gives us endless ways to add to the information which can be held by the original objects that are exposed to us.

FormDescription

The `FormDescription` object contains the properties for the forms supplied by Outlook are based. The only way to view these properties from the GUI is to open the form in Design mode and click on the **Properties** tab. Even though there are a lot of properties (22, to be exact) exposed by the `FormDescription` object, not all of them appear on the **Properties** tab.

These properties are not used by Outlook itself, which means that they can be changed through code. As you make changes to the different forms that you use, you can update these properties as required to ensure that all users are using the correct forms.

Actions and Action

The `Actions` collection is the holder for the `Action` objects. These objects are special actions that can be performed on an item to send it to other users or post it to a specific folder. Although the user can add custom actions, there are also a number of pre-defined actions. Most of the different item objects have `"Reply"`, `"Reply to All"`, `"Reply to Folder"` and `"Forward"` actions, even if they cannot be executed. The only way to be certain whether the action is implemented or not is to try it to see whether Outlook raises an error. We can add our own actions to a form in Design mode by viewing the **Actions** tab and clicking the **New...** button. To add an action through code, we must add an `Action` object to the item's `Actions` collection.

```
Dim omMail As MailItem
Dim omMailReply As MailItem
...
Set omMailReply = omMail.Actions("Reply").Execute
```

In the example above, we use the `"Reply"` action instead of the `Reply` method that the `MailItem` exposes. There is in fact no difference between the `Reply` method and the `Reply` action, but the `Action` object allows us to change certain details, such as the prefix added to the subject of a reply (usually **Re:**). Any changes made to this action will also be applied to the `Reply` method.

Attachments and Attachment

The `Attachments` collection holds all the `Attachment` objects — the files, Outlook items or other objects that are embedded in an item. If there are no attachments associated with an item, that item's `Attachment` collection will have a `Count` property with a value of zero.

The `Attachment` object can be any object, from a spreadsheet file to an image file. The file can even be in a format that the computer does not understand, which will cause an **Unknown File Format** error if the user attempts to open the attachment.

Recipients and Recipient

For any item that can be sent to another user (and even some that can't), there will be an associated `Recipients` collection. This collection contains `Recipient` objects — objects representing the users to whom the item is to be sent.

```
Dim omMail As MailItem
Dim orRecipient As Recipient

Set omMail = Application.CreateItem(olMailItem)
Set orRecipient = omMail.Recipients.Add("Iris Gifford")
```

In the example above, we create a `MailItem` and add a `Recipient`. To find out whether the recipient is valid (that is, if it is a correctly formatted email address, or it is a name which can be resolved from one of the address books), we can check the `Resolved` property exposed by the `Recipient` object. Each recipient can be assigned to a type, specifying which of the fields the recipient is added to: **To**, **CC** or **BCC**.

RecurrencePattern, Exceptions and Exception

The `RecurrencePattern` object is associated with the `AppointmentItem` and `TaskItem` objects only. This object allows you to set up a recurring appointment or task (that is, one which comes round at regular intervals). This object specifies how frequently this appointment or task recurs.

Sometimes, of course, an appointment will need to occur earlier or later than the other appointments in the same series. To accommodate this, the `RecurrencePattern` object has an associated `Exceptions` collection that contains all the `Exception` objects which represent the exceptions to the normal appointment.

The `RecurrencePattern` object can be accessed from the `AppointmentItem` or the `TaskItem` through the `GetRecurrence` method that is exposed by both of these items. There is also a Boolean `IsRecurring` property which indicates whether the item is a recurring appointment or task, again exposed by both the `AppointmentItem` and the `TaskItem`.

Inspectors

The `Inspectors` object is a collection of `Inspector` objects. These are the GUIs (Graphical User Interfaces) used to display individual Outlook items — the forms which are presented to the user when an item is opened for viewing or editing. The `Inspectors` collection gives us the ability to add new `Inspector` objects or to get a reference to an existing inspector. For each item object, there is a `GetInspector` method that will retrieve the `Inspector` associated with the item.

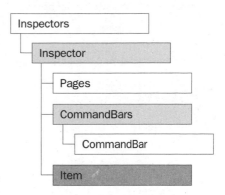

Pages

The `Pages` collection represents the different pages available on an Inspector. To understand these, open the `Inspector` object in Design mode by clicking on <u>T</u>ools | <u>F</u>orms | D<u>e</u>sign a Form. No matter which inspector you open, you will notice that there are five tabs with nothing on them, labeled P.2 to P.6. These are the pages that the `Pages` collection holds. The `Page` object belongs to the Office rather than to the Outlook object model, and as such is beyond the scope of this book.

Moreover, although controls and information can be added to the page through code, I would not advise this. I don't know about you, but I have a hard enough time placing controls on the GUI when I am looking at it, let alone working blind. So I suggest that you use the Form Designer to modify the inspector. Having said that, it is useful to know that you can make the page visible or invisible through the `Visible` property that the `Page` object exposes.

CommandBars and CommandBar

The `CommandBars` collection holds the different available `CommandBar` objects that each inspector can show. These `CommandBar` objects are the menus and toolbars that are available to the inspector. Each `CommandBar` object contains a collection of `CommandBarControls` which defines the menu options or toolbar buttons that will be made available on the menu or toolbar.

```
Dim omMail As MailItem
Dim ocbCommandBar As CommandBar
...
Set ocbCommandBar = omMail.GetInspector.CommandBars.Add("NewOne")
ocbCommandBar.Visible = True
```

In the sample above we create a new `CommandBar` called `"NewOne"`. We then set its `Visible` property to `True`, so that it appears on the toolbar. One point to note, at least with the current version, is that it is not possible to change the `CommandBar` objects of the default inspectors that come with Outlook. I would also suggest that if you need to add a new `CommandBar` to a form, you will find it easier to do it through the Form Designer rather than through code, since you can see the controls which you add.

If you have ever worked with the `CoolBar` control that comes with the Common Controls shipped with Visual Studio, this control will seem very familiar to you.

Item

This represents any of the Outlook items discussed in the `Items` section above.

Explorers

The `Explorer` object is the Outlook equivalent of Windows Explorer. It is the window that we see as soon as we open Outlook, which can display the Outlook Bar, the list of folders in the user's Mailbox, the contents of the folder, and a preview of the selected item. This window lets us navigate through the different folders that we have created, and open and read our mail.

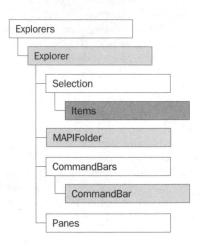

Selection

The `Selection` collection holds all of the selected items (that is, those items which are currently highlighted in blue) for a given `MAPIFolder`. This information can only be accessed through the `Explorer` object, because the `Explorer` object holds the folders and items being displayed in its panes (the panes are the windows containing the Outlook Bar, the Folder List, etc.). For more information on Outlook items, refer to the section above under the `MAPIFolder` object.

MAPIFolder

This `MAPIFolder` object is the same object as the one described in the section above on the `Folders` collection.

CommandBars and CommandBar

The `CommandBars` collection and `CommandBar` object are the same here as for the `Inspector` object discussed above.

Panes

The `Panes` collection holds the panes (the windows used to navigate through your folders) in the `Explorer` object. This indicates which panes can be shown. If you think about the normal Outlook window that you are familiar with, you would imagine that the Preview Pane, Folder List, Items list, and the Outlook Bar would all be Pane objects. However, in Outlook 2000 the only one of these that is actually an object accessible through VBA is the Outlook Bar — the pane on the left-hand side of the screen which contains groups of shortcuts to related `MAPIFolder` objects and/or file system folders.

You cannot add panes to or remove them from the `Panes` collection. To find out how many Pane objects are available for an explorer, you can check the `Count` property of the `Panes` Collection. But remember that, until further notice, this will always return one.

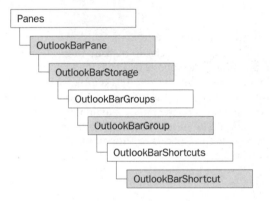

Example:

```
Dim oeExplorer As Explorer
Dim oobpPane As OutlookBarPane
Dim ogcGroups As OutlookBarGroups
Dim ogGroup As OutlookBarGroup

Set oeExplorer = Application.ActiveExplorer
Set oobpPane = oeExplorer.Panes.Item(1)
Set ogcGroups = oobpPane.Contents.Groups
Set ogGroup = ogcGroups.Add("WROX")
ogGroup.ViewType = olSmallIcon
ogGroup.Shortcuts.Add "Journal Wrox", "Journal Wrox"
```

This code gets a reference to the active explorer and then to the Outlook Bar Pane. We then add a new group called `"WROX"`. Once the group has been added, we set its `ViewType` property to display small icons. Finally, we add the `"Journal Wrox"` `MAPIFolder` that I have in my Personal Folders collection. (To run this code, you will of course have to change this reference to something appropriate to your own setup.)

OutlookBarPane

The `OutlookBarPane` object represents the Outlook Bar, and is the only explorer pane that we can access. This holds the `OutlookStorage` object, which tells us how the items in the pane are grouped together.

OutlookBarGroups and OutlookBarGroup

The `OutlookBarGroups` collection contains the `OutlookBarGroup` objects which hold the `OutlookBarShortcuts`. These objects allow us to group together related Outlook or file folders to give us easier access to these common elements. For example, I have the `"WROX"` group that was created in the code above, and in it I have mapped all my Outlook folders related to Wrox Press. I have also mapped the `Working` directory on my local hard drive.

OutlookBarShortcuts and OutlookBarShortcut

The `OutlookBarShortcuts` collection holds all the `OutlookBarShortcut` objects that are related and grouped together within the `OutlookBarGroup` object. These are the icons that appear on the Outlook Bar.

PropertyPages

The `PropertyPages` collection contains any custom property pages added by the user. The `PropertyPage` object provides a template which can be used to create your own property pages which can appear as a tab in the **Options** or **Properties** windows. The `PropertyPage` object does not contain any code; it is merely a template. The `Implements` keyword in a `PropertyPage` provides a shell which will allow Outlook to open your custom property pages. To make the `PropertyPage` available, use the `Add` method of the `PropertyPages` collection. The parent object of a `PropertyPage` is a `PropertyPageSite`; this object represents the **Options** or **Properties** dialog of which the custom **PropertyPage** forms one page.

Assistant

The `Assistant` object represents the Microsoft Office Assistant — the animated cartoon figure that can be set to appear when you ask for help, and which can sometimes be annoying, but at other times is amusing. This, of course, is just my opinion, and you probably have your own on this little guy. This object gives us the ability (amongst other things) to hide, show and activate the assistant.

COMAddIns

The `COMAddIns` collection contains all the currently available add-ins for Outlook. The only one available by default for Outlook is the **Microsoft VBA for Outlook Add-in**. You can use the `Update` method to refresh the collection and the `Count` method to find out how many add-ins are available to you.

LanguageSettings

The `LanguageSettings` object returns the language settings for Microsoft Office 2000 and informs the Office applications what language the Help Files are to be displayed in, etc. The language settings for Outlook cannot be changed through this object.

AnswerWizard

This represents the Office Answer Wizard, if this is installed. This object is beyond the scope of this book, but if you want to learn how to use it, you should check out the VBA Help Files that are shipped with Office and MSDN.

Summary

In this chapter we have walked through the entire Object Model exposed by Outlook 2000, including one or two objects which strictly speaking belong to the Office Object Model. We broke it down into a few chunks to make it easier to digest and remember, and we discussed each object and what these objects are used for.

This chapter is a lead-in for the rest of the book and this is where the real action starts. All of the objects outlined here are covered in greater depth throughout the later part of the book and in Appendix A.

3

Introduction to VBA

In this chapter we will take a look at the Visual Basic for Applications or VBA language. VBA is integrated into all Office 2000 products and is the language we will use to write the code in order to automate Outlook. The coverage of VBA in this chapter is not intended to be comprehensive. It simply serves as a refresher for those already familiar with VBA or as a taster for those who have not yet encountered the language.

Outlook provides the Visual Basic Editor as a programming environment for developers. You need to be familiar with this editor before we you can get stuck into Outlook 2000 VBA. So before we look the VBA fundamentals I'll give you a whistle stop tour of the Visual Basic Editor or VBE.

The Visual Basic Editor

The Visual Basic Editor or VBE is available with all of the Microsoft Office packages, such as Word and Excel, and so provides a common look and feel for developing VBA code. To get to the VBE you need to navigate through Tools I Macro I Visual Basic Editor.

The Visual Basic Editor is where code, incorporating the properties, methods and events of the Outlook objects, will be placed in order to automate Outlook. It typically looks as follows:

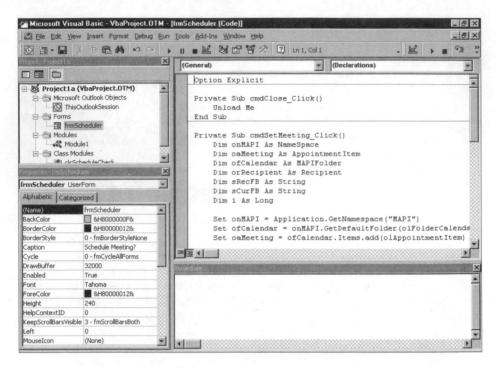

In the figure above you can see that the VBE is made up of a number of different window such as the **Project** explorer window and the **Properties** window. There are also other windows available and to set these windows to be visible or invisible within the VBE it is necessary to use the **View** menu. We'll now take a look at each of the windows in turn.

The Code Window

The **Code** window is where you will place the code to automate Outlook. There isn't a lot to say about this window and anyone who has already coded in Visual Basic or VBA should be familiar with this window. At the top of this window are two listboxes, on the left the **Object** box and on the right the **Procedure** box. By clicking on the left box a list of currently available forms, controls and other objects with procedures are displayed. Once one has been selected, the **Procedure** box can be used to find all possible procedures for the object.

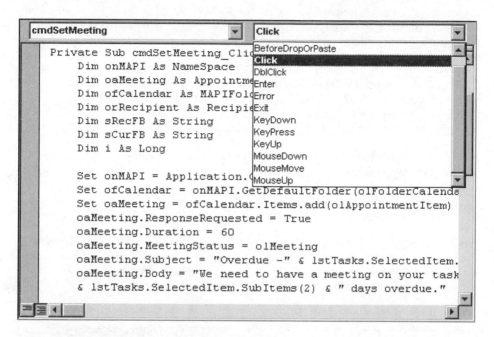

```
cmdSetMeeting              ▼    Click                      ▼
                                BeforeDropOrPaste           ▲
    Private Sub cmdSetMeeting_Cli   Click
    Dim onMAPI As NameSpace         DblClick
    Dim oaMeeting As Appointme      Enter
    Dim ofCalendar As MAPIFol       Error
    Dim orRecipient As Recipi       Exit
    Dim sRecFB As String            KeyDown
    Dim sCurFB As String            KeyPress
    Dim i As Long                   KeyUp
                                    MouseDown
    Set onMAPI = Application.       MouseMove
    Set ofCalendar = onMAPI.GetDefaultFolder(olFolderCalenda
    Set oaMeeting = ofCalendar.Items.add(olAppointmentItem)
    oaMeeting.ResponseRequested = True
    oaMeeting.Duration = 60
    oaMeeting.MeetingStatus = olMeeting
    oaMeeting.Subject = "Overdue -" & lstTasks.SelectedItem.
    oaMeeting.Body = "We need to have a meeting on your task
    & lstTasks.SelectedItem.SubItems(2) & " days overdue."
```

The Project Explorer Window

The Project Explorer window displays a tree view of all files that make up a project. As you can see from the figure below an Outlook project can be made up of a module called ThisOutlookSession and then any number of User Forms, Code Modules and Class Modules.

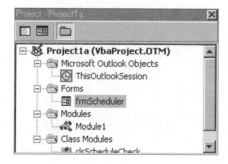

You can add new modules and forms or import and export existing files by right-clicking in this window. Alternatively you could use the Insert and File menus of the VBE.

ThisOutlookSession is a special class module, where the Outlook Application object and its six events are already exposed to you. It therefore makes sense to place code associated with application level events in this module. For example, any code that you want to run automatically when Outlook opens should be placed in the Application_Startup event.

A User form can be used to display a GUI to the user. These forms can be customized by adding controls from the Toolbox provided. New tools can be added to this Toolbox through the Tools | Additional Controls ... dialog. Code can then placed behind these controls to set the functionality of the form.

Code modules are used to write Outlook macros. Any Sub procedure placed in a module becomes a macro, which can be run through the Tools | Macro | Macros... dialog. Any code placed within a procedure here will be executed when the appropriate macro is run.

A class module is where we place code that provides a blue print for an object. Any number of objects based on this class can then be instantiated by using the New keyword.

```
Dim oMyObject as New oMyClass
```

It is here that you can write code to respond to non-application events that occur in Outlook. By declaring an Outlook object as a variable WithEvents in a class module you can code up any of its possible events. As you can see in the following figure, the object and its events become available in the Object and Procedure boxes.

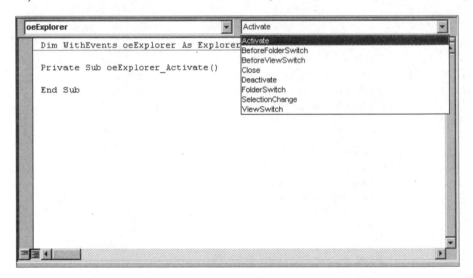

The Properties Window

The Properties window displays the properties of the currently active object that can be set at design time. In the VBE shown at the beginning of the chapter the Properties window shows all the design time properties for a user form.

The Immediate, Watches and Locals Windows

The Immediate, Watches and Locals windows are used for debugging purposes. The Immediate window functions much like the code window but is only available for use in break mode. This window allows you to execute commands, check and change variable values and do almost anything you might need to in order to figure out why your code isn't working properly.

The Watches window can be used to display the content of specified variables and properties and can also stop a routine when a certain condition is met. The Locals window, on the other hand, shows all the variables and their values as a routine is executed. If you haven't coded in VBA before you soon find these windows become your best friends.

Macros

If you have worked with Word or Excel for long enough, you will probably have come across macros before. With Office 2000 it is now possible to write macros for Outlook. You should note that it is not possible to record macros in the same way as you can in Word or Excel. It does, however, provide a way to Create, Run, Cancel, Step Into, Edit and Delete macros. Each macro comprises a sub procedure that sits in a code module.

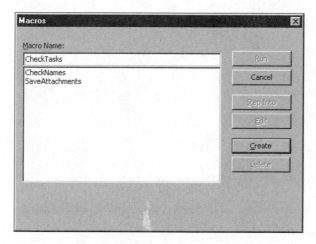

To create a new macro you simply need to enter a suitable macro name and click on the Create button. Outlook will then create a sub procedure of the same name in the first code module and display it in front of you. If no code modules are open it will automatically open one for you. The other options all work as you would expect. The Step Into option starts the macro in debug mode, allowing you to step through each line of code.

Object Properties, Methods and Events

An **object** in VBA represents an entity that you can describe and manipulate. In VBA these objects present interfaces to the outside world that we can access through our code. An object has attributes that describe it, known as **properties**. An object can also perform actions, known as **methods**. **Events** are things that happen to an object and through VBA you can write code to respond to these events.

An object is defined by a **class**. A class is a template from which an object is created. We can create many different objects from a single class and those objects are said to be **instances** of the class. The code to respond to Outlook object events is placed in a class module. This will be discussed later.

Here is an example using objects that are more familiar to us, to help explain the concept:

❏ John is an object of class Human

❏ Name, Age, Height and Weight are some of the properties of Humans

❏ For John these properties might equal John Smith, 43, 5' 11", and 190lbs respectively

❏ Walk, Sit and Blink would be methods for all Humans

❏ Dying would be an example of a Human event

Given the above statements, you could write VBA code to manipulate John, which would look something like this:

```
Sub SetUpPerson()

    John.Height = 71
    John.Weight = 190
    John.Age = 43

    John.Walk

End Sub
```

This style of programming provides VBA (and Visual Basic, which behaves in the same way) with a great deal of flexibility. With objects, properties and methods VBA can be used to do almost anything, as long as we have the right objects.

VBA itself has only a few objects, but Outlook has over 50 and it is through these objects that you can manipulate Outlook to do exactly what you want. In addition to setting property values, you can also retrieve them, and use that information however you wish.

Almost all your code in VBA will involve working with objects, so it is important to understand a few general rules that are almost always true:

❏ Objects are items to be manipulated

❏ They have properties and methods

❏ Properties are attributes of the object; they describe it

❏ Methods are actions that the object can perform; they do something

However, sometimes properties cause the object to do something and sometimes methods merely change attributes. Such properties and methods usually make sense when you encounter them.

Events

The code to respond to application level events should be placed in the ThisOutlookSession module of the Outlook VBE. The six application level events are listed in its Procedure box:

ItemSend	NewMail	OptionPagesAdd
Quit	Reminder	Startup

The code to respond to other Outlook objects' events should be placed in class modules and the object should be declared with the `WithEvents` keyword. For example to code the events of an `Explorer` object you might type

```
Dim WithEvents oeExplorer as Explorer
```

The `Explorer` object's events would then be found in the **Procedure** box of the class module. It is also necessary to ensure that an `Explorer` object is referenced when the class is instantiated so that Outlook knows which object's events to respond to.

This could be placed in the `Class_Initialize` procedure of the class module. This is called whenever an object is instantiated based on this class.

```
Private Sub Class_Initialize()
    Set oeExplorer = Application.Explorers
End Sub
```

Alternatively this could be placed in a Public Sub which is then called in order to instantiate the class.

```
Public Sub Initialize_handler()
    Set oeExplorer = Application.Explorers
End Sub
```

To do anything that is truly useful in VBA, you need to be able to store values, not only in object properties, but also in variables. Variables will be discussed later in the chapter.

Variables and Data Types

Variables are a concept of most programming languages. They are places to store information. These variables are then used throughout the program in place of the values they represent, allowing the same program to work with many different possible values. The use of variables usually takes one of only a few forms:

- ❑ Declaring the variable with the `Dim` keyword, which prepares it for use (`Dim X`)

- ❑ Storing values into the variable (`X=3`)

- ❑ Retrieving previously stored values out of the variable (`MsgBox X` or `Y = X + 3`)

That's all there is to it. Just three ways to work with variables, making it one of the simplest programming concepts. However, it is something that you will be using repeatedly throughout every program you write.

Declaring Variables

Before you can store values into a variable, VBA must know that the variable exists. Somewhere in our code we have to state that we are going to be using this certain name to refer to a variable. This is usually carried out right at the beginning of our code, and uses the `Dim` statement. The code below declares the variables X, Y, and Z:

```
Sub WorkingWithVariables()

    Dim X
    Dim Y
    Dim Z

    ...

End Sub
```

Once the variable is declared, VBA understands that it is a variable and allocates memory for you to store information. From that point on, anytime you use this variable's name in your code, VBA knows what it is and can treat it accordingly, as in this code:

```
Sub WorkingWithVariables()

    Dim X
    Dim Y
    Dim Z

    Z = 3
    Y = 4
    X = 1

    Z = Y / X
    X = Y + Z

End Sub
```

In the code above, numbers are being stored into the three variables, but you could store almost any type of information into them if you wished. In our programs we usually create our variables to hold specific types of information and VBA allows us to specify that type when we first create the variable. This is known as the **data type** of the variable and the next section covers the various data types available and how to determine which one to use.

Data Types

When we declare a variable, we can tell VBA what type of information that variable will contain by providing a data type. If we don't specifically tell VBA the data type for a variable, it assumes that the variable should be declared as a **variant**, which can hold any type of information but is very inefficient. More information on variants is given at the end of this section on data types. We specify a data type for a variable by adding `As <Data Type>` after the variable's declaration. For instance, in the code below, we are declaring X, Y, and Z as variables that will be used to hold **integers**:

```
Sub WorkingWithVariables()

    Dim X As Integer
    Dim Y As Integer
    Dim Z As Integer

    Z = 3
    Y = 4
    X = 1

    Z = Y / X
    X = Y + Z

End Sub
```

> It is tempting, especially to those used to other programming languages, to simplify the variable declarations shown above to: `Dim X, Y, Z As Integer`. Although this would not result in an error, it does not achieve the desired result. In VBA, it is possible to place multiple variable declarations onto one place, but each variable requires its data type to be specified separately. This makes the correct way to simplify those three variable declarations: `Dim X As Integer, Y As Integer, Z As Integer`. The first version of this line would have declared `X` and `Y` as variants and only `Z` as an integer.

There are many different data types available in VBA, and it can be difficult to be exactly sure which data type is required for a particular purpose. The types can be grouped into:

- ❑ Numeric variables, designed to hold various forms of numbers,
- ❑ String variables, designed to hold text,
- ❑ Date variables, actually for storing both date and time information,
- ❑ Boolean variables, for storing information that is binary (True/False, Yes/No),
- ❑ Object variables, used to represent objects,
- ❑ Variants, generic variables, capable of holding almost any data.

The definition and usage of these data types is covered below, in individual sections for each group.

Numeric Data Types

Since there are so many different types of applications that require numbers, and the accuracy, precision and size of numbers can vary so widely, there are several distinct data types in this category.

Integer	The most familiar of data types, this can store whole numbers from -32,768 to 32,767 (the standard range for a 16 bit, or two byte, number).

Long	The big brother of the Integer, this data type is referred to as a Long integer, being made up of 32 bits (four bytes). It is therefore capable of holding a much wider range of whole numbers than the Integer data type. You can store values between -2,147,483,648 and 2,147,483,647 into variables of this type.
Single	This is a Single-Precision Floating-Point value, using 4 bytes to store real numbers, which are limited more in precision than range. You can store positive numbers between 1.401298E-45 and 3.402823E38, and the opposite range of negative numbers.
Double	This is the same type of information as for Single, but using twice as many bytes to store the information (8 bytes). As with Single, it is the precision of this data type that is of primary concern. Both the Single and Double data types will be discussed in more detail after this table. A Double can hold values from 4.94065645841247E-324 to 1.79769313486232E308, and the opposite range for negative numbers.
Currency	As the name implies, this data type is designed to hold monetary values and, as such, is limited to a fixed number of decimals places (4). By fixing the decimal point and using 8 bytes for storage, this data type can accurately store values between -922,337,203,685,477.5808 and +922,337,203,685,477.5807, making it the best choice for financial transactions.
Byte	Using one byte to store integer values, variables of this type can store numbers between 0 and 255.
Decimal	This is the largest available numeric data type, capable of holding negative or positive numbers using up to 29 digits (the decimal point can be positioned anywhere within those 29 digits). This provides the Decimal data type with the ability to store a number as large as 79,228,162,514,264,337,593,543,950,335 negative or positive.
	You cannot declare a variable of type Decimal. This will be covered later, under the section on Variants.

Each data type is well suited for certain applications, such as the Currency data type, which should be used for monetary values.

Integer Values (Long Integer, Integer and Byte)

Integers are used in any situation that requires non-decimal values, such as for counters, although the Byte data type would actually be sufficient in most situations. Long integers are used in any situation that requires whole numbers that cover a wide range. This is often the data type used for ID values in databases, uniquely identifying some specific item such as a Customer, Product, or an Invoice.

Floating Point Values (Single and Double)

Single and Double data types are floating point numbers, meaning that they have a certain degree of precision. They manage to represent a wide range of values through manipulation of the decimal point. This is not really the place to go into an in-depth explanation of significant digits and scientific notation, but a quick overview will show you how these data types work.

> *The number 0.001 has 4 digits in it, and the decimal point is positioned after the first digit. This number could be expressed as 1 times 10^{-3}; they are the same. There is only one significant digit in this value, the 1. The number 2,322,000 is a seven digit number, but is equivalent to 2.322 times 10^6, so there are only 4 significant digits. Now, consider the number 2,322,000.001. In this case, there are 10, the zeroes are all significant because they separate non-zero values. Thinking of this another way, you could not display this number unambiguously without using all 10 digits.*

The Single data type supports values with up to 7 significant digits. This means that, although it could easily handle 2,322,000 or 0.001, it could not hold the value 2,322,000.001. This data type is useful for many things, but you must consider precision in its use. Use variables of type Single to store values that require low precision, such as interest rates (generally one or two digits of precision, 0.05 %, 6.9 %, etc) or values where it is acceptable to sacrifice some accuracy.

The Double data type supports values with up to 15 significant digits, which raises it to a level capable of handling most floating point information with acceptable accuracy. Doubles are often used as part of statistical or scientific calculations.

Monetary Values (Currency)

Many programs have used doubles to store monetary values, such as bank balances, payroll information, etc., but this is not a good idea. When dealing with money, you must not lose any information, every cent is important. Floating-point values deal only with a certain number of significant digits, and they are continually rounding values down to maintain that number. In the case of money, you should always work with a fixed-point data type, such as Integer, Long or the **Currency** data type.

> One successful method of storing monetary information, before the Currency data type was available, was to use Long integers and just assume two decimal places at the end. In reality, the Currency data type is doing almost the same thing, but with four decimal places.

The Decimal Data Type

The Decimal data type is an oddity, you cannot declare a variable of type Decimal, but it is possible to use it through a Variant (more information in the section on variants). This data type is really just a 12 byte integer value (capable of producing 29 digit numbers) that can have a decimal point anywhere within it. It is not a floating-point number, it does not round information to fit based on significant digits. This data type should only be necessary in unusual circumstances (such as complex scientific or statistical calculations) and should otherwise be ignored.

String Data Types

Strings are used to store any textual information and may comprise any combination of ASCII characters. There are only two types of strings:

Variable Length Strings (Regular)

When you declare a variable as `String`, you can store almost any amount of text into that variable (up to 2 billion characters). The realistic limit on how much you place into the `String` is dependent on your available memory, which would likely be exceeded before you reached 2 billion characters.

Fixed Length Strings

The variable declaration of a string can contain an additional piece of information, the **string length**, making the string fixed in size. A fixed length string can hold only that number of characters, and cannot grow beyond that length. The length information is added to your declaration by placing `*<length>` after the `As String`. The following code declares a fixed length string of 20 characters:

```
Dim FirstName As String * 20
```

Fixed length strings are used to save memory, but, in most cases, the small amount of space you could save is not worth the extra effort. The major exception to this would be situations where you are using a large number (hundreds or thousands) of these strings. Remember that you could end up using more space than you need if you create a fixed length string that is longer than your data.

Date

`Date` variables can be used to store date values, time values or a combined date/time value. Assigning a value to a `Date` variable is the only trick to using them. You have to use a special method of letting VBA know that you are dealing with dates, the # character. The code below demonstrates how to assign a specific date to a `Date` variable:

```
ExpiryDate = #08/12/98#
```

You have to do the same thing with time values, and when using both time and date values. An example of each method is listed below:

```
ExpiryDate = #4:00:00 PM#
ExpiryDate = #08/12/98 4:00:00 PM#
```

> Note that VBA uses your regional settings to determine what date/time formats to use. The statement above, using the date 8/12/98, could mean different things depending on whether your date format is set to Month/Day/Year or Day/Month/Year.

Boolean Variables

Often you need to store data that is binary (having only two possible values). **Boolean** variables are provided for this purpose, capable of storing only True or False. VBA provides two **constants** (special values represented by names, allowing you to use those names instead of the actual information), `True` and `False`, which make it easier to assign values to this type of variable. The code below shows several examples of setting Boolean variables:

```
Dim SendAsEmail As Boolean
Dim CollateCopies As Boolean
Dim ProductIsAvailable As Boolean

SendAsEmail = True
CollateCopies = False
ProductIsAvailable = Not ProductIsAvailable
```

The last line of code shows an example of using logic statements to manipulate Boolean values, in this case setting `ProductIsAvailable` to be the opposite of its current value. You can also use the logical operators, and these are discussed later.

Object Variables

Certain types of variables are capable of storing objects. These variables can be either generic variables that can hold any object, or variables that hold a single specific object type. These variables are declared like regular variables, using `As Object` to signify a generic object variable, and `As <Object Type>` to declare it as a specific type of object.

Once you have declared the variable though, you work with it a little differently. You must use the `Set` keyword when assigning a value to an object variable. The code below shows the declaration of both types of object variables and the use of the `Set` keyword:

```
Sub WorkingWithObjects()

    Dim oGeneric As Object
    Dim onMAPI As NameSpace

    Set onMAPI = Application.GetNameSpace("MAPI")
    Set oGeneric = onMAPI

End Sub
```

You can see from the example that you can use the generic object in exactly the same manner as the specific one, with the same effects. You will not get the wonderful code completion features of VBA when you are working with the generic object though, VBA doesn't pop up the list of object properties and methods for you automatically. Object variables will be used in all of the code samples in this book, but they are usually of a specific type.

Variants

When we originally started this discussion of variables, the example showed declaring variables without a data type. When that occurs, VBA automatically makes the variable a `Variant`, the default data type in both VBA and VB itself.

`Variant`s are variables that can hold any data type, performing automatic conversions as necessary, allowing you to assign any value to them without error. It is possible to determine the current data type stored in a `Variant` through the `VarType` function. This function returns a number that indicates which of the many different possible data types is currently being stored. VBA provides a series of **constants** listed below, that you can use in place of the various numeric values returned by this function:

Constant	Value	Constant	Value
vbEmpty	0	vbObject	9
vbNull	1	vbError	10
vbInteger	2	vbBoolean	11
vbLong	3	vbVariant	12
vbSingle	4	vbDataObject	13
vbDouble	5	vbDecimal	14
vbCurrency	6	vbByte	17
vbDate	7	vbArray	8192
vbString	8		

Despite their flexibility, or perhaps because of it, you should not use `Variant` variables unless you need to. If you know what you will be placing into the variable, then declare it as that type. This will avoid any problems of unwanted variable conversion, etc. There will be a few situations where you truly need a variable that can hold any data type, at which time a `Variant` will become essential, but these situations are not common.

Conversion between Data Types

For each type, only specific information can be stored, but there is some overlap and it is possible to convert data from one type to another. VBA will perform automatic conversions in most situations, such as in the code below:

```
Sub WorkingWithVariables()

    Dim X As Double
    Dim Y As Integer

    X = "3.5"
    Y = 32.2122
    MsgBox X
    MsgBox Y

End Sub
```

The code above would display a value of 3.5 for X, and 32 for Y. VBA converted the information appropriately in each case, even rounding the second value before placing it into an `Integer` variable.

Despite this automatic conversion, it is sometimes helpful to have a method of forcing a conversion into a specific data type, allowing you to control exactly what happens to your information. VBA provides a large group of conversion functions for this purpose, each designed to convert values into one specific data type:

CInt	Converts a value into an Integer, rounding if necessary.
CLng	Converts a value into a Long integer, rounding if necessary.
CDate	Converts a value into a Date, especially useful for converting Strings into Date variables. Capable of accepting a wide variety of date formats.
CDbl	Converts a value into a Double, potentially reducing its number of significant digits.
CCur	Converts a value into Currency.
CDec	Useful only when assigning the result to a Variant, this converts values into Decimal data types.
CBool	Converts into Boolean.
CStr	Converts anything into a String. For instance, Boolean variables become "True" or "False".

Arrays

An **array** is a series of values of the same data type, such as 10 variants, or 100 strings. Each value can be set or retrieved using its index or position in the array.

You can visualize an array as a row of values, each capable of holding an individual value.

In VBA, you declare an array just like a variable with the addition of the size of the array; this is shown below for several different sizes and types of arrays:

```
Sub WorkingWithArrays()

    Dim Numbers(10) As Integer
    Dim Names(30) As String
    Dim Stuff(100)

    Numbers(1) = 5
    Numbers(2) = Numbers(1) + 5
    Names(5) = "Duncan"
    Names(7) = "Fred"
    Names(23) = "Laura"

    MsgBox Names(5)

    Stuff(5) = "Duncan"
    Stuff(6) = 32

End Sub
```

Determining Array Bounds

When you specify the array size with a single number, this number determines the upper bound of the array and the lower bound is assumed. VBA, by default, places the lower bound of arrays at zero, so `Dim Names(30) As String` is creating an array with 31 positions in it. You can avoid this default behavior by including both the lower and upper bounds in your declaration, like this:

```
Dim Numbers(1 To 30) As Integer
```

Alternatively, you can change the default behavior of VBA through the `Option Base` statement. At the beginning of any VBA module (before any procedures), you can place a line of code that reads `Option Base 1` or `Option Base 0`. This line tells VBA what to use as the default lower bound for arrays in that module.

> 1 and 0 are not your only options for the lower bound of an array; you can just as easily create an array that starts at 10, 20, or even 5000. Just declare the array appropriately, `Dim X(5 to 342) As Integer`, for instance. You can only make the VBA default to 1 or 0 though. The `Option Base` statement will not accept any other values.

Multi-Dimensional Arrays

You can create arrays with more than one dimension by specifying **multiple index sizes**, which are particularly suited to certain applications. The result is a set of variables (all of the same type, just like in single dimension arrays) that can be referenced by their "co-ordinates". The code below declares two **multi-dimensional arrays**, which are illustrated immediately following:

```
Sub WorkingWithArrays()

    Dim Grid(1 To 8, 1 To 8) As Integer
    Dim Cube(1 To 8, 1 To 8, 1 To 8) As Single

    'Code to fill arrays with values would go here….

    Grid(3, 5) = 23
    Grid(5, 1) = Grid(2, 1) + Grid(3, 2)

    Cube(3, 3, 3) = Cube(2, 1, 5)
    Cube(8, 1, 5) = 53.3232

End Sub
```

`Multi-Dimensional` arrays take up a large amount of memory (the size of the data type * dimension 1 * dimension 2 * dimension 3 and so on…) so you should use them sparingly, and not make them any bigger than you need.

Dynamic Arrays

Sometimes you may be unsure of how large to make your array. Perhaps you are using one to store certain words as you find them in an Outlook item. When you are writing your code you have no way of knowing how many words you might find, so you can't determine how to declare the array. You could declare the array to be arbitrarily large, e.g. with 1000 elements, but that has two potential problems:

❑ What if there happened to be more than 1000 items? Your code could not handle it.

❑ What if there were less (and there usually would be)? You would be wasting memory.

Neither one of these problems can be ignored; you do not want to write code like that. Fortunately, VBA provides us with a way to deal with these issues, **dynamic arrays**. These arrays are declared without specifying their size, and then they can have their size set or adjusted at anytime.

The array is declared with empty parentheses to indicate that it is a dynamic array:

```
Dim Names() As String
```

Then the ReDim statement is used to set the size of the array:

```
ReDim Names(34)
```

> The ReDim **statement will erase any existing data in the array unless the** Preserve **keyword is added:**
>
> ```
> ReDim Preserve Names(68)
> ```
>
> **Of course, data would still be lost if the array was reduced in size, even if the** Preserve **keyword is used.**

Multi-dimensional dynamic arrays are also possible, although this is slightly limited. With multi-dimensional arrays, you can only adjust the size of the last dimension if you are using the Preserve keyword. However, if you are just calling ReDim (such as the first time you set the size of the array), you can set the number of dimensions and their size however you wish.

Constants

The last type of "variable" covered in this section is not really a variable at all. **Constants** cannot be changed through code, the very thing that defines variables. Like variables though, constants are used to associate a name with a value, allowing you to use that name in your code in place of the value itself. The difference is that the value is set as part of the constant's declaration, and cannot be changed (you can, of course, change its value by editing the declaration). The syntax for declaring a constant is shown below, with optional arguments shown enclosed between [and]:

```
[Public|Private] Const <Constant Name> [As <Data Type>] = <Value>
```

The optional Public or Private at the beginning of the declaration is used to control the constant's **scope**. Scope is discussed below. If you do not specify either Public or Private, then it is assumed that the constant is Private.

The other optional portion of this declaration is the data type - as with variables, the constant will be declared as a `Variant` if you do not specify otherwise. Several example constant declarations are shown below:

```
Const MaxLength = 20
Const CompanyName As String = "Java Jitters Inc."
Const YearEnd As Date = #08/12/99#
```

Using a constant in place of a particular value has several benefits, not the least of which is improving the readability of your code, the name `MaxLength` carries a great deal more meaning than the number 20. The other main benefit of using a constant becomes apparent when the value changes. If you have a program that uses a certain value (the name of your company, for example) in hundreds of different places in the code, you should use a constant and not the value itself. Then, if the company name were changed, however slightly, you would only have to make one change to your program, not search through all your code trying to find every place that the name was used.

Scope

Everything in Visual Basic has a certain **scope**, including variables and procedures. The scope of a procedure affects where it can be called from; if it is not visible to another procedure then it cannot be used. For variables it is the same concept, their scope determines where they (and therefore the information they carry) can be accessed. If you need a certain value to be visible to every piece of code in your project, that variable has to have the correct scope.

There are three distinct levels of scope possible in VBA:

❏ Global. Visible from any code in the same project.

❏ Module-Level. Visible from any code in the same module.

❏ Local. Visible only in the procedure it was declared in. (Does not apply to procedures, they always have a scope of at least module-level.)

Operators

The best way to view an operator is as a function exposed to us by VBA. The benefit of these operators is that we do not have to write our own and reinvent the wheel. I have grouped the different operators available to us into 4 groups, namely Arithmetical, Comparison, Concatenation and Logical.

Arithmetical Operators

+	Addition
–	Subtraction
*	Multiplication

/	Division
\	Integer division
^	Exponentiation
Mod	The remainder after integer division

Comparison Operators

The comparison operators are used to compare two variables or values and return a Boolean if the comparison expression is true. For example, 3 < 4 returns True.

It is important to be aware of what happens when you compare variables that are not of the same data type:

❑   If one is a numeric and the other is a variant and the variant cannot be converted to a numeric then an error is raised. Otherwise a numeric comparison is performed.

❑   If one variable is a string and the other is a variant data type except a Null then string comparison is performed.

❑   If one variable is numeric and the other is Empty then a numeric comparison is performed and Empty is treated as 0.

❑   If one variable is a string and the other is Empty then a string comparison is performed and Empty is treated as "".

<	Less than
<=	Less than or equal to
>	Greater than
>=	Greater than or equal
=	Equals to
<>	Not equal to

Concatenation

There are two concatenation operators: & and +. The & operator should be used for concatenation as it always works as you would expect, joining two strings. The result of using the + operator, on the other hand, depends on the data types used, and I have never found a good reason to use it for concatenation.

Logical

There is a total of six operators that allow us to evaluate expressions:

Not	NEGATION (x = Not y)
And	AND (x = a And b)
Or	OR (x = a Or b)
Xor	EXCLUSIVE OR (x = a Xor b)
Eqv	EQUIVALENCE (x = a Eqv b)
Imp	IMPLICATION (x = a Imp b)

Sub and Functions

The subs and functions are very similar. They are both made up of a series of VBA statements that can be executed whenever you want by calling the sub or function. Also parameters may be passed to the sub or function as arguments. Arguments are covered below. The only difference is that a function returns a value but a sub does not.

A sub is declared as follows:

```
Sub <ProcedureName>()

    Code

End Sub
```

The main procedure enclosing an Outlook macro is a sub. The `ProcedureName` corresponds to the macro name. Of course, the main sub may call other subs or functions.

Functions are declared slightly differently from subs:

```
Function <ProcedureName>() As <Data type>

    Code

End Sub
```

The keyword `Sub` is replaced with `Function` and the data type of the return value is indicated at the end of the declaration:

```
Function Squared(Number As Long) As Long

    Squared = Number * Number

End Function
```

> Like a variable, if you do not specify the data type returned by a function then it is considered to be a `Variant`.

In the code of the function, you return a value by a statement of the form `<Function Name> = <Value>`. That value is then returned to the code that called the function. At the calling end, you need to place brackets around the arguments you are sending to the function. The code below shows an example of calling a function.

```
X = Squared(34)
```

Arguments

Some procedures require information to be passed to them to be able to run - information that you supply when you call them. The pieces of information required are called the **arguments** or **parameters** of the procedure, and are specified in the procedure declaration. You specify parameters in the brackets after the procedure name by typing in a comma-separated list of variable names and data types, which look very similar to standard variable declarations:

```
Private Function ArgueFunction(FirstName As String, ByVal LastName
As String, Optional MiddleName)
```

ByRef and ByVal

You can pass any expression of the correct data type into a procedure, just like setting a variable of the same type, but when you pass an actual variable, procedures treat them differently. This difference in behavior occurs because variables can be passed into procedures in one of two ways, **by reference** or **by value.**

When a variable is passed **by reference**, the procedure works with the **actual variable** when it modifies the parameter.

When you pass a variable **by value**, only a **copy** of its contents are given to the procedure.

You can control how each parameter is passed to a procedure by modifying the procedure declaration. The keywords `ByRef` or `ByVal` can be placed in front of a parameter, making all variables passed to this parameter explicitly by reference or by value. These keywords affect each parameter individually, and any parameter that doesn't have a keyword in front of it is considered `ByRef` by default.

Optional Arguments

Many of the procedures that are supplied by Outlook or by VBA contain **optional arguments**, parameters that we can supply if needed but can also be skipped. The `MsgBox` function is good example of this, accepting five parameters, only one of which is required. Optional parameters allow us to make procedures easy to use; the user of the procedure need only supply the information that fits their current needs. To make a parameter optional in a procedure declaration that parameter must:

❑ Be after any required parameters, all optional parameters must fall at the end of the parameter list

❑ Have the `Optional` keyword before this parameter, and any that follow it in the parameter list

Optional parameters can have a default value specified; a value that the parameter will be assigned if none is supplied. Default values are added to the procedure declaration as an equal sign and value. The procedure declaration below illustrates the various parts of declaring an optional parameter:

```
Sub DisplayMessage(ByVal Message As String, Optional ByVal Title =
"My Message")
```

ParamArray

The last parameter in a procedure declaration may have the `ParamArray` keyword in front of it, signifying that it will accept an optional array of values as arguments. If a `ParamArray` argument is present in an argument list, there can be no optional parameters for the same procedure and you can't use the `ByVal` or `ByRef` keywords. Use of this keyword allows you to create procedures like the following example, one that can take a varying number of values and then work with those values to solve a problem:

```
Sub ParamArrayTest()

    SalaryAverage 32000, 34200, 50000

    SalaryAverage 34200, 34500, 50000

End Sub
```

```
Sub SalaryAverage(ParamArray Values())

    '...

End Sub
```

This type of function is useful, and it is extremely important to know that such abilities exist. However, it is slightly unusual and we will not need to use it anywhere in this book.

Summary

In this chapter we have looked at how to use the Visual Basic Editor and the Macro window that are offered by Outlook. We also took a cursory look at some of the fundamentals of VBA. This was intended to serve as a quick refresher for those who may already have worked with VBA, or as an appetizer for those who have not.

It was by no means comprehensive. Nor would it be practical to provide such VBA coverage in a book of this nature. But, armed with the information in this chapter and the code samples throughout the book, you should have a sound basis from which to increase your VBA programming skills. A much fuller account of VBA is provided in "Access 2000 VBA Programmer's Reference" also available from Wrox Press or if you're interested in learning more about VB "Beginning Visual Basic 6" by Peter Wright is probably the book for you.

Automating Outlook

The idea behind this chapter is to show you just how easy it is to automate Outlook and to get Outlook to work for you instead of you working for Outlook. This chapter is made up of two example applications that walk you through the process of using Outlook. The first application, an Overdue Tasks Scheduler, handles tasks that are overdue and arranges a meeting with their owner; this uses the Outlook object model as it is exposed to us through the VBA that comes with Outlook. The second is a mail merge program for sending personalized mails to a number of recipients; this application uses Visual Basic and shows how the Outlook object model can be accessed from outside Outlook. The code for both of these applications can be downloaded from the Wrox web site at http://www.wrox.com.

Overdue Tasks Scheduler

The Overdue Tasks Scheduler is designed to check for any overdue task upon startup of Outlook. Here an overdue task constitutes any task sent out by the user whose due date has passed and which is not marked as completed. If there are any such tasks, then details about the tasks are displayed in a form and the user may choose to send an meeting request to the delegate that is working on any particular overdue task.

This application is totally contained within Outlook.

The overdue tasks scheduler project comprises:

frmScheduler	A form to display a list of the overdue tasks and allow the user to decide which task to setup a meeting for.
clsScheduleCheck	A class module that performs the checking of the tasks and decides whether or not to show the form.

The only extra code needed will instantiate the class and should be placed in the code module ThisOutlookSession, always available in the Visual Basic Editor of Outlook.

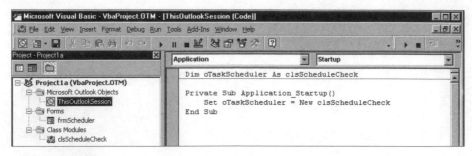

This code will cause the Overdue Task Scheduler to run when the Outlook application is started.

frmScheduler

The form used to display overdue tasks is relatively simple. It comprises two command buttons and a listview box, which will require a reference is the Microsoft Windows Common Controls 6.0 and may be accessed by right-clicking on the userform toolbox or using the Tools | References... of the VBE.

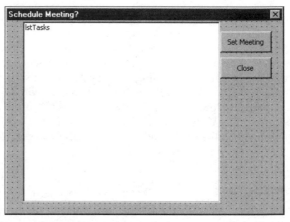

The properties of each control set at design time are given below.

Command button	Name:	cmdSetMeeting
	Caption:	Set Meeting
Command button	Name:	cmdClose
	Caption:	Close
	Cancel:	True
ListView	Name:	lstTasks
	FullRowSelect:	True
	LabelEdit:	1
	LabelWrap:	False
	View:	3

The next step is to check for overdue tasks and to fill this form with the appropriate information. This is achieved within the clsScheduler, which is instantiated as soon as Outlook opens. If we find any overdue tasks then we load the Schedule Meeting form showing the Task Name, Due Date, Days Overdue and Assignee for the task. This information is set in the class clsScheduler.

clsScheduler

This class requires two module level variables – one to hold a reference to the data source we are interested in and the second to hold a reference to the form that we have just created.

```
Private m_onMAPI As NameSpace
Private m_frmSchedule As frmScheduler
```

The first thing we need to happen when this class is instantiated is for the appropriate data source to be referenced. The overdue task check is then called.

```
Private Sub Class_Initialize()
    Set m_onMAPI = GetNamespace("MAPI")
    CheckSchedule
End Sub
```

CheckSchedule

The job of the `CheckSchedule` routine is to check all tasks in the **Tasks** folder to see if any of them are overdue. First we need to get a reference to the appropriate folder. Here we are assuming that all tasks are stored within the default **Tasks** folder of the user. You could, however, use the `PickFolder` method of the `NameSpace` object to allow the user to pick the appropriate folder.

```
Private Sub CheckSchedule()
    Dim otTask As TaskItem
    Dim ofTasks As MAPIFolder

    Set ofTasks = m_onMAPI.GetDefaultFolder(olFolderTasks)
```

Once we have the correct folder we need to work through each item of that folder to establish if any of the tasks that we have assigned to others are overdue and also not completed. This is simply achieved using the `DueDate` property and `Complete` property of each `TaskItem` object. We also ensure that the task is not something we have assigned ourselves by checking that there is at least one recipient. If an overdue task is found and it has not been completed, a reference is made to the `frmScheduler` and the details of this task are added to the `listview` of that form. The details of the task that we are interested in displaying in the form are the subject, due date, the number of days the task is overdue and the first recipient's name.

```
For Each otTask In ofTasks.Items
    If otTask.DueDate < Date And otTask.Complete = False And _
                otTask.Recipients.count > 0 Then

    With m_frmSchedule
        If m_frmSchedule Is Nothing Then
            Set m_frmSchedule = New frmScheduler
        End If
        m_frmSchedule.lstTasks.ListItems.add , _
        otTask.Subject, otTask.Subject
        m_frmSchedule.lstTasks.ListItems(otTask.Subject).SubItems(1) _
        = otTask.DueDate
        m_frmSchedule.lstTasks.ListItems(otTask.Subject).SubItems(2) _
        = Date - otTask.DueDate
        m_frmSchedule.lstTasks.ListItems(otTask.Subject).SubItems(3) _
        = otTask.Recipients(1).Name
    End With
    End If
Next
```

Once the checking for overdue tasks is complete, we check to see whether any such tasks exist and the frmScheduler has been instantiated. If so they are displayed within the form we created earlier. Finally the references to the last overdue `TaskItem` and the `Tasks` folder are released.

```
        If Not m_frmSchedule Is Nothing Then
            m_frmSchedule.Show vbModeless
        End If
        Set otTask = Nothing
        Set ofTasks = Nothing
    End Sub
```

The form displaying the overdue task data appears as follows:

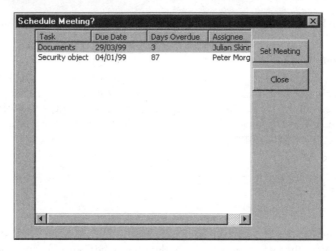

If the user decides to create a meeting by pressing the **Set Meeting** button, then an appointment is set up for the earliest possible time when both the user and the assignee are free. All the code to do this is placed in the **Set Meeting** command button `Click` event. If no meeting is desired the **Close** button is used to end this application.

```
Private Sub cmdClose_Click()
    Unload Me
End Sub
```

Setting a Meeting

If the user decides to request a meeting then the task in question should be selected and the **Set Meeting** button clicked. The first step when setting up the meeting is to get a reference to the user's **Calendar** MAPIfolder.

```
Private Sub cmdSetMeeting_Click()
    Dim onMAPI As NameSpace
    Dim oaMeeting As AppointmentItem
    Dim ofCalendar As MAPIFolder
    Dim orRecipient As Recipient
    Dim sRecFB As String
    Dim sCurFB As String
    Dim i As Long

    Set onMAPI = Application.GetNamespace("MAPI")
    Set ofCalendar = onMAPI.GetDefaultFolder(olFolderCalendar)
```

The next step up is to create the `AppointmentItem` object and set it up to be a meeting by setting the `MeetingStatus` property to be of type `olMeeting`. The duration of the meeting is also set and `ResponseRequested` property set so that the recipient will be prompted for a response. The subject and body of the meeting request are also set.

```
Set oaMeeting = ofCalendar.Items.add(olAppointmentItem)

oaMeeting.ResponseRequested = True
oaMeeting.Duration = 60
oaMeeting.MeetingStatus = olMeeting
oaMeeting.Subject = "Overdue -" & lstTasks.SelectedItem.Text
oaMeeting.Body = "We need to have a meeting on your task that is - " _
& lstTasks.SelectedItem.SubItems(2) & " days overdue."
```

We then add the assignee of the task to the `Recipients` collection of the `AppointmentItem`. We check, by using the `Resolve` method, that this recipient is held in the address book or has a valid email address and set the type property.

```
Set orRecipient =
oaMeeting.Recipients.add(lstTasks.SelectedItem.SubItems(3))
    orRecipient.Resolve
    orRecipient.Type = olTo
```

Finally we need to set the start date and time for the meeting. This is achieved by checking the `FreeBusy` property of both the recipient and the user. The meeting is assigned for the earliest possible time when both parties are free.

```
RecFB = orRecipient.FreeBusy(Now, 60)
sCurFB = onMAPI.CurrentUser.FreeBusy(Now, 60)

For i = Int((Now - CDate(Int(Now))) * 24) + 2 To Len(sRecFB)
    If Mid(sRecFB, i, 1) = 0 And Mid(sCurFB, i, 1) = 0 Then
        oaMeeting.start = CDate(Int(Now)) + CDbl(i - 1) / 24
        Exit For
    End If
Next
```

Once this is completed we then send the meeting request and release the object references.

```
oaMeeting.Send

Set orRecipient = Nothing
Set ofCalendar = Nothing
Set oaMeeting = Nothing
Set onMAPI = Nothing
End Sub
```

The result of this code is to produce the following meeting request sent to the task assignee.

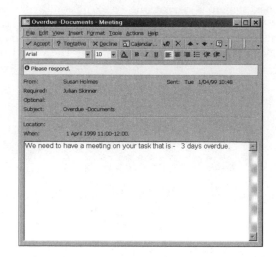

Mail Merge

The idea behind this sample application is to allow you to create your own personal mail templates — that is, pre-written mail messages — and then send mail based on this template to a number of selected recipients, personalized for each recipient. So, the idea is for a mail merge program which works just like Word Mail Merge, but for email rather than 'snail mail'. Note that this application is written in Visual Basic itself, not in Outlook VBA, so it demonstrates how the Outlook object model can be used to automate Outlook from outside. Note also that you will need to set references to the Microsoft DAO 3.6 Object Library and, of course, the Microsoft Outlook 9.0 Object Library; you will also need to add Microsoft Windows Common Controls components to the project. The code for the project is available for download from our website at http://www.wrox.com.

The application is made up of three different parts. The first is a form that simply gives us access to the other two parts of the application and opens the database that holds the templates; the second is a wizard that guides the user through the process of sending personalized mail based on a specific template; and the third allows the user to manage the templates themselves.

The whole project is contained within four different Visual Basic forms:

frmMailMerge	The opening screen which acts as the main menu for the application.
frmSelectTemplate	This form allows the user to select a template for editing, and also provides options to create or delete a template.
frmTemplateEditor	This is the form where the templates are actually designed or edited.
frmWizard	The wizard which guides the user through sending personalized email.

There is also one module, `MailMerge`, which serves merely to hold two public variables.

Main Menu Form

The opening form has three command buttons; clicking on the first selects opens the Mail Merge Wizard, which guides the user through the steps for sending out personalized mail; the second allows the user to create, edit or delete templates; and the third allows the user to quit the application.

Mail Merge Wizard

The Mail Merge Wizard walks us through the necessary steps to create an Electronic Mailer. There are three parts to the wizard; the first is the splash screen similar to that of most wizards you will have seen or used. This is simply a welcome screen informing the user what the purpose of the wizard is. The only options the user is given at this point are Cancel to exit the wizard and Next to go on to the next screen.

The second step prompts the user to select the recipients that we wish to have receive the mail. The names and email addresses of the potential recipients listed here are taken from the user's Contacts folder. There are also options to create and edit contacts.

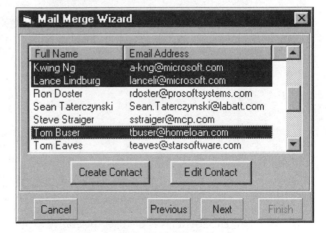

The final screen allows us to select the template on which the mail that is sent out to the recipients will be based. The user can also specify whether the items are to be saved in the Drafts folder or sent directly. If the Create Drafts for Review box is checked, the mails are saved in the Drafts folder, and the user can review them before they are sent. Otherwise, the mails will be sent when the user clicks on the Finish button.

Template Wizard

The other wizard in the Mail Merge application allows the user to create, edit and delete the templates used by the Mail Merge Wizard. There are two parts to the Template Wizard. The first form allows you to select the template that you want to edit or delete, and also gives you the option to create a new template.

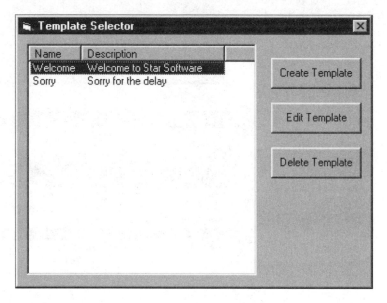

If the user elects to create or edit a template then the user is taken to the Template Editor form. This form gives the user the ability to add or modify the Body and Subject properties of the mails based on this template. Personalization is achieved using the Insert option on the form's menu bar; this provides the ability to include the first name, last name or full name of the recipient at any point in the text. This inserts a formula which will be replaced by the appropriate name for each recipient when mails based on this template are sent. The File menu allows us to save the template or to exit the Template Wizard.

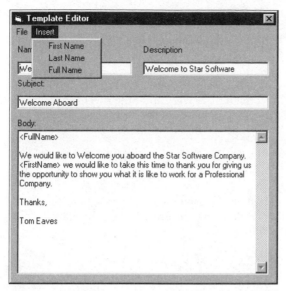

Now that we have seen *what* the Mail Merge application does, we need to take a look at *how* it does it.

MailMerge Module

This module contains only two lines, to declare variables for the template database and for the user's Mailbox name:

```
Public db As Database
Public strName As String
```

We define these here as public variables so that they are available to all the forms in the project.

frmMailMerge

This form does not deal directly with Outlook, but is very basic and it is useful to see how we set up the project for the other forms, so it is worth looking at the code. The form has three buttons, called cmdMailMerge, cmdTemplate and cmdQuit. We dimension two variables in the Declarations section at the top of the code:

```
Option Explicit
Private m_frmWizard As frmWizard
Private m_frmSelectTemplate As frmSelectTemplate
```

This allows us to create instances of the other forms when the user clicks one of the buttons to go on to the Mail Merge Wizard or the Template Wizard.

```
Private Sub Form_Load()
    Set db = OpenDatabase(Path and Filename of Template Database)
End Sub
```

As you can see, we open the database for the templates in the Load event of the form. I open the database here really just for the sake of convenience and to make sure it is ready for both parts of this application.

```
Private Sub cmdMailMerge_Click()
    Set m_frmWizard = New frmWizard
    m_frmWizard.Show
End Sub
```

When the `cmdMailMerge` button is clicked, we get a reference to a new `frmWizard` object, which gives us access to the next part of the application. Once we have this reference, we just show the form. If there were anything I wanted to do to the form before showing it, I could do it here, just before the form is displayed.

```
Private Sub cmdTemplate_Click()
    Set m_frmSelectTemplate = New frmSelectTemplate
    m_frmSelectTemplate.Show
End Sub
```

Behind the `cmdTemplate` button, we instantiate the `frmSelectTemplate` form and get a reference to it. Again, we just show this form, but if we needed to, we could alter the form before we showed it to the user.

```
Private Sub cmdQuit_Click()
    Unload Me
End Sub
```

The final button, `cmdQuit`, simply unloads the form, but we tidy up and make sure all our references have been freed in the form's `Unload` event.

```
Private Sub Form_Unload(Cancel As Integer)
    db.Close
    Set db = Nothing
    Set m_frmWizard = Nothing
    Set m_frmSelectTemplate = Nothing
End Sub
```

Here, we close the database connection and make sure we release all references to the forms and the database that we might have instantiated.

Mail Merge Wizard

The form for the Mail Merge Wizard contains a control array of three frames, `fmWizard()`, and a status bar, `sbWizard`. Each of the frames in the control array has controls of its own, which are only available when that frame is visible. The status bar control is not available in the default controls available with Visual Basic, but is included in Microsoft Common Controls. The status bar has four panels, **Cancel**, **Previous**, **Next** and **Finish**, which are used to handle navigation through the frames of the form (as well as some invisible panels which are used merely to space the visible panels nicely); the code behind this is given in the section entitled "Wizard Navigation" below.

In the Declarations section for the form, we define the following module variables to make them available to the wizard:

```
Private m_Index As Long
Private m_oOutlook As New Outlook.Application
Private m_oNameSpace As NameSpace

Private WithEvents Contact As ContactItem
```

Name	Data type	Description
m_Index	Long	Used to keep track of which frame the user is viewing at any one point.
m_oOutlook	Application object	Reference to the Outlook Application object.
m_oNameSpace	NameSpace object	Reference to the NameSpace object.
Contact	ContactItem	Reference to the ContactItem object. This variable is used to allow the user to edit or create contacts and it allows us to catch the events that the ContactItem exposes to us.

```
Private Sub Form_Load()
    Me.MousePointer = vbHourglass

    'Setup the Status Bar buttons
    sbWizard.Panels("Finish").Enabled = False
    sbWizard.Panels("Next").Enabled = True
    sbWizard.Panels("Cancel").Enabled = True
    sbWizard.Panels("Previous").Enabled = False

    'prepare a pointer at which slide we are currently looking at
    m_Index = 0

    'The first frame visible for view.
    fmWizard(m_Index).Visible = True

    'Get a reference to the MAPI Data Store
    Set m_oNameSpace = m_oOutlook.GetNamespace("MAPI")

    'If we are not logged in then Logon prompt the user
    'for which profile to use
    m_oNameSpace.Logon , , True

    'Load the Recipients Listbox
    Call AddRecipients

    'Load the Templates Listbox
    Call AddTemplates
    Me.MousePointer = vbNormal

End Sub
```

When the frmWizard form loads, we first setup the buttons on the status bar, making sure that they are all enabled or disabled as required. The m_Index variable is set to the 0 (indicating the first frame), since it is used to specify which frame the user is currently viewing. We then instantiate the NameSpace object and log on if the user is not already logged on. This logging on again is handled by Outlook, as you can only be signed into one Outlook profile at a time. Lastly, we load the list view for the recipients' names and email addresses and the combo box containing the template names by calling the AddRecipients and AddTemplates functions. The navigation of the wizard is covered below in the section entitled "Wizard Navigation".

AddRecipients Function

The `AddRecipients` function loads the recipients listview `lstRecipients` which appears in the second frame `fmWizard(1)`, with all the contacts from the user's Contacts `MAPIFolder` that have an email address assigned to them.

```
Private Sub AddRecipients()
    Dim oContact As ContactItem
    Dim oFolder As MAPIFolder
    Dim ifor As Integer
    Dim iSizeFullName As Integer
    Dim iMailName As Integer

    Me.MousePointer = vbHourglass

    'Get name of mailbox from user and validate it
    Do
        strName = InputBox("Please input the name of the mailbox " & _
                           "to look for contacts in.", "Input name")

        'Look for mailbox
        For ifor = 1 To m_oNameSpace.Folders.Count
            If m_oNameSpace.Folders(ifor) = strName Then
                Set oFolder = m_oNameSpace.Folders(strName).Folders("Contacts")
                Exit For
            End If
        Next

        'If folder not found, tell user and repeat input box
        If oFolder Is Nothing Then
            MsgBox Chr$(34) & strName & Chr$(34) & _
                   " is not a valid mailbox name.", vbExclamation
        End If
    Loop While oFolder Is Nothing

    'Make sure the recipient List is empty
    lstRecipients.ListItems.Clear
    For ifor = 1 To oFolder.Items.Count

        'Check to see if the current Item is a Contact Item
        If oFolder.Items(ifor).Class = olContact Then
            Set oContact = oFolder.Items(ifor)

            'Check to see if the Contact has a Email Address
            If oContact.Email1Address <> "" Then

                'This following code to used to set the width of the Columns
                'in the list box
                'This way we make sure that all names and Email Addresses
                'are fully shown.
                lblFullName.Caption = oContact.FullName
                If iSizeFullName < lblFullName.Width Then
                    iSizeFullName = lblFullName.Width
                End If
                lblMailName.Caption = oContact.Email1Address
                If iMailName < lblMailName.Width Then
                    iMailName = lblMailName.Width
                End If

                'Add the Contact to the Recipients List
                lstRecipients.ListItems.Add , oContact.Subject, _
                oContact.FullName

                lstRecipients.ListItems(oContact.Subject).SubItems(1) = _
                oContact.Email1Address
            End If
        End If
    Next
```

```
'Set the Widths of the Columns to the proper width
lstRecipients.ColumnHeaders(1).Width = iSizeFullName * 1.1
lstRecipients.ColumnHeaders(2).Width = iMailName * 1.1

'De-reference our internal Variable
Set oContact = Nothing
Set oFolder = Nothing

Me.MousePointer = vbNormal
End Sub
```

The first step for adding the recipients to the listview is to get a reference to the Contacts `MAPIFolder`. To do this we prompt the user to input the name of the mailbox from which the contacts will be taken. If this name is invalid (i.e. if the folder cannot be found), we repeat the input box until a valid name is entered. We then set `oFolder` to point to the Contacts `MAPIFolder` in this Mailbox, which is itself in the `Folders` collection of the MAPI data store referenced by `m_oNameSpace`. This a little bit easier to understand if you look at the following code.

```
Dim oTopLevelFolders As Folders
Dim oPersonalFolder As MAPIFolder
Dim oNextLevelFolders As Folders

Set oTopLevelFolders = m_oNameSpace.Folders
Set oPersonalFolder = oTopLevelFolders("Mailbox - User_Name")
Set oNextLevelFolders = oPersonalFolder.Folders
Set oFolder = oNextLevelFolders.Item("Contacts")
```

This code first gets a reference to the `Folders` collection immediately underneath the data store referenced by `m_oNameSpace`. We get a reference to the Mailbox folder in this top-level folder; then we go one layer further down and get a reference to the `Folders` collection at this level. This in turn gives us access to the Contacts `MAPIFolder`, which is the folder we're looking for. So the one line of code above has been expanded so you can see more clearly what I am doing.

Now before we actually load the list, we make sure that the list is empty. The next step is to walk through all of the objects in the Contacts `MAPIFolder`. To do this, I use the `Count` property rather than a `For Each` loop. The reason for this is that the Contacts `MAPIFolder` can hold both `ContactItem` objects and `DistListItem` objects. In this example, we only want contacts in the list, even though we could easily use the distribution list items as well. At the start of this loop, we check to see if the current item is a contact, and then that it has an email address. If both these conditions are matched, we can add it to the list.

Before we actually add the contact to the list, we set two labels (which are invisible to the user) to contain the values of the contact's email address and full name and then check their sizes against the longest names so far. This is to make sure that the columns in the list are properly sized. After we have done this we add the full name and the email address of the contact to the list. Once we have iterated through all the items in the Contacts `MAPIFolder`, we set the width of the fields in the listview to the proper size.

AddTemplates Function

The `AddTemplates` function loads the list of templates from which the user can select the template they would like to use for the personalized mail. These are placed in a combo box called `lstTemplates` which appears in the third frame `fmWizard(2)`.

```
Private Sub AddTemplates()
    Dim oRecordset As Recordset

    'Open a recordset that will hold the Templates
    'from the MailMerge database.
    Set oRecordset = db.OpenRecordset _
                        ("Select Description, TemplateID from Template;")

    'Check to see if we have any records
    If oRecordset.RecordCount <> 0 Then

        'If we have a record then move to the first record fo the set
        oRecordset.MoveFirst
        Do While Not oRecordset.EOF

            'Move through the recordset until we reach the End of File
            lstTemplates.AddItem oRecordset("Description")
            lstTemplates.ItemData(lstTemplates.NewIndex) = _
            oRecordset("TemplateID")
            oRecordset.MoveNext
        Loop
    End If

    oRecordset.Close

    'De-reference the Recordset
    Set oRecordset = Nothing
End Sub
```

The first step for adding the templates is to retrieve the template's `Description` and the `TemplateID` from the `Template` table in the `MailMerge` database. Once we have the recordset, we need to make sure that this database does actually contain records before we carry on. To do this, we check that the `RecordCount` is not equal to 0. This method for checking for records will only work if you have not modified the recordset first. If the recordset does contain records, we set the first record in the recordset as the current record. We then walk through the recordset until we reach the end of the file, adding each record to the list of templates. Notice that we use the `ItemData` property to hold the `TemplateID`. You will see the reason for this in the "Working with the `MailItem`" section later in this chapter. Finally, when we have extracted all the data we need, we close down the recordset and de-reference the recordset variable.

Wizard Navigation

Navigation through the different screens of the wizard (represented by the different frames on the form) is handled by the different buttons that are exposed on the status bar.

```
Private Sub sbWizard_PanelClick(ByVal Panel As MSComctlLib.Panel)

    Select Case Panel.Key

    'If user clicked the Next button
    Case "Next"
        m_Index = m_Index + 1
        If m_Index < 2 Then
            sbWizard.Panels("Finish").Enabled = False
        Else
            m_Index = 2
            Panel.Enabled = False
            sbWizard.Panels("Finish").Enabled = True
        End If
        sbWizard.Panels("Previous").Enabled = True
```

```
'If the user clicked the Previous button
Case "Previous"
    m_Index = m_Index - 1
    If m_Index > 0 Then
        sbWizard.Panels("Previous").Enabled = True
        sbWizard.Panels("Finish").Enabled = False
    Else
        m_Index = 0
        Panel.Enabled = False
    End If
    sbWizard.Panels("Next").Enabled = True

'If the user clicked the Finish button
Case "Finish"
    Call DoMerge

'If the user clicked the Cancel button
Case "Cancel"
    If MsgBox("Are you sure?", vbQuestion + vbYesNo) = vbYes Then
        Unload Me
    End If
End Select

'Turn all Frames invisible
fmWizard(0).Visible = False
fmWizard(1).Visible = False
fmWizard(2).Visible = False

'Turn the active Frame visible
fmWizard(m_Index).Visible = True

End Sub
```

We use StatusBar control that is shipped with Microsoft Windows Common Controls
to handle the navigation through the wizard. We have placed Cancel, Previous, Next
and Finish buttons on the status bar to allow us to move between the frames. For this
to work correctly, we need to use the Key property that is exposed by the Panel object
of the status bar. We assign a Key to each button by which we can identify it. In the
above code we check the Key property for the panel which the user clicked and which
is passed into this event handler as a parameter. We use this value as the basis for a
Select Case statement.

The first button is the Next panel. When this is pressed, we increment by one the
variable m_Index which indicates the current frame. Next, we check to see whether
we are on the last page of the wizard (i.e. m_Index = 2) or not (i.e. m_Index < 2). If
we are, we disable the current panel, which is the Next button, enable the Finish button
and set m_Index to 2. If we are not on the last page, we just make sure that the Finish
button is turned off. Finally, we ensure that the Previous button is enabled.

The second case is the Previous panel. Here we subtract one from the page indicator
m_Index. We then check the value of this to see whether we are on the first page of the
wizard or not. If we are on the first page, we disable the Previous button and set
m_Index to zero. If we are not on the first page, we ensure that the Finish panel is
disabled and enable the Previous button.

The third button we handle is the Cancel button. In this case, we check to see that the
user really does want to cancel. If they do, we unload the wizard; otherwise we do
nothing.

The last button we are interested in is the Finish button. If this is pressed, we actually create the email and, if desired, send it. This is carried out by the `DoMerge` function, which is covered below in the section on "Working with the Outlook `MailItem`".

The last step of the navigation is to show and hide the frames of the wizard as appropriate. We do this by hiding all of the frames (by setting their `Visible` property to `False`), and then displaying the current frame, which is referenced by the `m_Index` variable.

Working with Outlook Contacts

The first frame displayed to the user, `fmWizard(0)`, contains merely a label and a text box with a "Welcome" message. The second contains the listview control with the list of contacts which we built in the `AddRecipients` function. This screen also offers the user the ability to edit and create new contacts. To handle this, we use two buttons on the page, called `cmdCreateContact` and `cmdEditContact`.

```
Private Sub cmdCreateContact_Click()
    Set Contact = m_oOutlook.CreateItem(olContactItem)
    Contact.Display
End Sub

Private Sub cmdEditContact_Click()
    Dim oFolder As MAPIFolder

    Set oFolder = m_oNameSpace.Folders(strName).Folders("Contacts")
    Set Contact = oFolder.Items(lstRecipients.SelectedItem.Key)
    Contact.Display
End Sub
```

The first routine above creates a contact using the `CreateItem` method of the `Application` object and opens the inspector for this new item. The second just opens the inspector for the first selected contact in the list. The key to both of these routines is the fact that we are using the `Contact` variable that we declared in the Declarations for the form and which exposes the events that are raised by the `ContactItem`. So when we create the `ContactItem` above, we need to do no more than wait for the user to close the `ContactItem` that is being displayed. The `Contact_Close` event will then be raised and we can respond to the changes the user has made.

```
Private Sub Contact_Close(Cancel As Boolean)
    AddRecipients
End Sub
```

When the event is raised, all we have to do is reload the recipients list, by re-calling the `AddRecipients` function we used earlier. That's all there is do because the `ContactItem` handles all the work for us. All that we have to do is load the newly created contact or update the changed contact. The easiest way of doing this is just to reload the list.

Working with the Outlook MailItem

The next (and final) frame, `fmWizard(2)`, contains only two controls — a combo box called `lstTemplates` which contains the list of templates, from which the user must select the one on which the mail is to be based, and a checkbox called `chkDraft` which specifies whether the mail is to be sent directly, or saved in the Drafts folder so that the user can review it before sending it.

The last and most important function of this wizard is to create the `MailItem` and either save or send the message to the selected contacts. This occurs when the user clicks on the Finish panel and is handled by two subroutines called `DoMerge` and `ParseSubject`.

```
Private Sub DoMerge()
    Dim oRecordset As Recordset
    Dim oMail As MailItem
    Dim oListItem As ListItem
    Dim sSubject As String

    'Get Body and Subject information for the template selected by the user.
    Set oRecordset = db.OpenRecordset("Select Body, Subject from Template" & _
                " where TemplateID = " & lstTemplates.ItemData _
                (lstTemplates.ListIndex) & ";")

    'Check to make sure we have all of the information needed
    If oRecordset.RecordCount <> 0 Then
        oRecordset.MoveFirst
        For Each oListItem In lstRecipients.ListItems
            If oListItem.Selected Then
                Set oMail = m_oOutlook.CreateItem(olMailItem)

                'Add the Contact to the Mail message
                oMail.Recipients.Add oListItem.Key
                oMail.Recipients.ResolveAll

                'Add the Templates Subject to the Mails Subject
                oMail.Subject = oRecordset("subject")

                'Add the Updated Body of the Template to the Mail message
                oMail.Body = ParseSubject(oRecordset("Body"), oListItem.Key)

                'Check to see if the Draft is checked.
                If chkDraft Then
                    oMail.Save
                Else
                    oMail.Send
                End If

                'Set the Mail message to nothing
                Set oMail = Nothing
            End If
        Next
        Set oListItem = Nothing
    End If

    oRecordset.Close
    Set oRecordset = Nothing

End Sub
```

The first step is to get the `Body` and `Subject` for the mail from the template that the user has selected. We do this by creating a recordset from the MailMerge database. This recordset is set up to contain just one record — the template selected by the user. Then we iterate through the contacts in the listview. For each one that is selected, we create a new `MailItem` and add the contact as a recipient. We then update the `Subject` to the subject specified in the template, parse the body of the template to carry out the personalization and add it to the mail and save the message in the default (Drafts) folder if `chkDrafts` is checked; otherwise we send it straight away. Finally, we close the recordset and release the variable by setting it to `Nothing`. The process of parsing the body to personalize the mail is carried out by the `ParseSubject` function:

```
Private Function ParseSubject(Subject As String, Contact As String)
    Dim oContact As ContactItem
    Dim sTempSubject As String
    Dim oFolder As MAPIFolder
    sTempSubject = Subject

    'Retreive the Contact MAPIFolder
    Set oFolder = m_oNameSpace.Folders(strName).Folders("Contacts")

    'Get a reference to the Contact we are working on.
    Set oContact = oFolder.Items(Contact)

    'Replace the Tag <FullName> with the FullName property for the Contact
    Do While InStr(sTempSubject, "<FullName>") <> 0
        sTempSubject = Left$(sTempSubject, InStr _
                    (sTempSubject, "<FullName>") - 1) & oContact.FullName _
                    & Mid$(sTempSubject, InStr(sTempSubject, "<FullName>") _
                    + Len("<FullName>"))
    Loop

    'Replace the Tag <FirstName> with the FirstName property for the Contact
    Do While InStr(sTempSubject, "<FirstName>") <> 0
        sTempSubject = Left$(sTempSubject, InStr _
                    (sTempSubject, "<FirstName>") - 1) & _
                    oContact.FirstName & Mid$(sTempSubject, InStr _
                    (sTempSubject, "<FirstName>")  + Len("<FirstName>"))
    Loop

    'Replace the Tag <FirstName> with the LastName property for the Contact
    Do While InStr(sTempSubject, "<LastName>") <> 0
    sTempSubject = Left$(sTempSubject, InStr _
                (sTempSubject, "<LastName>") - 1) & oContact.LastName & _
                Mid$(sTempSubject, InStr(sTempSubject, "<LastName>") + _
                Len("<LastName>"))
    Loop

    'Pass the new Subject back
    ParseSubject = sTempSubject

    Set oContact = Nothing
    Set oFolder = Nothing

End Function
```

The first step of this routine is to get a reference to the contact that we are working with. To do this, we must first get a reference to the Contacts `MAPIFolder`. We then set the `oContact` variable to point the appropriate `ContactItem`. Now that we have the correct contact, we need to replace the tags with the proper information.

In this code we only use the `FullName`, `FirstName` and `LastName` properties of the contact, although it would not take much extra work to make this wizard utilize other properties. We run three loops to replace every occurrence of `<FullName>`, `<FirstName>` and `<LastName>` tags with the values in the `FullName`, `FirstName` and `LastName` properties of the `ContactItem`.

This method finally sends the parsed body back to the `DoMerge` function, which sets the `Body` property of the `MailItem` to this returned string.

Template Wizard

The second major section of the application allows the user to create, edit and delete the templates on which the mails are based. The code in this section does not use the Outlook model, so it is inappropriate to go over the code here in detail. Interested readers can examine the code for themselves; it is available for download from the Wrox web site at http://www.wrox.com.

Two forms are provided to help the user manage templates. The first, frmSelectTemplate, contains a listview control which allows the user to select a template for editing or deletion. This is populated with the available templates by a function called AddTemplates, which works in a similar way to the AddRecipients function in the Mail Merge Wizard form. There are also three command buttons, which give the user the options to create, edit or delete a template.

The second form, frmTemplateEditor, contains four text boxes containing the Name, Description, Subject and Body for the template. The user can add or edit the text in these at will. There is also a menu with options to save the template or quit the template, or to insert a tag representing the recipient's full name, first name or last name. Since these options are closely related to the Mail Merge Wizard section of the application, it is worth showing the code which inserts the tag:

```
Private Sub mnuFullName_Click()
    txtBody.Text = Left(txtBody.Text, txtBody.SelStart) _
    & " <FullName> " & Mid(txtBody.Text, _
    txtBody.SelStart + txtBody.SelLength + 1)
End Sub
```

The above code will be called when the user clicks on the Insert I FullName menu option. The code inserts the tag <FullName> over the currently selected text (or at the insertion point, if no text is selected) in the body.

So we have seen two Outlook applications in this chapter. The intention was to give you a flavour of what you can achieve with Outlook VBA and Visual Basic. Hopefully, you will now feel encouraged to go ahead and code up your own applications.

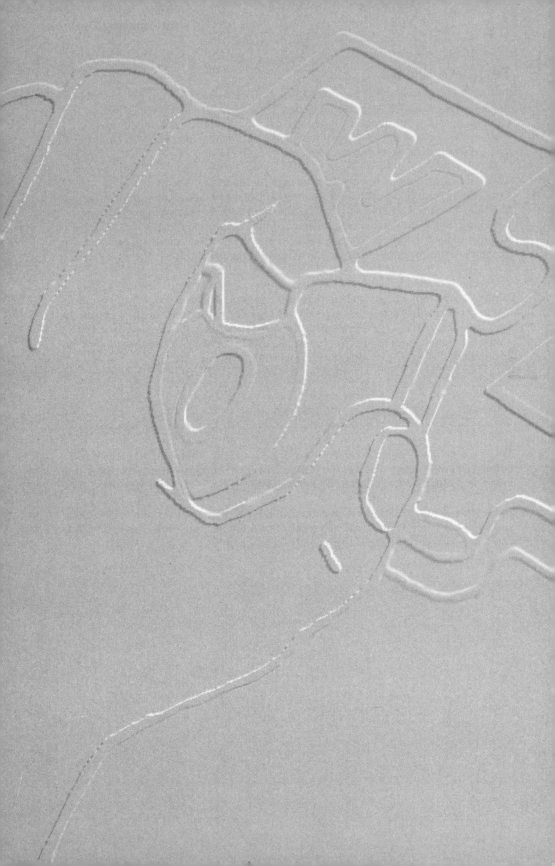

5

The Outlook Application

The `Application` object is the starting point for Outlook. It offers us the only way
into the Outlook Object Model and is really the heart and soul of Outlook. This object
gives us access to all the other objects, either directly or indirectly through other
objects.

By default if you open the Outlook GUI then the `Application` object has already
been instantiated. On the other hand if you want to use Outlook objects from another
language like Visual Basic then you will need to instantiate the `Application` object
and get a reference to it.

There are two ways to instantiate the object. The first uses early binding and an
example is shown below.

```
Dim oaOutlookApp As Outlook.Application

Set oaOutlookApp = New Outlook.Application
```

The late binding method uses the following syntax:

```
Dim oaOutlookApp As Object

Set oaOutlookApp = CreateObject("Outlook.Application")
```

The preferred method of instantiation is early binding. The reason is that with late
binding the application does not check whether a method or property is valid until
that method or property is actually called. This involves a lot of work and can greatly
increase an application runtime. With early binding the compiler will make these
checks at compile time. This means that less work takes place at runtime, a possible
disadvantage being a lack of flexibility.

Application Object Methods

ActiveExplorer Method

The `ActiveExplorer` method returns the topmost `Explorer` object. An `Explorer` object is a window that displays the contents of a `MAPIFolder`. For example, the window displayed when you first start up Outlook is an `Explorer`.

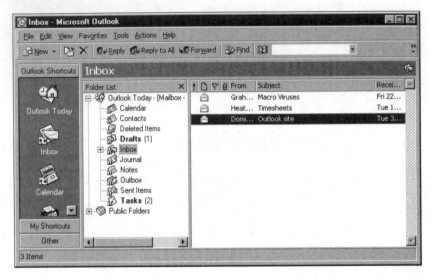

If there is no `Explorer` object open then `Nothing` is returned. More information on the Explorer object is given in chapter 7.

```
Set ExplorerObject = Application.ActiveExplorer
```

Example:

```
Dim oaOutlookApp As Application
Dim oeExplorer As Explorer
Dim sMessage As String

Set oaOutlookApp = Application
Set oeExplorer = oaOutlookApp.ActiveExplorer

If Not oeExplorer Is Nothing Then
    oeExplorer.WindowState = olMinimized

    sMessage = "You currently have - " &
oeExplorer.CurrentFolder.Items.count & _
                " items in " & oeExplorer.CurrentFolder.Name

    MsgBox sMessage
End If
```

In the example above we try to get a reference to the currently active `Explorer` object. If we are able to get a reference then we minimize this `Explorer` and display a message telling the user how many messages they have in the current folder.

To actually reference an `Explorer` object you first need to have an `Explorer` object shown. If Outlook is open then an `Explorer` object will automatically be available. Note that even if Outlook is instantiated from a different application and no `Explorer` object is visible, there is, oddly enough, still one available behind the scenes.

ActiveInspector Method

The `ActiveInspector` method returns the topmost `Inspector` object. An `Inspector` object is a window in which an Outlook item is displayed. This method will return `Nothing` if there is no `Inspector` object presently open. For more information on the `Inspector` object refer to chapter 7.

```
Set InspectorObject = Application.ActiveInspector
```

Example:

```
Dim oaOutlookApp As Application
Dim onMAPI As NameSpace
Dim oInspector As Inspector

Set oaOutlookApp = Application
Set onMAPI = oaOutlookApp.GetNamespace("MAPI")
Set oInspector = oaOutlookApp.ActiveInspector

If oInspector Is Nothing Then
    onMAPI.GetDefaultFolder(olFolderInbox).Items.GetFirst.Display
    Set oInspector = oaOutlookApp.ActiveInspector
End If

oInspector.Activate
MsgBox "You are currently viewing the item - " & _
        oInspector.CurrentItem.Subject
```

In the example above we are checking to see if there is an open `Inspector` object. If not, the first item of the Inbox is opened. A message box is then used to display the subject of the item being displayed.

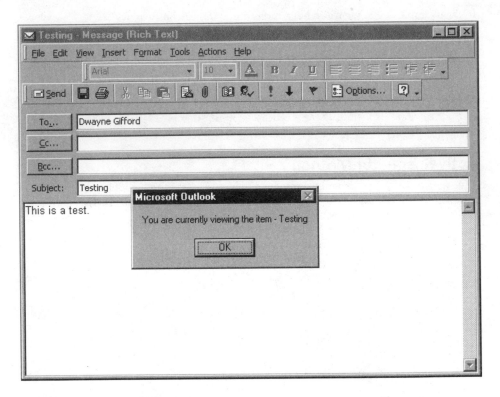

ActiveWindow Method

The `ActiveWindow` method returns the topmost window of Outlook. This could be either an `Explorer` or an `Inspector` object. If neither an `Explorer` or `Inspector` object is open then `Nothing` is returned.

```
Set Object = Application.ActiveWindow
```

One thing to be aware of here is if you try to assign this method to an `Inspector` object and the topmost window is an `Explorer` object then an error is raised. This also applies to the opposite situation. The following code offers a way to circumvent this problem.

```
If oaOutlookApp.ActiveWindow.Class = olInspector Then
    Set oiInspector =oaOutlookApp.ActiveWindow
Else
    Set oeExplorer = oaOutlookApp.ActiveWindow
End If
```

Here we establish what sort of window the topmost active window is before setting a reference to it. Alternatively you could also assign this object to an `Object` variable and make use of late binding.

CreateItem Method

The `CreateItem` method will create a new Outlook item based on the type set in the method's parameter

```
Set ItemObject = Application.CreateItem(ItemType)
```

Name	Data type	Description
ItemType	Long	Required, any of the olItemType contants.

The OlItemType constants are as follows:

Constant	Value	Description
olAppointment Item	1	Represents an Appointment Item
olContactItem	2	Represents a Contact Item
olJournalItem	4	Represents a Journal Item
olMailItem	0	Represents a Mail Item
olNoteItem	5	Represents a Note Item
olPostItem	6	Represents a Post Item
olTaskItem	3	Represents a Task Item

Example:

```
Dim oaOutlookApp As Application
Dim oDistList As DistListItem
Dim oRecipients As Recipients

Set oaOutlookApp = Application
Set oDistList = oaOutlookApp.CreateItem(olDistributionListItem)

Set oRecipients = oaOutlookApp.CreateItem(olMailItem).Recipients
oRecipients.Add "Iris Gifford"

oDistList.AddMembers oRecipients
oDistList.Display
```

In the example above we create a new Distribution List item. Notice the peculiar way used to add the recipients to the item. At the time of writing this book you cannot get a Recipients collection directly from the DistList object. So the work-around for this lack of functionality is to create the Recipients collection through a new item that offers the Recipients collection. In this case I am using a MailItem object.

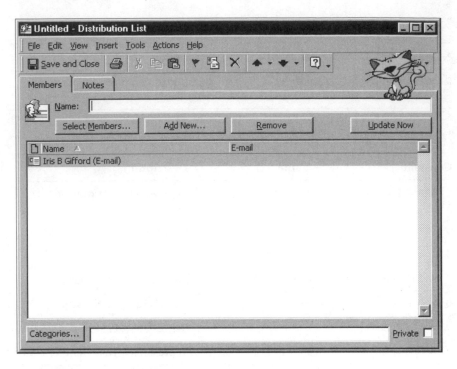

CreateItemFromTemplate Method

The `CreateItemFromTemplate` method creates and returns a new Outlook item based on an Outlook template (.oft).

```
Set ItemObject = Application.CreateItemFromTemplate(TemplatePath [,
InFolder])
```

Name	Type	Description
TemplatePath	String	Required, path and filename for the Outlook template.
InFolder	Variant	Optional, the location in which the new item is to be created. If omitted then the default folder for the item type is used.

It is possible to save each of the item objects as a template. That template file is simply a copy of the object at that point in time. So for example if you have added a BCC recipient to the mail item and then save it as a template, all new item objects created from this template will have this BCC recipient added to them.

Example:

```
Dim omail As MailItem

Set omail = Application.CreateItemFromTemplate("C:\Work\Test.oft")
omail.Display
```

Before running this code I created a template that had the subject and BCC set. The code simply uses this template to create a new `MailItem` object and displays it, as shown below.

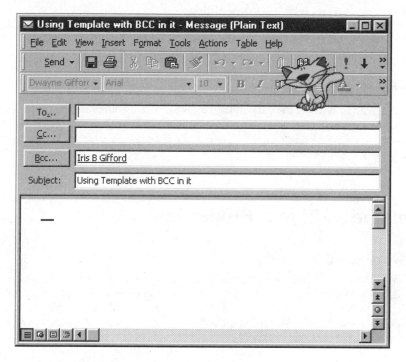

CreateObject Method

This method allows the developer to automate other applications from VBScript. Since this book is about automating Outlook, we will only take a cursory look at this method here. If you are familiar with Visual Basic then you may have used this method as it was originally the only way to instantiate a COM object.

```
Set ApplicationObject = Application.CreateObject(ObjectName)
```

Name	Data type	Description
ObjectName	String	Required, the class name of the object that you want to create.

GetNameSpace Method

The `GetNameSpace` method returns a `NameSpace` object providing access to the specified data source. Currently the only data source supported by Outlook is the Messaging Application Programming Interface or MAPI. For more information on the `NameSpace` object refer to chapter 6.

```
Set NameSpaceObject = Application.GetNameSpace(Type)
```

Name	Data type	Description
Type	String	Required, the name of the data source you wish to access.

Quit Method

The Quit method will log the current user out of the data source that they are logged into. This method will also close all open Explorer and Inspector windows. Any open items with unsaved information are closed and the user is prompted to see if they wish to save any changes.

```
Application.Quit
```

Application Object Properties

AnswerWizard Property

The AnswerWizard property will return a reference to the AnswerWizard object. This is the Microsoft Outlook Answer Wizard. It is can accessed via one of the tabs that appears in the Help window. This object allows us to add and remove files that Help accesses when the Answer Wizard is used. It does not, however, provide a way to search through the Answer Wizard.

```
Set AnswerWizardObject = Application.AnswerWizard
```

Application Property

The Application property will return the Application object for this session. This will set a reference to the Application object calling this property. It's hard to envisage a use for this property.

```
Set ApplicationObject = Application.Application
```

Assistant Property

The Assistant property returns the Assistant object. The Assistant object represents the Microsoft Office Assistant.

```
Set AssistantObject = Application.Assistant
```

Class Property

The Class property returns a unique value that identifies the object's type. This will be one of the OlObjectClass constants and since we are considering the Application object it will be olApplication or 0.

```
Long = Application.Class
```

COMAddIns Property

The COMAddIns property returns the COMAddIns collection. At the moment this collection is merely a representation of all the COM objects currently loaded in Outlook, since you cannot load or unload objects through this collection. This collection can be used to check which ActiveX objects are accessible in the current Outlook session and consequently to determine the currently available features.

```
Set COMAddInsCollection = Application.COMAddIns
```

Explorers Property

The Explorers property returns an Explorers collection. This collection will contain all of the currently open Explorer objects. An Explorer object is a window that displays the contents of a MAPIFolder. The Explorer object is covered in detail in chapter 7.

```
Set ExplorerObject = Application.Explorers
```

Inspectors Property

The Inspectors property returns the Inspectors collection, which contains all of the currently open Inspector objects. An Inspector object is a window in which an Outlook item is displayed. For more information on the Inspector object refer to chapter 7.

```
Set InspectorObject = Application.Inspectors
```

LanguageSettings Property

The LanguageSettings property will return the Microsoft Office LanguageSettings object. This object contains the language specific attributes for Outlook and retrieves all its information from the Registry. It is read-only and cannot be updated from Outlook.

```
Set LanguageSettingsObject = Application.LanguageSettings
```

Name Property

The Name property returns a string that represents the name for the Application object. This property is not updateable from the code and is set to be the value of Outlook.

```
String = Application.Name
```

Parent Property

The Parent property returns the parent object for the current Application object. This property will always be Nothing since this the Application object is at the top of the object model. This property would appear to be of limited use.

```
Set Object = Application.Parent
```

ProductCode Property

The `ProductCode` property returns a string that represents the GUID (Globally Unique Identifier) for Outlook.

```
String = Application.ProductCode
```

Session Property

The `Session` property returns a reference to the `NameSpace` object, which at present can only be the Messaging Application Programming Interface or MAPI.

```
Set NameSpaceObject = Application.Session
```

Version Property

The `Version` property returns a string that represents the Version number for the current Outlook Object Model.

```
String = Application.Version
```

Application Object Events

The best place to put code to respond to these application events is in the ThisOutlookSession class module. The reason is that in this class module the `Application` object is already set with its events exposed to you. If you click on the Object list box of the Visual Basic Editor and select the `Application` object you will see the events listed in the Procedure list box. To add your own code, select the desired event.

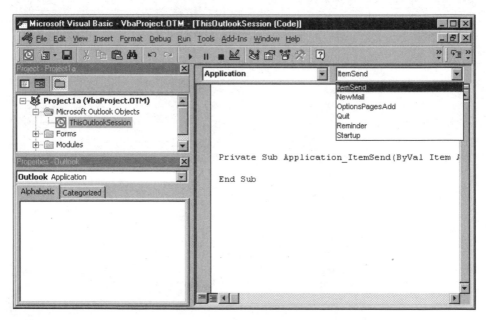

ItemSend Event

The ItemSend event occurs after the user clicks the Send button on the GUI or the Send method is executed through code.

```
Sub Application_ItemSend(ByVal Item As Object, Cancel As Boolean)
```

❑ Item refers to the item that is being sent. This means that the item may be changed through the event's code before it is sent.

❑ Cancel provides a mechanism to stop the item from being sent. This parameter is passed in as False. If it is set to True in the event's code then the item is not sent and the Inspector object for the item remains open.

Example:

```
Private Sub Application_ItemSend(ByVal Item As Object, Cancel As
Boolean)

    If InStr(Item.Subject, "Company Name") Then
        MsgBox "No messages with the company name" & _
               " are allowed to be sent."
        Cancel = True
    End If

End Sub
```

In the example above Outlook checks to see if the "Company Name" appears in the subject of the message. If it does then the ItemSend event is cancelled. Fortunately most of us do not work in such a secretive environment.

NewMail Event

The NewMail event occurs when new messages are received into the Inbox folder.

```
Private Sub Application_NewMail()
```

Example:

```
Private Sub Application_NewMail()
    Dim onMAPI As NameSpace
    Dim ofFolder As MAPIFolder
    Dim oItem As Object
    Dim omNewMail As MailItem

    Set onMAPI = GetNamespace("MAPI")
    Set ofFolder = onMAPI.GetDefaultFolder(olFolderInbox)
    Set omNewMail = ofFolder.Items.GetFirst

    If MsgBox("You have new mail from " & omNewMail.SenderName & _
              "Would you like to read it now?", _
              vbYesNo + vbQuestion) = vbYes Then
        omNewMail.Display
    End If
End Sub
```

When a new mail message is received by Outlook the user is informed of the sender's name. The user is then asked if they would like to read this new message. If so then the `Display` method of the `MailItem` is used to show the mail message to the user.

OptionsPageAdd Event

The `OptionsPageAdd` event occurs when the Options dialog is opened. This event provides the possibility of adding a custom Property page to this dialog.

```
Private Sub Application_OptionsPagesAdd(ByVal Pages As
PropertyPages)
```

The `Pages` parameter passes the collection of property pages that are displayed in the dialog box. Through this parameter, new pages may be added.

Quit Event

The `Quit` event occurs as Outlook shuts down.

```
Private Sub Application_Quit()
```

As of writing, the Quit event is actually called after the all GUI's have been closed. You cannot get a reference to any existing folder or item because they are no longer available. However, you can create, for example, a new `MailItem` and send it.

Reminder Event

The `Reminder` event is executed just before a reminder is sent. A reminder is the message that is sent at an interval before a meeting, appointment, etc. is due to take place. The `Reminder` event passes the item that the reminder is associated with as a parameter.

```
Private Sub Application_Reminder(ByVal Item As Object)
```

`Item` will be one of the following item objects:

- ❑ `AppointmentItem`
- ❑ `MailItem`
- ❑ `TaskItem`

The `Item` parameter for a reminder associated with a recurring appointment is the specific incidence of the appointment item **not** the master appointment.

Startup Event

The `Startup` event occurs after all the Addins have been loaded and after the `Explorer` has been shown.

```
Private Sub Application_Startup()
```

This event can be used to start Outlook VBA macros. For example, to initialize the Scheduler program covered in chapter 4, you could set a variable to equal clsScheduleCheck in this event's code.

```
Private Sub Application_Startup()

    Dim ocsClassSchedule As clsScheduleCheck
    Set ocsClassSchedule = New clsScheduleCheck

End Sub
```

The NameSpace Object

The NameSpace object gives us access to the data stores associated with Outlook. Presently there is only one type of data source available to the Namespace object. This is the **Messaging Application Programming Interface** (MAPI), which is a standard interface exposed by most mail servers. The MAPI defines how Outlook retrieves the data from the server and unless you plan on writing you own "Outlook" then that's as much as you need to know about MAPI.

Through the Namespace object we have access to the Addresslists, Folders, PropertyPages and SyncObjects collections.

❑   The AddressLists collection comprises a number of AddressList objects, which represent address books with various address entries.

❑   The Folders collection allows navigation through the MAPIFolders. A MAPIFolder object is any Outlook folder, such as the default folder **Inbox** or any user-created folder. This in turn allows us to navigate and manipulate the items within these folders.

❑   The SyncObjects collection of SyncObject objects allows us to set up profiles for handling synchronization of folders and their contents when working offline.

❑   The PropertyPages collection is used to add or remove a PropertyPage object or to derive information from existing pages. A PropertyPage object represents the custom property page that can be viewed for each Outlook folder.

In addition the NameSpace object provides access to information about the currently logged-on user.

So now that we know what the Namespace object is and what purpose it serves, we need a way to get a reference to one. There are two ways to access the NameSpace object. The first is through the GetNameSpace method exposed by the Application object.

```
Set NameSpaceObject = ApplicationObject.GetNameSpace(DataSource)
```

Datatype	Description
DataSource	Required String, presently only "MAPI" can be used.

Example:

```
Dim oOutlookApp as Outlook.Application
Dim onMAPI as NameSpace

Set oOutlookApp = New Outlook.Application
Set onMAPI = oOutlookApp.GetNameSpace("MAPI")
```

Firstly the two variables are declared and once a reference to the `Application` object is set the `GetNameSpace` method is employed. If working directly from VBA the `Application` object is automatically available and the `NameSpace` object may be set as follows.

```
Dim onMAPI as NameSpace
...
Set onMAPI =Application.GetNameSpace("MAPI")
```

The second way to access the `NameSpace` object is by using the `Session` method of any Outlook object that supports this method.

```
Dim onMAPI as NameSpace
...
Set onMAPI = Object.Session
```

NameSpace Object Methods

AddStore Method

The `AddStore` method is used to add a new personal folder (.pst) to the current user's profile. This method is equivalent to a user clicking on File I Open I Personal File Folder (.pst) … in Outlook.

```
NameSpaceObject.AddStore(StoreName)
```

Name	Data type	Description
StoreName	Variant	The path and filename for the PST file to be added

If the path that you have supplied is valid but the filename does not exist, a new PST file will be created in this path with the filename supplied. If the path is invalid an error is raised.

CreateRecipient Method

The `CreateRecipient` method creates a new `Recipient` object. A `Recipient` object is normally associated with an item that can be sent to someone (MailItem, AppointmentItem, TaskItem etc.). The `Recipient` object represents a person or distribution list of people to whom the item is sent. The `Recipient` object is covered in detail in chapter 10.

```
Set RecipientObject = NameSpaceObject.CreateRecipient(RecipientName)
```

Name	Data type	Description
RecipientName	String	Required, the name of the recipient.

Example:

```
Dim oRecipient As Recipient
Dim oNameSpace As NameSpace

Set oNameSpace = GetNamespace("MAPI")
Set oRecipient = oNameSpace.CreateRecipient("Iris Gifford")
oRecipient.Resolve

If oRecipient.Resolved Then
    MsgBox "We have a Valid Recipient"
Else
    MsgBox "Invalid Recipient"
End If
```

In the example above we get a reference to the `NameSpace` object by calling the `GctNameSpace` method exposed by the `Application` object. We then call the `CreateRecipient` method passing in the name of a recipient.

Although at this point we have created the `Recipient` object, we still need to ensure that it is a valid recipient. To do this we call the `Resolve` method, which checks if the recipient is in the Address Book associated with the user's profile. If it is not in the Address Book Outlook ensures that the name has an appropriate email address format. If the recipient is valid its `Resolved` property will be True, otherwise it will be set to False. If you try to send a message to an invalid recipient an error is raised explaining that one or more of the recipients was not recognized.

GetDefaultFolder Method

This method returns the default `MAPIFolder` object for the current profile based on the different folder types listed below. The `MAPIFolder` object represents a folder that you use in Outlook, such as the Inbox or any user-created folder. This method provides a way to **quickly** locate the default folder for any given type of item. The reason you might use this method is that you can locate a given folder without walking through the `Folders` collection.

```
Set MAPIFolderObject = NameSpaceObject. _
                    GetDefaultFolder(DefaultFolderName)
```

Name	Data type	Description
DefaultFolderName	Long integer	One of the OlDefaultFolder constants listed below

Constant	Value	Description
olFolderCalendar	9	Returns the Calendar folder
olFolderContacts	10	Returns the Contacts folder
olFolderDeletedItems	3	Returns the Deleted Items folder
olFolderDrafts	16	Returns the Drafts folder
olFolderInbox	6	Returns the Inbox folder
olFolderJournal	11	Returns the Journal folder
olFolderNotes	12	Returns the Notes folder
olFolderOutbox	4	Returns the Outbox folder
olFolderSentMail	5	Returns the Sent Mail folder
olFolderTasks	13	Returns the Tasks folder

Example:

```
Dim oFolder As MAPIFolder
Dim iFor As Integer
Dim oNameSpace As NameSpace
Dim oMail As MailItem

Set oNameSpace = GetNamespace("MAPI")
Set oFolder = oNameSpace.GetDefaultFolder(olFolderInbox)

For iFor = 1 To oFolder.Items.Count

    If oFolder.Items(ifor).Class = olMail Then
        Set oMail = oFolder.Items(ifor)

        If oMail.UnRead Then
            oMail.Display
        End If

    End If
Next
```

In the example above you can see that the GetDefaultFolder method is used to locate the user's Inbox without navigating through the Folders collection. Each of the items within this folder is checked to see if it is a MailItem that has not yet been read. If so the item is displayed.

> You should be aware that this method will return a folder that Outlook created for you when it was installed. So if you want to get a reference to one of your own folders of a particular type, you will need to make use of the `Folders` collection. The `Folders` collection is covered fully in chapter 8.

GetFolderFromID Method

The `GetFolderFromID` method is used to ease the transition between MAPI and OLE/Messaging applications and Outlook, by allowing you to locate a `MAPIFolder` object by its `EntryID` rather than its name. This is the old way of doing things. Since the advent of COM, it is normal to locate things by their key and not their ID.

The parameters of this method, `EntryFolderID` and `StoreID`, are system generated strings that uniquely identify the folder but are not words like Inbox or Contacts that we have become accustomed to. They are the unique ID's that the MAPI system assigns to the folder when it is created and these ID's will not change for the lifetime of the MAPIFolder.

```
Set MAPIFolderObject = NameSpaceObject.GetFolderFromID _
                            (EntryFolderID [, StoreID])
```

Name	Data type	Description
EntryFolderID	String	Required, a unique ID for the folder
StoreID	String	Optional, the server generated ID for the folder

Since most of us are familiar with the words like Inbox and Calendar here is an example that will first locate a default `MAPIFolder` for us, in this case the default Notes `MAPIFolder`. Once we have this reference we use the Notes `MAPIFolder` `EntryID` to create a new reference to the same `MAPIFolder`.

Example:

```
Dim oaOutlook As Application
Dim onMAPI As NameSpace
Dim ofFolder As MAPIFolder
Dim ofEntryFolder As MAPIFolder
Dim sEntryID As String

Set oaOutlookApp = Application
Set onMAPI = oaOutlookApp.GetNamespace("MAPI")

Set ofFolder = onMAPI.GetDefaultFolder(olFolderNotes)
sEntryID = ofFolder.EntryID

Set ofEntryFolder = onMAPI.GetFolderFromID(sEntryID)

ofEntryFolder.Display
```

Finally, when we have this reference we display this `MAPIFolder` in an `Explorer` object.

GetItemFromID Method

The GetItemFromID method returns a reference to an Outlook item identified by the EntryId and/or the StoreID. The EntryID and StoreID are unique ID's that are system generated, created when an item is placed in a MAPIFolder. They are only changed if the item is moved to a different MAPIfolder. The item returned can be any of the item types supported by Outlook, such as the MailItem or CalendarItem. All of the item objects for Outlook are covered in chapters 11 to 19.

```
Set ItemObject = NameSpaceObject.GetItemFromID _
                 (EntryItemID [, StoreID])
```

Name	Data type	Description
EntryItemID	String	Required, a unique ID for the item
StoreID	String	Optional, a unique ID for the item. Be aware that not all Outlook items support this property.

Like GetFolderFromID this method is used to ease the transition between MAPI and OLE/Messaging applications and Outlook. It allows older programs that use these ID's so that they may carry on without error. Other than that, however, it provides no benefit as we have become accustomed to using the key words like Inbox or Contact and not a huge string of apparently meaningless text.

GetRecipientFromID Method

The GetRecipientFromID method returns a reference to a Recipient object identified by the EntryID. The EntryID is created when the recipient is added to an Address Book. The advantage of this method is that it can be used to locate a recipient very quickly. It provides a way to reference a particular Recipient object without having to walk through the Recipients collection, but to do this you need to know the EntryID

```
Set RecipientObject = NameSpaceObject.GetRecipientFromID(EntryID)
```

Name	Data type	Description
EntryID	String	Required, the unique ID for the recipient.

A better way to locate a Recipient object is by using the Recipients collection exposed by different Outlook items. Once you have a reference to this collection you can use the Name property to get the required recipient. More information about the Recipients collection and the Recipient object can be found in chapter 10.

GetSharedDefaultFolder Method

The GetSharedDefaultFolder method returns the specified MAPIFolder object of a particular recipient based on the folder type supplied. This method comes into play when a user allows other users to access some of their default folders. The available MAPIFolder types can be any one of the OlDefaultFolder constants listed below.

To use this method successfully you require access to the MAPIFolder **and** you must supply a valid Recipient object. The best way to think of a Recipient object is a message addressee.

```
Set MAPIFolderObject = NameSpaceObject. _
            GetSharedDefaultFolder(RecipientObject,OlDefaultFolder)
```

Name	Data type	Description
RecipientObject	Recipient	Required, this must be a resolved Recipient object.
OlDefaultFolder	Long	Required, the type of folder you wish to return.

OlDefaultFolder can be any one of these constants:

Constant	Value	Description
olFolderCalendar	9	Returns the Calendar folder.
olFolderContacts	10	Returns the Contacts folder.
olFolderDeletedItems	3	Returns the Deleted Items folder.
olFolderDrafts	16	Returns the Drafts folder.
olFolderInbox	6	Returns the Inbox folder.
olFolderJournal	11	Returns the Journal folder.
olFolderNotes	12	Returns the Notes folder.
olFolderOutbox	4	Returns the Outbox folder.
olFolderSentMail	5	Returns the Sent Mail folder.
olFolderTasks	13	Returns the Tasks folder.

The following example has been written in Visual Basic, and shows you how to use the GetSharedDefaultFolder method.

```
Dim oaOutlook As New Outlook.Application
Dim onMAPI As NameSpace
Dim orUser As Recipient
Dim ofDwayneFolder As MAPIFolder

Set oaOutlook = Outlook.Application
Set onMAPI = oaOutlookApp.GetNameSpace("MAPI")

onMAPI.Logon , , True

Set orUser = onMAPI.CreateRecipient("Dwayne Gifford")
orUser.Resolve
```

```
If orUser.Resolved Then
    Set ofDwayneFolder = onMAPI.GetSharedDefaultFolder _
                     (orUser, olFolderContacts)
End If
```

The first step of the example is to get a reference to the Outlook `Application` object. We do this by including the `New` keyword in the declaration of `oaOutlook`. The next step is to get a reference to the MAPI data source. Be aware that since we are using Visual Basic and not VBA Outlook we will need to use the `Logon` method. Here the `Logon` method is used to show the Profile dialog for the user to select an appropriate profile.

It is now possible to create a reference to the `"Dwayne Gifford"` `Recipient` object and resolve it. The final step is to call the `GetSharedDefaultFolder` with the `Recipient` object and the type of `MAPIfolder` we wish to reference.

Logoff Method

The `Logoff` method will log the current user out of the current MAPI session.

```
NameSpaceObject.Logoff
```

Providing Prompt for Profile has been set in Outlook Options it is possible to make use of this method in order to call the `Logon` method again and login as a different user. This method is fully functional outside Outlook, for example in Visual Basic or VC++, but in the Outlook VBA this method will not actually log you out of the MAPI session.

Logon Method

Even with a reference to the `NameSpace` object we can't actually do anything with it until we login to a MAPI session. This can be achieved with the `Logon` method. If you try to use the `NameSpace` object without first calling this `Logon` method and you have set the Prompt for Profile in the Outlook Options you will be prompted to login by the Login dialog.

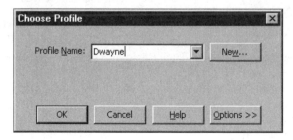

If Prompt for Profile isn't set, Outlook uses the default profile and automatically logs in for you. If there is a problem with the profile for some unknown reason then an error is raised.

The `Logon` method, then, allows you to explicitly login to a MAPI session through code.

```
NameSpaceObject.Logon([Profile,] [Password,] _
[ShowDialog,] [NewSession])
```

Name	Data type	Description
Profile	String	Optional, but if Prompt for Profile is set in Outlooks Options and ShowDialog is False then you must supply a valid profile.
Password	String	Optional, the password associated with the profile. Only required if the profile you are using needs one.
ShowDialog	Boolean	Optional, the default is False. If you set this to True then an Outlook Profile will be shown. You should be aware that this option is only used when you are interfacing to the Outlook Object Model from another application. If you can see your VBA code saved in Outlook, then you have already logged in to a data source.
NewSession	Boolean	Optional, the default is False. No matter what is set here you will never get a new session. Outlook only allows one session to run at any given time.

So you can see that the various options allow us some flexibility when we logon. We can either use the default profile or use another defined profile. We can also supply a password if required and we can choose whether to show the Profile dialog. On the other hand the NewSession option does nothing at the moment. You can only have one Outlook open at a time. So if you already have Outlook open then the NameSpace object will point to this copy of Outlook.

PickFolder Method

The PickFolder method shows the Select Folder dialog, which prompts the user to select one of the available MAPIFolder objects in the data source.

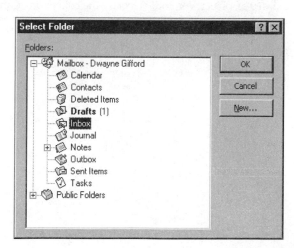

```
Set MAPIFolderObject = NameSpaceObject.PickFolder
```

If a `MAPIFolder` is selected then a reference to that `MAPIFolder` object is returned. If the user clicks on the **Cancel** button then `Nothing` is returned. This is demonstrated in the following example.

```
Dim onMapi As NameSpace
Dim ofFolder As MAPIFolder

Set onMapi = GetNamespace("MAPI")

Set ofFolder = onMapi.PickFolder

If ofFolder Is Nothing Then
  MsgBox "No Folder Selected, User Cancelled"
Else
  MsgBox "Folder - " & ofFolder.Name & " was selected by the user"
  ofFolder.Display
End If
```

We check if the user has selected a `MAPIFolder` or has the clicked the **Cancel** button by examining the `ofFolder` variable and an appropriate message is displayed.

NameSpace Object Properties

AddressLists Property

The `AddressLists` property returns a collection of `AddressList` objects, that is the root of the available Address Books for the current profile. This collection allows us to navigate to the available `AddressEntry` objects of the different Address Books in order to set recipients of Outlook items.

```
Set AddressListsCollection = NameSpaceObject.AddressLists
```

In the example below we use the `AddressLists` property of the `NameSpace` object to reference the collection and then walk through each one and display the `Name` of the `AddressList` object. We could declare the collection as an `AddressLists` variable but it is not necessary if we use the `For...Each` construct.

Example:

```
Dim onMAPI As NameSpace
Dim oalList As AddressList

Set onMAPI = Application.GetNamespace("MAPI")
For Each oalList In onMAPI.AddressLists
    MsgBox oalList.Name
Next
```

The `AddressLists` collection and `AddressList` object are covered fully in chapter 9.

Application Property

The `Application` property returns the `Application` object for the current session. This is clearly the Outlook `Application` object itself.

```
Set ApplicationObject = NameSpaceObject.Application
```

Class Property

The `Class` property returns a unique numeric value that identifies the type of the object. This will always be one of the `OlObjectClass` constants and in this case will be `olNameSpace` or 1.

```
Long = NameSpaceObject.Class
```

CurrentUser Property

The `CurrentUser` property returns the currently logged-in user as a `Recipient` object. So, this is another way to create a `Recipient` object that can be used with `GetDefaultSharedFolder` method or as an addressee on a mail message.

```
Set RecipientObject = NameSpaceObject.CurrentUser
```

By making use of this method you can also reduce the number of calls needed to get a valid `Recipient` object. Normally you would call the `CreateRecipient` method and then `Resolve` the newly-created recipient. Finally you would need to check the `Resolved` property to see if you had a valid recipient. Here you only have to set the recipient to equal the `CurrentUser` because the current user could not have logged in unless they were a valid recipient.

Example:

```
Dim onMapi As NameSpace
Dim orUser As Recipient
Dim ofDwayneFolder As MAPIFolder

Set onMapi = GetNamespace("MAPI")

Set orUser = onMapi.CurrentUser
Set ofDwayneFolder = onMAPI.GetSharedDefaultFolder(orUser,
olFolderContacts)
```

In the example above we first get the current user as a `Recipient` object and then we set a reference to the default shared **Contacts** folder for this recipient.

Folders Property

The `Folders` property returns the `Folders` collection for the object calling this property. In this case the object is the `NameSpace` object and so we retrieve the root of the `Folders` collection.

```
Set FoldersCollection = NameSpaceObject.Folders
```

In this case the referenced object is the `NameSpace` object but this property also applies to other `MAPIFolder` objects. From this root collection it is possible to navigate to and manipulate any Outlook folders and items within these folders. The `Folders` collection and `Folder` object are covered in detail in chapter 8.

Parent Property

The `Parent` property returns the parent object for the current object.

```
Set ApplicationObject = NameSpaceObject.Parent
```

Since here we are looking at the `NameSpace` object then the parent will always be the Outlook `Application` object. This should be obvious as the only way to reference a `NameSpace` object is through the `Application` object.

```
Set oNameSpace = oaApplication.GetNameSpace("MAPI")
```

Session Property

The `Session` property returns the `NameSpace` object for the current session and since here we are considering the `NameSpace` object then it will return itself. This property is therefore somewhat limited.

```
Set NameSpaceObject = NameSpaceObject.Session
```

SyncObjects Property

The `SyncObjects` property returns the `SyncObjects` collection for the current profile. The `SyncObjects` collection contains `SyncObject` objects, which hold synchronization profiles for a user. These profiles allow you to choose which rules to apply to synchronization when working offline.

```
Set SyncObjectsCollection = NameSpaceObject.SyncObjects
```

The `SyncObjects` collection and `SyncOject` object are discussed in detail below.

Type Property

The `Type` property returns a string that identifies the type of object we are currently looking at. In this case it will always return `MAPI`, since the only `type` currently support by Outlook is MAPI.

```
String = NameSpaceObject.Type
```

NameSpace Object Events

OptionsPageAdd Event

The `OptionsPageAdd` event will occur when a user opens the Tools | Option dialog or the Properties dialog of one of the available `MAPIFolder` objects shown in the `Explorer` window.

Syntax:

```
Private Sub NameSpaceObject_OptionsPagesAdd _
(ByVal Pages As PropertyPages, ByVal Folder As MAPIFolder)
```

Name	Description
Pages	Required, the collection of property pages that have been added to the dialog box.
Folder	Required, the MAPIFolder to which the **Properties** dialog pertains.

This event gives you the ability to add your own property page to the dialog before it is opened to the user, by using the Add method of the PropertyPages collection. This page must be an ActiveX control that implements a custom property page.

The SyncObjects Collection

Since the server on which a user's Mailbox is stored is usually a different machine from the client through which a user accesses their mail, it is frequently desirable for the user to have cached copies of the mailbox or of specific folders which are available even when working offline (for example, in case the network is unavailable). This process of keeping cached copies of folders is termed **synchronization**, and a specific pattern of folders to be cached is known as a **synchronization profile**. The SyncObjects collection contains all the synchronization profiles available for the current session, each of which is represented by a SyncObject and holds information about the folders that will be made available offline when that particular synchronization pattern is executed.

A reference is set to the SyncObjects collection through the NameSpace object.

```
Dim oscSyncObjects as SyncObjects
Dim onMAPI as NameSpace
...
Set onMAPI = Application.GetNamespace("MAPI")
Set oscSyncObjects = onMAPI.SyncObjects
```

SyncObjects Collection Method

Item Method

The Item method is used to retrieve a particular SyncObject object from within the SyncObjects collection, specified by an Index parameter.

```
Set SyncObjectObject = SyncObjectsCollection.Item(Index)
```

Name	Data type	Description
Index	Variant	A long integer representing the position of the SyncObject object within the collection or a string holding the name of the SyncObject object

SyncObjects Collection Properties

Application Property

The `Application` property returns the `Application` object for the `SyncObjects` collection. This will always be the Outlook `Application` object.

```
Set ApplicationObject = SyncObjectsCollection.Application
```

Class Property

The `Class` property returns a long integer that determines the object's type. This will be one of the `OlObjectClass` constants and for the `SyncObjects` collection is `olSyncObjects` or 73.

```
Long = SyncObjectsCollection.Class
```

Count Property

The `Count` property returns a long integer representing the number of `SyncObject` objects held in the `SyncObjects` collection.

```
Long = SyncObjectsCollection.Count
```

Parent Property

The `Parent` property returns the parent object for the referenced object. For the `SyncObjects` collection this property returns `Nothing`.

Session Property

The `Session` property returns the `NameSpace` object for the current session. There is only one such object and so this property returns the messaging application programming interface or MAPI.

```
Set NameSpaceObject = SyncObjectsCollection.Session
```

The SyncObject Object

A `SyncObject` object represents a specific synchronization profile — the pattern defining which folders will be made available offline when that particular profile is executed. It is not possible to set up a synchronization profile through code — this can only be achieved through the GUI.

A reference can be set to a `SyncObject` object by using the `Item` method of the `SyncObjects` collection. The `Index` parameter determines which `SyncObject` is returned. It can either be a long integer specifying the position of the `SyncObject` within the collection or a string holding the `Name` of the `SyncObject`.

```
Set SyncObjectObject = SyncObjectsCollection.Item(Index)
```

SyncObject Object Methods

Start Method

The `Start` method begins the synchronization process for the specified `SyncObject` and starts to prepare the folders defined by the `SyncObject` for offline availability. This method fires off the `SyncStart` event. Once the synchronization is complete and the cached folders have been fully updated, it will stop automatically.

```
SyncObjectObject.Start
```

> Please note that attempts to use this method during testing resulted in Outlook crashing. We would advise that synchronization is carried out through the **Tools** menu of the `Explorer`.

Stop Method

The `Stop` method prematurely terminates the synchronization process that was set in action with the `Start` method. It does not roll back the synchronization that has already occurred. If you execute this method then `SyncEnd` event will be fired.

```
SyncObjectObject.Stop
```

SyncObject Object Properties

Application Property

The `Application` property returns the `Application` object for the current session. This will be the Outlook `Application` object.

```
Set ApplicationObject = SyncObjectObject.Application
```

Class Property

The `Class` property returns a value that identifies the object's type. This will always be one of the `OlObjectClass` constants and in this case is `olSyncObject` or 72.

```
Long = SyncObjectObject.Class
```

Name Property

The `Name` property is the default property and returns the display name for the `SyncObject` object. This is the name shown in the **Tools | Synchronize** menu. It is a read-only property.

```
String = SyncObjectObject.Name
```

Parent Property

The `Parent` property returns the parent object for the referenced object. Since we are looking at the `SyncObject` object then the parent will be the `SyncObjects` collection.

```
Set SyncObjectsCollection = SyncObjectObject.Parent
```

Session Property

The `Session` property returns the `NameSpace` object for the current session. This will be the messaging application programming interface or MAPI.

```
Set NameSpaceObject = SyncObjectObject.Session
```

SyncObject Object Events

For the `SyncObject` object events to be fired it is necessary to use the `WithEvents` keyword and set a reference to the `SyncObject` of choice in a **Class Module**. Note that these events are not fired when synchronization is initiated through the GUI, and that we found that the `SyncObject`'s `Start` method caused Outlook to crash. We were therefore unable to get these events to fire.

OnError Event

The `OnError` event is fired if an error occurs while the synchronization is taking place.

```
Private Sub SyncObject_OnError(ByVal Code As Long, _
ByVal Description As String)
```

Name	Data type	Description
Code	Long	A unique value that identifies the error. It holds the `Number` property of the `Err` object in VBA.
Description	String	A description of the error. This is equivalent to the `Description` property exposed by the `Err` object.

Progress Event

The `Progress` event is raised periodically by Outlook as the synchronization process takes place. I feel that this event should be raised after each message is set or received, but this is not the case.

```
Private Sub SyncObject_Progress(ByVal State As OlSyncState, _
ByVal Description As String, ByVal Value As Long, ByVal Max As Long)
```

Name	Data type	Description
State	Long	Indicates whether synchronization is in process (olSyncState or 1) or has stopped (olSyncStopped or 0)
Description	String	This is a textual description of how the synchronization process is progressing
Value	Long	The number of items that have currently been synchronized
Max	Long	The total number of items that will be synchronized for this SyncObject

SyncEnd Event

The SyncEnd event is fired when the synchronization of a SyncObject has completed.

```
Private Sub SyncObject_SyncEnd()
```

SyncStart Event

The SyncStart event is supposed to occur immediately after the Start method for the SyncObject is executed. But note that during testing, this method caused Outlook to crash.

```
Private Sub SyncObject_SyncStart()
```

The PropertyPages Collection

The PropertyPages collection holds all of the PropertyPage objects representing custom property pages shown in the **Properties** dialog of a folder or the Outlook **Tools | Options** dialog.

The only way to set a reference to the PropertyPages collection is through the OptionsPagesAdd event that is exposed by the Application object and the NameSpace object. The PropertyPageSite object represents the dialog itself.

The syntax of the OptionsPagesAdd event of the Application object is given below. If a property page is added here, it will be displayed in the **Options** dialog.

```
Private Sub Application_OptionsPagesAdd(ByVal Pages As _
PropertyPages)
```

The OptionsPagesAdd event syntax for the NameSpace object is as follows:

```
Private Sub onMAPI_OptionsPagesAdd(ByVal Pages As PropertyPages, _
ByVal Folder As MAPIFolder)
```

Custom property pages added through this event are shown in the **Properties** dialog of a folder.

PropertyPages Collection Methods

Add Method

The Add method creates a new PropertyPage object and adds it either to the Properties dialog of the folders via NameSpace object event or to the Options dialog via Application object event.

>   PropertyPagesCollection.Add PropertyPage[, Title]

Name	Data type	Description
PropertyPage	Variant	Required, a PropertyPage object or the ProgID for the ActiveX Control that implements the property page object.
Title	String	Optional, the name to be displayed on the Property Page Tab.

For these examples it is necessary to set a reference to the ActiveX control for your project through the Tools | References... dialog.

Example:

```
Dim oppPropertyPage As PropertyPage

Set oppPropertyPage = CreateObject("OutlookPage.ctrPage")
Pages.Add oppPropertyPage, "Programmers Reference"
```

Or

```
Pages.Add "OutlookPage.ctrPage", "Programmers Reference"
```

The first example passes a PropertyPage object to the Add method and the second passes in the ProgID for the property page that we wish to add. The second method allows Outlook to instantiate the PropertyPage object.

I found that the Title parameter does not work correctly with the first example. The property page appears but with "Untitled" on the Tab. The second example seems to function correctly.

Item Method

The Item method returns a particular PropertyPage object from the PropertyPages collection.

```
Set PropertyPageObject = PropertyPagesCollection.Item(Index)
```

Name	Data type	Description
Index	Long	Required, this is the position of the PropertyPage object within the collection.

Note that these pages are only added when the OptionsPagesAdd event is invoked and they do not persist after the **Options** or **Properties** dialog has been closed. So to use this method you need to add the desired custom property pages first.

Remove Method

The Remove method deletes the PropertyPage object from the PropertyPages collection.

        PropertyPagesCollection.Remove Index

Name	Data type	Description
Index	Long	Required, this is the position of the PropertyPage object within the collection.

As with the Item method you need to add the desired custom property pages before you can remove one.

PropertyPages Collection Properties

Application Property

This property returns the Application object. It will be the Outlook Application object.

        Set ApplicationObject = PropertyPagesCollection.Application

Class Property

The Class property returns a long value that identifies the type of object. This will be one of the OlObjectClass constants and for the PropertyPages collection is olPropertyPages or 71.

        Long = PropertyPagesCollection.Class

Count Property

The Count property returns the number of PropertyPage objects in the collection.

        Long = PropertyPagesCollection.Count

Parent Property

This property returns the parent object for the `PropertyPages` collection. This will be the Outlook `Application` object itself.

```
Set ApplicationObject = PropertyPagesCollection.Parent
```

Session Property

The `Session` property returns the `NameSpace` object for the current session.

```
Set NameSpaceObject = PropertyPagesCollection.Session
```

The PropertyPage Object

The `PropertyPage` object represents a custom property page that can be added and displayed either in the Outlook **Options** dialog or a folder **Properties** dialog. The property page can be set up to react to the user clicking the **Apply** button on the dialog.

PropertyPage Object Methods

Apply Method

The `Apply` method interacts with Outlook and applies any changes to properties that have been set through property page. For this to work your property page must implement `PropertyPage`.

```
PropertyPageObject.Apply
```

It is then necessary to ensure that you place code in the ActiveX control to be executed when the `Apply` method is called. This should set the properties that the page displays.

```
Private Sub PropertyPage_Apply()
'Code to set properties to those shown on property page
End Sub
```

GetPageInfo Method

The `GetPageInfo` method can be used to return information about the property page. This could be set to anything from the opening of a Help File to simply showing a Message box.

```
PropertyPageObject.GetPageInfo HelpFile, HelpContext
```

Name	Data type	Description
HelpFile	String	The name of the help file associated with the custom property page
HelpContext	Long	The context ID of the help file associated with the custom property page

The code to react to this method should be placed in the ActiveX control of the property page. It is here that you would set up `HelpFile` and `HelpContext`. In the example below we choose simply to show a MsgBox when this method is called.

```
Private Sub PropertyPage_GetPageInfo(HelpFile As String, _
HelpContext As Long)
    MsgBox "This property page..."
End Sub
```

PropertyPage Object Property

Dirty Property

The `Dirty` property is set in the ActiveX control. Outlook queries this property when the `OnStatusChange` method occurs. It is a Boolean and should return True if the custom property page has been altered and hence the Apply button has been enabled.

```
Boolean = PropertyPageObject.Dirty
```

Example:

```
Private Property Get PropertyPage_Dirty() As Boolean
    PropertyPage_Dirty = True
End Property
```

In the example above the property page is set to be `Dirty`. This means that when Outlook checks this value it and finds it to be True it will enable the Apply button. Consequently, when the user clicks on the Apply or OK button the `Apply` method of the `PropertyPage` object will be called.

The PropertyPageSite Object

The `PropertyPageSite` object represents the dialog itself. It is used so that Outlook can ascertain what is happening to the property page, e.g. whether any of the properties has been changed or whether controls within the property page have been clicked.

A reference to this object should be set in the ActiveX control as follows:

```
Dim myPPSite As Outlook.PropertyPageSite
Set myPPSite = Parent
```

PropertyPageSite Object Methods

OnStatusChange Method

The `OnStatusChange` method is used to notify Outlook that the user has made a change to the property page. This in turns tells Outlook to query the page by checking the `Dirty` property.

```
PropertyPageSiteObject.OnStatusChange
```

Example:

```
Private Sub lblWelcome_Click()
     Dim opsSite As Outlook.PropertyPageSite
     Set opsSite = Parent
     opsSite.OnStatusChange
End Sub
```

In the example above I have added a label to the ActiveX control. When this label is clicked I notify Outlook that the property page has changed by calling the OnStatusChange method. This in turns checks the Dirty property of the property page to see if it has changed.

PropertyPageSite Object Properties

Application Property

The Application property returns the Outlook Application object.

```
Set ApplicationObject = PropertyPageSiteObject.Application
```

Class Property

The Class property returns a long value that identifies the type of object. This will be one of the OlObjectClass constants. In this case it is olOutlookPropertyPageSite or 70.

```
Long = PropertyPageSiteObject.Class
```

Parent Property

This property returns the parent object for the PropertyPageSite object. In this case it is the Outlook Application object.

```
Set ApplicationObject = PropertyPageSiteObject.Parent
```

Session Property

The Session property returns the NameSpace object for the current session.

```
Set NameSpaceObject = PropertyPageSiteObject.Session
```

Explorers and Inspectors

In this chapter we are going to examine the Outlook objects that are used to display mail information. Explorer objects are used to look at the contents of folders, while Inspector objects are used to view individual Outlook items. The remainder of the objects covered here are related to the appearance and functionality of Explorers and Inspectors and the items that they display.

The Explorers Collection

An Explorer object is a GUI that displays to the user the contents of MAPIFolder objects. I imagine the figure below is what comes to mind when someone thinks of Outlook. This is exactly what an Explorer object is. The Explorer object exposes the properties, methods and events that make this GUI.

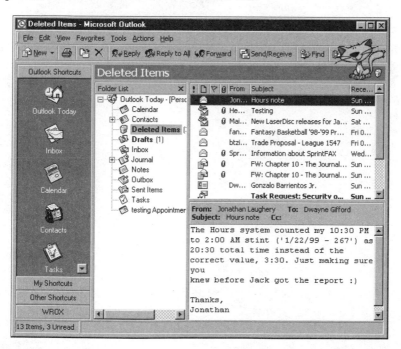

The `Explorers` collection holds all the `Explorer` objects that are available. However, not all `Explorer` objects are necessarily visible to the user. When a new `Explorer` is created through code it is added to the `Explorers` collection, but is invisible until its `Display` method is called.

The `Explorers` collection is accessed directly from the `Application` object.

```
Set ExplorersCollection = ApplicationObject.Explorers
```

Explorers Collection Methods

Add Method

The `Add` method creates a new `Explorer` object and adds it to the `Explorers` collection.

```
Set ExplorerObject = ExplorersCollection.Add(MAPIFolder[, DisplayMode])
```

Name	Data type	Description
MAPIFolder	MAPIFolder	Required, the `MAPIFolder` object the contents of which you wish the `Explorer` to display
DisplayMode	Long	Optional, one of the `OlFolderDisplayMode` constants, described below. The default is `olFolderDisplayNormal`.

OlFolderDisplayFolderOnly (1)   The `Explorer` has no **Outlook Bar** and no **Folder List** visible. However, both of these options are still available under the **View** menu.

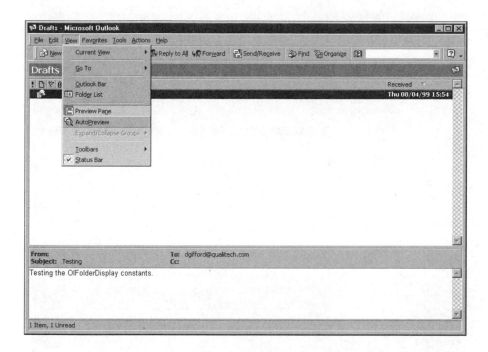

olFolderDisplayNoNavigation (2) This presents the same `Explorer` object as `olFolderDisplayFolderOnly` but this time you cannot open the Outlook Bar or the Folder List and you cannot move from the current folder.

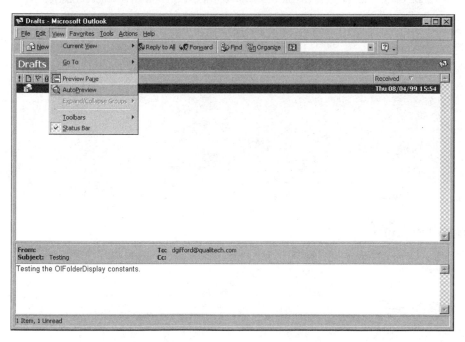

olFolderDisplayNormal (0) This is the view that you have set up and normally use. In my case it shows the Outlook Bar and Folder List. Yours may be a little different.

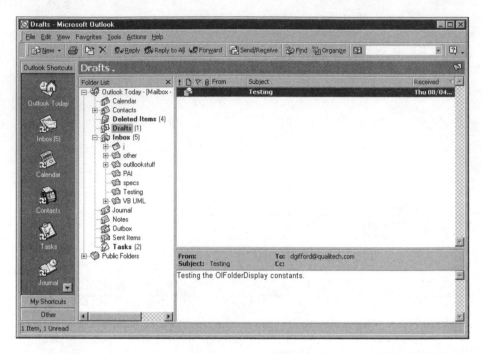

The code below is that used to display the Explorers shown above, where a different `OlFolderDisplay` constant was used for each figure. Note that although an Explorer is added with a particular display type, this will not be apparent until the `Display` method if the `Explorer` object is called.

```
Dim onMAPI As NameSpace
Dim oecExplorers As Explorers
Dim oeDrafts As Explorer
Dim ofDraftFolder As MAPIFolder


Set onMAPI = Application.GetNamespace("MAPI")
Set oecExplorers = Application.Explorers
Set ofDraftFolder = onMAPI.GetDefaultFolder(olFolderDrafts)

Set oeDrafts = oecExplorers.Add(ofDraftFolder, olFolderDisplayFolderOnly)

oeDrafts.Display
```

Item Method

The `Item` method returns a reference to a particular `Explorer` object within the collection.

```
Set ExplorerObject = ExplorersCollection.Item(Index)
```

Name	Data type	Description
Index	Long	Required, represents the position within the collection of the `Explorer` object that you wish to get a reference to.

Example:

```
Dim oecExplorers As Explorers
Dim oeExplorer As explorer

Set oecExplorers = Application.Explorers

If oecExplorers.count > 0 Then
    Set oeExplorer = oecExplorers.Item(1)
    oeExplorer.CurrentView = "By Follow-up Flag"

    If oeExplorer.WindowState = olMinimized Then
        oeExplorer.WindowState = olNormalWindow
    End If
End If
```

In this example a reference is set to the `Explorers` collection. If the collection is not empty a reference is set to the first `Explorer` object in the collection and its **View** is set to "By Follow-up Flag". If this `Explorer` object is originally minimized, it is returned to its Normal state. The **Inbox** was displayed in the first `Explorer` of my `Explorers` collection and so the result of this code was as shown in the figure below. For more information on `Views` refer to the `CurrentView` property exposed by the `Explorer` object.

Explorers Collection Properties

Application Property

The Application property returns the Application object for this session. Note that this will be the Outlook Application object. Since this is the root object for Outlook you should already have a reference to this object.

```
Set ApplicationObject = ExplorersCollection.Application
```

Class Property

The Class property returns a unique long integer value that identifies the object's type. This will be one of the OlObjectClass constants and for the Explorers collection will be olExplorers or 60.

```
Long = ExplorersCollection.Class
```

Count Property

The Count property returns a long integer that represents the number of Explorer objects in the Explorers collection.

```
Long = ExplorersCollection.Count
```

This property could be used to check whether the Explorers collection is empty and to call appropriate error handling code to prevent an error being raised when the Item method is used.

Parent Property

The Parent property returns the parent object for the Explorers collection. In this case we can only have one parent and that is the Application object.

```
Set ApplicationObject  = ExplorersCollection.Parent
```

Session Property

The Session property returns the NameSpace object for the current collection. Note that this will always be the Messaging Application Programming Interface or MAPI.

```
Set NameSpaceObject = ExplorersCollection.Session
```

Explorers Collection Event

NewExplorer Event

The NewExplorer event will occur whenever a new Explorer object is added to the Explorers collection. Remember that this will happen before the Explorer is shown.

For this event to be fired you need to make use of the WithEvents keyword. The following code should be placed in a **Class Module**.

```
Public WithEvents oecExplorers As Explorers
```

It is also necessary to set the chosen variable name, here `oecExplorers`, to be the `Explorers` collection in a procedure that is called from elsewhere. For example with the following code, the `Explorers` reference is automatically set when the class is instantiated

```
Private Sub Class_Initialize()
    Set oecExplorers = Application.Explorers
End Sub
```

The syntax of the event is as follows:

```
Private Sub oecExplorers_NewExplorer(ByVal Explorer As Explorer)
```

The `Explorer` parameter is the new `Explorer` object that is being added to the `Explorers` collection.

I tried many things with this event but nothing seemed to work. Also, if you look at the only example that Microsoft offers in the help file, they do nothing with the `Explorer` object that is passed in. Instead they minimize the active Explorer making sure that the new Explorer will be the topmost Window when displayed.

The Explorer Object

The `Explorer` object represents a window in which the contents of a folder are displayed.

A reference to an `Explorer` object can be set directly from the `Application` object by using the `ActiveExplorer` method. This will return the topmost Explorer if one exists.

```
Set ExplorerObject = ApplicationObject.ActiveExplorer
```

Alternatively an `Explorer` object can be accessed via the `MAPIFolder` the contents of which you want to display, using either the `GetExplorer` (for an invisible Explorer) or the `Display` method (for a visible Explorer).

```
Set ExplorerObject = MAPIFolderObject.GetExplorer

MAPIFolderObject.Display
Set ExplorerObject = Application.ActiveExplorer
```

Finally it is possible to get a reference to a particular `Explorer` object within the `Explorers` collection by using `Item` method.

```
Set ExplorerObject = ExplorersCollection.Item(Index)
```

Explorer Object Methods

Activate Method

The `Activate` method activates the `Explorer` object. This will force the `Explorer` object to be the active Window and the topmost Explorer.

```
ExplorerObject.Activate
```

Note that if you try to call the `Activate` method and the `Explorer` object has not been set you will receive an error. This scenario could occur if you use the `ActiveExplorer` method of the `Application` object as this will return `Nothing` if there are no `Explorer` objects. So to check for this you could use the following code.

```
If oeExplorer Is Nothing Then
```

Close Method

The `Close` method shuts down the `Explorer` object. No information associated with the `Explorer` object will be saved.

```
ExplorerObject.Close
```

Display Method

The `Display` method opens the `Explorer` object and causes it to be the topmost window for Outlook. Note that this method is available only for backward compatibility and the `Activate` method should be used for this purpose.

```
ExplorerObject.Display
```

IsPaneVisible Method

The `IsPaneVisible` method returns a `Boolean` value that determines whether a specific pane of the Explorer is visible.

```
Boolean = ExplorerObject.IsPaneVisible(Pane)
```

Name	Data type	Description
Pane	Long	Required, one of the `OlPane` constants, identifying the type of pane.

The `OlPane` constants:

Name	Value	Description
olOutLookBar	1	The bar that holds the shortcut buttons.
olFolderList	2	The list of Folders available to the current session.
olPreview	3	The Preview pane to allow you to view an item's content without opening it.

ShowPane Method

The `ShowPane` method allows you to display or hide a pane in the `Explorer` object and so control its appearance.

```
ExplorerObject.ShowPane(Pane, Visible)
```

Name	Data type	Description
Pane	Long	One of the OlPane constants, shown in the table above.
Visible	Boolean	Set to **True** to show the Pane, **False** to hide it.

Note that if you have created the Explorer object in olFolderDisplayNoNavigation mode then this method will have no effect. With the other display modes the panes become visible or invisible as expected.

Explorer Object Properties

Application Property

The Application property returns the Application object for this session. This will always be the Outlook Application object.

```
Set ApplicationObject = ExplorerObject.Application
```

Caption Property

The Caption method returns a string value that represents title at the top of the Explorer object.

```
String = ExplorerObject.Caption
```

Example:

```
Dim oecExplorers As Explorers
Dim ofRequiredFolder As MAPIFolder
Dim oeExplorer As Explorer
Dim sExpName As String
Dim bExplorerExists As Boolean

Set ofRequiredFolder = _
        Application.GetNamespace("MAPI").GetDefaultFolder(olFolderDrafts)
sExpName = ofRequiredFolder.Name & " - Microsoft Outlook"

Set oecExplorers = Application.Explorers
For Each oeExplorer In oecExplorers
    If sExpName = oeExplorer.Caption Then
        'bExplorerExists = True
        Exit For
    End If
Next

If bExplorerExists = False Then
    Set oeExplorer = oecExplorers.Add(ofRequiredFolder)
End If

oeExplorer.Activate
```

In this example the Caption property is used to check whether the MAPIFolder is already being displayed in an Explorer object. If it is the appropriate Explorer is activated. If there is no corresponding Explorer, then one is added to the Explorers collection and then activated. This is just an idea of what you could use this property for. Obviously there are other ways to achieve the same thing.

Class Property

The `Class` property returns a unique long integer value that identifies the object's type. This will be one of the `OlObjectClass` constants and in this instance will be `olExplorer` or `34`.

```
Long = ExplorerObject.Class
```

CommandBars Property

The `CommandBars` property returns the **Microsoft Office** `CommandBars` collection that represents all the toolbars and menus for the `Explorer` object.

```
Set CommandBarsCollection = ExplorerObject.CommandBars
```

CurrentFolder Property

The `CurrentFolder` property returns or sets the `MAPIFolder` object that is viewed in the `Explorer` object. This property can be used to change the folder that is viewed in an existing `Explorer` object, rather than adding a new one to the `Explorers` collection.

```
Set MAPIFolderObject = ExplorerObject.CurrentFolder
Set ExplorerObject.CurrentFolder = MAPIFolderObject
```

CurrentView Property

The `CurrentView` property returns or sets a string value that represents the View type for an `Explorer` object.

```
String = ExplorerObject.CurrentView
ExplorerObject.CurrentView = String
```

The different possible values for this property are shown under the View | Current View menu.

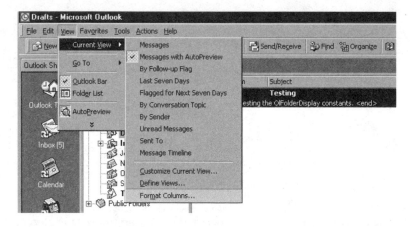

You can see that under this menu you can also build your own views or modify an existing one. This functionality is not yet offered through the Object Model.

Height Property

The `Height` property returns or sets a long integer value that represents the height of the `Explorer` object in pixels.

```
Long = ExplorerObject.Height
ExplorerObject.Height = Long
```

Left Property

The `Left` property returns or sets a long integer value that represents the position, in pixels, of left vertical edge of the `Explorer` object from the left edge of the screen.

```
Long = ExplorerObject.Left
ExplorerObject.Left = Long
```

Panes Property

The `Panes` property returns a `Panes` collection representing the panes displayed by an `Explorer` object. This object is covered in detail in the "Panes Collection" section later in this chapter.

```
Set PanesCollection = ExplorerObject.Panes
```

Parent Property

The `Parent` property returns the parent object for the `Explorer` object. This will be the `Application` object.

```
Set ApplicationObject = ExplorerObject.Parent
```

Selection Property

The `Selection` property returns the item objects for the `MAPIFolder` displayed in the Explorer. This will be an `Items` collection. If there are no items in the folder, for example it is a file-system folder or the Explorer is displaying **Outlook Today**, then this property returns an empty collection.

```
Set ItemsCollection = ExplorerObject.Selection
```

Session Property

The `Session` property returns the `NameSpace` object for the current collection. This will be the Messaging Application Programming Interface or MAPI.

```
Set NameSpaceObject = ExplorerObject.Session
```

Top Property

The Top property returns or sets a long integer value that represents the position, in pixels, of top horizontal edge of the Explorer object from the top of the screen.

```
Long = ExplorerObject.Top
ExplorerObject.Top = Long
```

Width Property

The Width property returns or sets a long integer value that represents the width of the Explorer object in pixels.

```
String = ExplorerObject.Width
ExplorerObject.Width = String
```

WindowState Property

The WindowState property returns or sets a long integer that indicates the window state for the Explorer object, i.e. whether it is minimized, maximized or of normal size.

```
Long  = ExplorerObject.WindowState
ExplorerObject.WindowState = Long
```

The WindowState property may take one of the OlWindowStates constants:

Name	Value	Description
olMaximized	1	The Explorer occupies the whole screen.
olMinimized	2	The Explorer is minimized to the Task Bar.
olNormal	3	The Explorer is in its normal state.

Explorer Object Events

For the Explorer events to be fired, code setting a reference to an Explorer object should be placed in a new **Class Module** within the Outlook project. This code will be used by all of the events supported by the Explorer object.

```
Public WithEvents oeExplorer As Explorer

Private Sub Class_Initialize()
    Set oeExplorer =Application.ActiveExplorer
End Sub
```

In the example code above you will notice that first we are creating a variable called oeExplorer that will allow us to respond to the events that the Explorer object exposes. Although this variable is set to the active explorer, this will be the Explorer that is active when the Class is instantiated. If the active Explorer changes but the Class is not re-instantiated, oeExplorer will no longer refer to the active Explorer. For this functionality use the NewExplorer event of the Explorers collection.

Activate Event

The `Activate` event occurs whenever the `Explorer` object is activated.

```
Private Sub oeExplorer_Activate()
```

Example:

```
Private Sub oeExplorer_Activate()
       If oeExplorer.WindowState <> olNormalWindow Then
              oeExplorer.WindowState = olNormalWindow
       End If
End Sub
```

In this example we ensure that the Explorer appears as a normal-sized window when it is activated.

BeforeFolderSwitch Event

The `BeforeFolderSwitch` event occurs before the folder shown in the Explorer is changed. This means that when a user or code changes the active folder in the Explorer this code is executed first and **then** the new `MAPIFolder` is shown. Since this event is called before the new `MAPIFolder` is actually shown it is possible to cancel the folder change and for the Explorer to appear unchanged.

Name	Description
NewFolder	The new `MAPIFolder` that the user has selected to view.
Cancel	Allows navigation to the new `MAPIFolder` to be canceled if set to True in the event's code.

Example:

```
Private Sub oeExplorer_BeforeFolderSwitch(ByVal NewFolder As Object, Cancel _
As Boolean)

       If NewFolder.Name = "Top Secret" Then
              Cancel = True
       End If
End Sub
```

In the example above we prevent the user from setting the active `MAPIFolder` to a folder named "Top Secret".

BeforeViewSwitch Event

The `BeforeViewSwitch` event occurs before a new view is activated. A View determines the appearance of the items shown in the right pane of the `Explorer` object. The available views are shown in the View | Current View menu, and this event is fired when a view different from the current one is selected either through the GUI or through code using the `CurrentView` property of the `Explorer` object.

Since this event occurs before the action is carried out, it is possible to cancel the event and force the view to remain unchanged.

```
Private Sub oeExplorer_BeforeViewSwitch(ByVal NewView As Variant, Cancel _
As Boolean)
```

Name	Description
NewView	The name of the new view that has been selected
Cancel	Allows the event to be canceled if set to True in the event's code.

Close Event

The Close event occurs when the Explorer object is closed. The method becomes available in the **Class Module** when the Explorer variable is declared. However, it is not mentioned in the help files and is not called unless the Explorer is the only Explorer in the collection.

```
Private Sub oeExplorer_Close()
```

Deactivate Event

The Deactivate event occurs when the Explorer loses focus.

```
Private Sub oeExplorer_Deactivate()
```

Example:

```
Private Sub oeExplorer_Deactivate()
    If oeExplorer.WindowState <> olMinimized Then
        oeExplorer.WindowState = olMinimized
    End If
End Sub
```

In the example above we ensure that the Explorer object is minimized when it loses focus.

FolderSwitch Event

The FolderSwitch event occurs when a new MAPIFolder is displayed in the Explorer. This event will occur after the BeforeFolderSwitch event is called.

```
Private Sub oeExplorer_FolderSwitch()
```

SelectionChange Event

The SelectionChange event occurs when the selected item or items highlighted in the right pane of the Explorer changes. This event will not occur if the current view is Outlook Today or Integrated File system.

```
Private Sub oeExplorer_SelectionChange()
```

ViewSwitch Event

The `ViewSwitch` event occurs when the current view changes and after the `BeforeViewSwitch` event. A view determines the appearance of the items shown in the right pane of the `Explorer` object and may changed through the GUI or through code.

```
Private Sub oeExplorer_ViewSwitch()
```

The Selection Collection

The `Selection` collection represents the Outlook items that are selected in an `Explorer` object. So if you look at the figure below, you can see that the `Selection` collection contains three items.

You will have as many selection collections as you have `Explorer` objects instantiated. It makes sense, then, that a reference to a `Selection` collection is set through the `Explorer` object using the `Selection` property.

```
Dim oeExplorer As Explorer
Dim oscSelection As Selection
...
Set oscSelection = oeExplorer.Selection
```

Selection Collection Methods

Item Method

The Item method returns a particular Outlook item from the Selection collection.

```
Set Object = SelectionCollection.Item(Index)
```

Name	Data type	Description
Index	Variant	Required, the position of the Outlook item in the Selection collection or the Subject property of the Outlook item

Example:

```
Dim oeExplorer As Explorer
Dim oscSelection As Outlook.Selection
Dim iFor As Integer
Dim odDocument As DocumentItem

Set oeExplorer = ActiveExplorer
Set oscSelection = oeExplorer.Selection
For iFor = 1 To oscSelection.count
    If oscSelection.Item(iFor).Class = olDocument Then
        Set odDocument = oscSelection.Item(iFor)
            odDocument.Display
    End If
Next
```

In the example above the Item method is used to examine the Class property of each Outlook item from the selected items of the currently active Explorer object. Any DocumentItem objects within this Selection collection are then displayed in an Inspector object.

Selection Collection Properties

Application Property

This property returns the Application object for this session. This will be the Outlook Application object.

```
Set ApplicationObject = SelectionCollection.Application
```

Class Property

The Class property returns a long value that identifies the type of object. This will be one of the OlObjectClass constants and for the Selection collection is olSelection or 74.

```
Long = SelectionCollection.Class
```

Count Property

The Count property returns the number of Outlook items in the referenced Selection collection.

```
Long = SelectionCollection.Count
```

Parent Property

This property returns the parent object for the Selection collection. In this case the parent will be the Explorer object that the Outlook items are selected from.

```
Set ExplorerObject = SelectionCollection.Parent
```

Session Property

The Session property returns the NameSpace object for the current session. This will always be the messaging application programming interface or MAPI.

```
Set NameSpaceObject = SelectionCollection.Session
```

The Panes Collection

The Panes collection contains the panes that are displayed by an Explorer object. Currently the only pane in the Panes collection is the OutlookBarPane object. The OutlookBarPane object represents the Outlook Bar in an Explorer object. The figure below shows an Outlook Bar pane of an Explorer.

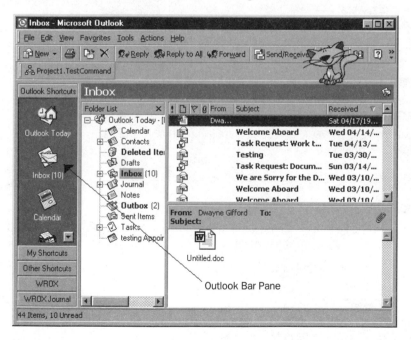

A reference to a `Panes` collection is made through the `Explorer` object that it is displayed in.

```
Dim oeExplorer as Explorer
Dim opcPanes as Panes
…
Set ocpPanes = oeExplorer.Panes
```

Panes Collection Method

Item Method

The `Item` method returns a particular `Pane` object from the `Panes` collection.

```
Set OutlookBarPaneObject = PanesCollection.Item (Index)
```

Name	Data type	Description
Index	Variant	Required, this is a long representing the position of the pane in the `Panes` collection or a string holding the name of the pane.

Since there is only one object in this collection, the only possibilities for the `Index` parameter are 1 or "OutlookBar" as shown below.

```
Set oobpPane = opcPanes.Item(1)
```

Or

```
Set oobpPane = opcPanes("OutlookBar")
```

Panes Collection Properties

Application Property

This property returns the `Application` object for this session. This is the Outlook `Application` object.

```
Set ApplicationObject = PanesCollection.Application
```

Class Property

The `Class` property returns a long value that identifies the type of object. This will be one of the `OlObjectClass` constants. For the `Panes` collection this is `olPanes` or `62`.

```
Long = PanesCollection.Class
```

Count Property

The `Count` property returns the number of panes in the collection. Currently this will only be one as Outlook 2000 only supports the Outlook Bar.

```
Long = PanesCollection.Count
```

Parent Property

This property returns the parent object for the `Panes` collection. In this case the parent will be the `Explorer` object displaying the panes.

```
Set ExplorerObject = PanesCollection.Parent
```

Session Property

The `Session` property returns the `NameSpace` object for the current session.

```
Set NameSpaceObject = PanesCollection.Session
```

The OutlookBarPane Object

The `OutlookBarPane` object represents the Outlook Bar that can be displayed in an Explorer. An example is shown in the last figure. This bar holds shortcuts for the different Outlook folders.

A reference to this object is made via the `Item` method of the `Panes` collection.

Either:

```
Dim opcPanes as Panes
Dim oobpBar As OutlookBarPane
…
Set oobpBar = opcPanes.Item(1)
```

or:

```
Dim opcPanes as Panes
Dim oobBbar As OutlookBarPane
…
Set oobpBar = opcPanes.Item("OutlookBar")
```

> The `OutlookBarPane` **object has no methods.**

OutlookBarPane Object Properties

Application Property

This property returns the `Application` object for this session. This is the Outlook `Application` object.

```
Set ApplicationObject = OutlookBarPaneObject.Application
```

Class Property

The `Class` property returns a long value that identifies the type of object. This will be one of the `OlObjectClass` constants. For the Outlook Bar, this is `olOutlookBarPane` or 63.

```
Long = OutlookBarPaneObject.Class
```

Contents Property

The `Contents` property returns the `OutlookBarStorage` object for the current `OutlookBarPane` object. This object represents a way of holding the objects of the Outlook Bar pane.

```
Set OutlookBarStorageObject = OutlookBarPaneObject.Contents
```

CurrentGroup Property

The `CurrentGroup` property is used to return or set the `OutlookBarGroup` object that is open in the `OutlookBarPane` object for the Explorer. This `OutlookBarGroup` object represents a group of shortcuts in the Outlook Bar pane.

```
Set OutlookBarGroupObject = OutlookBarPaneObject.CurrentGroup
Set OutlookBarPaneObject.CurrentGroup = OutlookBarGroupObject
```

Name property

The `Name` property returns, as a string, the name of the Outlook Bar pane. This will be "OutlookBar" since the only pane that is currently supported by Outlook 2000 is the Outlook Bar.

```
String = OutlookBarPaneObject.Name
```

Parent Property

This property returns the parent object for the `OutlookBarPane` object. In this case the parent will be `Explorer` object in which it is shown.

```
Set ExplorerObject = OutlookBarPaneObject.Parent
```

Session Property

The `Session` property returns the `NameSpace` object for the current session.

```
Set NameSpaceObject = OutlookBarPaneObject.Session
```

Visible Property

The `Visible` property is a Boolean value that can be used to return or set whether the Outlook Bar is visible in the `Explorer` object. To show the Outlook Bar, set this property to `True`. If set to `False`, the Outlook Bar will be hidden.

```
Boolean = OutlookBarPaneObject.Visible
OutlookBarPaneObject.Visible = Boolean
```

It is also possible to set or read this property through the `ShowPane` or `IsPaneVisible` methods of the `Explorer` object in which the Outlook Bar is displayed.

OutlookBarPane Object Events

Before these events can be fired it is necessary to declare `WithEvents`, a variable to hold a reference to the required `OutlookBarPane` object. This should be placed in a class module and the reference should be set where it will be called when the class is instantiated.

Example:

```
Dim WithEvents oobpBar As OutlookBarPane

Private Sub Class_Initialize()
    Set oobpBar = ActiveExplorer.Panes.Item("OutlookBar")
End Sub
```

BeforeGroupSwitch Event

The `BeforeGroupSwitch` event occurs before a new `OutlookBarGroup` object is opened in the Explorer. This could be as a result of code or the user switching between Outlook Bar Groups on the GUI. For example, if the user switches between the **Outlook Shortcuts** group and the **My Shortcuts** group, this event will be fired.

```
Private Sub oobpBar_BeforeGroupSwitch(ByVal ToGroup As OutlookBarGroup, _
                                      Cancel As Boolean)
```

Name	Description
ToGroup	The new group to be opened.
Cancel	If set to `True`, then the new group will not be opened.

Example:

```
Private Sub obpBar_BeforeGroupSwitch(ByVal ToGroup As OutlookBarGroup, Cancel
As Boolean)
    If ToGroup.Name = "WROX" Then
            Cancel = True
    End If
End Sub
```

In the example above we are checking to see if the new group is the WROX group and if it is then we stop the group from being opened.

BeforeNavigate Event

The `BeforeNavigate` event occurs when the user selects a shortcut to navigate to a new folder.

```
Private Sub oobpBar_BeforeNavigate(ByVal Shortcut As OutlookBarShortcut, _
                                   Cancel As Boolean)
```

Name	Description
Shortcut	The shortcut that user has selected.
Cancel	If set to `True`, then the navigation to the folder is stopped.

The OutlookBarStorage Object

The `OutlookBarStorage` object represents a way of holding the objects of the Outlook Bar pane. A reference is set via the `Contents` property of the associated `OutlookBarPane` object.

```
Dim oobpBar As OutlookBarPane
Dim oobsStorage As OutlookBarStorage
…
Set oobsStorage = oobpBar.Contents
```

> **The** `OutlookBarStorage` **object has no methods.**

OutlookBarStorage Object Properties

Application Property

This property returns the `Application` object for this session. This is the Outlook `Application` object.

```
Set ApplicationObject = OutlookBarStorageObject.Application
```

Class Property

The `Class` property returns a long value that identifies the type of object. This will be one of the `OlObjectClass` constants. For the `OutlookBarStorage` object this is `olOutlookBarStorage` or `64`.

```
Long = OutlookBarStorageObject.Class
```

Groups Property

The `Groups` property returns a reference to the `OutlookBarGroups` collection associated with the Outlook Bar pane. This is a set of Outlook Bar groups that can be shown in the Outlook Bar pane.

```
Set OutlookBarGroupsCollection = OutlookBarStorageObject.Groups
```

Parent Property

This property returns the parent object for the `OutlookBarStorage` object. In this case the parent is the `OutlookBarPane` object.

```
Set OutlookBarPaneObject = OutlookBarStorageObject.Parent
```

Session Property

The `Session` property returns the `NameSpace` object for the current session.

```
Set NameSpaceObject = OutlookBarStorageObject.Session
```

The OutlookBarGroups Collection

The OutlookBarGroups collection contains the references to the OutlookBarGroup objects that are held in the OutlookBarStorage collection. The OutlookBarGroup object represents a group on the Outlook Bar.

We cannot create a new OutlookBarGroups collection, but we can get a reference to an existing one through the Groups property of an OutlookBarStorage object:

```
Dim oobgcGroups As OutlookBarGroups
Dim oobstStorage As OutlookBarStorage
...
Set oobgcGroups = oobstStorage.Groups
```

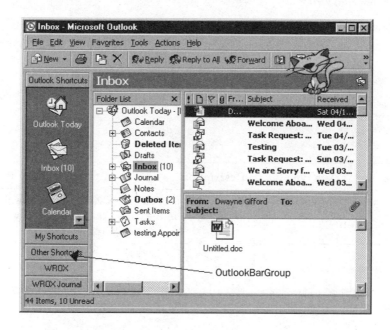

OutlookBarGroups Collection Methods

Add Method

The Add method gives us the ability to add a new OutlookBarGroup object to the collection.

```
Set OutlookBarGroup = OutlookBarGroupsCollection.Add Name[, Index]
```

Name	Data type	Description
Name	String	Required, the name for the group, which will appear on the Outlook Bar.
Index	Long	Optional, the position where the group is to appear in the Outlook Bar. A value of 1 represents the top position. The default is the bottom position on the bar.

For example, to add a new group called `"Wrox Group"` as the second group down in the bar, we would write:

```
Dim oobgcGroups As OutlookBarGroups
...
oobgcGroups.Add "Wrox Group", 2
```

Item Method

The `Item` method returns the `OutlookBarGroup` object from the `OutlookBarGroups` collection.

```
Set OutlookBarGroupObject = OutlookBarGroupsCollection.Item Index
```

Name	Data type	Description
Index	Variant	Required, this is the index value for the position of the group in the collection or the name of the `OutlookBarGroup` to be retrieved.

For example:

```
Set oobgGroup = oobgcGroups.Item(1)
```

Or

```
Set oobgGroup = oobgcGroups.Item("WROX Journal")
```

In the first example above we use the index to retrieve the first (i.e. topmost) group in the `OutlookBarGroups` collection. The second example uses the name of the `OutlookBarGroup` object to retrieve it from the collection.

Remove Method

The `Remove` method will delete the `OutlookBarGroup` from the `OutlookBarGroups` collection.

```
OutlookBarGroupsCollection.Remove Index
```

Name	Data type	Description
Index	Long	Required, the index number for the OutlookBarGroup object that you want to remove from the collection.

OutlookBarGroups Collection Properties

Application Property

This property returns the Application object for this session.

```
Set ApplicationObject = OutlookBarGroupsCollection.Application
```

Class Property

The Class property returns a long integer value that identifies the type of object; this is one of the olObjectClass constants. In this case, the value will be olOutlookBarGroups or 65.

```
Long = OutlookBarGroupsCollection.Class
```

Count Property

The Count property returns the number of OutlookBarGroup objects in the collection. If there are no OutlookBarGroup objects, Count will return zero.

```
Long = OutlookBarGroupsCollection.Count
```

Parent Property

This property returns a reference to the parent object for the OutlookBarGroups collection. This will always be the OutlookBarStorage object of the OutlookBarPane to which the groups belong.

```
Set OutlookBarStorageObject = OutlookBarGroupsCollection.Parent
```

Session Property

The Session property returns the NameSpace object for the current session.

```
Set NameSpaceObject = OutlookBarGroupsCollection.Session
```

OutlookBarGroups Collection Events

For these events to be fired, you need to use the WithEvents keyword. The following code should be placed in a Class Module.

```
Public WithEvents oogbcGroups As Groups
```

It is also necessary to set the chosen variable name, here oogbcGroups, to be the OutlookBarGroups collection in a procedure that is called from elsewhere. For example with the following code, the reference is automatically set when the class is instantiated

```
Private Sub Class_Initialize()
    Set oobgcGroups = ActiveExplorer.Panes.Item(1).Contents.Groups
End Sub
```

BeforeGroupAdd Event

The BeforeGroupAdd event occurs before the new group is actually added to the collection.

```
Private Sub oobgcGroups_BeforeGroupAdd(Cancel As Boolean)
```

Name	Description
Cancel	Setting this to True stops the group from being added.

BeforeGroupRemove Event

The BeforeGroupRemove event occurs before the group is actually removed, giving you a chance to stop the group from being removed.

```
Private Sub oobgcGroups_BeforeGroupRemove _
            (ByVal Group As OutlookBarGroup, Cancel As Boolean)
```

Name	Description
Group	The group that is about to be removed from the collection.
Cancel	Setting this to True cancels the removal of the group from the collection.

For example, the following code prevents the removal of the OutlookBarGroup called "WROX":

```
Private Sub oobgcGroups_BeforeGroupRemove _
            (ByVal Group As OutlookBarGroup, Cancel As Boolean)
    If Group.Name = "WROX" Then
        MsgBox "You cannot remove the Company Group"
        Cancel = True
    End If
End Sub
```

The example above checks the name of the group which is about to be removed to make sure that it is not the company group. If it is, we cancel the process of removing of the group by setting Cancel to True.

GroupAdd Event

The GroupAdd event occurs after the new group has been added to the OutlookBarGroups collection. This occurs after the BeforeGroupAdd event has been raised.

```
Private Sub oobgcGroups_GroupAdd(ByVal NewGroup As OutlookBarGroup)
```

Name	Description
NewGroup	The new group being added to the collection.

The OutlookBarGroup Object

The OutlookBarGroup object represents a group of shortcuts on the Outlook Bar. Each of these groups appears on the bar as one of those gray tabs which slide up and down as you open and close them. An OutlookBarGroup can contain shortcuts to MAPIFolder objects, to file system folders or web sites.

An OutlookBarGroup can be created through the Add method of the OutlookBarGroups collection. To get a reference to an existing OutlookBarGroup, use the Item method of the OutlookBarGroups collection. Both of these methods are discussed above in the section on the OutlookBarGroups collection.

> The OutlookBarGroup object has no methods.

OutlookBarGroup Object Properties

Application Property

This property returns the Application object for this session.

```
Set ApplicationObject = OutlookBarGroupObject.Application
```

Class Property

The Class property returns a long value that identifies the type of the object; this will be one of the OlObjectClass constants. In this case, the value will be olOutlookBarGroup or 66.

```
Long = OutlookBarGroupObject.Class
```

Name Property

This property returns a string value representing the name for the OutlookBarGroup. This value is set when the group is added to the collection.

```
String = OutlookBarGroupObject.Name
```

Parent Property

The Parent property returns a reference to the parent object for the OutlookBarGroup object. This will always be the OutlookBarStorage object for the OutlookBarPane to which the group belongs.

```
Set OutlookBarStorageObject = OutlookBarGroupObject.Parent
```

Session Property

The `Session` property returns the `NameSpace` object for the current session.

```
Set NameSpaceObject = OutlookBarGroupObject.Session
```

Shortcuts Property

The `Shortcuts` property returns a reference to the `OutlookBarShortcuts` collection for the `OutlookBarGroup` object. This collection contains all the objects representing the shortcuts in the group.

```
Set OutlookBarShortcutsCollection = OutlookBarGroupObject.Shortcuts
```

ViewType Property

The `ViewType` property returns or sets the style for the icons that the group will display. The long integer value can be either of the `OlOutlookBarViewType` constants.

```
OutlookBarGroupObject.ViewType = Long
Long = OutlookBarGroupObject.ViewType
```

Constant	Value	Description
olLarge _Icon	1	The icons shown in the group will be large icons.
olSmall _Icon	2	The icons shown in the group will be small icons.

The OutlookBarShortcuts Collection

The `OutlookBarShortcuts` collection holds the `OutlookBarShortcut` objects in the Outlook Bar group. An `OutlookBarShortcut` object represents a shortcut in the group that links you to a MAPIFolder, URL or a system folder. When you click on one of these links you will be taken to the target the link points to.

A reference is set to the `OutlookBarShortcuts` collection through the `Shortcuts` method of an `OutlookBarGroup` object.

```
Dim oobgGroup As OutlookBarGroup
Dim oobscShortcuts As OutlookBarShortcuts
...
Set oobscShortcuts = oobgGroup.Shortcuts
```

OutlookBarShortcuts Collection Methods

Add Method

The `Add` method adds a new `OutlookBarShortcut` object to the collection and returns a reference to it.

```
Set OutlookBarShortcutObject = OutlookBarShortcutsCollection.Add _
                                    (Target, Name[, Index])
```

Name	Data type	Description
Target	Variant	Required, the target for the shortcut. If this is an Outlook folder then this should be set to the MAPIFolder object. If it is a Web page or system folder then it should be a string holding the URL or path name.
Name	String	Required, the name to represent the shortcut.
Index	Long	Optional, the position where the shortcut will appear in the group.

Example:

```
Dim oobgGroup As OutlookBarGroup
Dim oobscShortcuts As OutlookBarShortcuts
Dim ofFolder1 As MAPIFolder

Set oobgGroup = ActiveExplorer.Panes.Item(1).Contents.Groups(1)
Set oobscShortcuts = oobgGroup.Shortcuts

Set ofFolder1 = Application.GetNamespace("MAPI"). _
            GetDefaultFolder(olFolderInbox).Folders(1)
oobscShortcuts.add ofFolder1, "Folder 1", 2
```

The example above adds the first child folder of the default Inbox folder as a shortcut on the Outlook Bar. In the figure below you can see that it appears second in the list, set by the Index parameter, with "Folder 1" underneath it. Note that this is **not** the name of the folder.

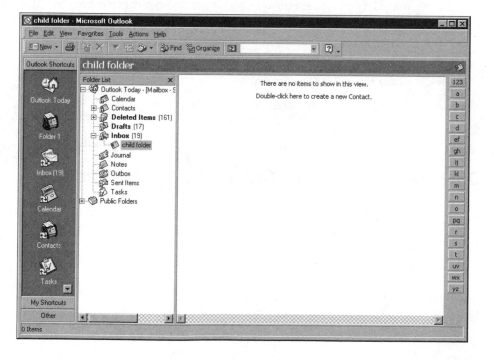

Example:

```
Dim oobgGroup As OutlookBarGroup
Dim oobscShortcuts As OutlookBarShortcuts
Dim ofFolder1 As MAPIFolder

Set oobgGroup = ActiveExplorer.Panes.Item(1).Contents.Groups(1)
Set oobscShortcuts = oobgGroup.Shortcuts

Set ofFolder1 = Application.GetNamespace("MAPI"). _
               GetDefaultFolder(olFolderInbox).Folders(1)
oobscShortcuts.add "http:\\www.wrox.com", "Wrox"
```

In this second example a shortcut to the Wrox Web site is placed at the bottom of the other shortcuts.

Item Method

The Item method returns a particular OutlookBarShortcut object from the OutlookBarShortcuts collection.

```
Set OutlookBarShortcutObject = OutlookBarShortcutsCollection.Item(Index)
```

Name	Data type	Description
Index	Variant	Required, a long representing the position of the OutlookBarShortcut object within the collection or a string holding its name.

Remove Method

The Remove method deletes the specified OutlookBarShortcut object from the OutlookBarShortcuts collection.

```
OutlookBarShortcutsCollection.Remove Index
```

Name	Data type	Description
Index	Long	Required, represents the position of the OutlookBarShortcut object within the collection.

OutlookBarShortcuts Collection Properties

Application Property

This property returns the Application object for this session.

```
Set ApplicationObject = OutlookBarShortcutsCollection.Application
```

Class Property

The `Class` property returns a long value that identifies the type of object. This will be one of the `OlObjectClass` constants. For this collection it is `olOutlookBarShortcuts` or 67.

```
Long = OutlookBarShortcutsCollection.Class
```

Count Property

The `Count` property returns the number of `OutlookBarShortcut` objects in the collection. If there are no shortcuts in the collection then zero will be returned.

```
Long = OutlookBarShortcutsCollection.Count
```

Parent Property

This property returns the parent object for the `OutlookBarShortcuts` collection. In this case the parent is the associated `OutlookBarGroup` object.

```
Set OutlookBarGroupObject = OutlookBarShortcutsCollection.Parent
```

Session Property

The `Session` property returns the `NameSpace` object for the current session.

```
Set NameSpaceObject = OutlookBarShortcutsCollection.Session
```

OutlookBarShortcuts Collection Events

Before these events can be fired it is necessary to declare `WithEvents`, a variable to hold a reference to the required `OutlookBarShortCuts` collection. This should be placed in a class module and the reference should be set where it will be called when the class is instantiated.

Example:

```
Dim WithEvents oobscShortcuts As OutlookBarShortcuts

Private Sub Class_Initialize()
    Set oobscShortcuts = _
            ActiveExplorer.Panes.Item(1).Contents.Groups(1).Shortcuts
End Sub
```

BeforeShortcutAdd Event

The `BeforeShortcutAdd` event occurs before a new shortcut is added to the `OutlookBarShortcuts` collection.

```
Private Sub oobscShortcuts_BeforeShortcutAdd(Cancel As Boolean)
```

Name	Data type	Description
Cancel	Boolean	If set to True, the shortcut will not be added.

BeforeShortcutRemove Event

The `BeforeShortcutRemove` event occurs before a shortcut is removed giving you a opportunity to stop the shortcut from being removed.

```
Private Sub oobscShortcuts_BeforeShortcutRemove _
(ByVal Shortcut As OutlookBarShortcut, Cancel As Boolean)
```

Name	Description
Shortcut	The shortcut that is about to be removed
Cancel	If set to True then the shortcut will not be removed from the collection.

ShortcutAdd Event

The `ShortcutAdd` event occurs when a new shortcut is added to the `OutlookBarShortcuts` collection. This event will occur after the `BeforeShortcutAdd` event is executed.

```
Private Sub oobscShortcuts_ShortcutAdd(ByVal NewShortcut As _
OutlookBarShortcut)
```

Name	Description
NewShortcut	The new shortcut being added to the collection.

The OutlookBarShortcut Object

This object represents a shortcut displayed in the Outlook Bar. A reference is set to it via the `Item` method of the `OutlookBarShortcuts` collection explained above.

> **The** `OutlookBarShortcut` **object has no methods.**

OutlookBarShortcut Object Properties

Application Property

This property returns the `Application` object for this session.

```
Set ApplicationObject = OutlookBarShortcutObject.Application
```

Class Property

The `Class` property returns a long value that identifies the type of object. This will be one of the `OlObjectClass` constants. For this object it is `olOutlookBarShortcut` or `68`.

```
Long = OutlookBarShortcutObject.Class
```

Name Property

This property returns a string value representing the name shown under the Outlook Bar shortcut. This value is set when the shortcut is added to the collection.

```
String = OutlookBarShortcutObject.Name
```

Parent Property

This property returns a reference to the parent object for the `OutlookBarShortcut` object. In this case the parent is the `OutlookBarGroup` object.

```
Set OutlookBarGroupObject = OutlookBarShortcutObject.Parent
```

Session Property

The `Session` property returns the `NameSpace` object for the current session.

```
Set NameSpaceObject = OutlookBarShortcutObject.Session
```

Target Property

The `Target` property is a variant value that identifies what the shortcut is linked to. This value is set when a new shortcut is created through the `Add` method exposed by the `OutlookBarShortcuts` collection or by the user adding a shortcut through the GUI.

```
Variant = OutlookBarShortcutObject.Target
```

If the value returned is a string then it holds either the path of a system folder or the URL of a Web page. If a `MAPIFolder` object is returned then the shortcut is an Outlook folder. Lastly, if a non-Outlook object is returned the shortcut is a system folder.

The Inspectors Collection

The `Inspectors` collection holds all the `Inspector` objects that have been created. An `Inspector` object is the GUI that Outlook items are displayed in. These `Inspector` objects have a different appearance depending on what type of item is being displayed. The example below shows an Inspector for a `JournalItem` object.

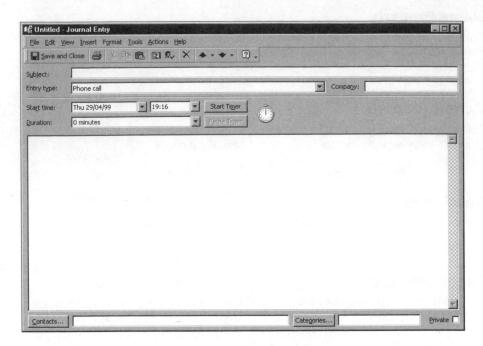

Inspector objects are not necessarily visible to the eye. They can be instantiated without being displayed on the screen. Such Inspector objects are still part of the Inspectors collection.

The Inspectors method of an Application object is used to set a reference to the Inspectors collection.

```
Set oicInspectors = ApplicationObject.ActiveInspector
```

Inspectors Collection Methods

Add Method

The Add method is used to instantiate a new Inspector object and add it to the Inspectors collection.

```
Set InspectorObject = InspectorsCollection.Add(Item)
```

Name	Description
Item	The Outlook item to be displayed.

Example:

```
Dim onMAPI As NameSpace
Dim ofInbox As MAPIFolder
Dim iFor As Integer
Dim oiInspector As Inspector
Dim omMail As MailItem

Set onMAPI = Application.GetNamespace("MAPI")
Set ofInbox = onMAPI.GetDefaultFolder(olFolderInbox)
For iFor = 1 To ofInbox.Items.count
    If ofInbox.Items(iFor).Class = olMail And ofInbox.Items(iFor).UnRead Then
        Set omiMail = ofInbox.Items(iFor)
        Set oiInspector = Application.Inspectors.Add(omiMail)
        oiInspector.Activate
    End If
Next
```

In this example a reference is set to the user's Inbox. Then each item in this folder is checked to see if it is a `MailItem` object that has not yet been read. Each such item is added to `Inspectors` collection using the `Add` method and then displayed on screen using the `Activate` method of the `Inspector` object. The result of this when run on my Inbox was as follows.

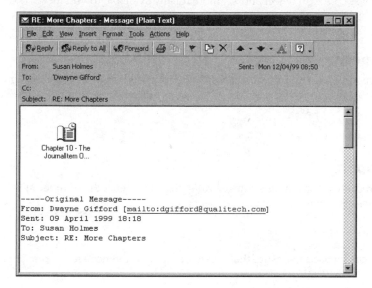

Item Method

The `Item` method is used to get a reference to a specific `Inspector` object that has already been created.

```
Set InspectorObject = InspectorsCollection.Item(Index)
```

This method takes one parameter, `Index`, which determines the particular object within the collection. Although this `Index` is a variant, if you enter any value other than a long integer representing the position of the Inspector within the collection an error will be raised.

Example:

```
Dim oiInspector As Inspector
If Application.Inspectors.count > 0 Then

    Set oiInspector = Application.Inspectors.Item(1)
    If oiInspector.WindowState = olMinimized Then
        oiInspector.WindowState = olNormalWindow
    End If
End If
```

In the example above, providing that the Inspectors collection is not empty, a reference is set to the first Inspector object. If this Inspector is in a minimized state, then it is displayed at its normal size.

Inspectors Collection Properties

Application Property

The Application property returns the Application object for this session. This is the Outlook Application object and is automatically available to you in VBA.

```
Set ApplicationObject = InspectorsCollection.Application
```

Class Property

The Class property returns a unique value that identifies the type of object being referenced. This will be one of the OlObjectClass constants and for an Inspector object is olInspectors or 61.

```
Long = InspectorsCollection.Class
```

Count Property

The Count property returns a long integer value that represents the number of Inspector objects in the Inspectors collection.

```
Long = InspectorsCollection.Count
```

This property can be used to ensure that we do not try to reference an Inspector object that does not exist.

```
If Application.Inspectors.count > 0 Then
...
End If
```

Parent Property

The Parent property returns the parent object for the Inspectors collection. In this case the only possible parent is the Application object.

```
Set ApplicationObject = InspectorsCollection.Parent
```

Session Property

The `Session` property returns the `NameSpace` object for the current collection. This will be the only data source available to Outlook, i.e. the MAPI.

```
Set NameSpaceObject = InspectorsCollection.Session
```

Inspectors Collection Events

For `Inspectors` collection events to be fired it is necessary to ensure the following code is placed in a **Class Module** and that this class is instantiated.

```
Dim WithEvents oicInspectors As Inspectors

Private Sub Class_Initialize()
    Set oicInspectors = Application.Inspectors
End Sub
```

NewInspector Event

The `NewInspector` event occurs when a new Inspector is instantiated.

```
Private Sub oicInspectors_NewInspector(ByVal Inspector As Inspector)
```

There are a number of things you can do with this event. You can set which command bars are visible and modify the item that the Inspector holds. In the example the user is given a warning if they have 5 or more items already open.

Example:

```
Dim lNoofItems As Long

lNoofItems = oicInspectors.count

If lNoofItems > 5 Then MsgBox "WARNING: You have " & lNoofItems - 1 & " items
open already!!!", vbExclamation
```

The Inspector Object

As was said in the introduction to the "Inspectors Collection" section, an `Inspector` object is the GUI that holds an Outlook item. It is possible for an `Inspector` object to exist but not to be made visible to the user. When visible its appearance will depend upon the type of item being displayed.

There are two ways to create a new `Inspector` object. The first employs the `GetInspector` property of an Outlook item and the second uses the `Display` method of the item.

```
Set InspectorObject = Object.GetInspector
Set InspectorObject = Object.Display
```

To get a reference to an existing `Inspector` object, you can either use the `ActiveInspector` method of the `Application` object to reference the active or topmost Inspector, or the `Item` method of the `Inspectors` collection to reference a particular `Inspector` object within the collection, specified by an `Index` parameter. The latter method is described above.

```
Set InspectorObject = ApplicationObject.ActiveInspector
Set InspectorObject = InspectorsCollection.Item(Index)
```

Inspector Object Methods

Activate Method

The Activate method makes the referenced Inspector object the topmost window on your screen.

```
InspectorObject.Activate
```

Close Method

The Close method closes the Inspector object and removes it from the Inspectors collection.

```
InspectorObject.Close(SaveMode)
```

Name	Data type	Description
SaveMode	Long	Required, determines whether any changes are saved and whether the user is prompted to save any changes. It will be one of the OlInspectorClose constants, given below.

Constant	Value	Description
olDiscard	1	Close without prompting to save, discard any changes.
olPromptForSave	2	Prompt the user to save or discard any changes.
olSave	0	Save any changes unconditionally.

Display Method

The Display method displays the Inspector object for the user to view. This method is only included for backwards compatibility and the Activate method can be used instead.

```
InspectorObject.Display([Modal])
```

The parameter Modal is an optional Boolean parameter. If set to True the Inspector object will be modal, otherwise it will be modeless.

HideFormPage Method

The `HideFormPage` method can be used to hide the different Form pages that make up the current `Inspector` object. The `Inspector` object shown below possesses five different Form pages: General, Details, Activities, Certificates and All Fields.

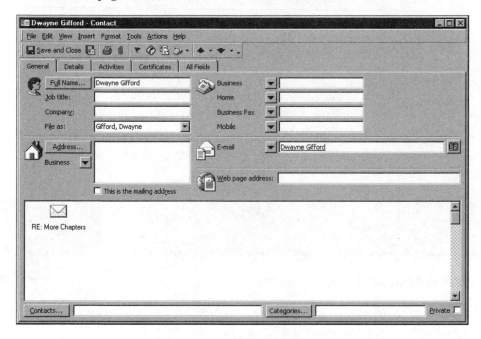

```
InspectorObject.HideFormPage(PageName)
```

The `PageName` parameter specifies which form page is to be hidden.

Example:

```
Dim oiInspector As Inspector
Dim ocFirstContact As ContactItem

Set ocFirstContact =
Application.GetNamespace("MAPI").GetDefaultFolder(olFolderContacts). _
        Items.GetFirst
ocFirstContact.Display
Set oiInspector = Inspectors.Item(1)

oiInspector.HideFormPage "All Fields"
oiInspector.HideFormPage "General"
```

The above code was used to display the same `ContactItem` as above, but the General and All Fields pages were hidden, as shown below.

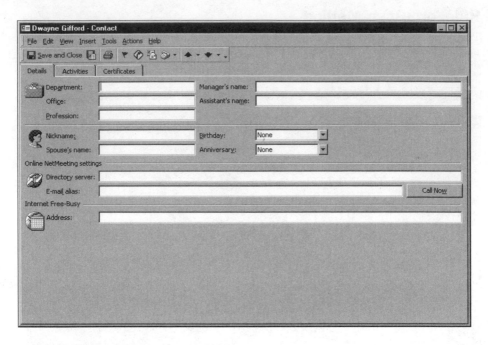

IsWordMail Method

The `IsWordMail` method identifies whether a mail message associated with the `Inspector` object is displayed in Word or an Outlook `Inspector` object. This method returns True if the message is displayed in Word.

```
Boolean = InspectorObject.IsWordMail
```

SetCurrentFormPage Method

The `SetCurrentFormPage` method works in the similar way to the `ShowFormPage` method, that is it ensures that the specified page is visible on the `Inspector`. In addition, it causes this page to be brought to the front in the `Inspector` object.

```
InspectorObject.SetCurrentFormPage FormPage
```

Name	Data type	Description
FormPage	String	This is the name of the form page that you wish to be topmost on the `Inspector` object

ShowFormPage Method

The `ShowFormPage` method displays a form page on an `Inspector` object. However, it will not necessarily be the focus of the GUI.

```
InspectorObject.ShowFormPage FormPage
```

Name	Data type	Description
FormPage	String	This is the name of the form page that you wish to be visible on the Inspector object

In this example we reuse the code shown in the HideFormPage method. The ShowFormPage method is used to display the **All Fields** page, but it is the **Certificates** page that has the focus, having been displayed with the SetCurrentFormPage method.

```
Dim oiInspector As Inspector
Dim ocFirstContact As ContactItem

Set ocFirstContact =
Application.GetNamespace("MAPI").GetDefaultFolder(olFolderContacts).Items.Get
First
ocFirstContact.Display
Set oiInspector = Inspectors.Item(1)

oiInspector.HideFormPage "All Fields"
oiInspector.HideFormPage "General"
oiInspector.SetCurrentFormPage "Certificates"
oiInspector.ShowFormPage "All Fields"
```

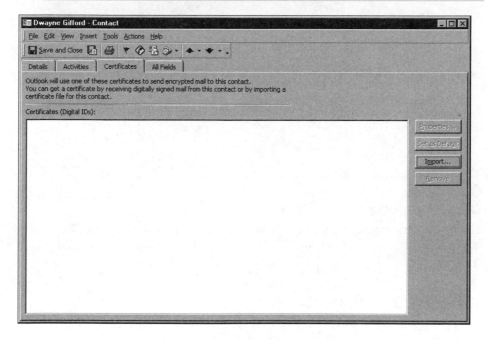

Inspector Object Properties

Application Property

The `Application` property returns the current `Application` object. This will be the Outlook `Application` object.

```
Set ApplicationObject = InspectorObject.Application
```

Caption Property

The `Caption` property returns the current caption for the `Inspector` object. The caption is the title bar text, as shown below.

```
String = InspectorObject.Caption
```

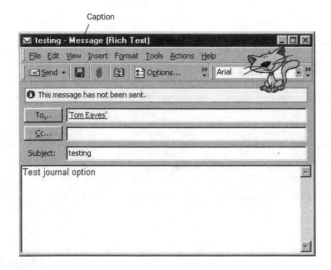

Class Property

The `Class` property returns a unique value that identifies the object's type. This is one of the `OlObjectClass` constants and in this case will be `olInspector` or 35.

```
Long = InspectorObject.Class
```

CommandBars Property

The `CommandBars` property returns the Microsoft Office `CommandBars` collection that represents all the toolbars and menus for the `Inspector` object

```
Set CommandBarsCollection = InspectorObject.CommandBars
```

CurrentItem Property

The `CurrentItem` property returns the current item being displayed in the `Inspector` object.

```
Set ItemObject = InspectorObject.CurrentItem
```

Since an `Inspector` object can display any of the Outlook items, this property may return any of a number of different objects. Therefore before setting a reference to the item, it is best to check the `Class` property of the returned object.

Example:

```
If Inspector.CurrentItem.Class = olMail Then
    Set oMail = Inspector.CurrentItem
End If
```

You should take care if you intend to use the returned object without explicitly setting a reference to it - Outlook will not show you a list of the available methods and properties and these methods and properties are not identical for the different Outlook items.

EditorType Property

The `EditorType` property will return a long integer value that defines the type of editor that the item will be displayed in.

```
Long = InspectorObject.EditorType
```

The following is a list of valid editor types.

Name	Value	Description
olEditorHTML	2	The editor is an HTML editor.
olEditorRTF	3	The editor is an RTF editor.
olEditorText	1	The editor is a Text editor.
olEditorWord	4	The editor is Microsoft Word.

Height Property

The `Height` property is long integer value that returns or sets the height of the `Inspector` object in pixels.

```
Long = InspectorObject.Height
InspectorObject.Height = Long
```

HTMLEditor Property

The `HTMLEditor` property returns the HTML Document object model for the current item being displayed. This property is only valid if the `EditorType` property is `olEditorHTML` and is only available for the current item.

```
Set Object = InspectorObject.HTMLEditor
```

Once you have the HTML Document object model you can now work with it in the same way as for Outlook's object model.

Left Property

The `Left` property is a long integer value that returns or sets the position in pixels of the left vertical edge of the Inspector window from the left edge of the screen.

```
Long = InspectorObject.Left
InspectorObject.Left = Long
```

ModifiedFormPages Property

The `ModifiedFormPages` property returns the `Pages` collection. The `Inspector` object below is displaying a collection of five pages. These are Outlook pages and you can only make changes to the top one, **General**. It is possible to add your own pages to a **Pages** collection.

```
Set PagesCollection = InspectorObject.ModifiedFormPages
```

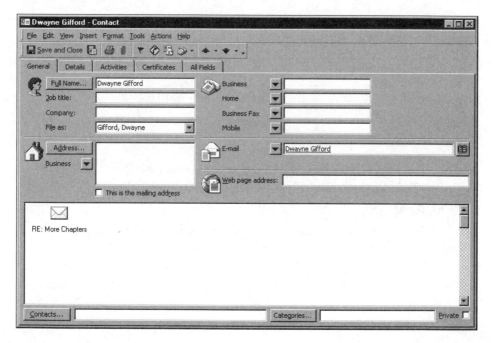

You can add a page to the collection and get a reference to it. Through code you can add up to five custom pages and change their appearance. An example of this is given later in the chapter. These added pages are also available in the **Forms Designer** and I recommend that you work with them from there.

Parent Property

The `Parent` property returns the parent object for the current object. This will always be the Outlook `Application` object.

```
Set ApplicationObject = InspectorObject.Parent
```

Session Property

The `Session` property returns to the `NameSpace` object for the current collection. This will be the MAPI.

```
Set NameSpaceObject = InspectorObject.Session
```

Top Property

The `Top` property holds a long integer value that returns or sets the position, in pixels, of the topmost horizontal edge of the `Inspector` window from the top of the screen.

```
Long = InspectorObject.Top
InspectorObject.Top = Long
```

Width Property

The `Width` property holds a long integer value that returns or sets the width of the `Inspector` window in pixels.

```
Long = InspectorObject.Width
InspectorObject.Width = Long
```

WindowState Property

The `WindowState` property returns or sets the window state for the `Inspector` object, i.e. whether it is minimized on the Task Bar, maximized to occupy the entire screen or is in its intermediate normal state.

```
Long = InspectorObject.WindowState
InspectorObject.WindowState = Long
```

The `WindowState` property may take one of the following `OlWindowState` constants.

Name	Value	Description
`olMaximized`	1	The Inspector occupies the entire screen
`olMinimized`	2	The Inspector is minimized on the Task Bar
`olNormal`	3	The Inspector is shown in its normal state

WordEditor Property

The WordEditor property returns the Word Document Object Model for the current item being displayed. This property is only valid if the EditorType property is set to olEditorWord and if IsWordMail is set to True. This object model will only be available for the current item and will need to be reset for each item.

```
Set Object = InspectorObject.WordEditor
```

For more information on how to use this object refer to the "Word 2000 VBA Programmers Reference" by Wrox Press. Once you have a reference to the Word Document Object Model you can work with it in a similar way to Outlook's Object Model.

Inspector Object Events

For the Inspector events to be fired, code setting a reference to an Explorer object should be placed in a new Class Module within the Outlook project. This code will be used by all of the events supported by the Explorer object.

Example:

```
Public WithEvents oeExplorer As Explorer

Private Sub Class_Initialize()
    Set oiInspector = Application.Inspectors.Item(1)
End Sub
```

> Note that none of the Events for the Inspector object is available fo VBScript.

Activate Event

The Activate event occurs when the Inspector window is activated either through code using the Activate method or through the GUI.

```
Private Sub oiInspector_Activate()
```

The example below ensures that the WindowState is normal and that the All Fields page is not shown

Example:

```
Private Sub oiInspector_Activate()
    If oiInspector.WindowState <> olNormalWindow Then
            oiInspector.WindowState = olNormalWindow
    End If
    oiInspector.HideFormPage "All Fields"
End Sub
```

Close Event

The Close event is called when the Inspector is shutdown. The method is available in the Class Module, but it is not mentioned in the help files.

```
Private Sub oiInspector_Close()
```

It is not possible to do anything with the `Inspector` object itself before it is fully closed. You can, however, set focus of other objects.

Deactivate Event

The `Deactivate` event occurs when the `Inspector` loses focus.

```
Private Sub oiInspector_Deactivate()
```

Example:

```
Private Sub oiInspector_Deactivate()
    If oiInspector.WindowState <> olMinimized Then
            oiInspector.WindowState = olMinimized
    End If
End Sub
```

In this example the `Inspector` is minimized when it loses focus.

The Pages Collection

The `Pages` collection holds any pages that have been modified for a given item displayed in an `Inspector` object. This means that for an item whose pages have not been modified the `Pages` collection will be empty. If the main page is modified then it is automatically added to the `Pages` collection. It is also possible to add up to five custom pages to an Outlook item. As these pages are customized they too will be added to the `Pages` collection.

Pages are usually added and customized through the **Forms Designer**, found through the **Tools | Forms | Design This Form** of the Outlook item. However, they can also be added through code, as will be demonstrated below.

A reference to a `Pages` collection is set through the `ModifiedFormPages` property of the `Inspector` object holding the Outlook item.

```
Dim oiInspector As Inspector
Dim opcPages As Pages
…
Set opcPages = oiInspector.ModifiedFormPages
```

Pages Collection Methods

Add Method

The `Add` method creates and returns a new customizable page for an Outlook item. You can only add up to five custom pages. If you try to add more than this an error is raised telling you that no more custom pages are available.

```
PagesCollection.Add Name
```

Name	Data type	Description
Name	String	Required, the name shown on the tab of the newly created page.

Example:

```
Dim oiInspector As Inspector
Dim opcPages As Outlook.Pages
Dim olabel As Label
Dim oText As TextBox

Set oiInspector = ActiveInspector
Set opcPages = oiInspector.ModifiedFormPages

'Add the new page to the Active Inspector
     opcPages.Add ("Author Information")
     opcPages("Author Information").Enabled = True
'Add a FirstName Label to the new Page
     Set olabel = opcPages("Author
Information").Controls.Add("Forms.Label.1", "lblFirstName", True)
     olabel.Caption = "First Name:"
     opcPages("Author Information").Controls("lblFirstName").Left = 50
     opcPages("Author Information").Controls("lblFirstName").Top = 10
'Add a FirstName TextBox to the new Page
     Set oText = opcPages("Author Information").Controls. _
     Add("Forms.TextBox.1", "txtFirstName", True)
     oText.Text = "Dwayne"
     opcPages("Author Information").Controls("txtFirstName").Left = 100
     opcPages("Author Information").Controls("txtFirstName").Top = 10
     opcPages("Author Information").Controls("txtFirstName").Width = 100
'Add a LastName Label to the new Page
     Set olabel = opcPages("Author Information").Controls. _
     Add("Forms.Label.1", "lblLastName", True)
     olabel.Caption = "Last Name:"
     opcPages("Author Information").Controls("lblLastName").Left = 220
     opcPages("Author Information").Controls("lblLastName").Top = 10
     'Add a FirstName TextBox to the new Page
     Set oText = opcPages("Author Information").Controls. _
     Add("Forms.TextBox.1", "txtLastName", True)
     oText.Text = "Gifford"
     opcPages("Author Information").Controls("txtLastName").Left = 270
     opcPages("Author Information").Controls("txtLastName").Top = 10
     opcPages("Author Information").Controls("txtLastName").Width = 100
'Add a BookTitle Label to the new Page
     Set olabel = opcPages("Author Information").Controls. _
     Add("Forms.Label.1", "lblBookTitle", True)
     olabel.Caption = "Book Title:"
     opcPages("Author Information").Controls("lblBookTitle").Left = 50
     opcPages("Author Information").Controls("lblBookTitle").Top = 40
'Add a BookTitle TextBox to the new Page
     Set oText = opcPages("Author Information").Controls. _
     Add("Forms.TextBox.1", "txtBookTitle", True)
     oText.Text = "Outlook 2000 VBA Programmers Reference"
     opcPages("Author Information").Controls("txtBookTitle").Left = 100
     opcPages("Author Information").Controls("txtBookTitle").Top = 40
     opcPages("Author Information").Controls("txtBookTitle").Width = 275
'Add a Publisher Label to the new Page
     Set olabel = opcPages("Author Information").Controls. _
     Add("Forms.Label.1", "lblPublisher", True)
     olabel.Caption = "Publisher:"
     opcPages("Author Information").Controls("lblPublisher").Left = 50
     opcPages("Author Information").Controls("lblPublisher").Top = 70
'Add a Publisher TextBox to the new Page
     Set oText = opcPages("Author Information").Controls. _
     Add("Forms.TextBox.1", "txtPublisher", True)
     oText.Text = "WROX Publishing"
     opcPages("Author Information").Controls("txtPublisher").Left = 100
     opcPages("Author Information").Controls("txtPublisher").Top = 70
     opcPages("Author Information").Controls("txtPublisher").Width = 275
     opcPages("Author Information").Controls("txtPublisher").Enabled = False
End If
```

In the example above we get a reference to the active `Inspector` object. We then use the add method to create a new page called "Author Information". Once the page is added we can modify it. I have added some text boxes and labels to hold Author Information.

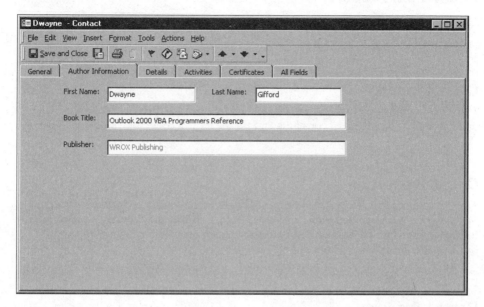

In the figure you can see the "Author Information" page is added and the form controls are shown.

Item Method

The `Item` method returns a particular customized page from the `Pages` collection.

```
PagesCollection.Item Index
```

Name	Data type	Description
Index	Variant	Required, either a long representing the position of the page within the `Pages` collection or a string holding the name of the page

Remove Method

The `Remove` method deletes a page from the `Pages` collection.

```
PagesCollection.Remove Index
```

Name	Data type	Description
Index	Long	Required, represents the position of the page within the `Pages` collection

Pages Collection Properties

Application Property

The `Application` property returns the `Application` object for this session. This will be the Outlook `Application` object.

```
Set ApplicationObject = PagesCollection.Application
```

Class Property

The `Class` property returns a long value that identifies the type of object. This will be one of the `OlObjectClass` constants and for the `Pages` collection is `olPages` or `36`.

```
Long = PagesCollection.Class
```

Count Property

The `Count` property returns the number of pages in the `Pages` collection. If the item has never been customized then `Count` will hold zero. The maximum possible value for this property is six. This corresponds to the main page being customized and the five possible additional custom pages.

```
Long = PagesCollection.Count
```

Parent Property

This property returns a reference to the parent object for the `Pages` collection. In this case the parent will be the `Inspector` object that holds the Outlook item whose pages comprise the `Pages` collection

```
Set InspectorObject = Pagescollection.Parent
```

Session Property

The `Session` property returns a reference to the `NameSpace` object for the current session.

```
Set NameSpaceObject = PagesCollection.Session
```

8

Outlook Folders

The `Folders` collection represents the available folders at any given level of the folder hierarchy. The concept of the `Folders` collection is recursive in nature, meaning that you can have as many levels of folders as you want. The screenshot below shows a typical folder hierarchy indicating the different folder levels.

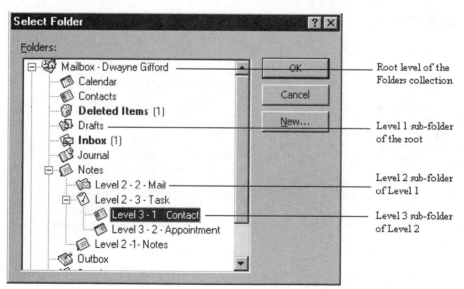

You can see that the folders collection of the Mailbox – Dwayne Gifford folder contains a number of individual `Folder` objects, Calendar, Contacts, etc. Each folder can contain Outlook items and `MAPIFolders`.

The various properties, methods and events of the `Folders` collection and `MAPIFolder` object allow navigation to and manipulation of these folders and the items that they contain.

There are two ways to get a reference to a `Folders` collection. The first is through the `NameSpace` object. This will return the root `Folders` collection

Syntax:

```
Dim ofcFolders as Folders
Dim onMAPI as NameSpace
...
Set ofcFolders = onMAPI.Folders
```

The second is from a `MAPIFolder` object. This will return the `Folders` collection representing all folders contained by the specified MAPIFolder.

```
Dim ofcFolders as Folders
Dim ofFolder as MAPIFolder
...
Set ofcFolders = ofFolder.Folders
```

For example if we choose the Notes folder to be the `MAPIFolder` then the `ofcFolders` collection would contain all folders starting Level 2...

Folders Collection Methods

Add Method

The `Add` method will create and return a new `MAPIFolder` object in the current `Folders` collection.

```
Set MAPIFolderObject = FoldersCollection.Add(Name [, Type])
```

Name	Data type	Description
Name	String	Required, the name of the folder that you see in Outlook.
Type	Long	Optional, can be one of the `OlDefaultFolder` constants. If no type is supplied then the new `MAPIFolder` will inherit its `Type` from the parent `MAPIFolder`.

Valid `OlDefaultFolder` constants for this method are as follows:

Constant	Value	Description
olFolderCalendar	9	Creates a new Calendar folder
olFolderContacts	10	Creates a new Contacts folder

Constant	Value	Description
olFolderDrafts	16	Creates a new Drafts folder
olFolderInbox	6	Creates a new Inbox folder
olFolderJournal	11	Creates a new Journal folder
olFolderNotes	12	Creates a new Notes folder
olFolderTasks	13	Creates a new Tasks folder.

The following constants are not valid when trying to create a new folder:

Constant	Value	Description
olFolderDeletedItems	3	Represents a DeletedItems folder
olFolderOutbox	4	Represents a Outbox folder
olFolderSentMail	5	Represents a SentMail folder

Example:

```
Dim onMAPI As NameSpace
Dim ofChosenFolder As MAPIFolder

Set onMAPI = Application.GetNamespace("MAPI")
Set ofChosenFolder = onMAPI.PickFolder

ofChosenFolder.Folders.Add "Inbox 2", olFolderInbox
```

In the above example, the user is prompted by the **Pick Folder** dialog to choose one of their folders. A new folder called "**Inbox 2**" is then created in the chosen. The figure below shows the newly created "**Inbox 2**" MAPIFolder in the original **Inbox** MAPIFolder.

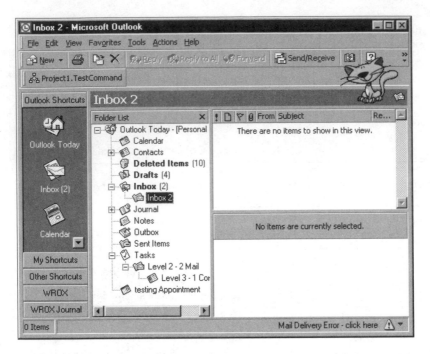

More details on the `PickFolder` method of the `NameSpace` object are given in chapter 6.

GetFirst Method

The `GetFirst` method allows you to navigate to the first `MAPIFolder` object in the referenced collection. If there is no `MAPIFolder` object in the collection then `Nothing` is returned.

```
Set MAPIFolderObject = FoldersCollection.GetFirst
```

It is always wise to first get a reference to the `Folders` collection before you use the `Get` methods on the collection.

Example:

```
Dim onMAPI As NameSpace
Dim ofRootFolder As Folders
Dim ofFirstFolder as MAPIFolder

Set onMAPI = Application.GetNamespace("MAPI")
Set ofRootFolder = onMAPI.Folders
Set ofFirstFolder = ofRootFolder.GetFirst

MsgBox ofFirstFolder
```

This simple example first sets a reference to the root folders collection. It then uses the `GetFirst` method to get the first folder within this collection, having first declared it to be a `MAPIFolder`. Finally its name is displayed in a message box.

GetLast Method

The GetLast method works in a similar fashion to the GetFirst method except it will return the last MAPIFolder in the collection. If there are no folders in the collection it will return Nothing.

```
Set MAPIFolder = FoldersCollection.GetLast
```

GetNext Method

The GetNext method moves to the next MAPIFolder in the collection.

```
Set MAPIFolderObject = FoldersCollection.GetNext
```

Example:

```
Dim ofcPersonalFolders As Folders
Dim ofFolder As MAPIFolder

Set ofcPersonalFolders = Application.GetNamespace _
                        ("MAPI").Folders.GetFirst.Folders
Set ofFolder = ofcPersonalFolders.GetFirst

Do Until ofFolder Is Nothing
    MsgBox ofFolder.Name
    Set ofFolder = ofcPersonalFolders.GetNext
Loop
```

In the example above we walk through the folders of the first Folders collection within the Root folders collection for the current profile. For my profile the first collection within the root folder collection is my **Personal Folder**. A reference is first set to this folder and then the GetFirst and GetNext methods are used to move through each of the folders in this collection. A Do Until loop is employed to check when the end of the Folders collection is reached and the name of each folder is displayed in a message box.

GetPrevious Method

The GetPrevious method provides a way to move to a previous MAPIFolder object in the current collection

```
Set MAPIFolderObject = FoldersCollection.GetPrevious
```

Again, I hate to repeat myself but it is always wise to get a reference to the collection that you want to work with before you use any of the Get methods of the Folders collection.

Item Method

The Item method provides a way to reference a particular MAPIFolder. This can be achieved by using the index number of the MAPIFolder within the collection or by using the name of the MAPIfolder.

```
Set MAPIFolderObject = FoldersCollection.Item(Index)
```

Name	Data type	Description
Index	Variant	Required, either a long representing the position of the MAPIFolder object within the collection or its name as a string.

Example:

```
Dim onMAPI As NameSpace
Dim ofInbox As MAPIFolder
Dim ofFolder As MAPIFolder

Set onMAPI = Application.GetNamespace("MAPI")

Set ofInbox = onMAPI.Folders.GetFirst.Folders.Item("Inbox")
Set ofFolder = onMAPI.Folders.GetFirst.Folders(2)
```

In this example we get references to two different folders. For the first variable, ofInbox, we pick the folder by its name. The second variable, ofFolder, is set to the second folder within the first folder in the root folders using the index of the folder. For my personal setup this gives me a reference to the **Contacts** folder, although this may differ for you. Because Item is the default method it is not necessary to type it explicitly, as shown in the last line of code.

Remove Method

The Remove method will take the MAPIFolder referenced by the index parameter and permanently remove it from the Folders collection.

FoldersCollection.Remove *Index*

Name	Data type	Description
Index	Long	Required, represents the position of the MAPIFolder object within the collection that you wish to remove.

> Be aware that when a folder is removed with this method, it will remove ALL folders and items within that folder without providing a warning.

Example:

```
Dim onMAPI As NameSpace
Dim ofFolder As MAPIFolder
Dim iFor As Integer

Set onMAPI = Application.GetNamespace("MAPI")
Set ofFolder = onMAPI.GetDefaultFolder(olFolderInbox)

ofFolder.Folders.Add "Inbox 3", olFolderInbox

For iFor = 1 To ofFolder.Folders.count
```

```
        If ofFolder.Folders.Item(iFor).Name = "Inbox 3" Then
            ofFolder.Folders.Remove iFor
            Exit For
        End If
Next
```

In this example we first add a `MAPIFolder` to the `ofFolder` object. We then walk through the `Folders` collection to locate the `MAPIFolder`. Once we do locate it we use the `Remove` method to delete it from the collection and exit the `For...Loop`.

Folders Collection Properties

Application Property

The `Application` property returns the `Application` object for the `Folders` collection. This will be the Outlook `Application` object.

```
Set ApplicationObject = FoldersCollection.Application
```

Class Property

The `Class` property returns a unique value that identifies an object's type. This will be one of the `OlObjectClass` constants and in this case will be `olFolders` or 15.

```
Long = FoldersCollection.Class
```

Count Property

The `Count` property returns a long integer representing the number of `MAPIFolder` objects in the collection.

```
Long = FoldersCollection.Count
```

Example:

```
Dim onMAPI As NameSpace
Dim ofcPersonalFolders As Folders
Dim ofFolder As MAPIFolder
Dim iFor As Integer

Set onMAPI = Application.GetNamespace("MAPI")
Set ofcPersonalFolders = onMAPI.Folders.Item _
                    ("Mailbox - Dwayne Gifford").Folders

For iFor = 1 To ofcPersonalFolders.Count
    Set ofFolder = ofcPersonalFolders.Item(iFor)
    MsgBox ofFolder.Name
Next
```

In this example a reference is set to the `Folders` collection of the **Mailbox – Dwayne Gifford** folder. The `Count` property is then used to set the upper limit of the `For...Next` construct, which is used to display the name of each of the folders within the collection.

Parent Property

The `Parent` property returns the parent object of the `Folders` collection. This may either be the `NameSpace` object or a `MAPIFolder` object.

```
Set MAPIFolderObject= FoldersCollection.Parent
```

Session Property

The `Session` property returns the `NameSpace` object for the current collection. You should already have this object if you have a reference to a `Folders` collection.

```
Set NameSpaceObject = FoldersCollection.Session
```

Folders Collection Events

For the `Folders` collection events to be fired it is necessary to use the `WithEvents` keyword and set a reference to a `Folders` collection within a sub that will be called before the event. For illustration purposes only I have set a reference to the Deleted Items folders collection.

Example:

```
Dim WithEvents ofcFolders As Folders

Private Sub Class_Initialize()
    Set ofcFolders = Application.GetNamespace("MAPI"). _
        GetDefaultFolder(olFolderDeletedItems).Folders
End Sub
```

FolderAdd Event

The `FolderAdd` event occurs when a new `MAPIFolder` object is added to a collection.

```
Sub FoldersCollection_FolderAdd(ByVal Folder As MAPIFolder)
```

Name	Data type	Description
Folder	MAPIFolder	The new `MAPIFolder` object that is being added to the `Folders` collection.

Example:

```
Private Sub ofcFolders_FolderAdd(ByVal Folder As MAPIFolder)

    If Folder.UnReadItemCount <> 0 Then
        MsgBox "This folder has unread items. You may  " & _
            "want to reinstate it.", vbExclamation
    End If

End Sub
```

In this example the user is warned if they delete a folder with unread items in it. When this happens, the deleted folder is added to the `folders` collection of the DeletedItems folder, triggering the `FolderAdd` event. Firstly `ofcFolders` is set to be the Deleted Items `Folders` collection. This will be called when an object based on this class is instantiated.

Within the `FolderAdd` event, a newly created folder is checked for unread items. If they exist, the user is warned.

FolderChange Event

The `FolderChange` event occurs when one of the `MAPIFolder` objects, in the chosen `Folders` collection, is changed.

```
Sub FoldersCollection_FolderChange(ByVal Folder As MAPIFolder)
```

Name	Data type	Description
Folder	MAPIFolder	The `MAPIFolder` object that is being changed to the `Folders` collection.

FolderRemove Event

The `FolderRemove` event occurs when one of the `MAPIFolder` objects is deleted from the chosen `Folders collection`.

```
Sub FoldersCollection_FolderRemove()
```

MAPIFolder Object

A `MAPIFolder` object is a container that can hold either folders or Outlook items, or more likely both. A reference to a `MAPIFolder` object can be set by using the:

- ❑ `GetDefaultFolder`, `GetFolderFromID` and `GetSharedDefaultFolder` methods of the `NameSpace` object
- ❑ `Item`, `GetFirst`, `GetLast`, `GetNext` and `GetPrevious` methods of a `Folders` collection

Syntax:

```
Set ofFolder = onMAPI.GetFolderFromID(sEntryID, sStoreID)
```

or

```
Set ofFolder = onMAPI.GetDefaultFolder(olFolderInbox)
```

or

```
Set ofFolder = onMAPI.GetSharedDefaultFolder(orRecipient, _
olFolderInbox)
```

or

```
Ser ofFolder = onMAPI.Folders.Item("Inbox")
```

or

```
set ofFolder = onMAPI.Folders.GetFirst
```

These methods are covered fully in Chapter 6 and earlier in this chapter.

MAPIFolder Object Methods

CopyTo Method

The `CopyTo` method takes the currently referenced `MAPIFolder` and makes a copy of it and its contents in the specified destination `MAPIFolder`.

> `MAPIFolderObject.CopyTo(DestinationFolderObject)`

Name	Data type	Description
Destination FolderObject	MAPIFolder	Required, the `Folder` object that you wish to hold the copy in

Example:

```
Dim onMAPI As NameSpace
Dim ofStart As MAPIFolder
Dim ofDestination As MAPIFolder

Set onMAPI = Application.GetNamespace("MAPI")
Set ofStart = onMAPI.GetDefaultFolder(olFolderInbox)
Set ofDestination = onMAPI.GetDefaultFolder(olFolderOutbox)

ofStart.CopyTo ofDestination
```

In this example we are creating a copy of the **Inbox** folder in the **Outbox** folder. If there is already a folder called **Inbox** here then the method will add a sequence number to the end of the new object. The `CopyTo` method is likely to be used to create back-ups of important folders.

Delete Method

The `Delete` method provides a way to remove a `MAPIFolder` object. It will delete this `MAPIFolder` object from its parent `Folders` collection.

> `MAPIFolderObject.Delete`

This method works in the same way as the delete option on the GUI. However, if the folder is located within the `Deleted Items` folder, there is no warning massage or option to cancel the delete.

Display Method

The `Display` method displays a **new** `Explorer` for the `MAPIFolder` with the current object as the active `MAPIFolder`. An `Explorer` is an Outlook window that shows the contents of a folder. So if you already have an Outlook window open for the user, this method will open a new Outlook window in front of the user with the contents of the specified `MAPIFolder` visible. It will not make any changes to the old `Explorer`. The `Explorer` object is fully covered in chapter 7.

> `MAPIFolderObject.Display`

Example:

```
Dim onMAPI As NameSpace
Dim ofFolder As MAPIFolder

Set onMAPI = Application.GetNamespace("MAPI")
Set ofFolder = onMAPI.GetDefaultFolder(olFolderInbox)

ofFolder.Display
```

In the above example the `ofFolder` variable is set to the default Inbox folder. Then a new `Explorer` object is opened with this `MAPIFolder` object as the active folder.

GetExplorer Method

The `GetExplorer` method returns an invisible `Explorer` object that has the specified `MAPIFolder` object as its active folder. Once you have this `Explorer` object you can use the `Activate` method of the `Explorer` object to show it.

MAPIFolderObject.GetExplorer([*DisplayMode*])

Name	Data type	Description
DisplayMode	Long	Optional, one of the `OlFolderDisplayMode` constants. If omitted `olFolderDisplayNormal` is used by default.

The result of using each of the `OlFolderDisplayMode` constants is shown below.

OlFolderDisplayFolderOnly (1) displays, next to the Folder name, a drop-down list of folders available. All navigation buttons are also available. Notice the figure below has all navigation buttons on the toolbar.

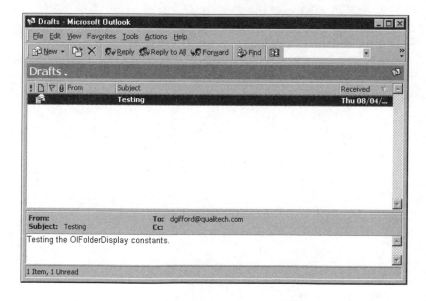

olFolderDisplayNoNavigation (2) displays the current `MAPIFolder` and the user is unable to navigate to any other `MAPIFolder` object. Notice that the navigational buttons on the toolbar are invisible.

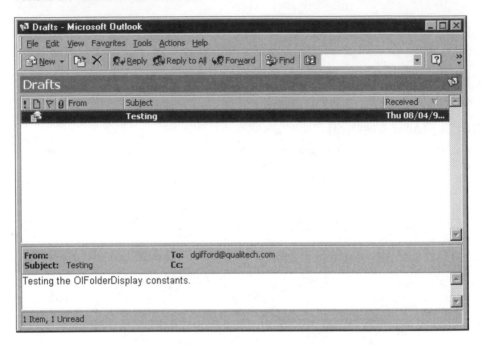

olFolderDisplayNormal (0) displays the `Explorer` just as it appears when you open Outlook.

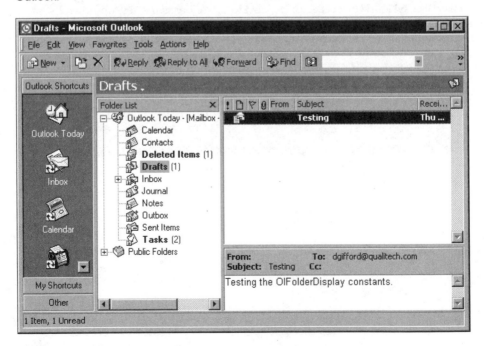

Example:

```
Dim onMAPI As NameSpace
Dim ofFolder As MAPIFolder
Dim oeExplorer As explorer

Set onMAPI = Application.GetNamespace("MAPI")
Set ofFolder = onMAPI.GetDefaultFolder(olFolderDrafts)

Set oeExplorer = ofFolder.GetExplorer(olFolderDisplayNoNavigation)
oeExplorer.Activate
```

This code was used to show the second `Explorer` object in the set of three above, displaying the default **Drafts** folder with no folder navigation available. The `Activate` method of the `Explorer` object is used to show the `MAPIFolder` to the user. Note that the optional display mode parameter only comes into play when the `Explorer` object methods are used to show it and not the `Display` method of the `MAPIFolder`.

MoveTo Method

The `MoveTo` method moves a `MAPIFolder` to a specified `MAPIFolder` object.

```
MAPIFolderObject.Move(DestinationFolderObject)
```

Name	Data type	Description
Destination FolderObject	MAPIFolder	Required, the destination `Folder` object that you wish to move the `FolderObject` to.

MAPIFolder Object Properties

Application Property

The `Application` property will return the parent application object of the `MAPIFolder` object. This will be the Outlook `Application` object.

```
Set ApplicationObject = MAPIFolderObject.Application
```

Class Property

The `Class` property returns a unique value that identifies the object's type. This will be one of the `OlObjectClass` constants and in this case will be `olFolder` or 2.

```
Long = MAPIFolderObject.Class
```

DefaultItemType Property

The `DefaultItem` property returns the default item type for the `MAPIFolder`. This property specifies what type of Outlook item a folder possesses by default, i.e. if you create a new `item` without supplying the `Type` then its type will be set according to the `DefaultItemType` of the folder it is added to.

```
Long = MAPIFolderObject.DefaultItemType
```

The value returned will be one of the following `OlItemType` contants:

Constant	Value	Description
olAppointmentItem	1	An Appointment item
olContactItem	2	A Contact item
olJournalItem	4	A Journal item
olMailItem	0	A Mail item. This is the default item for Outlook and the default type for all `MAPIFolder` objects that hold Mail type Items.
olNoteItem	5	A Note item
olPostItem	6	A Post item
olTaskItem	3	A Task item

DefaultMessageClass Property

The `DefaultMessageClass` property returns, as a string, the Message Class, or type of message, for the `MAPIFolder`. This is the `MessageClass` property that, if not otherwise explicitly set, is assigned to an Outlook item by default when added to a folder. This value identifies the default `Inspector` object in which an item will be shown.

```
String = MAPIFolderObject.DefaultMessageClass
```

The possible values that will be returned are as follows:

IPM.Activity	IPM.Appointment	IPM.Contact
IPM.Note	IPM.StickyNote	IPM.Task

There is a one-to-one relationship between this property and the `DefaultItemType` property

Example:

```
Dim onMAPI As NameSpace
Dim ofcRoot As Folders
Dim ofPersonalFolder As MAPIFolder
Dim ofcPFolders As Folders
Dim ofFolder As MAPIFolder

Set onMAPI = Application.GetNamespace("MAPI")
Set ofcRoot = onMAPI.Folders
Set ofPersonalFolder = ofcRoot.Item("Mailbox - Dwayne Gifford")
Set ofcPFolders = ofPersonalFolder.Folders
```

```
For Each ofFolder In ofcPFolders
    Debug.Print ofFolder.Name, ofFolder.DefaultMessageClass,
ofFolder.DefaultItemType
Next
```

This example walks through my **Personal** folders and displays both the
`DefaultMessageClass` and `DefaultItemType` properties in the **Immediate**
Windo . The results are shown below.

Folder Name	DefaultMessageClass	DefaultItemType
Calendar	IPM.Appointment	1
Contacts	IPM.Contact	2
Deleted Items	IPM.Note	0
Drafts	IPM.Note	0
Inbox	IPM.Note	0
Journal	IPM.Activity	4
Notes	IPM.StickyNote	5
Outbox	IPM.Note	0
Sent Items	IPM.Note	0
Tasks	IPM.Task	3

Description Property

The `Description` property sets
or returns a string value that
provides information about the
`MAPIFolder`. This property can
be viewed in the **Description** box
that you see in the **Properties** box
for the `MAPIFolder`. For
compatibility it corresponds to
the PR_COMMENT property
used in MAPI.

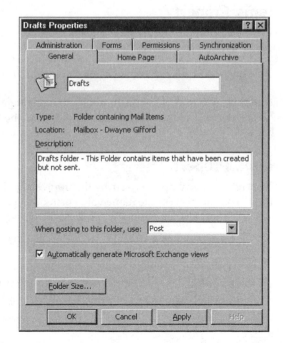

```
String = MAPIFolderObject.Description
MAPIFolderObject.Description = String
```

I would suggest that if you are creating important MAPIFolders through code on a user's machine then it is worth using this Description property to tell the user the purpose of the folder and that it should not be deleted.

EntryID Property

The EntryID property returns a unique ID for the MAPIFolder. It is created when the MAPIFolder is created or moved to a different folder. It may be used in conjunction with the GetFolderFromID method of the NameSpace object.

```
String  = MAPIFolderObject.EntryID
```

This property is here for backwards compatibility with MAPI.

Folders Property

The Folders property returns the collection of folders that belong to the specified MAPIFolder, i.e. the sub-folders of the current object.

```
Set FoldersCollection = MAPIFolderObject.Folders
```

These Folders collections are recursive in nature, i.e. any one of the MAPIFolder objects in the Folders collection can contain its own Folders collection. The only way to ensure that you are at the bottom of a hierarchy of folders is to check that the Count property of the Folders collection equals 0.

Items Property

The Items property returns the collection of items within the specified MAPIFolder object.

```
Set ItemsCollection = MAPIFolderObject.Items
```

From this collection we have the ability to navigate around and work with the various Outlook Items. The Items collection and each of the Outlook items are covered fully in chapters 12 to 19.

Name Propert

The Name property returns a string that represents the name of the MAPIFolder object. You can also set the name value using this property. The Name property of the folders is shown when you view the Outlook folders hierarchy.

```
String = MAPIFolderObject.Name
MAPIFolderObject.Name = String
```

If, within a particular Folders collection, you try to set the Name property of a MAPIFolder to the name of an already existing MAPIFolder an error will be raised.

Parent Property

The `Parent` property returns the parent object for the current object. In this case since we are looking at a `MAPIFolder` object the parent will be the `MAPIFolder` object directly above it in the folders hierarchy or the `Namespace` object for the current session.

```
Set Object = MAPIFolderObject.Parent
```

UnReadItemCount Property

The `UnReadItemCount` property returns a long integer representing the number of messages within the current `MAPIFolder` that have not been read.

```
Long = MAPIFolderObject.UnReadItemCount
```

StoreID Property

The `StoreID` property returns a unique ID of the `MAPIFolder` object. This value is set when the object is created or moved to a new `Folders` collection. It is not clear why two unique ID's, i.e. the `EntryID` and the `StoreID` are required.

```
String = MAPIFolderObject.StoreID
```

Session Property

The `Session` property returns the `NameSpace` object for the current session. This will be the `MAPI`.

```
Set NameSpaceObject = MAPIFolderObject.Session
```

WebViewAllowNavigation Property

The `WebViewAllowNavigation` property returns or sets a Boolean value indicating the "navigation mode" for the Web view.

```
Boolean = MAPIFolderObject.WebViewAllowNavigation
MAPIFolderObject.WebViewAllowNavigation = Boolean
```

By setting this to **True** the user has ability to use the **Back** and **Forward** buttons for Web navigation.

WebViewOn Property

The `WebViewOn` property returns or sets a Boolean value indicating the Web "view state" for the current `MAPIFolder` object. If set to **True** then Outlook is told to display the Web page specified in the `WebViewURL` property.

```
Boolean = MAPIFolderObject.WebViewOn
MAPIFolderObject.WebViewOn = Boolean
```

WebViewURL Property

The `WebViewURL` property returns or sets a string value indicating the URL of the web page assigned to this `MAPIFolder` object.

```
String = MAPIFolderObject.WebViewURL
MAPIFolderObject.WebViewURL = String
```

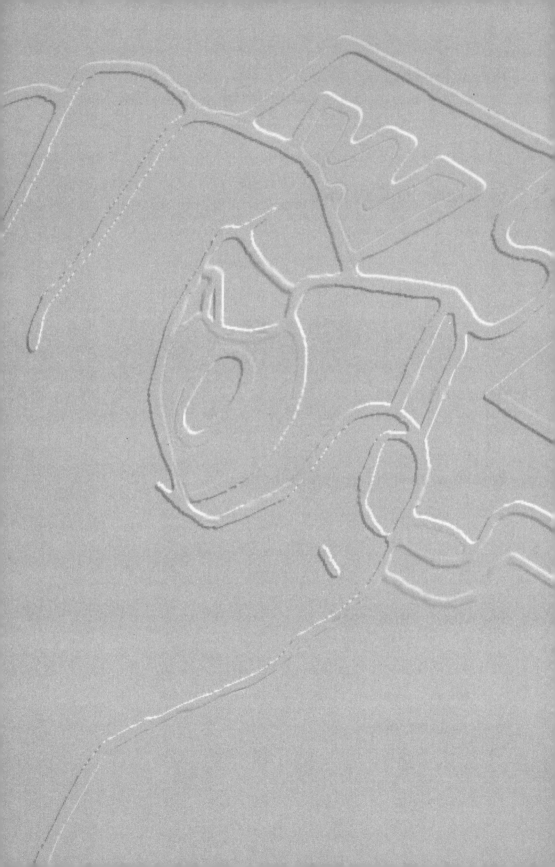

The Address Book

The best way to think of the AddressLists and AddressEntries collections is to consider the Address Book that comes with Outlook.

In the screenshot below some of the entries in the **Show Names from the:** dropdown box represent the AddressList objects. In this case we have four AddressList objects - **Global Address List, Recipients, Contacts** and **Level 3 – 1 – Contact**. The first two are server lists and the last two are local lists. In this example **Star Software** and **STAR** are folders in the hierarchy that contain no address information directly. The sum of these four AddressList objects gives the AddressLists collection.

The collection of entries in the body of the dialog make up the AddressEntries collection for the AddressList object shown and each of these entries, such as **Dwayne Gifford** represents an AddressEntry object.

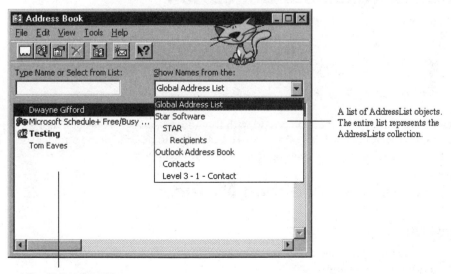

A list of AddressList objects. The entire list represents the AddressLists collection.

A list of AddressEntry objects. The entire list represents the AddressEntries collection.

If we use an analogy to telephone directories then the AddressLists collection would be a collection of telephone directories, like the Yellow Pages and White Pages. Each of these directories is analogous to an AddressList object. Within each directory there is a number of names, addresses and telephone numbers. Each single entry of a name, address and number is equivalent to an AddressEntry object and the collection of all entries in a single directory compares to an AddressEntry collection.

One thing to note about the Address Book is that even though the individual AddressList objects shown in the screen shot belong to a recursive folder hierarchy, they in fact all belong directly to the root AddressLists collection.

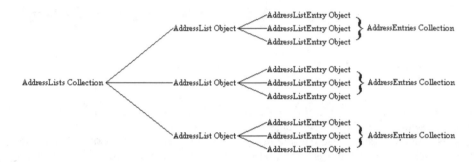

Presently, it is impossible to add new AddressList objects via the AddressLists collection. However, if you add a Contact MAPIFolder object then this will add a new AddressList object in the AddressLists collection.

The AddressLists Collection

The only way to reach the AddressLists collection is through the NameSpace object.

```
Dim AddressListCollection as AddressLists
Dim onMAPI as NameSpace
…
Set AddressListsCollection = onMAPI.AddressLists
```

In fact there is very little that you can do with the AddressLists collection. It is possible to set a reference to an AddressList object or to determine the number of AddressList objects in the collection via the Count property.

AddressLists Collection Methods

Item Method

The Item method provides a way to access a specific AddressList object within the AddressLists collection.

```
Set AddressListObject = AddressListsCollection.Item(Index)
```

Since the Item method is the default method for the AddressLists collection you can omit the word Item from code.

```
Set AddressListObject = AddressListsCollection (Index)
```

Name	Data type	Description
Index	Variant	Required. This can either be a number which represents the position of the AddressList object within the AddressLists collection or it can the name of the AddressList object as a string.

AddressLists Collection Properties

Application Property

The Application property returns the Application object for this session. This will be the Outlook Application object that is already in use.

```
Set ApplicationObject = AddressListsCollection.Application
```

Class Property

The Class property returns a unique long integer value used to identify the type of object that we currently are referencing. This will always be one of the OlObjectClass Constants and in this case it will be olAddressLists or value 20.

```
Long = AddressListsCollection.Class
```

Count Property

The Count property returns the number of AddressList objects in the collection.

```
Long = AddressListsCollection.Count
```

Example:

```
Dim onMAPI As NameSpace
Dim oalcAddressLists As AddressLists
Dim oalAddressList As AddressList
Dim intFor As Integer

Set onMAPI = Application.GetNamespace("MAPI")
Set oalcAddressLists = onMAPI.AddressLists

For intFor = 1 To oalcAddressLists.count
    Set oalAddressList = oalcAddressLists.Item(intFor)
    Debug.Print oalAddressList.Name
Next
```

In the example above the `Count` property is used to set the upper limit of the `For...Next` construct, which displays the name of each `AddressList` object. For the Address Book shown in the screenshot above this will display the following in the Immediate Windo :

Global Address List
Recipients
Contacts
Level 3 – 1 – Contact

Parent Property

The `Parent` property returns the parent object for the `AddressLists` collection.

```
Set NameSpaceObject = AddressListsCollection.Parent
```

As stated at the beginning of this chapter the only way to reference the `AddressLists` collection is through the `NameSpace` object. This method therefore will always return the Messaging Application Programming Interface or MAPI.

Session Property

The `Session` property returns the `NameSpace` object for the current collection. As there is currently only one data source for Outlook, this property will be set to the `MAPI`.

```
Set NameSpaceObject = AddressListsCollection.Session
```

The AddressList Object

The `AddressList` object quite simply contains a list of addresses. Each of these addresses is held in an `AddressEntry` object. So if you think back to the example we used above with the White Pages Yellow Pages phone books, each of these books is analogous to an `AddressList` object and each of the domestic or commercial entries within them is an `AddressEntry` object.

The only way to get a reference to this object is through the `Item` method of the `AddressLists` collection.

```
Dim AddressListObject As AddressList

AddressListObject = AddressListsCollection.Item(Index)
```

The `Index` parameter can be either a long integer denoting the position of the `AddressList` object within the `AddressLists` collection or the name of the `AddressList` object as a string.

Note that the `AddressList` object has no methods, in particular no Add method. So you might be asking yourself how do we add new `AddressList` objects? To add a new `AddressList` object you need to add a new Contact `MAPIFolder` object or use the Services tab of the Tools | Services dialog box.

In the present release of Outlook there is no way through code to make a contacts folder that has been newly created through code, to appear in the Address Book. So presently there is only one way available to make a new Contact Folder appear in the Address Book and that is via the Outlook GUI.

> **The AddressList object possesses no methods.**

AddressList Object Properties

AddressEntries Property

The AddressEntries property returns a reference to the AddressEntries collection for the AddressList object.

        Set AddressEntriesCollection = AddressListObject.AddressEntries

The AddressEntries collection contains a number of AddressEntry objects, which each represent a person or process to which a message may be sent.

Application Property

The Application property returns a reference to the Application object for this session. This will be the Outlook Application object.

        Set ApplicationObject = AddressListObject.Application

Class Property

The Class property returns a unique value used to identify the type of object that we are currently referencing. This will be one of the OlObjectClass constants and in this case it will return olAddressList or value 7.

        Long = AddressListObject.Class

ID Property

The ID property returns a unique value that is created when the AddressList object is created. This value will not change between sessions and the only way to force a new ID is to remove the AddressList object from Outlook and then recreate it again.

        String = AddressListObject.ID

Index Property

The Index property returns a long integer value identifying the object's position in the AddressLists collection. This value can change between sessions. The first object in the collection will have Index 1.

        Long = AddressListObject.Index

Name Property

The `Name` property returns a string value that represents the display name that you see in the Address Book. This is equivalent to the name of a `MAPIFolder` object of type `olFolderContacts` if the **Show in Address Book** property has been set to **True**.

```
String = AddressListObject.Name
```

This is a read-only property meaning that you cannot change the name with this property.

Parent Property

The `Parent` property returns the parent object for the `AddressList` object. The parent object of the `AddressList` object will always be an `AddressLists` collection, since the only way to reference an `AddressList` object is via the `AddressLists` collection.

```
Set AddressListsCollection = AddressListObject.Parent
```

IsReadOnly Property

The `IsReadOnly` property returns a Boolean value that determines whether the `AddressList` object may be modified. If set to **True** you may not add or remove `AddressEntry` objects within the `AddressEntries` collection of the `AddressList` object. You should be aware that this property does not affect your ability to modify individual `AddressEntry` objects belonging to the `AddressList` object

```
Boolean = AddressListObject.IsReadOnly
```

If you intend to write a routine that adds/removes `AddressEntry` objects to/from the `AddressEntries` collection, then it would be wise to check the `AddressList` object's permissions first via this property to prevent errors being raised.

Session Property

The `Session` property returns a reference to the `NameSpace` object for the current collection. This will be the MAPI `NameSpace` object.

```
Set NameSpaceObject = AddressListObject.Session
```

The AddressEntries Collection

The `AddressEntries` collection is a collection of `AddressEntry` objects for a given `AddressList` object. Thinking back to our telephone directories analogy, the `AddressEntries` collection can be thought of as the holder of the references to all of the entries in the phone book.

An `AddressEntries` collection must be associated with an `AddressList` object. For a `ContactItem` to appear in an `AddressEntries` collection as an `AddressEntry` object you must first assign a value to its `EmailAddress` property.

```
Dim oalAddressList as AddressList
Dim oaecAddresses As AddressEntries
...
Set oaecAddresses= oalAddressList.AddressEntries
```

AddressEntries Collection Methods

Add Method

The Add method creates and returns a new AddressEntry object in the AddressEntries collection.

```
Set AddressEntryObject = AddressEntriesCollection.Add _
                (Type[, Name][, Address])
```

Name	Data type	Description
Type	String	Required, the type of address that you are adding, such as Internet Mail or Microsoft Mail Address.
Name	String	Optional, the display name for the AddressEntry object
Address	String	Optional, the email address for the AddressEntry object

> At the time of writing the Add method will raise an error no matter what value you enter in the Type parameter of this method if you are not connected to a Microsoft Exchange Server.

Now if you think about it, it doesn't make sense to add a new AddressEntry without a display name. The display name and the ID are the only ways to locate the AddressEntry object so even though this is optional, I think you should use this parameter.

Also, note that the AddressEntry object is not committed to the AddressEntries collection until the AddressEntry Update method has been called.

GetFirst Method

The GetFirst method gives you away to navigate to the first AddressEntry object in the referenced collection. If there is no AddressEntry object in the collection then Nothing is returned.

```
Set AddressEntryObject = AddressEntriesCollection.GetFirst
```

It is always wise to first get a reference to the AddressEntries collection before you use the Get methods on the collection.

GetLast Method

The `GetLast` method works in a similar fashion to the `GetFirst` method except that it clearly takes you to the last `AddressEntry` in the collection. It will return `Nothing` if there is no `AddressEntry` object in the collection.

```
Set AddressEntryObject = AddressEntriesCollection.GetLast
```

GetNext Method

The `GetNext` method moves to the next `AddressEntry` object in the collection. If there is no object to move to then `Nothing` will be returned.

```
Set AddressEntryObject = AddressEntriesCollection.GetNext
```

Example:

```
Dim onMAPI As NameSpace
Dim oaecAddresses As AddressEntries
Dim oaeAddress As AddressEntry

Set onMAPI = Application.GetNamespace("MAPI")
Set oaecAddresses = onMAPI.AddressLists.Item(1).AddressEntries
Set oaeddress = oaecAddresses.GetFirst

Do Until oaeAddress Is Nothing
    Debug.Print oaeAddress.Name
    Set oaeAddress = oaecAddresses.GetNext
Loop
```

In this example the `GetFirst` and `GetNext` method are used to display the name of each `AddressEntry` object within the `AddressEntries` collection of the first `AddressList` object in the `AddressLists` collection.

GetPrevious Method

The `GetPrevious` method provides a way to move to a previous `AddressEntry` object in the current collection. If there are no earlier `AddressEntry` objects in the collection then `Nothing` is returned.

```
Set AddressEntryObject = AddressEntriesCollection.GetPrevious
```

Item Method

The `Item` method returns a specific `AddressEntry` object referenced by the Index.

```
Set AddressEntryObject = AddressEntriesCollection.Item(Index)
```

Name	Data type	Description
Index	Variant	Required. This can either be a long representing the position of the `AddressEntry` object in the `AddressEntries` collection or a string containing the name of the `AddressEntry` object.

Example:

```
Set oAddressEntry = oAddressList.AddressEntries.Item(1)
```
Or
```
Set oAddressEntry = oAddressList.AddressEntries.Item("Dominic")
```

In the first example above we set a reference to the first `AddressEntry` in the `AddressEntries` collection. In the second example we set a reference to the first `AddressEntry` object with a name of "Dominic".

Sort Method

The `Sort` method allows you to arrange the collection by a valid property for the type of `AddressEntry` that is contained within the collection.

```
AddressEntriesCollection.Sort([Property], [Descending])
```

Name	Data type	Description
Property	String	Optional, the name of one of the properties of an `AddressEntry` object.
Descending	Long	Optional, determines how the `AddressEntry` objects are sorted.

The `Descending` parameter may be one of the `OlSortOrder` constants.

Name	Value	Description
olAscending	1	The collection is sorted in ascending order.
olDescending	2	The collection is sorted in descending.
olSortNone	0	This sort order is not changed.

At the time of writing this method did not appear to be working reliably.

AddressEntries Collection Properties

Application Property

The `Application` property returns the `Application` object for this session. This will be the Outlook `Application` object.

```
Set ApplicationObject = AddressEntriesCollection.Application
```

Class Property

The `Class` property returns a unique value used to identify the type of object that is currently referenced. This will be one of the `OlObjectClass` constants. In this case it will be `olAddressEntries` or value `21`.

```
Long = AddressEntriesCollection.Class
```

Count Property

The Count property returns the number of AddressEntry objects within the collection.

```
Long = AddressEntriesCollection.Count
```

Parent Property

The Parent property returns the parent object for the AddressEntries collection. As we said at the start of this chapter there is only one way to get to the AddressEntries collection and that is through an AddressList object. So the parent in this case will always be the particular AddressList object to which the collection belongs.

```
Set Object = AddressEntriesCollection.Parent
```

Session Property

The Session property returns to the NameSpace object for the current collection. Since we only have one type of NameSpace object this must return a reference to the Messaging Application Programming Interface or MAPI.

```
Set NameSpaceObject = AddressEntriesCollection.Session
```

The AddressEntry Object

An AddressEntry object holds information about a person to whom mail messages may be sent. There are two ways to reference an AddressEntry object. The first is by adding a Recipient object to one of the different item objects available. Remember if you try to access the AddressEntry property before first resolving the recipient then this property will automatically call the Resolve method for you. For more information on the Recipient object refer to chapter 10. The second way to reference a particular AddressEntry is via an AddressEntries collection.

```
Set AddressEntryObject = RecipientObject.AddressEntry
```

or

```
Set AddressEntryObject = AddressEntriesCollection.Item(Index)
```

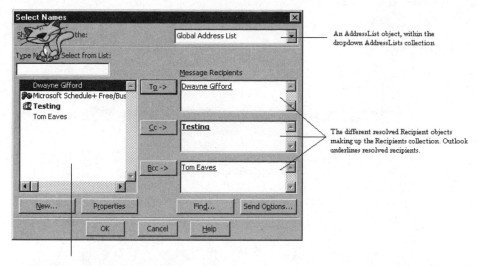

An AddressList object, within the dropdown AddressLists collection

The different resolved Recipient objects making up the Recipients collection. Outlook underlines resolved recipients.

The AddressEntries collection comprising four AddressEntry objects

I bet you have seen the above figure before, it's the dialog that appears if you click on the To, CC or BCC buttons on an Outlook item. You can see that it comprises three different collections.

❑ The first is the `AddressLists` collection and its `AddressList` object. This is on the right of the figure at the top.

❑ The second collection is the `AddressEntries` collection and its `AddressEntry` objects. This is on the left side of the figure.

❑ The last is the `Recipients` collection and its `Recipient` objects for the current item. This list is located down the right side of the figure. It also has each of the `Recipient` objects broken out by their `Type` property.

AddressEntry Object Methods

Delete Method

The `Delete` method removes the `AddressEntry` object from the `AddressEntries` collection.

```
AddressEntryObject.Delete
```

Example:

```
Dim onMAPI As NameSpace
Dim oaecAddresses As AddressEntries
Dim oaeAddress As AddressEntry

Set onMAPI = Application.GetNamespace("MAPI")
Set oaecAddresses = onMAPI.AddressLists.Item(1).AddressEntries
Set oaeAddress = oaecAddresses.GetFirst

oaeAddress.Delete
```

The above example deletes the first `AddressEntry` object from an `AddressEntries` collection.

Details Method

The `Details` method opens a modal dialog box to show you detailed information about the `AddressEntry` object.

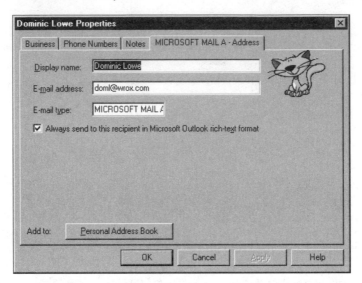

If you click the **OK** button in this box then the `Update` method will be fired and any changes to the `AddressEntry` will be committed to the Messaging system.

```
AddressEntryObject.Details([hWnd])
```

Name	Data type	Description
hWnd	Long	Optional, the handle of the parent window. If you supply this option then the dialog becomes the child to the supplied parent. By leaving it empty then the window is opened modally.

The following code was used to display the figure shown above.

```
Dim onMAPI As NameSpace
Dim oaecAddresses As AddressEntries
Dim oaeAddress As AddressEntry

Set onMAPI = Application.GetNamespace("MAPI")
Set oaecAddresses = onMAPI.AddressLists.Item _
                ("Personal Address Book").AddressEntries
Set oaeAddress = oaecAddresses.GetFirst

oaeAddress.Details
```

If you have just created a new `AddressEntry` object using the `Add` method of the `AddressEntries` collection, but have given no details for that object, the `Details` method of the new `AddressEntry` object will display a new `ContactItem` dialog for you to fill in.

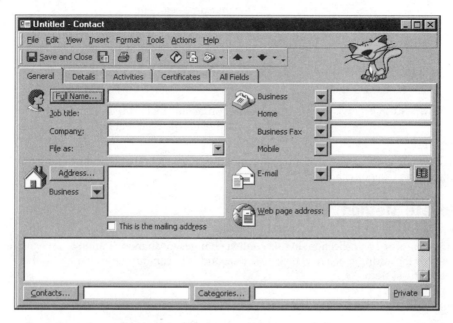

GetFreeBusy Method

The `GetFreeBusy` method returns a string representing a month's worth of free/busy information for the AddressEntry. This is the information available in the **Calendar** `MAPIFolder` object of Outlook for the given time period.

```
String = AddressEntryObject.GetFreeBusy(Start, MinPerChar[,
CompleteFormat])
```

Name	Data type	Description
Start	Date	Required, the start date of the period of free/busy information.
MinPerChar	Long	Required, the number of minutes per character represented in free/busy string.
CompleteFormat	Boolean	Optional, determines the level of detail in the returned string. False is default.

If the `CompleteFormat` option is set to **False** then the returned string is made up of 0's indicating that the `AddressEntry` is free for that time interval and 1's indicating that they are busy. If this parameter is set to **True**, then more detailed information is returned. This complete information will be made up of the `OlBusyStatus` constants.

Name	Value	Description
olBusy	2	The contact for that AddressEntry is busy for that time segment.
olFree	0	The contact for that AddressEntry is available for the time segment.
olOutOfOffice	3	The contact for that AddressEntry is out of the office for the time segment.
olTentative	1	The contact for that AddressEntry is tentative for the time segment.

An example of the use of FreeBusy information is given in the second example of the Automating Outlook chapter.

Update Method

The Update method has two purposes. The first is to commit changes to the local AddressEntries collection. In this context changes mean modification to an existing object or the addition of a new object. The second is to commit these changes to the messaging system.

> AddressEntryObject.Update([MakePermanent], [RefreshObject])

Name	Data type	Description
MakePermanent	Boolean	Optional, determines whether Outlook adds/updates the object to the messaging system. If set to False then the changes are not committed to the messaging system. True is the default setting.
RefreshObject	Boolean	Optional, by setting this value to True Outlook will reload all of the properties for the current object. False is default setting.

If the Update method fails then an error is raised.

Example:

```
Dim onMAPI As NameSpace
Dim oaecAddresses As AddressEntries
Dim oaeAddress As AddressEntry

Set onMAPI = Application.GetNamespace("MAPI")
Set oaecAddresses = onMAPI.AddressLists.Item _
              ("Personal Address Book").AddressEntries
Set oaeAddress = oaecAddresses.Add("Microsoft Mail Address")
oaeAddress.Name = "Dominic Lowe"
```

```
On Error GoTo DialogBox
oaeAddress.Address = "doml@wrox.com"

oaeAddress.Update
Exit Sub

DialogBox:
oaeAddress.Details
```

Notice that the Name property becomes the display name shown is the previous figure, and the Address property becomes the email address. The idea behind this code is to allow the user to try to commit a new AddressEntry object to the messaging system. If an error is raised then the dialog will be displayed prompting the user to make the necessary changes and then use the **OK** button to commit.

> At the time of writing of this book the Details method raises an error if the Update method has not been called first.

AddressEntry Object Properties

Address Property

The Address property returns or updates the **Email Address** field shown in the above figure. This is the email address that a message will be sent to if this AddressEntry is used as a Recipient object for an item.

```
String = AddressEntryObject.Address
AddressEntryObject.Address = String
```

Application Property

The Application property returns the Application object for this session. This will be the **Outlook** Application object.

```
Set ApplicationObject = AddressEntryObject.Application
```

Class Property

The Class property returns a unique value used to identify the type of object that we currently are referencing. This is one of the OlObjectClass constants and for the object in question it will be olAddressEntry or value 8.

```
Long = AddressEntryObject.Class
```

DisplayType Property

The DisplayType property identifies the type of AddressEntry and this consequently identifies the type of message system we are dealing with. It tells us if we are dealing with a user or distribution list. This property will hold one of the OlDisplayType constants.

```
Long = AddressEntryObject.DisplayType
```

Name	Value	Description
olAgent	3	The recipient is an Agent.
olDistList	1	The recipient is a Distribution List.
olForum	2	The recipient is a Forum.
olOrganization	4	The recipient is an Organization
olPrivateDistList	5	The recipient is a Private Distribution List.
olRemoteUser	6	The recipient is a Remote User.
olUser	0	The recipient is a User.

ID Property

The ID property holds a unique string value assigned to the AddressEntry object when it is created. This ID will not change between sessions unless someone deletes the AddressEntry and then adds it back to an AddressList object.

```
String = AddressListObject.ID
```

Manager Property

The Manager property allows you to read the manager for the AddressEntry object providing you have the requisite permissions. This is another AddressEntry object.

```
Set AddressEntryObject = AddressEntryObject.Manager
```

When I was at Microsoft you could double click on your manager and find out who their manager was. You could do this until you reached Bill Gates. At this point you could not go any farther.

Members Property

If the current AddressEntry object is of type olDistList or olPrivateDistList then the Members property returns the AddressEntries collection holding all of the AddressEntry objects for this list. olDistList and olPrivateDistList are different type of distribution lists. The first is a global distribution and the second is for the current profile only. If the AddressList object is of any other type the Members property will return Nothing.

```
Set AddressEntriesCollection = AddressEntryObject.Members
```

Example:

```
Dim onMAPI As NameSpace
Dim oaecAddresses As AddressEntries
Dim oaeAddress As AddressEntry
Dim sMembers As String

Set onMAPI = Application.GetNamespace("MAPI")
```

```
Set oaecAddresses = onMAPI.AddressLists.Item _
    ("Global Address List").AddressEntries
    For Each oaeAddress In oaecAddresses
    sMembers = " "
        If oaeAddress.DisplayType = olDistList Then
            For iFor = 1 To oaeAddress.Members.count
                sMembers = sMembers &
oaeAddress.Members.Item(iFor).Name
            Next
            MsgBox sMembers
        End If
    Next
```

In the example above each AddressEntry is checked to see if it is of type olDistList. If it is then a message box displays a list of the members of the distribution list.

Now if we were to add a new AddressEntry to the members collection, we would actually be adding a new AddressEntry to the distribution list.

Name Property

The Name property returns or updates the display name as a string for the AddressEntry object.

```
String = AddressEntryObject.Name
AddressEntryObject.Name = String
```

If you set the AddressEntry to be a Recipient object for a mail message then this Name property becomes the Name property of the recipient and if you looked at the message then you would see this property displayed for the user to view.

Parent Property

The Parent property returns the parent object for the AddressEntry object. This either could be the Recipient object or the AddressEntries collection depending how this AddressEntry object was referenced.

```
Set Object = AddressEntryObject.Parent
```

Session Property

The Session property returns the NameSpace object for the current collection. This will be the Messaging Application Programming Interface or MAPI.

```
Set NameSpaceObject = AddressEntryObject.Session
```

Type Property

The Type property returns or updates a string value, such as "Microsoft Mail Address", that indicates the type of AddressEntry object that is referenced.

```
String = AddressEntryObject.Type
AddressEntryObject.Type = String
```

10

Recipients

A `Recipients` collection comprises a number of `Recipient` objects. Each such object in Outlook represents a resource or user. Most commonly a `Recipient` object is a mail addressee. So a `Recipients` collection works hand in hand with any Outlook item that can be sent to other people - each of these items has its own `Recipients` collection.

Whenever a new item is created it is possible to set up a new `Recipients` collection and whenever an existing item is referenced it is possible to examine the `Recipients` collection associated with it. This collection represents **all** the addressees on a mail message, i.e. in the To, CC and BCC fields.

To set a reference to a `Recipients` collection it is first necessary to have an Outlook item that can be sent, such as a `MailItem` or `AppointmentItem` object.

Example:

```
Dim orcRecipients As Recipients
Dim omMail as MailItem
...
Set orcRecipients = omMail.Recipients
```

If the `MailItem` is newly created and no addressees have been set, then the `Recipients` collection will have no `Recipient` objects associated with it. So each `Recipients` collection may have any number of members, from zero upwards.

Once we have a reference to a `Recipients` collection we can add or remove `Recipient` objects. It is also possible to ensure that all of its members are valid addressees and to examine the Calender schedule for each member.

Recipients Collection Methods

Add Method

The `Add` method creates a new `Recipient` object and adds it to the `Recipients` collection. Once created, all the methods and properties that a `Recipient` object exposes are available. These methods and properties are covered in detail later in this chapter.

```
RecipientsCollection.Add(Name)
```

Name	Data type	Description
Name	String	Required, the name of the new recipient.

It is worth noting that this method simply sets the name of the `Recipient` object. It does not mean that this recipient is valid, i.e. the recipient represents a real addressee.

Example:

```
Dim omTestMail As MailItem
Dim orcTestRecipients As Recipients

Set omTestMail = Application.CreateItem(olMailItem)
Set orcTestRecipients = omTestMail.Recipients

orcTestRecipients.Add "Dwayne Gifford"
orcTestRecipients.Add "Mickey Mouse"

omTestMail.Display
```

In the above example a reference to a `Recipients` collection is set. Two `Recipient` objects are added and then the `MailItem` is displayed, as below.

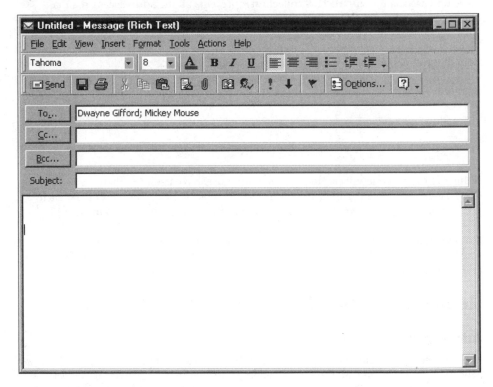

Although it is clear that the second recipient is not valid, it is still added and displayed. An error would not be raised until the item was sent. To check for the validity of recipients you would need to use either the `ResolveAll` method of the `Recipients` collection or the `Resolve` method available for all `Recipient` objects. Details of these methods are given within in this chapter.

Item Method

The `Item` method provides a way to access a particular `Recipient` object within the collection.

```
Set RecipientObject = RecipientsCollection.Item(Index)
```

Name	Data type	Description
Index	Variant	Required, the name of the recipient or the index number representing the position of the recipient within the collection.

Remove Method

The `Remove` method removes from the collection a `Recipient` object referenced by the index. Note that you cannot use the `Recipient` name to identify the `Recipient` object in question. The reason is that it is possible to have two recipients with the same name, making identification of the correct recipient impossible.

```
RecipientsCollection.Remove(Index)
```

Name	Data type	Description
Index	Long	Required, must be an index value representing the position of the recipient within the collection.

If you do try to use the name of the recipient here you will receive a type mismatch error.

ResolveAll Method

The `ResolveAll` method will attempt to resolve each recipient in the collection against the Address Book. If the recipient is not held within the Address Book this method will check to see if the recipient name has a valid email format. This method returns a Boolean that is set to True if all recipients were resolved and to False if one or more recipients are not valid.

```
Boolean = RecipientsCollection.ResolveAll
```

If all recipients are resolved then this method will also set the Boolean `Resolved` property of each `Recipient` object to True and the `Address` property is set to the email address of the recipient. If one or more of the recipients are unresolved then these two properties of each recipient object are not set.

Example:

```
Dim omMailItem As MailItem
Dim orcRecipients As Recipients
Dim orRecipient As Recipient

Set omMailItem = Application.CreateItem(olMailItem)
Set orcRecipients = omMailItem.Recipients

orcRecipients.Add "Dwayne Gifford"
orcRecipients.Add "abc@MyCompany.com"
'orcRecipients.Add "Mickey Mouse"

For Each orRecipient In orcRecipients
    Debug.Print orRecipient.Name & " - " & orRecipient.Resolved & _
                            " - " & orRecipient.Address
Next

If orcRecipients.ResolveAll = True Then

    For Each orRecipient In orcRecipients
            Debug.Print orRecipient.Name & " - " & _
                orRecipient.Resolved & " - " & orRecipient.Address
    Next
Else
    Debug.Print "Recipients have not been resolved"
    For Each orRecipient In orcRecipients
            Debug.Print orRecipient.Name & " - " & _
                orRecipient.Resolved & " - " & orRecipient.Address
    Next
End If
```

The above example executes the `ResolveAll` method. If this method returns **True**, it then proceeds to examine the `Resolved` and `Address` properties of each recipient. The results of this code are shown below.

Dwayne Gifford - False -
abc@MyCompany.com - False -

Dwayne Gifford (E-mail) - True - dgifford@qualitech.com
abc@MyCompany.com - True - abc@MyCompany.com

If the third `Recipient.Add` line is included, then the `Resolved` property for each recipient remains at its default value and the `Address` property is not set.

Dwayne Gifford - False -
abc@MyCompany.com - False -
Mickey Mouse - False -

Recipients have not been resolved
Dwayne Gifford - False -
abc@MyCompany.com - False -
Mickey Mouse - False -

Recipients Collection Properties

Application Property

The `Application` property returns the `Application` object for the current session. Note that this will return a reference to the same object Outlook `Application` object that you are already using.

```
Set ApplicationObject = RecipientsCollection.Application
```

Example:

```
Dim oaOutlookApp As Application
Dim oaRecipient As Application
Dim omMessage As MailItem
Dim orcRecipients As Recipients

Set oaOutlookApp = Outlook.Application

Set omMessage = oaOutlookApp.CreateItem(olMailItem)
omMessage.To = "Dwayne Gifford"

Set orcRecipients = omMessage.Recipients

Set oaRecipient = orcRecipients.Application
```

In this example we set a reference to the `Application` object both directly and indirectly through the `Recipients` collection. If you now look at the `oaRecipient` and the `oaOutlookApp` objects you will notice that they are the same objects, having the same properties set. Now you could use `oaRecipient` to work on the current recipients and leave the other untouched.

Count Property

The `Count` property returns the number of `Recipient` objects in the collection.

```
Long = RecipientsCollection.Count
```

Example:

```
Dim onMAPI As NameSpace
Dim omMessage As MailItem
Dim orcRecipients As Recipients
Dim strRec As String
Set onMAPI = Application.GetNamespace("MAPI")
Set omMessage =
onMAPI.GetDefaultFolder(olFolderInbox).Items.GetFirst
Set orcRecipients = omMessage.Recipients
orcRecipients.ResolveAll
strRec = "The recipients of this mail message were "
For iFor = 1 To orcRecipients.count
  strRec = strRec & orcRecipients.Item(iFor).Name & " "
Next

MsgBox strRec
```

In the example above the names of the recipients of a mail message are shown. The `Count` property is used to set the upper limit on the `For...Next` loop.

Parent Property

The `Parent` property returns the parent object for the `Recipients` collection.

```
Set Object = RecipientsCollection.Parent
```

You should take care to ensure that you use an object variable, as there is no guarantee which type of object will be returned. Be aware that by doing this the object becomes late bound.

Class Property

The `Class` property returns a unique long value that identifies the type of object. This will be one of the `OlObjectClass` constants and in this case we are looking at `olRecipients` or 17.

```
Long = RecipientsCollection.Class
```

Session Property

The `Session` property returns the `NameSpace` object for the current collection. Since we only have one, this will be the MAPI.

```
Set NameSpaceObject = RecipientsCollection.Session
```

The Recipient Object

The `Recipient` object represents a resource or user. In the majority of cases this will be a mail message addressee. A resource can be thought of as a meeting room or anything that is in demand and needs to be scheduled for use. The best way to think of a `Recipient` object is as the object behind the name you see on the **To**, **CC** or **BCC** line of a mail message, appointment, journal entry or task.

So now we know what a `Recipient` object is, we need a way to get create one. To accommodate this we can use either the `CreateRecipient` or `CurrentUser` methods of a `NameSpace` object, or the `Add` method of a `Recipients` Collection.

```
Set RecipientObject = NameSpaceObject.CreateRecipient(RecipientName)

Set RecipientObject = NameSpaceObject.CurrentUser

Set RecipientObject = ItemObject.Recipients.Add(RecipientName)
```

With the first two methods it is possible to create a recipient that does not belong to a `Recipients` collection and so is not associated with a mail message. However, until a recipient is linked to a mail message it is of limited use.

We can also set a reference to an existing `Recipient` object using the `Item` method of a `Recipients` collection, discussed above.

Although a recipient might seem a rather limited object, it is in fact quite powerful. Not only can it be used to access the recipient's `AddressEntry` object and provide information such as the address and name of a recipient, but it also allows us to check their availability for a meeting and to track the status of an item that has been sent, i.e. whether it has been received, read etc.

Recipient Object Methods

Delete Method

The `Delete` method removes the currently selected recipient from a `Recipients` collection.

    RecipientObject.Delete

FreeBusy Method

The `FreeBusy` method returns as a string a month's worth of free/busy information for the `Recipient` object. This is the information you can view in the **Calendar** folder of Outlook.

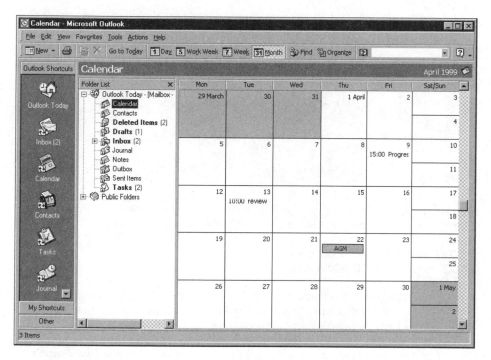

    String = RecipientObject.FreeBusy(Start, _
        MinPerChar[, CompleteFormat])

Name	Data type	Description
Start	Date	Required, the start date of the returned period of free/busy information.
MinPerChar	Long	Required, the number of minutes each character represents in free/busy string.
CompleteFormat	Boolean	Optional, used to determine the detail of information returned. **False** is default.

If the `CompleteFormat` option is set to **False** then the string returned is made up of 0's (for free) and 1's (for busy). For more detail this parameter should be set to **True**. The string will then comprise the following `OlBusyStatus` constants

Constant	Value	Description
olBusy	2	The recipient is busy for that time segment.
olFree	0	The recipient is available for the time segment.
olOutOfOffice	3	The recipient is out of the office for the time segment.
olTentative	1	The recipient is tentative for the time segment.

The following example displays the Free/Busy information, shown in the screenshot above.

```
Dim onMAPI As NameSpace
Dim orCurrUser As Recipient
Dim strFBInfo As String

Set onMAPI = Application.GetNamespace("MAPI")
Set orCurrUser = onMAPI.CurrentUser

strFBInfo = orCurrUser.FreeBusy(#3/29/1999#, 60 * 24)
Debug.Print strFBInfo

strFBInfo = orCurrUser.FreeBusy(#3/29/1999#, 60 * 24, True)
Debug.Print
```

Here we display the information in day intervals. The first line shows the Free/Busy information in its simple form and the second in the more detailed format.

000000000000100010000000001000000
000000000000100020000000001000000

Now, it more likely that you would want to have this information in hour or even half-hour intervals. Clearly this will result in a very long Free/Busy string. You will need some way to identify which day and hour each constant represents.

Obviously there are a number of ways to do this. The example below shows a simple way to break the string into more manageable chunks.

```
Dim onMAPI As NameSpace
Dim orCurrUser As Recipient
Dim strFBInfo As String
Dim strHold(30) As String
Dim strText As String

Set onMAPI = Application.GetNamespace("MAPI")
Set orCurrUser = onMAPI.CurrentUser

strFBInfo = orCurrUser.FreeBusy(#3/29/1999#, 30, True)

For iFor = 1 To 30
```

```
      strHold(iFor) = Left$(strFBInfo, 48)
      strFBInfo = Mid$(strFBInfo, 49)

      If iFor > 1 Then
              strText = strText & vbCrLf & strHold(iFor)
      Else
          strText = strHold(iFor)
      End If
Next
```

A 30-slot array of strings is set up to contain the Free/Busy information for the thirty 24-hour periods. We have split up the 30-day period and made it easier to handle. The type of manipulation you need to perform will depend upon the particular situation.

Resolve Method

The `Resolve` method checks if the `Recipient` object is in the Address Book. If so then the recipient is valid. If the recipient is not found in the Address Book but has a valid email address format, then it is also a valid recipient.

```
Boolean = RecipientObject.Resolve
```

If the recipient is valid then this method will return **True** and the `Resolved` property of the recipient will be similarly set. The recipient's `Address` property is also set. Any method that requires a `Recipient` object, must ensure that the recipient is valid to prevent an error being raised.

An alternative to this method is to use the `ResolveAll` method of the `Recipients` collection, which validates all members of the collection. This method and its limitations are discussed earlier in this chapter.

Recipient Object Properties

Address Property

The `Address` property returns or sets the email address for the current recipient. Note that if this property has not been set directly through code and the `Resolve` method has not been called then this property will return an empty string.

```
String = RecipientObject.Address
RecipientObject.Address = String
```

You should be aware that no validation is performed on this property. If the mail is sent and the address is invalid, a mail failure message will be returned.

AddressEntry Property

The `AddressEntry` property returns the `AddressEntry` object for the recipient. The `AddressEntry` object contains information about a person or resource. It is covered in detail in chapter 9.

```
Set AddressEntryObject = RecipientObject.AddressEntry
```

If the recipient has not yet been resolved, then the Resolve method for the recipient is called automatically. If the recipient cannot be resolved then an error is raised.

Application Property

The Application property returns the Application object for the Recipient object. This will be the Outlook Application object.

```
Set ApplicationObject = RecipientObject.Application
```

AutoResponse Property

The AutoResponse property returns or sets the string value that will be sent as an auto response. This means that as soon as the recipient receives the mail message a response made up of the AutoResponse string is sent back to the originator. I was unable to get this property to work reliably during testing.

```
String = RecipientObject.AutoRepsonse
RecipientObject.AutoResponse = String
```

Class Property

The Class property returns a unique value that identifies an object's type. This will be one of the OlObjectClass constants and since we are considering the Recipient object it will be olRecipient or 4.

```
Long = RecipientObject.Class
```

DisplayType Property

The DisplayType property returns a long integer representing what kind of recipient you have. It will be one of the OlDisplayType constants.

```
Long = RecipientObject.DisplayType
```

Constant	Data type	Description
olAgent	3	The recipient is an Agent Recipient
olDistList	1	The recipient is a Distribution List
olForum	2	The recipient is a Forum
olOrganization	4	The recipient is an Organization
olPrivateDistList	5	The recipient is a Private Distribution List
olRemoteUser	6	The recipient is a Remote User
olUser	0	The recipient is a User

To date I have only seen a distribution list, a private distribution list, a remote user and a user as a Recipient object.

EntryID Property

The `EntryID` property returns a unique ID for the recipient. This ID is created when the recipient is created. It is permanent and will not change between sessions unless the recipient is removed and recreated.

```
String = RecipientObject.EntryID
```

This property is available for backwards compatibility with MAPI. The value is not normally used with Outlook as you can use the index value to locate a recipient in a `Recipients` collection. Also there is no method of a recipient that requires this unique ID.

Index Property

The `Index` property returns a long integer that represents this `Recipient` object's position within the `Recipients` collection.

```
Long = RecipientObject.Index
```

MeetingResponseStatus Property

The `MeetingResponseStatus` property returns the status of the recipient for a meeting, i.e. whether the recipient accepted, declined etc. the meeting. This will be one of the `OlMeetingResponse` constants. Note, however, that unless the item sent to the recipient is a task item or an appointment item then this property will return `olResponseNone`.

```
Long = RecipientObject.MeetingResponseStatus
```

Constant	Value	Description
olResponseAccepted	3	The recipient has accepted the meeting
olResponseDeclined	4	The recipient has declined the meeting
olResponseNone	0	No response status was set
olResponseNotResponded	5	No response has been received
olResponseOrganized	1	The meeting has been assigned to a task
olResponseTentative	2	A tentative response was received

Name Property

The `Name` property returns the name of the recipient. This is the display name, i.e. the one you see in the TO, CC or BCC line.

```
String = RecipientObject.Name
```

As you can imagine this property gives you the name of the recipient. There are no hidden tricks here - if you use the following code then the Name property will return "Dwayne Gifford".

```
Set orRecipient = ApplicationObject.CreateRecipient _
                      ("Dwayne Gifford")
```

Parent Property

The Parent property returns the parent object for the current object.

```
Set Object = RecipientObject.Parent
```

If the recipient is associated with an Outlook item via a Recipients collection, then that item is the parent object. If, on the other hand, the recipient was created using the CreateRecipient or CurrentUser methods of the NameSpace object then the parent object is set to Nothing.

Resolved Property

The Resolved property returns a Boolean indicating whether the recipient has been validated against the Address Book or has a valid format. If True is returned then the recipient is valid.

```
Boolean = RecipientObject.Resolved
```

Session Property

The Session property returns the NameSpace object for the current session. Since at present there is only one data source, this will be the messaging application programming interface or MAPI.

```
Set NameSpaceObject = RecipientObject.Session
```

TrackingStatus Property

The TrackingStatus property returns or sets the tracking status for the recipient. The tracking status describes the progress of a mail message. The value of this property will be one of the OlTrackingStatus constants and if no tracking information is available for the item or none was set then olTrackingNone is returned.

```
Long = RecipientObject.TrackingStatus
RecipientObject.TrackingStatus = Long
```

Constant	Value	Description
olTrackingDelivered	1	The recipient has received the item
olTrackingNone	0	No tracking was set
olTrackingNotDelivered	2	The recipient has not yet received the item

Constant	Value	Description
olTrackingNotRead	3	The recipient has not yet read the item
olTrackingRead	6	The recipient has read the item
olTrackingRecallFailure	4	The originator is unable to retrieve the mail message back from the recipient
olTrackingRecallSuccess	5	The originator was able to retrieve back from the recipient. If the message is unread and the recall was successful, no evidence of the message being sent remains in the recipients mailbox.
olTrackingReplied	7	The recipient has replied to the item

If tracking was turned on for the item to which the recipient is associated, it is possible to use this property to check the status of this tracking for this recipient.

TrackingStatusTime Property

The TrackingStatusTime property returns or sets the tracking status date and time for a recipient. This means that when the TrackingStatus property changes, for example from olTrackingNotRead to olTrackingRead, the time of this change is recorded in the TrackingStatusTime property.

```
Date = RecipientObject.TrackingStatusTime
RecipientObject.TrackingStatusTime = Date
```

Type Property

The Type property returns or sets the type of the recipient, which in turn depends upon the type of its associated item.

```
Long = RecipientObject.Type
RecipientObject.Type = Long
```

The recipient's Type can be any of the following depending on the item itself.

JournalItem			
	olAssociated Contact	1	The recipient is an associated contact. The recipient object of a JounalItem appears to serve no purpose.

MailItem			
	olBCC	3	The recipient is a BCC recipient
	olCC	2	The recipient is a CC recipient
	olOriginator	0	The recipient is originator of the item
	olTo	1	The recipient is a To recipient
MeetingItem			
	olOptional	2	The recipient is an optional participant for the meeting
	olOrganizer	0	The recipient is the originator of the meeting
	olRequired	1	The recipient is a required participant for the meeting
	olResource	3	The recipient is a resource, such as a meeting room
TaskItem			
	olFinalStatus	3	The task is in irs final status
	olUpdate	2	The task has been updated

As you can see from this property the `Recipient` object type is really dependent upon the item object that it is associated with.

11

Outlook Items

The `Items` collection holds all the **Outlook** items in a given `MAPIFolder` object. There are a number of different **Outlook** items. For example the simple mail messages that we receive and send are `MailItem` objects. It is also possible to set up appointments with other people using the `AppointmentItem` objects. These are just a couple of the different items exposed to us by **Outlook**.

Most users see **Outlook** as a means to send and receive mail messages. From this viewpoint, all the items that are seen in the **Inbox** folder make up an `Items` collection. The same is true for any **Outlook** `MAPIFolder` – all the items within such a folder comprise an `Items` collection.

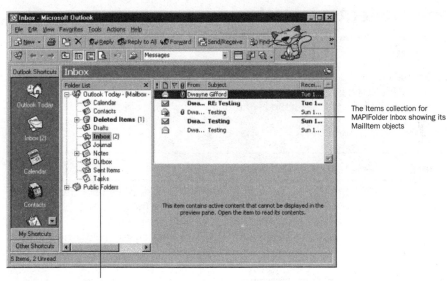

The Items collection for MAPIFolder Inbox showing its MailItem objects

The Inbox MAPIFolder

The following is a list of Outlook items. All these items will be covered in detail in chapters 12 to 19.

AppointmentItem	ContactItem	DistListItem
DocumentItem	JournalItem	MailItem
MeetingItem	NoteItem	PostItem
RemoteItem	ReportItem	TaskItem
TaskRequestAcceptItem	TaskRequestDeclineItem	TaskRequestItem
TaskRequestUpdateItem		

All Outlook items, except the `NoteItem` object, support the same events. Therefore to avoid repetition, these events will also be covered in this chapter, rather than in each individual Outlook item chapter. The `NoteItem` object supports no events.

There is only one way to set a reference to an `Items` collection and that is via the `Items` property of a `MAPIFolder` object.

```
Set ItemsCollection = MAPIFolderObject.Items
```

Once a reference to an `Items` collection is set, it can be used navigate to a particular item within a `MAPIFolder` object and to add and remove items.

Items Collection Methods

Add Method

The `Add` method creates and returns a new item. This is only one of three ways to create new items in Outlook. The others being the `CreateItem` and `CreateItemFromTemplate` methods of the `Application` object.

```
Set Object = ItemsCollection.Add([Type])
```

Name	Data type	Description
`Type`	Variant	Optional, represents the type of Outlook item to be created. It can be any of the `OlItemType` constants given below or one of the `MessageClass` values for customized forms that you may have created.

Constant	Value	Description
`olAppointmentItem`	1	Represents an Appointment item
`olContactItem`	2	Represents a Contact item
`olJournalItem`	4	Represents a Journal item

Constant	Value	Description
olMailItem	0	Represents a Mail item
olNoteItem	5	Represents a Note item
olPostItem	6	Represents a Post item
olTaskItem	3	Represents a Task item

If the Type parameter is omitted from the Add method then the item created will be of the default type for the folder that the Items collection belongs to. This default type for the folder is set using the DefaultItemType property.

Example:

```
Dim oicDraftItems As Items
Dim omNewMailItem As MailItem
Set oicDraftItems = Session.GetDefaultFolder(olFolderDrafts).Items
Set omNewMailItem = oicDraftItems.Add(olMailItem)
omNewMailItem.Save
```

The above example creates and saves a new mail item in the Items collection for the Drafts MAPIFolder.

Find Method

The Find method searches through the Items collection based on a filter and returns the first suitable item.

```
Set Object = ItemsCollection.Find(Filter)
```

Name	Data type	Description
Filter	String	Required, a conditional expression that returns a Boolean. If the filter returns True the item is selected. The filter is not case sensitive.

A filter string can be made up of several filter clauses connected by the logical operators Not, And or Or.

A filter clause evaluates to True or False and comprises a literal property name surrounded by square brackets, a comparison operator and a value the property is to be compared against, for example:

[Location] = 'Room 101'

The following comparison operators may be used:

>	greater than	<	less than
>=	greater than or equal to	<=	less than or equal to
=	equal to	<>	not equal to

The following properties may not be used within a filter clause:

Body	Categories	Children
Class	Companies	CompanyLastFirst NoSpace
CompanyLast FirstSpaceOnly	ContactNames	Contacts
Conversation Index	DLName	Email1EntryID
Email2EntryID	Email3EntryID	EntryID
HTMLBody	IsOnlineMeeting	LastFirstAndSuffix
LastFirstNoSpace	LastFirstNo SpaceCompany	LastFirstSpaceOnly
LastFirstSpace OnlyCompany	MemberCount	NetMeetingAlias
NetMeetingAuto Start	NetMeeting OrganizerAlias	NetMeetingServer
NetMeetingType	RecurrenceState	ReplyRecipients
ReceivedBy EntryID	RecevedOnBehalf OfEntryID	ResponseState
Saved	Sent	Submitted
VotingOptions		

In the examples below, an Items collection referencing ContactItem objects is filtered. In the first example, the first ContactItem that has its Location property set to 'Room 101' will be returned. In the second example two filter clauses are used. An item is only returned if the BusinessAddressCity property is set to 'Jacksonville' **and** the BusinessAddressState is set to 'Fl'.

```
Dim onMAPI As NameSpace
Dim oicContacts As Items
Dim ocR101 As ContactItem

Set onMAPI = Application.GetNamespace("MAPI")
Set oicContacts = onMAPI.GetDefaultFolder(olFolderContacts).Items
Set ocR101 = oicContacts.Find("[Location] = 'Room 101'")
```

Or

```
Dim onMAPI As NameSpace
Dim oicContacts As Items
Dim ocJacksonville As ContactItem

Set onMAPI = Application.GetNamespace("MAPI")
Set oicContacts = onMAPI.GetDefaultFolder(olFolderContacts).Items
Set ocJacksonville = oicContacts.Find("[BusinessAddressCity] " & _
                      " = 'Jacksonville' and [BusinessAddressState] = 'Fl'")
```

If no item satisfying the conditions within the filter is found, then `Nothing` is returned.

FindNext Method

The `FindNext` method returns the next item that meets the filter criteria set with the `Find` method – see above.

```
Set Object = ItemsCollection.FindNext
```

If you call `FindNext` method before the `Find` method, `Nothing` is returned and consequently an error will be raised if you try to access the `Object`.

GetFirst Method

The `GetFirst` method returns the first item in the referenced collection. If there is no item in the collection then `Nothing` is returned.

```
Set Object = ItemsCollection.GetFirst
```

It is always wise to first get a reference to the `Items` collection before using the Get methods.

GetLast Method

The `GetLast` method returns the last item in the `Items` collection. If the collection is empty it will return `Nothing`.

```
Set Object = ItemsCollection.GetLast
```

GetNext Method

The `GetNext` method returns the next item in the referenced collection. If the end of the collection is reached then `Nothing` is returned.

```
Set Object = ItemsCollection.GetNext
```

It is always wise to first get a reference to the `Items` collection before using the Get methods.

Example:

```
Dim onMAPI As NameSpace
Dim ofInbox As MAPIFolder
Dim oicInboxItems As Items
Dim omUnreadMail As Object
Set onMAPI = Application.GetNamespace("MAPI")
Set oicInboxItems = onMAPI.GetDefaultFolder(olFolderInbox).Items
Set omUnreadMail = oicInboxItems.GetFirst
Do Until omUnreadMail Is Nothing
    If omUnreadMail.UnRead = True Then omUnreadMail.Display
    Set omUnreadMail = oicInboxItems.GetNext
Loop
```

In this example the `GetFirst` and `GetNext` methods are used to walk through all items in the **Inbox** `MAPIFolder Items` collection. Any unread messages are displayed.

GetPrevious Method

The `GetPrevious` method returns a reference to the previous item in the current collection. If the start of the collection is reached then `Nothing` is returned.

```
Set Object = ItemsCollection.GetPrevious
```

Item Method

The `Item` method returns a particular item from the `Items` collection, specified by the parameter `Index`.

```
Set Object = ItemsCollection.Item(Index)
```

Name	Data type	Description
`Index`	Variant	Required, a long representing the position of the item within the `Items` collection or a string being the `Subject` property for the item

> The Subject may be used as the index for all types of items except ContactItem. For this item the default property FullName is used.

This is an important method since you will no doubt need to work with the items in different folders. For example I could imagine you might need to monitor an **Inbox** for customers requesting a product that your company sells. By using the `Item` method you could walk through all the items in the collection for the **Inbox** and then post the information to the sales database for shipment and billing.

Example:

```
Dim onMAPI As NameSpace
Dim oicNewMail As Items
Dim dbSales As Database
Dim oiMail As MailItem
Dim iFor As Integer

Set onMAPI = Application.GetNamespace("MAPI")
Set oicNewMail = onMAPI.GetDefaultFolder(olFolderInbox).Items

'Open the Sales Database
Set dbSales = OpenDatabase("C:\Work\Wrox\Sales.MDB")

For iFor = oicNewMail.count To 1 Step -1

    If oicNewMail.Item(iFor).UnRead And _
        oicNewMail.Item(iFor).Class = olMail Then
Set oiMail = oicNewMail.Item(iFor)
'Log the information to the Sales database.
        dbSales.Execute "Insert Into Inquiry (Subject, Description) " & _
                        "Values('" & oiMail.Subject & "', '" & _
                        oiMail.Body & "')"
        oiMail.Delete
    End If
Next
```

In the above example we walk through the `Items` collection of the Inbox `MAPI folder` looking for `MailItem` objects that have not yet been read. If any such object is found its subject and body information is logged to a sales database and in this case deleted. Alternatively these `MailItem` objects could be moved to another folder.

Note that since the items are being deleted it is necessary to move backwards through the collection. The sample code shown for the `Restrict` method below demonstrates how to make this code cleaner and work faster

Remove Method

The `Remove` method deletes an item, specified by its index, from the collection

```
ItemsCollection.Remove(Index)
```

Name	Data type	Description
Index	Long	Required, the position of the item within the `Items` collection.

If you try to remove an item that does not exist then an error will be raised.

ResetColumns Method

The `ResetColumns` method clears any cached properties set with `SetColumns` method. For more information on cached properties refer to the `SetColumns` method.

```
ItemsCollection.ResetColumns
```

If called before any properties have been cached with the `SetColumns` method, the `ResetColumns` method will do nothing.

Restrict Method

The `Restrict` method works in a similar way to the `Find` method, except that it returns a new collection of all items matching the filter criteria that were applied.

```
Set ItemsCollection = ItemsCollection.Restrict(Filter)
```

Name	Data type	Description
Filter	String	Required, a conditional expression that returns a Boolean. If the filter returns True the item is selected. The filter is not case sensitive.

A filter string can be made up of several filter clauses connected by the logical operators Not, And or Or.

A filter clause evaluates to True or False and comprises a literal property name surrounded by square brackets, a comparison operator and the value the property is to be compared against, for example

[Location] = 'Room 101'

The following comparison operators may be used:

>	greater than	<	less than
>=	greater than or equal to	<=	less than or equal to
=	equal to	<>	not equal to

The following properties may not be used within a filter clause:

Body	Categories	Children
Class	Companies	CompanyLast FirstNoSpace
CompanyLastFirst SpaceOnly	ContactNames	Contacts
ConversationIndex	DLName	Email1EntryID
Email2EntryID	Email3EntryID	EntryID
HTMLBody	IsOnlineMeeting	LastFirstAndSuffix
LastFirstNoSpace	LastFirstNo SpaceCompany	LastFirstSpaceOnly
LastFirstSpace OnlyCompany	MemberCount	NetMeetingAlias
NetMeeting AutoStart	NetMeeting OrganizerAlias	NetMeetingServer
NetMeetingType	RecurrenceState	ReplyRecipients
ReceivedByEntryID	RecevedOnBehalf OfEntryID	ResponseState
Saved	Sent	Submitted
VotingOptions		

Example:

```
Dim onMAPI As NameSpace
Dim oicNewMail As Items
Dim dbSales As Database
Dim oiMail As MailItem
Dim oicItems As Items
Dim iFor As Integer

Set onMAPI = Application.GetNamespace("MAPI")
Set oicNewMail = onMAPI.GetDefaultFolder(olFolderInbox).Items
```

```
'Open the Sales Database
Set dbSales = OpenDatabase("C:\Work\Wrox\Sales.MDB")
Set oicItems = oicNewMail.Restrict("[UnRead] = True And [MessageClass]" & _
               " = 'IPM.Note'")
For iFor = oicItems.count To 1 Step -1
    Set oiMail = oicItems(iFor)
    dbSales.Execute "Insert Into Inquiry (Subject, Description) Values('" _
                & oiMail.Subject & "', '" & oiMail.Body & "')"
    oiMail.Delete
Next
```

This code fulfills the same purpose as that shown for the Item method. Here, though, the Restrict method is used to limit the number of Item objects we need to walk through. This is achieved by setting a reference to an Items collection that only contains unread, IPM.Note items. The MessageClass property is used instead of the Class property, as the Class property is not permitted to appear in the Filter parameter. Once a reference to this collection is set, we move backwards through the collection logging item information to a sales database and deleting the item.

SetColumns Method

The SetColumns method caches properties of items in order to provide fast access to these properties. When a property is cached Outlook loads this property into memory instead of leaving it on the hard disk. This way you get a quicker response when the property is accessed

```
ItemsCollection.SetColumns(Columns)
```

Name	Data type	Description
Columns	String	Required, a list of properties for the items, separated by commas.

Note that any property that returns an object or is in the list below will cause an error.

Body	Categories	Children
Class	Companies	Contacts
DLName	EntryID	HTMLBody
MemberCount	Recurrence State	Reply Recipients
ResponseState	Saved	Sent
Submitted	VotingOptions	

This list of properties could change with new releases of Outlook.

The example below uses the `SetColumns` method to cache the `ReceivedTime` property for subsequent and speedier use with the `Sort` method. A reference is set to the collection of items in the Inbox that are unread and are not mail items. This collection is then sorted in order of time received and displayed for the user.

Example:

```
Dim onMAPI As NameSpace
Dim oicInboxItems As Items
Dim oicItems As Items
Dim oiTask As Object

Set onMAPI = GetNamespace("MAPI")
Set oicInboxItems = onMAPI.GetDefaultFolder(olFolderInbox).Items
Set oicItems = oicInboxItems.Restrict("[UnRead] = True And " &_
               "[MessageClass] <> 'IPM.Note'")

oicItems.SetColumns "[ReceivedTime]"
oicItems.Sort "[ReceivedTime]"
Set oiTask = oicItems.GetLast
Do While Not oiTask Is Nothing
    oiTask.Display
    Set oiTask = oicItems.GetLast
Loop
```

The reason the `GetLast` method is used to get the next item in the collection is that as the previous item is displayed, its `UnRead` property changes from True to False and it is removed from the `oicItems` collection.

Sort Method

The `Sort` method arranges the collection by a valid property for the type of item that is contained within the collection. Note that if the property can be multi-valued then it cannot be used with this method.

```
ItemsCollection.Sort(Property [, Descending])
```

Name	Data type	Description
`Property`	String	Required, a valid single-valued property for the items contained within the collection
`Descending`	Boolean	Optional, default is False. If set to True the items will be sorted in ascending order

Example:

```
Dim onMAPI As NameSpace
Dim oicNewMail As Items
Dim oicItems As Items
Dim a As MailItem

Set onMAPI = Application.GetNamespace("MAPI")
Set oicNewMail = onMAPI.GetDefaultFolder(olFolderInbox).Items

Set oicItems = oicNewMail.Restrict("[UnRead] = True And " & _
               "[MessageClass] = 'IPM.Note'")

oicItems.Sort "[ReceivedTime]", True
```

In the example above the `Restrict` method is used to set a reference to an items collection containing only unread, IPM.Note items. This collection is then sorted in descending order according the `ReceivedTime` property to allow us to work with the newest items first. The indices of this collection are reset accordingly.

Items Collection Properties

Application Property

The `Application` property returns the `Application` object for this session. This will be the **Outlook** `Application` object.

```
Set ApplicationObject = ItemsCollection.Application
```

Class Property

The `Class` property returns a unique long integer value that identifies the object's type. This will be one of the `OlObjectClass` constants and for the `Items` collection is `olItems` or 16.

```
Long = ItemsCollection.Class
```

Count Property

The `Count` property returns a long integer value that represents the number of items in the `Items` collection.

```
Long = ItemsCollection.Count
```

The `Count` property could be used to ensure that a collection is not empty before access to its elements is attempted.

IncludeRecurrences Property

The `IncludeRecurrences` property returns or sets a Boolean value indicating whether the items referenced by the collection may be actual instances of recurring items. This property is valid for `AppointmentItem` objects only. It should be set to **True** if the `Items` collection is to include recurring objects. More information about these objects is given in Chapter 17. By default this property will be **False**.

```
Boolean = ItemsCollection.IncludeRecurrences
ItemsCollection.IncludeRecurrences = Boolean
```

This property will only take affect if the `Items` collection contains recurring `AppointmentItem` objects and is sorted in ascending order according to start date. In this case, if the collection includes a recurring appointment with no end date, the `Count` property of the collection will return 2,147,483,647 or the largest possible long integer.

Parent Property

The `Parent` property returns the parent object for the `Items` collection. Since the only way to reference an `Items` collection is through a `MAPIFolder` then the `Parent` property will always return a `MAPIFolder` object.

```
Set MAPIFolderObject = ItemsCollection.Parent
```

Session Property

The `Session` property returns to the `NameSpace` object for the current collection. This will be the messaging application programming interface or MAPI.

```
Set NameSpaceObject = ItemsCollection.Session
```

Items Collection Events

The code to respond to `Items` collection events should be placed in a **Class Module**. It is necessary to declare the variable using the `WithEvents` keyword and to reference the `Items` collection you require. Here we are referencing the `Items` collection for the default **Inbox** `MAPIFolder`.

```
Dim WithEvents oicItems As Items

Private Sub Class_Initialize()
    Set oicItems = Application.GetNamespace("MAPI").GetDefaultFolder & _
                   (olFolderInbox)
End Sub
```

ItemAdd Event

The `ItemAdd` event occurs whenever a new item is added to the appropriate folder.

```
Private Sub oicItems_ItemAdd(ByVal Item As Object)
```

The `Item` parameter passed to this procedure is the particular item that has been added.

ItemChange Event

The `ItemChange` event occurs whenever any property of an item within the collection is changed.

```
Private Sub oicItems_ItemChange(ByVal Item As Object)
```

The `Item` parameter passed to this procedure is the particular item that has been modified.

ItemRemove Event

The `ItemRemove` event occurs whenever an item is deleted from the collection.

```
Private Sub oicItems_ItemRemove()
```

Item Object Events

There are sixteen different types of item available:

AppointmentItem	ContactItem	DistListItem
DocumentItem	JournalItem	MailItem
MeetingItem	NoteItem	PostItem
ReportItem	RemoteItem	TaskItem
TaskRequest AcceptItem	TaskRequest DeclineItem	TaskRequestUp dateItem
TaskRequestItem		

Since all of the different items support different properties and methods I have covered them in their own individual chapters. However, all of these objects support a common set of events that will be covered here in this chapter to avoid repetition in later chapters. The only exception is the NoteItem which does not support any events at all.

To code up these events you need to make use of the WithEvents keyword that is offered with VBA or VB, and to set a reference to the appropriate item.

For the purposes of illustration we shall be using the MailItem object to illustrate the syntax and functionality of these events. However, the events apply to all items bar the NoteItem and the code should be modified accordingly.

The following code, placed in a **Class Module,** is used to set a reference to the first mail item of the default **Inbox** folder.

Example:

```
Dim WithEvents omMail As MailItem

Private Sub Class_Initialize()
    Dim onMAPI As NameSpace

    Set onMAPI = Application.GetNamespace("MAPI")
    Set omMail = onMAPI.GetDefaultFolder(olFolderInbox).Items.GetFirst
End Sub
```

The item events are then made available in the procedure listbox as shown below.

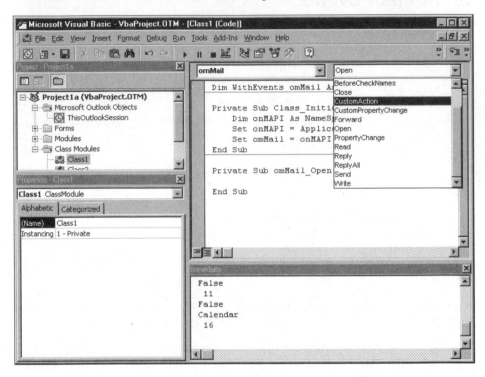

AttachmentAdd Event

The `AttachmentAdd` event is called just before an attachment is added to the item.

```
Private Sub omMail_AttachmentAdd(ByVal Attachment As Attachment)
```

This event passes the attachment as a parameter and provides an opportunity to make changes to the attachment and/or to the message itself.

So if for example your administrator has encouraged you not to send mail messages greater than 1 Meg in size, this event could be used to check a `MailItem` object's size and issue a warning if it exceeds the guidelines.

Example:

```
Private Sub omMail_AttachmentAdd(ByVal Attachment As Attachment)

Dim orMailRec As Recipient

   If Attachment.Type = olByValue Then
      omMail.Save
      If omMail.Size > 10 Then
         MsgBox "Your mail is now of size " & omMail.Size / 1000000 & _
                "MB. Please zip the attachment if you have not " & _
                "done so already.", vbExclamation
      End If
   Else
```

```
      For Each orMailRec In omMail.Recipients
         If InStr(orMailRec.Address, "@") Then
            MsgBox "You cannot send a linked attachment to an external" & _
                   "recipient.You may want to ammend this mail message.", _
                   vbExclamation
         End If
      Next
   End If

   End Sub
```

A second check is also performed to see if the user has linked the attachment and if any of the recipients are on an external mail server. If this is the case the user is informed of the potential problem.

AttachmentRead Event

The `AttachmentRead` event occurs after you have been asked if you would like to save the attachment to disk or to read it.

```
Private Sub omMail_AttachmentRead(ByVal Attachment As Attachment)
```

The attachment that is being opened is passed via the `Attachment` parameter. It is possible to manipulate the item and/or the attachment when this event is called.

BeforeAttachmentSave Event

The `BeforeAttachmentSave` event occurs before an attachment is saved. It is possible to manipulate the item and/or the attachment within this event's code.

```
Private Sub Item_BeforeAttachmentSave(ByVal Attachment As _
Outlook.Attachment, _
Cancel As Boolean)
```

Name	Description
`Attachment`	The attachment that is about to be saved
`Cancel`	Determines whether the attachment will be saved. By default this is set to False, but setting it to True within the event's code cancels the attachment save.

BeforeCheckNames Event

The `BeforeCheckNames` event is fired just before the recipients of the item are resolved. Recipients are resources or people to whom the item is addressed. If a recipient is a member of the current session's address book or their name is of a valid email format, then the recipient will be resolved.

```
Private Sub omMail_BeforeCheckNames(Cancel As Boolean)
```

The `Cancel` parameter may be used to stop the recipient names being checked. By default `Cancel` will be set to False. If reset to True in this event's code the recipients will not be resolved.

This event is called if the user employs Tools | Check Names through the GUI or if the user clicks the Send button. Calling the `Send` method through code will also fire this event

If the `Send` method is used and the `BeforeCheckNames` is canceled by setting `Cancel` to True in the event's code, the mail message will not be sent.

In this example the current user is added as a BCC recipient of the mail item. The `Cancel` parameter is then set to True. Now if the user adds a recipient to the message and then moves on to add a message to the body of the item the user-added recipient will be validated but the current user will not be added. When the user clicks on the Send button the current user will be added and the message will remain in create mode in front of the user.

Example:

```
Private Sub omMail_BeforeCheckNames(Cancel As Boolean)
    omMail.BCC = onMAPI.CurrentUser
    Cancel = True
End Sub
```

Clearly this is not the most practical of examples, but I wanted to demonstrate when the `BeforeCheckNames` event is fired and when it is not.

Close Event

The `Close` event is fired whenever the `Inspector` object that is associated with the item is closed. This event is not fired by setting the item to `Nothing`.

```
Private Sub omMail_Close(Cancel As Boolean)
```

Setting the `Cancel` parameter to True will stop the close event and cause the item to remain open.

Example:

```
Private Sub Item_Close(Cancel As Boolean)
    If omMail.Sent = False Then
        If MsgBox("Would you like to send the Item before closing", _
                vbYesNo + vbQuestion) = vbYes Then
            If omMail.Recipients.count > 0 Then
                omMail.Send
            Else
                MsgBox "This message cannot be sent as there are " & _
                    "no recipients."
            End If
        End If
    End If
End Sub
```

In this example the mail message if checked to see if it has been sent. If not the user is asked if they wish to send it and a check is included to ensure that the item has at least one recipient.

CustomAction Event

The `CustomAction` event occurs whenever a custom or user-defined action is executed on the item. Custom actions can be created through code or through the Tools | Forms | Design this Form on the GUI. The `Action` object is covered in detail later in this chapter.

```
Private Sub omMail_CustomAction(ByVal Action As Object, ByVal Response _
As Object, Cancel As Boolean)
```

Name	Description
`Action`	Represents the action to be executed
`Response`	Represents the new item created as a result of the action
`Cancel`	Determines whether the custom action will actually be executed. The default is set to False. If set to True the action is canceled.

CustomPropertyChange Event

The `CustomPropertyChange` occurs whenever any of the custom properties is modified.

```
Private Sub omMail_CustomPropertyChange(ByVal Name As String)
```

The `Name` parameter is the name of the property that is modified.

This event corresponds to the `PropertyChange` event but it will only be fired when a **user-defined** property is changed.

Example:

```
Private Sub Class_Initialize()
    Dim oupAuthorName As UserProperty

    Set onMapi = GetNamespace("MAPI")
    Set omMail = CreateItem(olMailItem)
    omMail.Recipients.Add "Iris Gifford"
    omMail.Recipients.Add "Tom Eaves"
    omMail.Recipients.ResolveAll

    Set oupAuthorName = omMail.UserProperties.Add("AuthorName", olText)
    omMail.Display
End Sub
```

```
Private Sub omMail_CustomPropertyChange(ByVal Name As String)
    If Name = "AuthorName" Then
            omMail.UserProperties(Name).Value = omMail.SenderName
    End If
End Sub
```

In the example above a custom property called `AuthorName` is first created. This property for the `MailItem` object in question is of `Text` type. If this property is modified at any time, it is set to the `SenderName` property of the item.

Forward Event

The `Forward` event occurs whenever an item is Forwarded.

```
Private Sub omMail_Forward(ByVal Forward As Object, Cancel As Boolean)
```

Name	Description
Forward	This is the new item created if the event is completed.
Cancel	Determines whether the item will actually be forwarded. The default is set to **False**. If set to **True** the forward is canceled.

Example:

```
Private Sub omMail_Forward(ByVal Forward As Object, Cancel As Boolean)
    If omMail.Sensitivity = olConfidential Then
        MsgBox "This message cannot be forwarded"
        Cancel = True
    End If
End Sub
```

The above code is used to ensure that a confidential mail message cannot be forwarded. A message is displayed to the user to inform them of the situation.

Open Event

The `Open` event occurs when an item is opened in an `Inspector` object. This event is fired just before the Inspector is displayed and can be canceled by setting the `Cancel` parameter to **True**.

```
Private Sub omMail_Open(Cancel As Boolean)
```

Example:

```
Private Sub omMail_Open(Cancel As Boolean)
    If omMail.CreationTime = #1/1/4501# Then
        omMail.BCC = omMail.Session.CurrentUser
    End If
End Sub
```

In the example above the current user is added as a BCC recipient to a newly created `MailItem` object. The creation time of a new item is set to 1/1/4501.

> Note that simply setting a reference to an item will not fire this event.

PropertyChange Event

The `PropertyChange` event occurs when one of the default item properties is changed. This does not include any of the `UserProperties` properties.

```
Private Sub omMail_PropertyChange(ByVal Name As String)
```

The Name parameter passes the name of the property that has been modified. So, for example, if the Subject property of the referenced item were changed this event would be called.

Read Event

The Read event is called when the item is opened for the first time after the class setting a reference to it has been instantiated. If the item is closed and then reopened only the Open event is fired. If a new item is created and a reference set to it when the class is instantiated then the Read event is not fired.

```
Private Sub omMail_Read()
```

Reply Event

The Reply event occurs whenever an item is replied to. This event is fired **before** the reply GUI is displayed and consequently it is possible to cancel the reply by setting the Cancel to **True** in the event's code.

```
Private Sub omMail_Reply(ByVal Response As Object, Cancel As Boolean)
```

Name	Description
Response	This is the new item created to hold the reply.
Cancel	Determines whether the item will actually be replied to. The default is set to **False**. If set to **True** the reply is canceled.

Example

```
Private Sub omMail_Reply(ByVal Response As Object, Cancel As Boolean)

    Dim iaAttachment As Attachment
            If MsgBox("Would you like to send the Attachments as well?" , _
                vbQuestion + vbYesNo) = vbYes Then

            For Each iaAttachment In omMail.Attachments
                stempname = "C:\Windows\Temp\new" & iaAttachment.FileName
                iaAttachment.SaveAsFile stempname
                Response.Attachments.Add _
                stempname, iaAttachment.Type, iaAttachment.Position, _
                iaAttachment.DisplayName
                Response.Send
            Next

        End If
        Set iaAttachment = Nothing

End Sub
```

This code example allows the user to return the attachments that were sent with the original message. This is useful because if the user opens and alters any attachments, they can automatically return the amended attachments to the sender. The reason the that the word "new" is attached to the beginning of the attachment filename is that the original name is already in use by Outlook and so trying to use it will cause an error.

ReplyAll Event

The `ReplyAll` event occurs whenever the `ReplyAll` method is executed. This event is fired before the ReplyAll GUI is displayed and so can be canceled if required.

```
Private Sub omMail_ReplyAll(ByVal Response As Object, Cancel As Boolean)
```

Name	Description
Response	This is the new item created to hold the reply.
Cancel	Determines whether the item will actually be replied to. The default is set to False. If set to True the replyall is canceled.

Send Event

The `Send` event occurs when the `Send` method is executed either through code or by the clicking on the Send button in the GUI.

```
Private Sub omMail_Send(Cancel As Boolean)
```

It is possible to stop the item from being sent by setting the `Cancel` parameter from its default of False to True in the event's code.

Example:

```
Private Sub omMail_Send(Cancel As Boolean)
    omMail.BCC = omMail.Session.CurrentUser
    omMail.Recipients.ResolveAll
End Sub
```

This example adds the current user to the `MailItem` as a BCC recipient. After adding a new recipient it is necessary to resolve it in order to prevent an error being raised.

Write Event

The `Write` event occurs whenever the item is saved either through code or through the GUI.

```
Private Sub omMail_Write(Cancel As Boolean)
```

It is possible to prevent any changes being saved via the `Cancel` parameter. If set to True in the event's code the save will be canceled.

In this example we combine the `Open` and `Write` events to provide the possibility of saving a backup of the original message when a save is made.

Example:

```
Dim WithEvents omMail As MailItem
Dim omTempMail As MailItem
Dim bTempCopy As Boolean

Private Sub omMail_Open(Cancel As Boolean)
    bTempCopy = True
    Set omTempMail = omMail.Copy
End Sub
```

```
Private Sub omMail_Write(Cancel As Boolean)
    Dim a As MAPIFolder
    If bTempCopy = False Then
        If MsgBox("Would you like to save a backup of the original?", _
            vbYesNo) = vbYes Then
            omTempMail.Move Application.Session.PickFolder
        End If
    End If
    bTempCopy = False
End Sub
```

In this example a copy of the original message is made when it is opened. Because the
Copy method will trigger the Write event of the item being copied it is necessary to
use a flag, bTempCopy, to inform the Write event not to run the code within it. When
the Write event proper is called the user is asked if they wish to save a backup copy.
If they do, then the temporary copy omTempMail of the original is moved to the folder
of their choice.

The Attachments Collection

The Attachments collection holds all of the Attachment objects that are associated
with an Outlook item. The Attachment object itself represents a document or the link
to a document that is contained within an item. Every Outlook item has an attachments
collection except a NoteItem object. For objects apart from the DocumentItem and
ReportItem objects, attachments are displayed in the body of the item as shown
below.

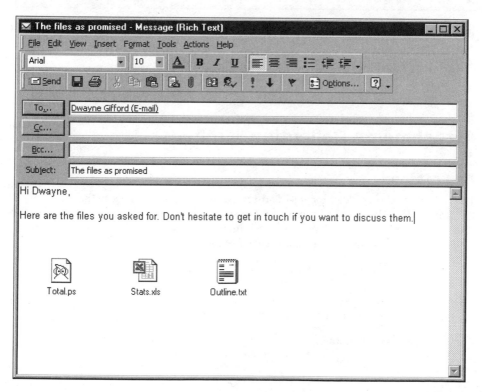

To access the attachments of the `DocumentItem` and `ReportItem` objects via the Outlook GUI, you need to use the **Preview Pane**.

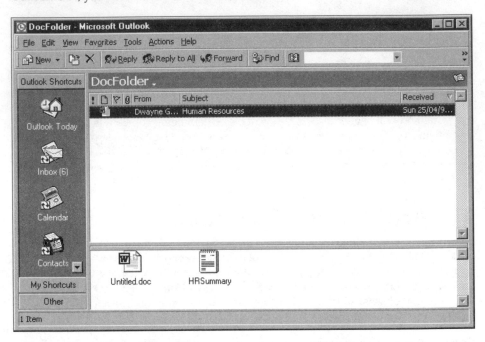

The only way to get a reference to an `Attachments` collection is through an **Outlook** item.

```
Dim omMail As MailItem
Dim oacAttachments As Attachments
...
Set oacAttachments = omMail.Attachments
```

Attachments Collection Methods

Add Method

The `Add` method provides a means of adding an `Attachment` object to the `Attachments` collection and can be used to set a reference to the added attachment. This will add the attachment to the **Outlook** item associated with the `Attachments` collection. The attachment may also be an **Outlook** item.

```
Set AttachmentObject = AttachmentsCollection.Add(FileName _
                           [, Type][, Position][, DisplayName])
```

Name	Data type	Description
FileName	Variant	Required, the file and path name of a file or the Outlook item that will become the attachment.

Name	Data type	Description
Type	Long	Optional, represents the type of attachment and must be one of the OlAttachmentType constants given below.
Position	Long	Optional, the position of the attachment within the body of the message, in terms of characters of body text. If omitted the attachment is placed at the end of the body text.
Display Name	String	Optional, the name that will appear under the attachment in the body of the item. If omitted the file name will be shown.

The Type parameter may take one of the following OlAttachmentType constants:

Name	Value	Description
olByReference	4	Creates the attachment as a shortcut to the file
olByValue	1	Creates the attachment as a copy of the original item or file
olEmbeddedItem	5	Creates the attachment as a shortcut to an Outlook item

In the following example it is necessary to have a file named Outline.txt in your My Documents folder.

Example:

```
Dim omMail As MailItem
Dim oacAttachments As Attachments
Dim oaProject As Attachment

Set omMail = Application.CreateItem(olMailItem)
omMail.Body = "Enclosed is the project outline that you requested." & _
            vbCrLf & " Let me know what you think."

Set oacAttachments = omMail.Attachments
oacAttachments.add "C:\My Documents\Outline.txt", olEmbeddeditem, 53, _
                "Project Outline"

omMail.Display
```

In the example above a new MailItem object is created and a message placed in its body. A reference to its Attachments collection is made and the Add method is used to add an attachment. This attachment takes the form of a link or shortcut to the text file Outline.txt and is placed at the 53rd character within the body text. Finally the new mail message is displayed.

The result is shown below.

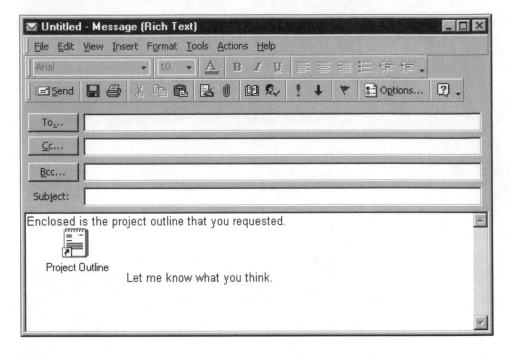

Item Method

The Item method returns a particular Attachment object from the Attachments collection.

```
Set AttachmentObject = AttachmentsCollection.Item(Index)
```

Name	Data type	Description
Index	Variant	Required, a number representing the position of the attachment within the collection.

Remove Method

The Remove method removes the Attachment object indicated by the Index value from the Attachments collection.

```
AttachmentsCollection.Remove(Index)
```

Name	Data type	Description
Index	Variant	Required, a number representing the position of the attachment within the collection.

Attachments Collection Properties

Application Property

The `Application` property returns the `Application` object for this session. This can only be the Outlook `Application` object.

```
Set ApplicationObject = AttachmentsCollection.Application
```

Class Property

The `Class` property holds a unique value that identifies the type of object we are referencing. This will be one of the `OlObjectClass` constants and in this case will be set to `olAttachments` or `18`.

```
Long = AttachmentsCollection.Class
```

Count Property

The `Count` property returns a long integer value that represents the number of `Attachment` objects in the `Attachments` collection. This property could be used to prevent errors being raised, by checking its value to ensure that an `Attachments` collection is not empty before a reference is set to one of its `Attachment` objects.

```
Long = AttachmentsCollection.Count
```

Parent Property

This property returns the parent object for the `Attachments` collection. In this case the parent is one of the Outlook items that the `Attachments` collection belongs to.

```
Set Object = AttachmentsCollection.Parent
```

Session property

The `Session` property returns the `NameSpace` object for the current collection. This can only be the messaging application programming interface or MAPI.

```
Set NameSpaceObject = AttachmentsCollection.Session
```

Attachment Object

An `Attachment` object represents a document or link to a document that is added to an Outlook item. It may also be another Outlook item embedded within the parent item.

Attachment Object Methods

Delete Method

The `Delete` method removes the current `Attachment` object from the `Attachments` collection.

```
AttachmentObject.Delete
```

SaveAsFile Method

The `SaveAsFile` method provides a means to save the attachment to disk.

```
AttachmentObject.SaveAsFile Path
```

Name	Data type	Description
Path	String	Required, the path name and file name where the attachment is to be saved

Example:

```
Dim sFoldername As String
Dim onMAPI As NameSpace
Dim omMail As MailItem
Dim ofInbox As MAPIFolder
Dim oacAttachments As Attachments
Dim oaAttachment As Attachment

sFoldername = InputBox("Please enter the name of the folder where " & _
                       "you would like to save your attachments", _
                       "Attachment Save", "C:\My Documents")
If sFoldername <> "" Then
    Set onMAPI = GetNamespace("MAPI")
    Set ofInbox = onMAPI.GetDefaultFolder(olFolderInbox)
    For iFor = 1 To ofInbox.Items.count
        If ofInbox.Items(iFor).Class = olMail And _
        ofInbox.Items(iFor).Attachments.count <> 0 Then
            Set omMail = ofInbox.Items(iFor)
            Set oacAttachments = omMail.Attachments
            For Each oaAttachment In oacAttachments
                oaAttachment.SaveAsFile sFoldername & "\" & _
                                        oaAttachment.FileName
            Next
        End If
    Next
End If
```

The example above is designed to save the attachments of mail items in the Inbox to a user-specified folder. Each item in the default Inbox folder is checked to see if it is a mail item with attachments. If so the attachments are saved to the folder specified by the user. The user may choose not to save the attachments by clicking cancel on the Inputbox.

Attachment Object Properties

Application Property

The `Application` property returns the `Application` object for this session, which will be the Outlook `Application` object.

```
Set ApplicationObject = AttachmentObject.Application
```

Class Property

The `Class` property returns a long integer value that identifies the type of object we are referencing. This will be one of the `OlObjectClass` constants and for an `Attachment` object is `olAttachment` or 5.

```
Long = AttachmentObject.Class
```

DisplayName Property

The `DisplayName` property holds a string value and is used to return or set the name that is shown under the attachment, in the body of the item. This can be different from the filename.

```
String = AttachmentObject.DisplayName
AttachmentObject.DisplayName = String
```

FileName Property

The `FileName` property returns a string value that holds the file name of the attachment. It does not include the path name.

```
String = AttachmentObject.FileName
```

Index Property

The `Index` property returns a long integer value representing the `Attachment` object's current position in the `Attachments` collection.

```
Long = AttachmentObject.Index
```

Parent Property

The `Parent` property returns the parent object for the `Attachment` object. This is the Outlook item to which the attachment belongs.

```
Set Object = AttachmentObject.Parent
```

PathName Property

The `PathName` property returns a string value that represents the full path including file name of the attachment. This property is only valid for linked files.

```
String = AttachmentObject.PathName
```

Position Property

The `Position` property is a long integer value that is used to return or set the position of the attachment in the body of the Outlook item. The position is measured as the number of characters, including spaces and carriage return line feeds, from the start of the body text. So if you set the `Position` property to be 34, then there will be 33 characters to the left of the attachment.

```
Long = AttachmentObject.Position
AttachmentObject.Position = Long
```

Session Property

The `Session` property returns the `NameSpace` object for the current session. This will be the messaging application programming interface or MAPI.

```
Set NameSpaceObject = AttachmentObject.Session
```

Type Property

The Type property holds a long integer value that identifies the type of attachment.

```
Long = AttachmentObject.Type
```

The possible types of attachment are:

Constant	Value	Description
olByReference	4	Creates the attachment as a shortcut to the file.
olByValue	1	Creates the attachment as a copy of the original item or file
olEmbeddedItem	5	Creates the attachment as an Outlook item

The Links Collection

The Links collection holds a collection of Link objects. A Link object represents an item associated with another Outlook item. Every Outlook item has a Links collection associated with it, although it may be an empty collection. Currently Link objects may only be items of the type ContactItem object.

The only way to get a reference to a Links collection is through one of the Outlook items. In the example below we use a journal item.

```
Dim ojJournal As JournalItem
Dim olcLinks as Links
...
Set olcLinks = ojJournal.Links
```

Links Collection Methods

Add Method

The Add method creates a new Link object and adds it to the Links collection. Presently, only a contact item can be linked to another item.

```
Set LinkObject = LinksCollection.Add(Item)
```

Name	Data Type	Description
Item	Object	Required, the Outlook item to be added to the Links collection

Example:

```
Dim onMAPI As NameSpace
Dim ofFolder As MAPIFolder
Dim ofContact As MAPIFolder
Dim ocContact As ContactItem
Dim olcLinks As Links
Dim iFor As Integer
```

```
Set onMAPI = Application.GetNamespace("MAPI")
Set ofFolder = onMAPI.PickFolder

If Not ofFolder Is Nothing Then
    Set ofContact = onMAPI.GetDefaultFolder(olFolderContacts)
    Set ocContact = ofContact.Items.Find("[FullName] = 'Dwayne Gifford'")
    For iFor = 1 To ofFolder.Items.count
        Set olcLinks = ofFolder.Items(iFor).Links
        olcLinks.add ocContact
        ofFolder.Items(iFor).Save
    Next
End If
```

In the example above the contact **Dwayne Gifford** is added as a Link object to each of the Outlook items in a user-specified folder.

Item Method

The Item method returns a specified Link object from the Links collection.

```
Set LinkObject = LinksCollection.Item(Index)
```

Name	Data type	Description
Index	Variant	Required, this can be either the name of the Link object or a long value representing the position of the Link object within the collection.

Remove Method

The Remove method deletes the Link object from the Links collection.

```
LinksCollection.Remove Index
```

Name	Data type	Description
Index	Long	Required, the position of the Link object within the collection.

Links Collection Properties

Application Property

The Application property returns the Application object for this session. This will be the Outlook Application object.

```
Set ApplicationObject = LinksCollection.Application
```

Class Property

The Class property holds a long value that identifies the type of object. This will be one of the OlObjectClass constants and for a Links collection is olLinks or 76.

```
Long = LinksCollection.Class
```

Count Property

The Count property returns, as a long, the number of Link objects in the collection.

```
Long = LinksCollection.Count
```

Example:

```
Dim onMAPI As NameSpace
Dim ofFolder As MAPIFolder
Dim olcLinks As Links
Dim olLink As Link
Dim sLinks As String
Dim iFor As Integer
Dim iFor1 As Integer

Set onMAPI = Application.GetNamespace("MAPI")
Set ofFolder = onMAPI.PickFolder

If ofFolder Is Nothing Then Exit Sub

For iFor = 1 To ofFolder.Items.count
    Set olcLinks = ofFolder.Items(iFor).Links
    sLinks = ""
    If olcLinks.count > 0 Then
        For iFor1 = 1 To olcLinks.count
            Set olLink = olcLinks(iFor1)
            sLinks = sLinks & olLink.Name & vbCrLf
        Next
        MsgBox "Item " & ofFolder.Items(iFor).Subject & _
                " has the followling links:" & vbCrLf & sLinks
    End If
Next
```

In the example above the user is asked to choose a folder. The code then runs through each item in the folder and, if the item has contacts linked to it, displays a list of the Link objects.

Parent Property

This property returns the parent object for the Links collection. In this case the Parent property will return a reference to the Outlook item to which the Links collection belongs.

```
Set Object = LinksCollection.Parent
```

Session Property

The Session property returns a reference to the NameSpace object for the current session. This will be the MAPI.

```
Set NameSpaceObject = LinksCollection.Session
```

The Link Object

A Link object represents an item associated with another Outlook item. Currently it can only be a ContactItem object.

A reference to a Link object is set through the Links collection using the Item method. The Item method, discussed above, takes a parameter used to specify the Link object required.

This may either be a long integer representing the position of the `Link` object within the collection or a string holding the name of the link.

```
Dim olcLinks as Links
Dim olLink as Link
...
Set olLink = olcLinks.Item("Link Name")
```

Link Object Properties

Application Property

This property returns the `Application` object for this session. This will be the Outlook `Application` object.

```
Set ApplicationObject = LinkObject.Application
```

Class Property

The `Class` property returns a unique long value that identifies the type of object. This will be one of the `OlObjectClass` constants and in this case is `olLink` or `75`.

```
Long = LinkObject.Class
```

Item Property

The `Item` property returns the Outlook item that is represented by the `Link` object. If the `ContactItem` object that has been added as a link to an Outlook item is deleted or moved from its Contacts folder, then subsequent use of the `Item` property will result in an error being raised.

```
Set ContactItemObject = LinkObject.Item
```

Name Property

The `Name` property returns a string value holding the name of the `Link` object. Currently this is the same as the `Subject` property of the `ContactItem` object.

```
String = LinkObject.Name
```

Parent Property

The `Parent` property returns a reference to the parent object of the `Link` object. This will be the Outlook item to which the `Link` object is associated.

```
Set Object = LinkObject.Parent
```

Session Property

The `Session` property returns the `NameSpace` object for the current session. This will be the MAPI.

```
Set NameSpaceObject = LinkObject.Session
```

Type Property

The `Type` property returns a long integer value that identifies the type of object that the `Link` object represents. This will be one of the `OlObjectClass` constants and since the only object that is currently supported by the `Link` object is a `ContactItem` object, it will be set to `olContact` or `40`.

```
Long = LinkObject.Type
```

The UserProperties Collection

The `UserProperties` collection holds the `UserProperty` objects for an Outlook item. Each of the items that are exposed by Outlook has a `UserProperties` collection, although it may be empty. A `UserProperty` object represents a user-defined property for the item.

A reference to a `UserProperties` collection is set via the Outlook item to which it belongs. For illustration purposes, the following code uses a `MailItem` object.

```
Dim omMail as MailItem
Dim oucUserProperties as UserProperties
…
Set oucUserProperties = omMail.UserProperties
```

UserProperties Collection Methods

Add Method

The `Add` method creates a new `UserProperty` object and adds it to the `UserProperties` collection.

```
Set UserPropertyObject = UserPropertiesCollection.Add(Name, _
                         Type[, AddToFolderFields][, DisplayFormat])
```

Name	Data type	Description
Name	String	Required, the name for the user property.
Type	Long	Required, determines the data type of the user property and must be one of the `OlUserPropertyType` constants given below.
AddToFolder Fields	Boolean	Optional, **True** if the property will be added to the folder fields. This in turns makes this property available to the **Form Designer**. This also allows you to add the property as a column in the `Explorer` object, which can then be used to sort the order of the items in the folder.
Display Format	Long	Optional, the index value of the display format for the `Type` of the custom property.

The `Type` parameter should be set to one of the following `OlUserPropertyType` constants:

Name	Value	Description
olCombination	19	The user property holds a variant
olCurrency	14	The user property holds a currency value
olDateTime	5	The user property holds a date/time value
olDuration	7	The user property holds a number that represents how long something took to complete
olFormula	18	The user property holds a formula
olKeywords	11	The user property holds a delimited string
olNumber	3	The user property holds a number
olPercent	12	The user property holds a percentage value
olText	1	The user property holds a text value
olYesNo	6	The user property holds a Boolean value

Example:

```
Dim onMAPI As NameSpace
Dim ofDrafts As MAPIFolder
Dim omMail As MailItem
Dim oucProperties As UserProperties
Dim ouRep As UserProperty

Set onMAPI = Application.GetNamespace("MAPI")
Set ofDrafts = onMAPI.GetDefaultFolder(olFolderDrafts)
Set omMail = ofDrafts.Items.add(olMailItem)
Set oucProperties = omMail.UserProperties
Set oupProperty - oucProperties.add("Representative", olText, True, 1)

oupProperty.Value = "Dominic"
omMail.Save
```

In the example we create a new `MailItem` object in the **Drafts** folder. With this item we then add a new user property called "Representative" to the `UserProperties` collection. This text property is added to the folder fields. At the same time we set the `DisplayFormat` to be the first format available to the `Text` type. The `DisplayFormat` for each `Type` parameter is shown on the GUI for adding new fields. This can be accessed through the **View | Current View | Customize Current View …** menu.

Then click on the Fields button and New Field to see the form shown below. So the Number Type parameter has 9 possible display formats.

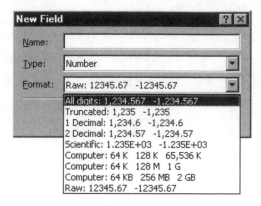

Find Method

The Find method locates and returns a particular UserProperty object, specified by its name. If there is no user property with that name then Nothing is returned.

```
Set UserPropertyObject = UserPropertiesCollection.Find(Name [, Custom])
```

Name	Data type	Description
Name	String	Required, the name of the property
Custom	Boolean	Optional, set to True if a user property and False if a system property. The default is True.

Example:

```
Dim onMAPI As NameSpace
Dim ofDrafts As MAPIFolder
Dim omMail As MailItem
Dim oucProperties As UserProperties
Dim ouRepresentative As UserProperty

Set onMAPI = GetNamespace("MAPI")
Set ofDrafts = onMAPI.GetDefaultFolder(olFolderDrafts)
Set omMail = ofDrafts.Items(1)
Set oucProperties = omMail.UserProperties
Set ouRepresentative = oucProperties.Find("Representative", True)
```

In the example above we set a reference to the first MailItem object in the Drafts folder. The Find method is then used to search for a user property of the item named "Representative".

Item Method

The Item method returns a particular UserProperty object from the UserProperties collection.

```
Set UserPropertyObject = UserPropertiesCollection.Item(Index)
```

Name	Data type	Description
Index	Variant	Required, this is used to identify the user property required. It may be either the name of the user property or a long.

Remove Method

The Remove method deletes a UserProperty object from the UserProperties collection.

```
UserPropertiesCollection.Remove Index
```

Name	Data type	Description
Index	Long	Required, a number representing the position of the UserProperty object within the collection.

UserProperties Collection Properties

Application Property

This property returns the Application object for this session. This will be the Outlook Application object.

```
Set ApplicationObject = UserPropertiesCollection.Application
```

Class Property

The Class property returns a long value that identifies the type of object. This will be one of the OlObjectClass constants. For a UserProperties collection it holds olUserProperties or 38.

```
Long = UserPropertiesCollection.Class
```

Count Property

The Count property returns a long giving the number of UserProperty objects in the collection.

```
Long = UserPropertiesCollection.Count
```

Parent Property

The Parent property returns the parent object for the UserProperties collection. This property will hold a reference to the Outlook item that the UserProperties collection belongs to.

```
Set Object = UserPropertiesCollection.Parent
```

Session Property

The Session property returns the NameSpace object for the current session. This is the messaging application programming interface or MAPI.

```
Set NameSpaceObject = UserPropertiesCollection.Session
```

The UserProperty Object

A UserProperty object represents a user-defined property for the item.

UserProperty Object Methods

Delete Method

The Delete method deletes the referenced UserProperty object from the UserProperties collection.

```
UserPropertyObject.Delete
```

UserProperty Object Properties

Application Property

This property returns the Application object for this session. This will be the Outlook Application object.

```
Set ApplicationObject = UserPropertyObject.Application
```

Class Property

This property returns a long value that identifies the type of object. This will be one of the OlObjectClass constants. In this case it holds olUserProperty or 39.

```
Long = UserPropertyObject.Class
```

Formula Property

The Formula property is a string value that returns or sets the formula for the user property.

```
String = UserPropertyObject.Formula
UserPropertyObject.Formula = String
```

Name Property

The Name property returns a string value, which holds the name for the UserProperty object. This was assigned when the custom property was added to the collection.

```
String = UserPropertyObject.Name
```

Parent Property

This property returns the parent object for the UserProperty object. This will reference the Outlook item that the UserProperty object belongs to.

```
Set Object = UserPropertyObject.Parent
```

Session Property

The Session property returns the NameSpace object for the current session.

```
Set NameSpaceObject = UserPropertyObject.Session
```

Type Property

The Type property returns a long integer value indicating the data type of the user property.

```
Long = UserPropertyObject.Type
```

This will be one of the OlUserPropertyType constants.

Constant	Value	Description
olCombination	19	The user property holds a variant
olCurrency	14	The user property holds a currency value
olDateTime	5	The user property holds a date/time value
olDuration	7	The user property holds a number that represents how long something took to complete
olFormula	18	The user property holds a formula
olKeywords	11	The user property holds a delimited string
olNumber	3	The user property holds a number
olPercent	12	The user property holds a percentage value
olText	1	The user property holds a text value
olYesNo	6	The user property holds a Boolean value

ValidationFormula Property

The ValidationFormula property is a string value that can be used to return or set a descriptive string for the validation formula. It does not have any functionality.

```
String = UserPropertyObject.ValidationFormula
UserPropertyObject.ValidationFormula = String
```

ValidationText Property

The ValidationText property is a string value that is used to return or set a message that can be shown if validation fails.

```
String = UserPropertyObject.ValidationText
UserPropertyObject.ValidationText = String
```

Value Property

The Value property is a variant that returns or sets the value of the custom property.

```
Variant = UserPropertyObject.Value
UserPropertyObject.Value = Variant
```

The Actions Collection

The Actions collection holds a collection of Action objects for an Outlook item. An Action object represents a unique action that can be executed on the Outlook item.

A reference is set to an Actions collection through an Outlook item. This can be any of the Outlook items and in the example below the JournalItem object is used.

```
Dim ojJournal As JournalItem
Dim oacActions as Actions
...
Set oacActions = ojJournal.Actions
```

Actions Collection Methods

Add Method

The Add method provides a means to add a custom Action object to the Actions collection for the current item. It returns a reference to the new Action object.

```
Set ActionObject = ActionsCollection.Add
```

The reference to the Action object returned by this method can then be used to set the properties and functionality of the custom action. A custom action inherits the functionality of an existing action.

Item Method

The Item method returns a particular Action object from the Actions collection. The Action object returned is specified by an index parameter.

```
Set ActionObject = ActionsCollection.Item(Index)
```

Name	Data type	Description
Index	Variant	Required, this can either be a string holding the name of the Action object or a long representing the position of the Action object within the collection.

Remove Method

The Remove method deletes a specified Action object from the Actions collection.

```
ActionsCollection.Remove Index
```

Name	Data type	Description
Index	Long	Required, a long representing the position of the Action object within the collection.

Actions Collection Properties

Application Property

This property returns the `Application` object for this session. This will be the Outlook `Application` object.

```
Set ApplicationObject = ActionsCollection.Application
```

Class Property

The `Class` property returns a long value that identifies the type of object. This will be one of the `OlObjectClass` constants and in this case is `olActions` or `33`.

```
Long = ActionsCollection.Class
```

Count Property

The `Count` property returns the number of `Action` objects within the collection.

```
Long = ActionsCollection.Class
```

Parent Property

This property returns the parent object for the `Actions` collection. This property will reference the Outlook item that the `Actions` collection belongs to.

```
Set Object = ActionsCollection.Parent
```

Session Property

The `Session` property returns the `NameSpace` object for the current session.

```
Set NameSpaceObject = ActionsCollection.Session
```

The Action Object

An `Action` object represents a unique action that can be executed on the Outlook item. There is a small number of Outlook actions and it is possible to add user-defined actions to an item's `Actions` collection. These custom actions inherit their functionality from the existing Outlook actions via the `CopyLike` property described below. This means that any new actions are merely copies of an existing Outlook action with fairly superficial cosmetic changes.

A reference is set to an existing `Action` object through the `Item` method of the `Actions` collection to which it belongs. This method is described above.

```
Dim oaAction as Action
...
Set oaAction = oacActions.Item(Index)
```

To create and reference a new `Action` object employ the `Add` method of an `Actions` collection.

```
Dim oaAction as Action
...
Set oaAction = oacActions.Add
```

Action Object Methods

Delete Method

The `Delete` method removes the current `Action` object from an `Actions` collection.

```
ActionObject.Delete
```

Execute Method

The `Execute` method carries out the action and returns the new Outlook item that is created when the action is executed.

```
Set Object = ActionObject.Execute
```

Action Object Properties

Application Property

This property returns the `Application` object for this session. This is the Outlook `Application` object.

```
Set ApplicationObject = ActionObject.Application
```

Class Property

The `Class` property returns a long value that identifies the type of object. This will be one of the `OlObjectClass` constants and in this case is `olAction` or `32`.

```
Long = ActionObject.Class
```

CopyLike Property

The `CopyLike` property is a long integer that is used to return or set the inheritance style for the action. When the action is executed a new item is created and this property determines how the properties are copied over to the new item.

```
Long = ActionObject.CopyLike
ActionObject.CopyLike = Long
```

`CopyLike` property holds one of the `OlActionCopyLike` constants.

Name	Value	Description
olForward	2	The new item will only have the body and subject of the original item.
olReply	0	Default. The new item will have the originator of the item in the **TO** line and the subject and body of the original item.
olReplyAll	1	The new item will have all recipients of the original item in the **CC** line and the originator in the **TO** line. The subject and body will be copied from the original.
olReplyFolder	3	A new post item is created with the conversation, body and **Post To** copied from the original.
olRespond	4	As olReply, but a message requesting the user to respond is added to the GUI of the original item.

In the example below a custom action named "Forward with BCC" is added to the first item in the user's default **Inbox**.

Example:

```
Dim onMAPI As NameSpace
Dim omMail As MailItem
Dim omForwardBCC As MailItem
Dim ofInbox As MAPIFolder
Dim oaAction As Action
Dim oacActions As Actions

Set onMAPI = GetNamespace("MAPI")
Set ofInbox = onMAPI.GetDefaultFolder(olFolderInbox)
Set omMail = ofInbox.Items.GetFirst
Set oacActions = omMail.Actions
Set oaAction = oacActions.add

oaAction.Enabled = True
oaAction.Prefix = "Outlook Project"
oaAction.ReplyStyle = olIndentOriginalText

oaAction.CopyLike = olReply
oaAction.Name = "ReplyOP"

omMail.Actions.Item("ReplyOP").Execute
```

The Enabled property is set to **True**, which means this property can be executed. Then a prefix of "Outlook Project:" is added to the subject and the ReplyStyle property is set so that the original text will be indented. Finally the functionality is set via the CopyLike property to olReply.

Enabled Property

The `Enabled` property holds a read/write Boolean value that determines whether or not the action is enabled. The default for this property is True, which means that the action can be executed on the Outlook item.

```
Boolean = ActionObject.Enabled
ActionObject.Enabled = Boolean
```

MessageClass Property

The `MessageClass` property returns the message class for the item that will be created upon execution of the action. For custom actions it returns an empty string.

```
String = ActionObject.MessageClass
ActionObject.MessageClass = String
```

Name Property

The `Name` property is a string value that is used to return or set the display name for the action.

```
String = ActionObject.Name
ActionObject.Name = String
```

Parent Property

This property returns the parent object for the `Action` object. This will be the particular Outlook item to which the action belongs.

```
Set Object = ActionObject.Parent
```

Prefix Property

The `Prefix` property returns or sets a string value that represents the prefix to be used in the subject of the item created when the action is carried out. A colon will be added automatically at the end of the prefix.

```
String = ActionObject.Prefix
ActionObject.Prefix = String
```

ReplyStyle Property

The `ReplyStyle` property holds a long integer value that is used to return or set the formatting to be used for the new item.

```
Long = ActionObject.ReplyStyle
ActionObject.ReplyStyle = Long
```

The `ReplyStyle` property holds one of the `OlActionReplyStyle` constants:

Constant	Value	Description
olOmitOriginalText	0	The original text is not included in the reply.
olEmbedOriginalItem	1	The original item is included in the reply as an attachment.

Constant	Value	Description
olInclude OriginalText	2	The original text is included in the reply.
olIndentOriginalText	3	The original text is included in the reply and indented.
olLinkOriginalItem	4	A shortcut to the original item is included in the text as an attachment.
olUserPreference	5	The user's default reply style is used.
olReplyTick OriginalText	1000	The original text is included with a greater than sign before each line.

ResponseStyle Property

The ResponseStyle property is a long integer value used to return or set the response to be used when the action is executed via the GUI of the Outlook item.

```
Long = ActionObject.ResponseStyle
ActionObject.ResponseStyle = Long
```

The ResponseStyle property holds one of the OlActionResponseStyle constants:

Constant	Value	Description
olOpen	0	The new item is opened for the user to edit.
olPrompt	2	The user is asked if they would like to edit the message before it is sent.
olSend	1	The item is sent without providing the user with an opportunity to make changes.

Session Property

The Session property returns the NameSpace object for the current session. This will be the messaging application programming interface or MAPI.

```
Set NameSpaceObject = ActionObject.Session
```

ShowOn Property

The ShowOn property returns or sets a long integer value that represents where the action is made available on the GUI when the Outlook item that the action belongs to is opened.

```
Long = ActionObject.Showon
ActionObject.Showon = Long
```

The `ShowOn` property will hold one of the `OlActionShowOn` constants:

Constant	Value	Description
olDontShow	0	The action is not available on the GUI.
olMenu	2	The action is shown in the **Actions** menu.
olMenuandToolbar	1	The action is shown on the **Toolbar** and in the **Actions** menu.

FormDescription Object

The `FormDescription` object represents the general properties for an **Outlook** form. At the moment, this is all that we can actually do with this object: we cannot make any changes to the form other than set the properties that define the form for Outlook. We cannot programmatically place controls on the form or define its appearance.

If you want to design a form, you must open an instance of the pre-existing form that most closely resembles the form you want to create in design mode. To do this, you must select **Tools | Forms | Design a Form…**. I would recommend at the moment that you use this Form Designer to create your new forms rather than the `FormDescription` object. The reason for this is that in the designer you can develop the form in one go, whereas with this object, you would have to use the form designer for the physical design of the form anyway.

We can get a reference to an item's `FormDescription` object through its `FormDescription` property. For example, to get a `MailItem`'s `FormDescription`, we might write:

```
Dim omMail As MailItem
Dim ofdDescription As FormDescription
...
Set ofdDescription = omMail.FormDescription
```

FormDescription Method

PublishForm Method

The `PublishForm` method saves the definition of the `FormDescription` object to the specified form registry.

FormDescriptionObject.PublishForm(*Registry*[, *Folder*])

Name	Data type	Description
Registry	Long	Required, defines the class of the form and is one of the `olFormRegistry` constants.
Folder	MAPIFolder object	Optional, except if `Registry` is `olFolderRegistry`. Equates to a valid `MAPIFolder` object.

Registry can be any of the following `OlFormRegistry` constants:

Constant	Value	Description
olDefaultRegistry	0	The item is handled without regard to its form class.
olPersonalRegistry	2	Only the current profile can access the forms.
olFolderRegistry	3	The form is exposed to any user with access to the folder.
olOrganization Registry	4	The form is to be shared across the entire enterprise: all users in the organization have access to the form.

The following code demonstrates the use of this method:

```
Dim ofdDescription As FormDescription
Dim ocContact As ContactItem

Set ocContact = CreateItem(olContactItem)
Set ofdDescription = ocContact.FormDescription
With ofdDescription
    .Comment = "New custom Form WROX."
    .Name = "Wrox Contact"
    .DisplayName = "WROX Contact Item"
    .Number = "1.1"
    .Version = "2.0"
    .Password = "WROX"
    .Locked = True
    .PublishForm olDefaultRegistry
End With
```

In the example above we create a new `ContactItem` object and get a reference to its `FormDescription` object. Once we have this reference we set its properties as desired. It is particularly important that we set the `Name` property, since the `PublishForm` method will cause an error if this value is not set

Once we have set the appropriate properties we then use the `PublishForm` method to commit the custom form to the default registry. This form will now appear in the Personal Forms Library under its display name **WROX Contact Item** if the user selects <u>T</u>ools | <u>F</u>orms | Ch<u>o</u>ose Form... or <u>T</u>ools | <u>F</u>orms | <u>D</u>esign a Form... In order to modify this form, the user will be required to enter the password that we set in the code.

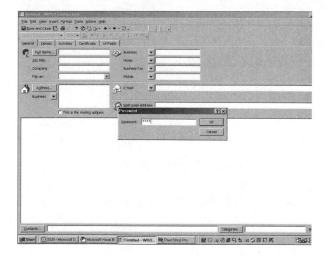

FormDescription Properties

Application Property

The `Application` property returns the `Application` object for this session. This property does not appear on the GUI.

```
Set ApplicationObject = FormDescriptionObject.Application
```

Category Property

The `Category` property is a string value that returns or sets the category that is to be used by the custom form; this property can be used to group together related forms.

```
String = FormDescriptionObject.Category
FormDescriptionObject.Category = String
```

CategorySub Property

The `CategorySub` property is a string value that returns or sets the sub-category that is to be used by the custom form; this property can be used to group forms within a specific `Category`.

```
String = FormDescriptionObject.CategorySub
FormDescriptionObject.CategorySub = String
```

Class Property

This returns one of the `OlObjectClass` constants which identifies the type of the object in question. For a `FormDescription` object, the value is `olFormDescription` or 37.

```
Long = FormDescriptionObject.Class
```

Comment Property

The `Comment` property is a string value that returns or updates the comment for the `FormDescription`. This is a description designed to explain the function of the form.

```
String = FormDescriptionObject.Comment
FormDescriptionObject.Comment = String
```

ContactName Property

The `ContactName` property is a string value that returns or sets the name of the person that should be contacted for more information on the current custom form.

```
String = FormDescriptionObject.ContactName
FormDescriptionObject.ContactName = String
```

DisplayName Property

The `DisplayName` property is a string value that returns or sets the name that will be shown in the **Choose Form...** dialog box.

```
String = FormDescriptionObject.DisplayName
FormDescriptionObject.DisplayName = String
```

> Note that setting the `DisplayName` to a given value also causes the `Name` property to be set to the same value if the `Name` property is an empty string. Otherwise the `Name` property remains unchanged.

Hidden Property

The `Hidden` property is a Boolean value which indicates whether the form is to be made available from the Outlook menus and the Choose Form... dialog. Setting this to `True` means that this form can only be instantiated by other custom forms (in the same way that we cannot directly create a `MeetingItem` or `TaskRequestItem`). The default value for this property is `False`.

```
Boolean = FormDescriptionObject.Hidden
FormDescriptionObject.Hidden = Boolean
```

Icon Property

The `Icon` property is a string value that returns or sets the path and filename for the large icon for items based on the custom form.

```
String = FormDescriptionObject.Hidden
FormDescriptionObject.Hidden = String
```

Locked Property

The `Locked` property is a Boolean value that returns or sets whether changes can be made to the custom form. If set to **False**, users are permitted to make changes; if set to `True`, they will have to enter a password before they can access the form in design mode. For this property to have any effect you must also set a password on the custom form.

```
Boolean = FormDescriptionObject.Locked
FormDescriptionObject.Locked = Boolean
```

MessageClass Property

The `MessageClass` property returns a string identifying the type of item currently in use. Since we are creating a new form, we will need to use this property to link an item object to the form. This property will be set to the original item's `MessageClass` with a period and the `Name` property appended. This property is read-only and cannot be updated.

```
String = FormDescriptionObject.MessageClass
```

MiniIcon Property

The `MiniIcon` property is a string value that returns or sets the path and filename for the small icon for items based on the custom form.

```
String = FormDescriptionObject.MiniIcon
FormDescriptionObject.MiniIcon = String
```

Name Property

The `Name` property is a string value that returns or sets the caption for the form. It is also appended to the form's `MessageClass`.

```
String = FormDescriptionObject.Name
FormDescriptionObject.Name = String
```

> Note that setting the `Name` to a given value will also set the `DisplayName` property to that value if this has not already been set. Otherwise, the `DisplayName` property remains unchanged.

Number Property

The `Number` property is a string value that returns or sets a number that can be used to help identify the form.

```
String = FormDescriptionObject.Number
FormDescriptionObject.Number = String
```

OneOff Property

The `OneOff` property is a Boolean value that returns or sets whether the form is to be kept as a custom form or used only once and discarded. By default the `OneOff` property is `False`, specifying that Outlook is to retain the custom form.

```
Boolean = FormDescriptionObject.OneOff
FormDescriptionObject.OneOff = Boolean
```

Parent Property

This property returns a reference to the parent object for the current `FormDescription` object. This will always be the Outlook item from which the reference to the `FormDescription` object was obtained.

```
Set Object = FormDescriptionObject.Parent
```

Password Property

The `Password` property is a string value that returns or sets the password that a user will have to enter in order to modify the custom form. To force the user to enter a password, `Locked` must be set to `True`. The password property is case-sensitive, so that, for example, `"Bob"` and `"bob"` are not the same.

```
String = FormDescriptionObject.Password
FormDescriptionObject.Password = String
```

ScriptText Property

The `ScriptText` property returns a string value containing all of the VBScript code for the custom form.

```
String = FormDescriptionObject.ScriptText
```

Session Property

The `Session` property returns a reference to the `NameSpace` object for the current session.

```
Set NameSpaceObject = FormDescriptionObject.Session
```

Template Property

The `Template` property is a string value that returns or sets the filename for the Word template that is to be used by the custom form. This is only valid if `UseWordMail` is set to `True`.

```
FormDescriptionObject.Template = String
```

UseWordMail Property

The `UseWordMail` property is a Boolean value, which returns or sets whether items based on the form are to use `Word` as the default editor. The default value is `False`, indicating that Word is not the default editor.

```
Boolean = FormDescriptionObject.UseWordMail
FormDescriptionObject.UseWordMail = Boolean
```

Version Property

The `Version` property is a string value that can be used to return or set a version number for the form; this could be used to identify different versions of a custom form.

```
String = FormDescriptionObject.Version
FormDescriptionObject.Version = String
```

12

Contacts

In Outlook a contact is someone with whom you communicate via email on a professional or personal basis. A `ContactItem` object is used to hold information about a particular contact and to access that information in a useful manner. This information is held in up to 144 different properties that the `ContactItem` object exposes to us. A typical contact item displayed in an Explorer is shown below.

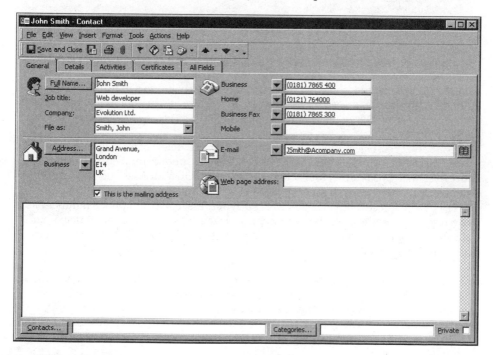

In this figure you can see just a handful of the properties that the `ContactItem` object has to offer.

There are two ways to create a new `ContactItem` object through code. The first uses the `CreateItem` of the `Application` object.

```
Dim ocContact As ContactItem
Set ocContact = Application.CreateItem(olContactItem)
```

The second employs the `Add` method of an `Items` collection. An `Items` collection holds all the Outlook items that sit in a particular `MAPIFolder`, and is covered in detail in chapter 11.

```
Dim oicItems As Items
Dim ocContact As ContactItem
…
Set ocContact = oicItems.Add(olContactItem)
```

To set a reference to an existing `ContactItem` object it is necessary to navigate via the `MAPIFolder` in which it resides and use the `Item` method of the `Items` collection held in that `MAPIFolder`. In the example below a reference is set to the first contact item in the default **Contacts** folder.

Example:

```
Dim ofContacts As MAPIFolder
Dim oicItems As Items
Dim ocContact As ContactItem

Set ofContacts =
Application.GetNamespace("MAPI").GetDefaultFolder(olFolderContacts)
Set oicItems = ofContacts.Items
Set ocContact = oicItems.Item(1)
```

The `Item` method of the items collection may also take a string parameter to identify the particular contact item. The property of the `ContactItem` object used as the identifier in this method is the default `Subject` property but this in turn depends upon which properties are set for the contact item. More information is given about the `Subject` property later in the chapter.

The `ContactItem` object allows you to create, edit and delete contact information. According to Microsoft this includes several addresses, phone numbers and e-mail addresses. In fact you can set four addresses, three e-mail addresses and 19 telephone numbers. If that isn't enough for you, then you can always set up more with the `UserProperties` covered in chapter 11. Each address, email and phone number has its own set of properties, which to me seems a strange way to set up the contact item. Collections would seem more suited to this purpose and would allow you to have as many addresses, emails etc. as you want.

Another type of item that can be held in a **Contacts** folder is the `DistList` object. This represents a group of contacts, related to one another in some way, held under a common name. This object can then be used as a recipient of an Outlook item and means that the user does not have to type in each of the individual email addresses. More details on this object are given later in the chapter.

ContactItem Methods

Close Method

The `Close` method is used to shutdown the `Inspector` object that is showing the contact information.

```
ContactItem.Close(SaveMode)
```

Name	Data type	Description
SaveMode	Long	Required, determines whether any changes to the `DocumentItem` are saved or discarded when the item closes and whether the user is asked if they wish to save any changes.

The `SaveMode` parameter will be one of the `OlInspectorClose` constants given below.

Constant	Value	Description
olDiscard	1	Discard all changes to the item and without prompting
olPromptForSave	2	Prompt the user to **Save** or **Discard** the item
olSave	0	Save the changes without prompting the user

Note that if the item is not open then this method will still have an effect. If you make a change to an item through code, using the `Close` method with `olPromptForSave` or `olSave`, then the user will either be prompted to save changes or the changes will be saved without prompting.

Copy Method

The `Copy` method creates a new `ContactItem` object that holds identical information to the current contact item.

```
Set ContactItem = ContactItem.Copy
```

The following code could be run to create a backup of contact items before contact information in a particular folder is updated.

Example:

```
Dim onMAPI As NameSpace
Dim ofContactFolder As MAPIFolder
```

```
Dim ofArchiveFolder As MAPIFolder
Dim ocContact As ContactItem
Dim ocOldContact As ContactItem
Dim iFor As Integer

Set onMAPI = Application.GetNamespace("MAPI")
Set ofContactFolder = onMAPI.PickFolder
Set ofArchiveFolder =
ofContactFolder.Folders.add(ofContactFolder.Name & "Archive",
olFolderContacts)

For iFor = 1 To ofContactFolder.Items.count
    If ofContactFolder.Items.Item(iFor).MessageClass = _
            "IPM.Contact" Then
        Set ocContact = ofContactFolder.Items.Item(iFor)
        Set ocOldContact = ocContact.Copy
        ocOldContact.Move ofArchiveFolder
    End If
Next
```

In the example above the user is asked to choose the folder whose contacts they want to make a back-up of. A sub-folder of that folder is then created with the same name as the original but with the string "Archive" appended. Each ContactItem object in the chosen folder is then copied and the copy moved into the new Archive sub-folder.

Delete Method

The Delete method removes the current ContactItem object from the Items collection holding it.

```
ContactItem.Delete
```

Display Method

The Display method will activate an Inspector object for the current ContactItem object. If the contact item is already open then this method will bring the Inspector to the front of the screen. Otherwise this method will open an new Inspector object in which to display the contact.

```
ContactItem.Display(Modal)
```

Name	Data type	Description
Modal	Boolean	Required, determines whether the Inspector object is shown modally, True, or in a modeless state, False.

This method displays the ContactItem object and can be used to set a reference to the Inspector object. If you wish simply to set a reference to the Inspector object but not make it visible to the user employ the GetInspector property, which is explained later in the chapter.

ForwardAsVcard Method

The `ForwardAsVcard` method sends the current contact item as an attachment to a `MailItem` object.

```
Set MailItemObject = ContactItem.ForwardAsVcard
```

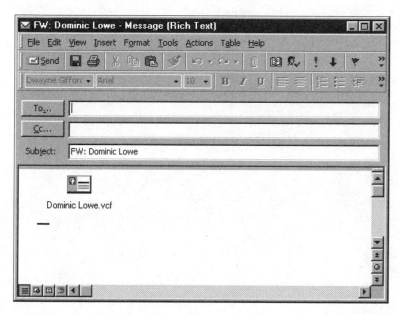

As the above figure shows, the `ContactItem` object for "Dominic Lowe" is attached to a mail item that can be sent. When the recipient of such a mail opens the attachment it appears in the form of a contact item. For information on the `MailItem` object refer to chapter 13.

Move Method

The `Move` method moves the current `ContactItem` object to a new MAPIFolder. It makes sense to move a contact to a folder that supports `ContactItem` objects. However, there is no such restriction and if a contact is moved to a different type of folder, such as the **Notes** folder, it will be transformed into the appropriate item type. The figure below shows a contact that has been moved to the **Notes** folder.

```
ContactItem.Move NewFolder
```

Name	Description
NewFolder	Required, an existing MAPIFolder object.

This method could be used to move all contacts that work at the same company to a company-specific **Contacts** folder.

Example:

```
Dim onMAPI As NameSpace
Dim offolder As MAPIFolder
Dim bFolderExists As Boolean
Dim ofWROXFolder As MAPIFolder
Dim ocContact As ContactItem
Set onMAPI = Application.GetNamespace("MAPI")
Set offolder = onMAPI.PickFolder
bFolderExists = False
For iFor = 1 To offolder.Folders.count
    If offolder.Folders(iFor).Name = "WROX" Then
        bFolderExists = True
        Exit For
    End If
Next

If bFolderExists = True Then
    Set ofWROXFolder = offolder.Folders.Item("WROX")
Else
    Set ofWROXFolder = offolder.Folders.add("WROX",
olFolderContacts)
End If

For iFor = 1 To offolder.Items.count
    If offolder.Items(iFor).MessageClass = "IPM.Contact" Then
        Set ocContact = offolder.Items(iFor)
        If ocContact.CompanyName = "WROX" Then
            ocContact.Move ofWROXFolder
        End If
    End If
Next
ofWROXFolder.Display
```

The example above prompts the user to select a folder and then checks to see if the WROX sub-folder exists. If it does then a reference to it is set, otherwise a WROX folder is created. We then move through the chosen folder looking for contacts that work for WROX. Any that are found are moved to the WROX sub-folder, which is then displayed to the user.

PrintOut Method

The `PrintOut` method is used to print the contact item, creating a hard copy of the contact information.

```
ContactItem.PrintOut
```

This method uses your default printer settings and only prints the properties that are located on the first two tabs of the ContactItem object GUI.

Save Method

The `Save` method is used to save the `ContactItem` object to the current MAPIFolder or if this is a new contact item then it is saved to the default MAPIFolder, which is the Outlook created Contacts folder.

```
ContactItem.Save
```

SaveAs Method

The `SaveAs` method allows you to save the `ContactItem` object to disk.

```
ContactItem.SaveAs(Path [, Type])
```

Name	Data type	Description
Path	String	Required, a valid path and filename for the new file
Type	Long	Optional, determines the form the saved file takes

The `Type` must be one of the following `OlSaveAsType` constants given below.

Constant	Value	Description
olMSG	3	Outlook Message format
olRTF	1	Rich Text Format
olTemplate	2	Outlook Template
olTXT	0	Text file
olVCard	7	Virtual business card format

ContactItem Properties

Because the `ContactItem` object exposes 144 different properties I am going to move away from the strictly alphabetical format used in other chapters. I am going to group together the Address properties, Email properties and the Telephone properties to avoid needless repetition. The other properties will be covered as usual.

Addresses

There are 28 properties available for addresses, each address comprising 7 properties. The four different Address types are Business, Home, Mailing and Other.

BusinessAddress	HomeAddress
BusinessAddressCity	HomeAddressCity

Table Continued on Following Page

BusinessAddressCountry	HomeAddressCountry
BusinessAddressPostalCode	HomeAddressPostalCode
BusinessAddressPostOfficeBox	HomeAddressPostOfficeBox
BusinessAddressState	HomeAddressState
BusinessAddressStreet	HomeAddressStreet
MailingAddress	OtherAddress
MailingAddressCity	OtherAddressCity
MailingAddressCountry	OtherAddressCountry
MailingAddressPostalCode	OtherAddressPostalCode
MailingAddressPostOfficeBox	OtherAddressPostOfficeBox
MailingAddressState	OtherAddressState
MailingAddressStreet	OtherAddressStreet

In fact only three different addresses can be set, as the Mailing address will be a copy of one of the other addresses, depending on the value of the SelectedMailingAddress property, discussed later. Note that if the Mailing address fields are changed then the associated address fields also change, and vice versa.

> As each of the seven properties is described below a pseudo-property name will be used which is the same as the property name but with the type of address replaced with an asterisk, e.g. *Address will be used to represent the BusinessAddress, HomeAddress, MailingAddress and OtherAddress properties.

All of these properties are free form string properties, meaning you can enter whatever text you wish.

*Address

This property sets or returns the complete address for the contact.

```
String = ContactItem.*Address
ContactItem.*Address = String
```

If you set this property through code it will also set the AddressState and AddressCity properties. If no commas are placed in the string then the Address and the AddressState is set to the whole string and properties other than these two are set to empty strings. If commas are used as address field separators, everything before the last comma is set to be the AddressCity and everything after the final comma is set as the AddressState property.

> It is probably wise to use the individual address fields if you want to set addresses through code.

*AddressCity

The *AddressCity property is used to return or set the city field of the address as a string. Changing this property will also change the appropriate part of the Address property.

```
String = ContactItem.*AddressCity
ContactItem.*AddressCity = String
```

*AddressCountry

The *AddressCountry property is used to return or set the country field of the address as a string. Changing this property will also change the appropriate part of the Address property.

```
String = ContactItem.*AddressCountry
ContactItem.*AddressCountry = String
```

*AddressPostalCode

The *AddressPostalCode property is used to return or set the postal code field of the address as a string. Changing this property will also change the appropriate part of the Address property.

```
String = ContactItem.*AddressPostalCode
ContactItem.*AddressPostalCode = String
```

*AddressPostOfficeBox

The *AddressPostOfficeBox property is used to return or set the post office box field.

```
String = ContactItem.*AddressPostOfficeBox
ContactItem.*AddressPostOfficeBox = String
```

*AddressState

The *AddressState property is used to return or set the state field of the address as a string. Changing this property will also change the appropriate part of the Address property.

```
String = ContactItem.*AddressState
ContactItem.*AddressState = String
```

*AddressStreet

The *AddressStreet property is used to return or set the street field of the address as a string. Changing this property will also change the appropriate part of the Address property.

```
String = ContactItem.*AddressStreet
ContactItem.*AddressStreet = String
```

Telephone Numbers

There are 19 different telephone properties available from the `ContactItem` object:

AssistantTelephoneNumber	Business2TelephoneNumber
BusinessFaxNumber	BusinessTelephoneNumber
CallbackTelephoneNumber	CarTelephoneNumber
CompanyMainTelephoneNumber	Home2TelephoneNumber
HomeFaxNumber	HomeTelephoneNumber
ISDNNumber	MobileTelephoneNumber
OtherFaxNumber	OtherTelephoneNumber
PagerNumber	PrimaryTelephoneNumber
RadioTelephoneNumber	TelexNumber
TTYTDDTelephoneNumber	

Any one of the above properties allows you to return or update a telephone or fax number. All these properties hold string values.

```
String = ContactItem.TelephoneNumber
ContactItem.TelephoneNumber = String
```

EMAIL Information

There is a total of 12 email properties available to the `ContactItem` object.

Email1Address	Email2Address	Email3Address
Email1AddressType	Email2AddressType	Email3AddressType
Email1DisplayName	Email2DisplayName	Email3DisplayName
Email1EntryID	Email2EntryID	Email3EntryID

These properties are required by the `Recipient` object. This is the information that is returned when you resolve a `Recipient` object that has a corresponding `ContactItem` object. For more information on the `Recipient` object refer to chapter 10.

> A pseudo-property, where an asterisk replaces the number of the email, will be used to cover all three properties, one for each email.

Email*Address

The `Email*Address` property returns or sets an email address for the contact. You must ensure that this is a valid email address, as Outlook will not. If an invalid address is used on an outgoing Outlook item you will receive system generated "undeliverable mail" message.

```
String = ContactItem.Email*Address
ContactItem.Email*Address = String
```

Email*AddressType

This property returns or sets the email type for the contact. These properties are free form strings but should match an existing mail transport, such as SMTP.

```
String = ContactItem.Email*AddressType
ContactItem.Email*AddressType = String
```

Email*DisplayName

The Email*DisplayName property returns a string holding the email display name for the contact. This is set by Outlook to be the FullName property with "(E-mail *)" appended.

```
String = ContactItem.Email*DisplayName
```

Email*EntryID

This property returns the email EntryID for the contact. This is created when the email entry is saved.

```
String = ContactItem.Email*EntryID
```

Most of the remaining properties can be found somewhere on the contact item GUI. Although some of them do not appear on the first two tabs, the majority of the properties are shown in the All Fields tab of the GUI.

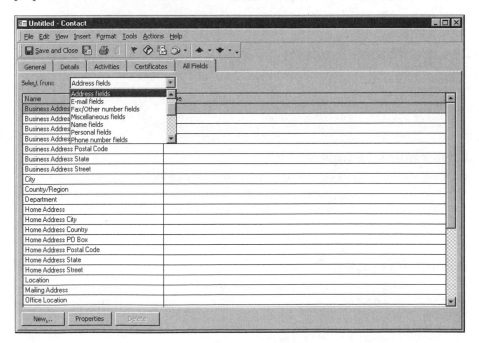

Account Property

The `Account` property returns and updates the account for the contact. This is a free form string that can hold any text value you wish.

```
String = ContactItem.Account
ContactItem.Account = String
```

Actions Property

The `Actions` property returns a reference to the `Actions` collection available for the `ContactItem` object. These are special actions that can be executed on the `ContactItem` object. The actions in this collection are **Reply, Reply to All, Forward** and **Reply to Folder**. They can all be executed but it is difficult to imagine why you might want to use them.

```
Set ActionsCollection = ContactItem.Actions
```

Anniversary Property

The `Anniversary` property returns and sets the date of an anniversary for the contact. If it has not been set then this property will return a value of **01/01/4501**.

```
Date = ContactItem.Anniversary
ContactItem.Anniversary = Date
```

Application Property

The `Application` property returns the `Application` object for the current session. This will be the **Outlook** `Application` object.

```
Set ApplicationObject = ContactItem.Application
```

AssistantName Property

The `AssistantName` property can be used to return or set the name of the assistant for the contact.

```
String = ContactItem.AssistantName
ContactItem.AssistantName = String
```

Attachments Property

The `Attachments` property can be used to set a reference to the `Attachments` collection for the `ContactItem` object. Attachments are documents or links to documents added to an **Outlook** item and are covered in detail in chapter 11.

```
Set AttachmentsCollection = ContactItem.Attachments
```

BillingInformation Property

The `BillingInformation` property is used to set or return the billing information for the contact. This property is free form string and can hold anything.

```
String = ContactItem.BillingInformation
ContactItem.BillingInformation = String
```

Birthday Property

The Birthday property is used to return or set the birthday date for the contact. If no birthday date has been set for the contact then 01/01/4501 will be returned.

```
Date = ContactItem.Birthday
ContactItem.Birthday = Date
```

Body Property

The Body property returns or sets the text seen in the body of the contact. This is also where the attachments are shown but they do not form part of the body.

```
String = ContactItem.Body
ContactItem.Body = String
```

BusinessHomePage Property

The BusinessHomePage property returns or sets the URL for the web page for the business of the contact.

```
String = ContactItem.BusinessHomePage
ContactItem.BusinessHomePage = String
```

Categories Property

The Categories property returns or sets the categories for the ContactItem object. If more than one category is associated with the contact, they should be separated by commas. Categories are used to group items that are related to one another in some way.

```
String = ContactItem.Categories
ContactItem.Categories = String
```

The advantage of assigning items to different categories is that you can then search for the items by category.

Children Property

The Children property can be used to return or set the names of the children of the contact. This is a free form string and any text can be entered.

```
String = ContactItem.Children
ContactItem.Children = String
```

Class Property

The Class property returns a long integer value that identifies the object's type. This will be one of the OlObjectClass constants and for a contact item is olContact or 40.

```
Long = ContactItem.Class
```

Companies Property

The `Companies` property is used to return or set the company names that are associated with the contact. This is a free form string and can be set to whatever text you wish.

```
String = ContactItem.Companies
ContactItem.Companies = String
```

CompanyAndFullName Property

The `CompanyAndFullName` property holds the concatenated string of the `CompanyName` and the `FullName` properties of the contact. This property and the 10 other similar properties seem a little pointless as you could manipulate the string values returned by these properties in any way you wish.

```
String = ContactItem.CompanyAndFullName
```

CompanyLastFirstNoSpace Property

The `CompanyLastFirstNoSpace` property returns a string holding the company name, last name and first name of the contact without any spaces in between. This property seems somewhat redundant.

```
String = ContactItem.CompanyLastFirstNoSpace
```

CompanyLastFirstSpaceOnly Property

The `CompanyLastFirstSpaceOnly` property returns a string holding the company name, last name and first name of the contact with a space between the last name and first name of the contact.

```
String = ContactItem.CompanyLastFirstSpaceOnly
```

284

CompanyName Property

The CompanyName property is used to return or set the name of the company for whom the contact works.

```
String = ContactItem.CompanyName
ContactItem.CompanyName = String
```

ComputerNetworkName Property

The ComputerNetworkName property returns or sets the name of the computer network for the contact. This is a free form string property.

```
String = ContactItem.ComputerNetworkName
ContactItem.ComputerNetworkName = String
```

ConversationIndex Property

The ConversationIndex property returns the index of the conversation thread. This property appears to be redundant for this particular item. It does, however, return a string whose ASCII value is 22.

```
String = ContactItem.ConversationIndex
```

ConversationTopic Property

The ConversationTopic property returns the topic of conversation for the contact. This property seems to be set to the contact's name if the ContactItem object is created by moving a mail message from the contact to a contacts folder. Otherwise it holds an empty string. This property would appear to be of limited use.

```
String = ContactItem.ConversationTopic
```

CreationTime Property

The CreationTime property holds the date and time that the contact information was created. For a newly created contact, this property holds 01/01/4501.

```
Date = ContactItem.CreationTime
```

CustomerID Property

The CustomerID property is used to return or set the customer ID for the contact. This is not something that Outlook generates. It is simply a string that can be assigned to the contact by the user in order to identify it.

```
String = ContactItem.CustomerID
ContactItem.CustomerID = String
```

Department Property

The Department property can be used to return or set the name or number of the department that the contact works in. This property corresponds to the department field on the Details tab of the GUI.

```
String = ContactItem.Department
ContactItem.Department = String
```

EntryID Property

The `EntryID` property returns, as a string, the unique ID for the contact. This ID is generated when the `ContactItem` object is created. This property is not displayed in the GUI.

```
String = ContactItem.EntryID
```

FileAs Property

The `FileAs` property returns or sets the string that holds the default name under which the contact is filed. This property allows you to group related contacts together. By default this property will be set to a concatenated string of the contact's last and first name. Setting this property to something else will not affect the `LastName` or `FirstName` properties.

```
String = ContactItem.FileAs
ContactItem.FileAs = String
```

FirstName Property

The `FirstName` property is used to return or set the first name for the contact. Changing this property will also reset the `FullName` property to reflect the change.

```
String = ContactItem.FirstName
ContactItem.FirstName = String
```

FormDescription Property

The `FormDescription` property allows you to get a reference to the `FormDescription` object associated with the `ContactItem` object.

```
Set FormDescriptionObject = ContactItem.FormDescription
```

The `FormDescription` object holds the properties that determine the appearance of the GUI in which an item is displayed. I would actually suggest that you work with forms in the **Forms Designer** that comes with the GUI and is accessed via the **Tools | Forms** menu. This designer allows you to customize the original forms that come with Outlook. Detailed information on the `FormDescription` object is given in chapter 11.

FTPSite Property

The `FTPSite` property returns or sets the FTP site name for the contact. If this is set to a string not starting http://, then http:// is prefixed. Beyond this, no validation is performed.

```
String = ContactItem.FTPSite
ContactItem.FTPSite = String
```

FullName Property

The `FullName` property is used to return or set the whole unparsed name for the contact.

```
String = ContactItem.FullName
ContactItem.FullName = String
```

When reset through code Outlook will parse the string into the other name properties as follows:

Name1	Name2	Name3	Name4	Name5
Title	FirstName	MiddleName	LastName	Suffix

This means that if the `FullName` property is set to "Mr John Smith", the `MiddleName` property is set to "Smith" and the `LastName` and `Suffix` properties are set to empty strings.

> It is probably safest to set each of the name properties separately rather than with the `FullName` property. Any changes made to the five other name properties will reset the `FullName` property appropriately.

FullNameAndCompany Property

The `FullNameAndCompany` property returns the last name, first name and company name as a concatenated string.

```
String = ContactItem.FullNameAndCompany
```

Gender Property

The `Gender` property returns or sets the gender of the contact.

```
Long = ContactItem.Gender
ContactItem.Gender = Long
```

The `Gender` property will be set to one of the `OlGender` constants:

Constant	Value	Description
olFemale	1	Identifies the contact as a female.
olMale	2	Identifies the contact as a male.
olUnspecified	0	Default, no gender has been set for the contact.

GetInspector Property

The `GetInspector` property returns a reference to the `Inspector` object for the contact item. An Inspector is a GUI in which Outlook items are displayed. For the more information on the `Inspector` object refer to Chapter 7.

```
Set InspectorObject = ContactItem.GetInspector
```

If the contact item is already open this property will return a reference to the Inspector holding it. Otherwise a new Inspector, holding the `ContactItem` object, will be added to the `Inspectors` collection.

This method will not display the contact. To display the contact item, either user the `Display` method of the `ContactItem` object or use the `Activate` method of the `Inspector` object, once you have a reference to it.

GovernmentIDNumber Property

The `GovernmentIDNumber` property returns or sets the government ID number for the contact. This is a string and can be set to anything you wish.

```
String = ContactItem.GovernmentIDNumber
ContactItem.GovernmentIDNumber = String
```

Hobby Property

The `Hobby` property can be used to set or return the hobbies of the contact. This is a string and no restrictions are set on its content.

```
String = ContactItem.Hobby
ContactItem.Hobby = String
```

Importance Property

The `Importance` property allows you to view or change the current importance for a contact. This will not affect the `Importance` property of any items sent to or received from the contact.

```
Long = ContactItem.Importance
ContactItem.Importance = Long
```

This property should be set to one of the `OlImportance` constants.

Constant	Value	Description
olImportanceHigh	2	The item is of high importance
olImportanceLow	0	The item is of low importance
olImportanceNormal	1	The item is of normal importance

Initials Property

The `Initials` property is used to return or set a string holding the initials for the contact. By default the `Initials` property is made up the initial letters of the first name, middle name and last name of the contact. The `Initials` property may be set through code and saved to any value you like, but as soon as the contact is opened again the `Initials` property will be set back to its default name-dependent value.

```
String = ContactItem.Initials
ContactItem.Initials = String
```

InternetFreeBusyAddress Property

The `InternetFreeBusyAddress` property allows you to retrieve or set the URL for the contact's Free/Busy information. This string property is only available for a contact of type Internet Only. If this is set to a string not starting http://, then http:// is prefixed. Beyond this, no validation is performed.

```
String = ContactItem.InternetFreeBusyAddress
ContactItem.InternetFreeBusyAddress = String
```

JobTitle Property

The `JobTitle` property return or sets the job title for the contact. This property holds a string and can be set to whatever you like.

```
String = ContactItem.JobTitle
ContactItem.JobTitle = String
```

Journal Property

The `Journal` property holds a Boolean that determines whether transactions with the contact are logged in the Journal folder. This read/write property holds True if transactions with the contact are to be monitored.

```
Boolean = ContactItem.Journal
ContactItem.Journal = Boolean
```

The Journal folder holds `JournalItem` objects, which are used to track chosen events of the user and their contacts. For more information on the `JournalItem` object refer to chapter 16.

Language Property

The `Language` property can be used to return or set the language for the contact. This property is simply available to the user for their information and does not affect how Outlook works. It is free form string and no validation is performed to check if a valid language has been set.

```
String = ContactItem.Language
ContactItem.Language = String
```

LastFirstAndSuffix Property

The `LastFirstAndSuffix` property returns the last name, first name and the suffix for the contact as a concatenated string.

```
String = ContactItem.LastFirstAndSuffix
```

LastFirstNoSpace Property

The `LastFirstNoSpace` property returns a concatenated string of the last name and first name of the contact without a space between the names.

```
String = ContactItem.LastFirstNoSpace
```

LastFirstNoSpaceCompany Property

The `LastFirstNoSpaceCompany` returns the last name, first name and the company name for the contact as a string. One thing to beware of here is that if either the company name or the first name and last name are not set then this property will return an empty string.

```
String = ContactItem.LastFirstNoSpaceCompany
```

LastFirstSpaceOnly Property

The `LastFirstSpaceOnly` property returns a string holding the last and first name of the contact with a space between them.

```
String = ContactItem.LastFirstSpaceOnly
```

LastFirstSpaceOnlyCompany Property

The `LastFirstSpaceOnlyCompany` property returns a string holding the last name, first name and the company name of the contact, with a space between the last and first name.

```
String = ContactItem.LastFirstSpaceOnlyCompany
```

LastModificationTime Property

The `LastModificationTime` property returns the time and date that the contact was last changed. For a newly created contact this will be set to 01/01/4501.

```
Date = ContactItem.LastModificationTime
```

LastName Property

The `LastName` property is used to return or set the last name of the contact as a string. Changing this property will also reset the `FullName` property to reflect the change.

```
String = ContactItem.LastName
ContactItem.LastName = String
```

LastNameAndFirstName Property

The `LastNameandFirstName` property returns a string holding the last and first names of the contact.

```
String = ContactItem.LastNameAndFirstName
```

ManagerName Property

The `ManagerName` property can be used to set or return the name of the manager of the contact. This is a string property.

```
String = ContactItem.ManagerName
ContactItem.ManagerName = String
```

MessageClass Property

The MessageClass property returns or sets the type of message of the current item. This string property is used to identify which form is associated with the item, so that the appropriate properties of the form are exposed. It can also be used to determine the type of item that you have referenced, if it is ambiguous.

```
String = ContactItem.MessageClass
ContactItem.MessageClass = String
```

For a ContactItem object this property will return IPM.Contact. If this property is set through code to be something other than IPM.Contact and the item saved, the contact item will be transformed to a different type of object.

MiddleName Property

The MiddleName property can be used to return or set the middle name of the contact. Changing this property will also reset the FullName property to reflect the change.

```
String = ContactItem.MiddleName
ContactItem.MiddleName = String
```

Mileage Property

The Mileage property allows you to enter or read a string value representing the mileage associated with the contact.

```
String = ContactItem.Mileage
ContactItem.Mileage = String
```

NetMeetingAlias Property

The NetMeetingAlias property can be used to return or set the Alias or user ID that the contact uses for net meetings.

```
String = ContactItem.NetMeetingAlias
ContactItem.NetMeetingAlias = String
```

NetMeetingServer Property

The NetMeetingServer property returns or sets the name of the server that this contact uses for online meetings.

```
String = ContactItem.NetMeetingServer
ContactItem.NetMeetingServer = String
```

NickName Property

The NickName property returns or sets the nickname for the contact. This free form string may be set to any text you wish.

```
String = ContactItem.NickName
ContactItem.NickName = String
```

NoAging Property

The `NoAging` property holds a Boolean value that specifies whether the `ContactItem` object can be archived. If an AutoArchive is attempted on this `ContactItem` object it will only be archived if this property is set to False. The default is False.

```
Boolean = ContactItem.NoAging
ContactItem.NoAging = Boolean
```

OfficeLocation Property

The `OfficeLocation` property can be used to return or set the location of the contact's office. This is free form and can hold anything.

```
String = ContactItem.OfficeLocation
ContactItem.OfficeLocation = String
```

OrganizationalDNumber Property

The `OrganizationalIDNumber` property returns or sets the ID number of the organization for which the contact works. This string property is not set by Outlook and is provided purely as an aid to the user.

```
String = ContactItem.OrganizationaIDNumber
ContactItem.OrganizationaIDNumber =String
```

OutlookInternalVersion Property

The `OutlookInternalVersion` property returns a long integer that identifies the Build number for the version of Outlook in which the item was created.

```
Long = ContactItem.OutlookInternalVersion
```

OutlookVersion Property

The `OutlookVersion` property returns a string holding the version number of the Outlook application in which the item was created.

```
String = ContactItem.OutlookVersion
```

Parent Property

This property returns a reference to the parent object for the current `ContactItem` object. This property will be the folder in which the contact is held. A newly created `ContactItem` object is automatically held in the Outlook default Contacts folder.

```
Set MAPIFolderObject = ContactItem.Parent
```

PersonalHomePage Property

The `PersonalHomePage` property returns or sets the Home Page URL for the contact. If this is set to a string not starting http://, then http:// is prefixed. Beyond this, no validation is performed.

```
String = ContactItem.PersonalHomePage
ContactItem.PersonalHomePage = String
```

Profession Property

The `Profession` property can be used to return or set the profession of the contact.

```
String = ContactItem.Profession
ContactItem.Profession = String
```

ReferredBy Property

The `ReferredBy` property can be used to return or set the name of the person or persons that referred the contact. Note that this is only a string field and not a `ContactItem` object itself.

```
String = ContactItem.ReferredBy
ContactItem.ReferredBy = String
```

Saved Property

The `Saved` property can be used to determine whether the `ContactItem` object has changed since it was last saved. If this Boolean property holds **True** than no changes have been made.

```
Boolean = ContactItem.Saved
```

This property can be used to decide if it would be sensible to prompt the user to save changes.

Example:

```
Dim ocContact as ContactItem
Dim iRepsonse as Integer

...

If Not ocContact.Saved Then
    iResponse = MsgBox("Would you like to save changes", _
                vbYesNo + vbQuestion)
    If iResponse = vbYes Then
            ocContact.Save
    End If
End If
```

In the above example the `Saved` property is examined to check if the contact item has been modified since it was last saved. If it has then the user is prompted to save changes, and if they accept the `Save` method is executed.

SelectedMailingAddress Property

The `SelectedMailingAddress` property sets or returns a long integer that identifies the type of address that the mailing address is a copy of.

```
Long = ContactItem.SelectedMailingAddress
ContactItem.SelectedMailingAddress = Long
```

The `SelectedMailingAddress` property will hold one of the following `OlMailingAddress` constants.

Constant	Value	Description
olBusiness	2	The Mailing Address is a copy of the Business Address
olNone	0	No Mailing Address has been selected
olHome	1	The Mailing Address is a copy of the Home Address
olOther	3	The Mailing Address is a copy of the Other Address

When this property is set, Outlook copies the corresponding address to the mailing address properties. If the SelectedMailingAddress property is set to olNone and then one of the mailing address properties is set, the SelectedMailingAddress property will change to olBusiness.

Sensitivity Property

The Sensitivity property returns or sets the level of sensitivity for the contact. This property does not affect the sensitivity of Outlook items sent to or received from the contact.

```
Long = ContactItem.Sensitivity
ContactItem.Sensitivity = Long
```

The property will hold one of OlSensitivity constants.

Constant	Value	Description
olConfidential	3	Treat the contact item as being confidential in nature
olNormal	0	The contact item contains no sensitive information
olPersonal	1	Treat the contact item as being personal in nature
olPrivate	2	Treat the contact item as being private in nature

Session Property

The Session property returns a reference to the NameSpace object for the current session. As there is only one type of NameSpace object available this will be the messaging application programming interface or MAPI.

```
Set NameSpaceObject = ContactItem.Session
```

Size Property

The `Size` property returns a long integer representing the size of the contact item in bytes.

```
Long = ContactItem.Size
```

Spouse Property

The `Spouse` property can be used to return or set a string holding the name of the contact's spouse.

```
String = ContactItem.Spouse
ContactItem.Spouse = String
```

Subject Property

The `Subject` property returns or sets as a string the default property for the contact.

```
String = ContactItem.Subject
ContactItem.Subject = String
```

If the `FileAs` property is set but none of the name properties is then the `Subject` property is by default equal to the `FileAs` property. If any of the name properties, bar the `Title` property, are set then the subject is set to their concatenated string.

On the other hand if the `Subject` property is set through code to a certain string value, then it will remain as that value, even when the contact is re-opened.

Suffix Property

The `Suffix` property returns or sets the suffix for the contact. This property is a string data type and can be set to any text. Changing this property will also reset the `FullName` property to reflect the change.

```
String = ContactItem.Suffix
ContactItem.Suffix = String
```

Title Property

The `Title` property returns or sets a string value holding the title for the contact. Changing this property will also reset the `FullName` property to reflect the change.

```
String = ContactItem.Title
ContactItem.Title = String
```

UnRead Property

The `UnRead` property can be used to return or set a Boolean value, which is supposed to identify whether the item has been read.

```
Boolean = ContactItem.Unread
ContactItem.Unread = Boolean
```

This property is really of no use to the ContactItem object and this is reflected in its behavior. If a new contact item is created then this property holds the value True, but as soon as it is saved the property is set to False. It is possible to set this property to True, through code but as soon as you save the changes, it is set back to False.

The User Properties

The four properties User1, User2, User3, User4 have the same functionality and so to avoid repetition only one will be described.

The User1 property is used to return or set a Schedule+ user name for the contact. Schedule + is an old mailing system. This property holds a string and no validation is performed on it.

```
String = ContactItem.User1
ContactItem.User1 = String
```

UserCertificate Property

The UserCertificate property returns or sets a string holding the name of the authentication certificates or Digital IDs for the contact. These files are normally issued by the administrator or some security authority and are used to authenticate a digital signature or to send encrypted mail.

```
String = ContactItem.UserCertificate
ContactItem.UserCertificate = String
```

UserProperties Property

The UserProperties property returns a reference to the UserProperties collection for the ContactItem object. This property provides a way to interface with the user properties of ContactItem object.

```
Set UserPropertiesCollection = ContactItem.UserProperties
```

For more information on the UserProperties collection and the UserProperty object refer to chapter 11.

WebPage Property

The WebPage property returns or sets the URL for the contact's web page. If this is set to a string not starting http://, then http:// is prefixed. Beyond this, no validation is performed.

```
String = ContactItem.WebPage
ContactItem.WebPage = String
```

YomiCompanyName Property

The YomiCompanyName property returns or sets a string value holding the Japanese phonetic rendering of the company name for the contact.

```
String = ContactItem.YomiCompanyName
ContactItem.YomiCompanyName = String
```

YomiFirstName Property

The `YomiFirstName` property returns or sets a string value holding the Japanese phonetic rendering of the first name for the contact.

```
String = ContactItem.YomiFirstName
ContactItem.YomiFirstName = String
```

YomiLastName Property

The `YomiLastName` property returns or sets a string value holding the Japanese phonetic rendering of the last name for the contact.

```
String = ContactItem.YomiLastName
ContactItem.YomiLastName = String
```

DistListItem Object

The `DistListItem` object holds a distribution list or a list of recipients who are grouped together under a particular name. These recipients are related to one another in some fashion and the distribution list name usually reflects their connection. This `DistListItem` object allows us to send a mail message to a number of people without having to type in all the individual names.

A `DistListItem` object is shown below. You can add, select and remove members of the distribution list through code just as you can through the GUI.

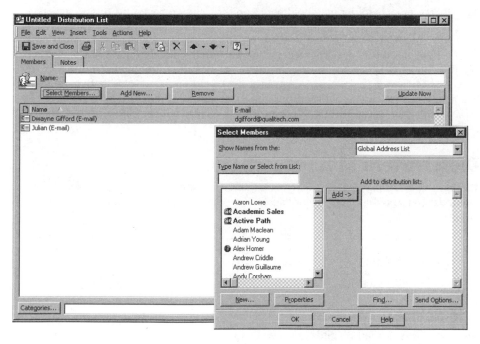

It is possible to create a new `DistListItem` object using the `CreateItem` method of the `Application` object.

```
Dim odDistList As DistListItem
...
Set odDistList = Application.CreateItem(olDistributionListItem)
```

Another way to create a new `DistListItem` object is by using the `Add` method of an `Items` collection held in a folder that supports contacts and distribution lists.

```
Dim oicItems As Items
Dim odDistList As DistListItem
...
Set odDistList = oicItems.add(olDistributionListItem)
```

To set a reference to an existing `DistListItem` object it is necessary to work with the `Item` method of the `Items` collection held in the relevant folder.

Example:

```
Dim onMAPI As NameSpace
Dim ofContact As MAPIFolder
Dim odDistList As DistListItem

Set onMAPI = Application.GetNamespace("MAPI")
Set ofContact = onMAPI.GetDefaultFolder(olFolderContacts)
Set odDistList = ofContact.Items.Item(1)
```

Note that a contacts folder may hold both `ContactItem` objects and `DistListItem` objects.

As of writing this object does not seem to have the full functionality that you would expect of a distribution list. The `AddMembers` and `RemoveMembers` methods require that you to pass a `Recipients` collection. However, the `DistListItem` object offers no way to create a `Recipients` collection, and the work around is to create a temporary `MailItem`, `AppointmentItem`, `JournalItem` or `TaskItem` object in order to create one.

DistListItem Methods

The following is a list of methods that are identical to the `ContactItem` object methods, and so will not be covered again. For details refer back to the `ContactItem` object.

Close	Copy	Delete	Display
Move	PrintOut	Save	SaveAs

AddMembers Method

The `AddMembers` method adds new members to the distribution list in the form of a `Recipients` collection.

```
DistListItem.AddMembers RecipientsCollection
```

The strange thing with this method is that it requires a `Recipients` collection to be passed into it. But the only way create a `Recipients` collection is via one of the `MailItem`, `MeetingItem`, `PostItem`, `TaskItem` or `AppointmentItem` objects. So to use this method a new item of one of these types needs to be created and a reference set to its `Recipients` collection.

Example:

```
Dim onMAPI As NameSpace
Dim ofContacts As MAPIFolder
Dim odDistList As DistListItem
Dim omMail As MailItem
Dim orcRecipients As Recipients

Set onMAPI = Application.GetNamespace("MAPI")
Set ofContacts = onMAPI.GetDefaultFolder(olFolderContacts)
Set odDistList = ofContacts.Items.add(olDistributionListItem)
odDistList.DLName = "Test"

Set omMail = Application.CreateItem(olMailItem)
Set orcRecipients = omMail.Recipients
orcRecipients.add "Dwayne Gifford"
orcRecipients.add "John Smith"
orcRecipients.ResolveAll

odDistList.AddMembers orcRecipients
odDistList.Save
```

In the example you will notice that once the `DistListItem` object is set up a `MailItem` object is created and a reference set to its `Recipients` collection. Then the new members for the distribution list are added to the `Recipients` collection and resolved to check that they are valid. The `ResolveAll` method does not raise an error if a recipient is not valid, but simply returns **False**. If any of the recipients are invalid this code will not add the new members to the distribution list. So in a real application some error handling would be called for here. Finally the recipients are added to the distribution list by making use of the `AddMembers` method. If you try to add a recipient that already exists in the distribution no error is raised and the recipient is not added.

GetMember Method

The `GetMember` method provides a way to retrieve a member of the `DistListItem` object.

```
Set RecipientObject = DistListItem.GetMember(Index)
```

Name	Value	Description
Index	Long	Required, the position of the recipient within the list of members that makes up the distribution list

RemoveMembers Method

The `RemoveMembers` method deletes specified members from the distribution list.

```
DistListItem.RemoveMembers RecipientsCollection
```

Again, just like the AddMembers method we need to pass in a Recipients collection. As of this writing the DistListItem object does not have a Recipients collection associated with it, so it is necessary to create a MailItem, MeetingItem, PostItem, TaskItem or AppointmentItem object and use its Recipients collection. An example of this is given below.

Example:

```
Dim onMAPI As NameSpace
Dim ofContacts As MAPIFolder
Dim odDistList As DistListItem
Dim omMail As MailItem
Dim orcRecipients As Recipients

Set onMAPI = Application.GetNamespace("MAPI")
Set ofContacts = onMAPI.GetDefaultFolder(olFolderContacts)
Set odDistList = ofContacts.Items.Item("Test")

Set omMail = Application.CreateItem(olMailItem)
Set orcRecipients = omMail.Recipients

orcRecipients.add "John Smith"
orcRecipients.ResolveAll

odDistList.RemoveMembers orcRecipients
odDistList.Save
```

The above code works in conjunction with the code given in the AddMembers method. Here a reference is set to the existing DistListItem object named "Test". Then a new MailItem object is created and a reference set to its Recipients collection. A **new** MailItem object is used to ensure that the collection is empty. The members that are to be removed from the distribution list are added to the Recipients collection, which is then resolved to see if the recipients are valid. If any of the recipients are invalid then no members will be removed. The ResolveAll method returns a Boolean value of **False** if any recipient is not valid, so suitable error-handling could be used in a real application. Finally the RemoveMembers method is employed to remove the recipients from the distribution list.

DistListItem Properties

The following is a list of properties that are identical to the ContactItem object. To avoid repetition they will not be covered again here and the reader should refer to the ContactItem object for the details of these properties.

Actions	Application	Attachments	Billing Information
Categories	Class	Companies	Conversation Index
Conversation Topic	Creation Time	EntryID	Form Description
GetInspector	Importance	LastModification Date	MessageClass

Mileage	NoAging	OutlookInternal Version	Outlook Version
Parent	Saved	Sensitivity	Session
Size	Subject	UnRead	User Properties

Body Property

The Body property is a string that can be set or retrieved and is displayed in the Notes tab of the distribution list GUI. It could, for example, be used to keep information about how distribution list members are related.

```
String = DistListItem.Body
DistListItem.Body = String
```

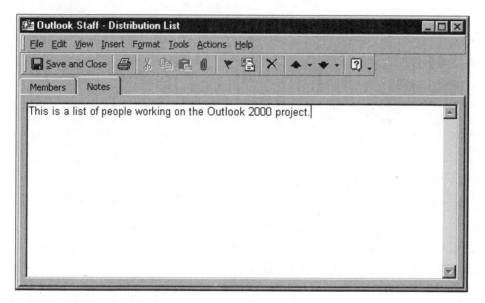

DLName Property

The DLName property is used to return or set the name of the distribution list. This is a string property that should be set to a name reflecting the nature of the distribution list, although could be set to almost anything.

```
String = DistListItem.DLName
DistListItem.DLName = String
```

Links Property

The Links property provides access to the Links collection. The Links collection is a grouping of Outlook items, currently only contact items, that have been linked to the current item. This can be used to group contact items that are somehow related to the distribution list. The Links collection and Link object are covered in Chapter 11.

MemberCount Property

The MemberCount property returns the number of members that belong to the distribution list.

```
Long = DistListItem.MemberCount
```

Note that if another distribution list is added to the referenced DistListItem object this will only count as one member and not the total number of members held in that distribution list.

Contacts

13

Mail Messages

In this chapter, we will be looking at the `MailItem` object, the `RemoteItem` object and the `ReportItem` object. The easiest of the three to understand is the `MailItem` object, which represents the familiar email message that we have been sending and receiving for the last seven years or more. But when laptops became popular, the `RemoteItem` object also became important. This is because most users would not wait to have all their mail downloaded, either because it would cost a lot or because they could be waiting for hours. So to get around this, most of the good server programs are starting to offer objects of this type. These allow you to see what the message is about before you decide whether to bring it across to the client. Moreover, as the Internet got more and more popular, so did the `ReportItem` object, due to the frequency of bad address information. I don't know about you, but for me making sure I type the email address correctly takes a lot of extra effort. The `ReportItem` object informs me if the message did not reach all the recipients, and which recipients did not get it.

The `RemoteItem` and `ReportItem` objects can only be referenced; we are unable to create them ourselves. The system does that for us.

There are two ways to create a new `MailItem`, and one way to get a reference to an existing mail message. To get a reference to an existing entry, we must first obtain a reference to a `MAPIFolder` that holds mail entries.

For example, to retrieve a `MailItem` with the subject `"Copy Method"` from the Inbox folder we could use the following code:

```
Dim ofFolder As MAPIFolder
Dim omMail As MailItem

Set ofFolder = Application.GetNamespace("MAPI").GetDefaultFolder _
                (olFolderInbox)
Set omMail = ofFolder.Items("Copy Method")
```

To create a new `MailItem`, we can either use the `Add` method that is exposed by the `MAPIFolder` object's `Items` collection or the `CreateItem` method that is exposed by the `Application` object.

For example:

```
Dim ofFolder As MAPIFolder
Dim omMail As MailItem
...
Set omMail = ofFolder.Items.Add(olMailItem)
```

Or:

```
Dim omMail As MailItem
Set omMail = Application.CreateItem(olMailItem)
```

The MailItem Object

The `MailItem` object represents a mail message and can reside in any of the `MAPIFolder` objects that support it. Most people think that this is the core of outlook, and it used to be the only feature that most mail clients used. However, this has changed: as you have probably already realized by now, Outlook offers many more possibilities than this, and the `MailItem` is really just one small piece of the puzzle.

MailItem Methods

ClearConversationIndex Method

The `ClearConversationIndex` method provides us a way of clearing the conversation index. This string value indicates the position of the mail in the conversation: each time a user replies to or forwards the item, the ASCII value of the conversation index increases by 5. The `ClearConversationIndex` method resets the conversation index to the character with an ASCII value of 22, as if this were a new conversation.

```
MailItem.ClearConversationIndex
```

Close Method

The `Close` method shuts down the `Inspector` object that is currently showing the `MailItem`.

```
MailItem.Close(SaveMode)
```

Name	Data type	Description
SaveMode	Long	Required, one of the OlInspectorClose constants.

The `OlInspectorClose` constants are as follows:

Constant	Value	Description
olSave	0	Save the item without prompting the user.

Constant	Value	Description
olDiscard	1	Discard all changes to the item without prompting.
olPromptForSave	2	Prompt the user to save or discard the item.

Even if the Inspector object for the MailItem has not been opened, any changes made to the item will be saved if SaveMode is set to olSave, or the user will be prompted if it is set to olPromptForSave. If SaveMode is set to olDiscard, note that any changes will not be lost until the object is uninstantiated (e.g. when the macro comes to an end).

Copy Method

The Copy method creates a new mail that is identical to the current MailItem.

```
Set MailItem = MailItem.Copy
```

For example:

```
Dim onMAPI As NameSpace
Dim ofMyFolders As MAPIFolder
Dim ofInbox As MAPIFolder
Dim ofArchive As MAPIFolder
Dim omMail As MailItem
Dim omCopy As MailItem
Dim ifor As Integer

Set onMAPI = Application.GetNameSpace("MAPI")
Set ofMyFolders = onMAPI.Folders("Mailbox - Dwayne Gifford")
Set ofInbox = ofMyFolders.Folders("Inbox")

For ifor = 1 To ofInbox.Folders.Count
    If ofInbox.Folders(ifor) = "Archive" Then
        Set ofArchive = ofMyFolders.Folders(ifor)
        Exit For
    End If
Next

If ofArchive Is Nothing Then
    Set ofArchive = ofInbox.Folders.Add("Archive", olFolderInbox)
End If

For ifor = 1 To ofInbox.Items.Count
    If ofInbox.Items(ifor).Class = olMail Then
        If ofInbox.Items(ifor).SenderName = "Tom" _
        And InStr(ofInbox.Items(ifor).Subject, "Chapter") Then
            Set omMail = ofInbox.Items(ifor)
            Set omCopy = omMail.Copy
            omCopy.ClearConversationIndex
            omCopy.Subject = omCopy.Subject & " - Copied"
            omCopy.Move ofArchive
        End If
    End If
Next ifor
```

In this example, we first get a reference to the Inbox and check whether there is a `MAPIFolder` called `"Archive"` directly underneath this. If there is, we set a reference to it; otherwise we create it. When we have this reference, we walk through the `Items` collection of the Inbox to select all items which are `MailItem` objects (by checking their `Class` property). Amongst these items, we check for mail sent by Tom (using the `SenderName` property) which has the keyword `"Chapter"` contained somewhere in the subject (using the VB `InStr` keyword). If we do find an item for which both these conditions are met, we get a reference to it. At which point we create a copy of the original mail, reset the conversation index, change the subject and move the new `MailItem` to our `"Archive"` folder.

Delete Method

The `Delete` method does just that — it removes the current `MailItem` from the `Items` collection.

```
MailItem.Delete
```

No surprises here — if you execute this method, the `Item` is deleted from the folder that it belonged to.

Display Method

The `Display` method activates the `Inspector` object for the current `MailItem`.

```
MailItem.Display([Modal])
```

Name	Data type	Description
Modal	Boolean	True to display the Inspector window modally; False for modeless display.

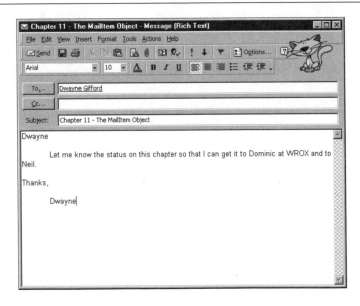

For example, the code below iterates through the Inbox and displays any mail items sent by Tom with the word "Chapter" in the subject:

```
Dim onMAPI As NameSpace
Dim ofMyFolders As MAPIFolder
Dim ofInbox As MAPIFolder
Dim omMail As MailItem
Dim ifor As Integer

Set onMAPI = Application.GetNameSpace("MAPI")
Set ofMyFolders = onMAPI.Folders("Mailbox - Dwayne Gifford")
Set ofInbox = ofMyFolders.Folders("Inbox")

For ifor = 1 To ofInbox.Items.Count
   If ofInbox.Items(ifor).Class = olMail Then
      If ofInbox.Items(ifor).SenderName = "Tom" _
      And InStr(ofInbox.Items(ifor).Subject, "Chapter") Then
         Set omMail = ofInbox.Items(ifor)
            omMail.Display
      End If
   End If
Next ifor
```

This code starts by getting a reference to the Inbox; it then looks through the items in it, checking for any mail items that were sent by Tom Eaves with the word "Chapter" in the subject. If such an item is found, we get a reference to it and display it to the user.

Forward Method

The Forward method creates a new mail item containing the body and the subject (by default with a prefix "FW: ") of the original item. This is similar to a Reply or ReplyAll message, except that no recipients are added.

```
Set MailItem = MailItem.Forward
```

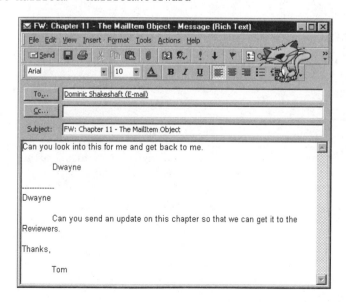

Example:

```
Dim onMAPI As NameSpace
Dim ofMyFolders As MAPIFolder
Dim ofInbox As MAPIFolder
Dim omMail As MailItem
Dim omForward As MailItem
Dim sSubject As String
Dim ifor As Integer

Set onMAPI = Application.GetNameSpace("MAPI")
Set ofMyFolders = onMAPI.Folders("Mailbox - Dwayne Gifford")
Set ofInbox = ofMyFolders.Folders("Inbox")

For ifor = 1 To ofInbox.Items.Count
    If ofInbox.Items(ifor).Class = olMail Then
        If ofInbox.Items(ifor).SenderName = "Tom" _
        And InStr(ofInbox.Items(ifor).Subject, "Chapter") Then
            Set omMail = ofInbox.Items(ifor)
            Set omForward = omMail.Forward
            sSubject = "Can you look into this for me and get back to me."
            sSubject = sSubject & vbCrLf & vbCrLf & vbTab & "Dwayne"
            sSubject = sSubject & vbCrLf & vbCrLf & "-------------"
            sSubject = sSubject & vbCrLf
            omForward.Body = sSubject & omMail.Body
            omForward.Recipients.Add "Dominic"
            omForward.Recipients.ResolveAll
            omForward.Send
        End If
    End If
Next ifor
```

This code sample iterates through the Inbox looking for any `MailItem` objects sent by Tom (that is, with "Tom" as the `SenderName`) and with the word "Chapter" in the subject. If any mail messages are found which match both criteria, they are forwarded to Dominic to look at. You will notice that the figure above is a screenshot of a mail being forwarded to Dominic.

Move Method

The `Move` method allows us to take the current `MailItem` and move it to a new `MAPIFolder` which supports `MailItem` objects.

```
MailItem.Move DestFldr
```

Name	Data type	Description
DestFldr	MAPIFolder object	Required, equates to an existing MAPIFolder object.

One possible use for this method is to move all related mail items that are related to a specific folder:

```
Dim onMAPI As NameSpace
Dim ofMyFolders As MAPIFolder
Dim ofInbox As MAPIFolder
Dim ofWROX As MAPIFolder
Dim omMail As MailItem
Dim iFor As Integer

Set onMAPI = Application.GetNameSpace("MAPI")
Set ofMyFolders = onMAPI.Folders("Mailbox - Dwayne Gifford")
Set ofInbox = ofMyFolders.Folders("Inbox")

For iFor = 1 To ofMyFolders.Folders.Count
    If ofMyFolders.Folders(iFor) = "WROX" Then
        Set ofWROX = ofMyFolders.Folders(iFor)
        Exit For
    End If
Next

If ofWROX Is Nothing Then
    Set ofWROX = ofMyFolders.Folders.Add("WROX", olFolderInbox)
End If

For iFor = ofInbox.Items.Count To 1 Step -1
    If ofInbox.Items(iFor).Class = olMail Then
        If ofInbox.Items(iFor).SenderName = "Tom" Then
            Set omMail = ofInbox.Items(iFor)
            omMail.Move ofWROX
        End If
    End If
Next iFor
```

In the example above we first get a reference to the Inbox. We then look for a `"WROX"` folder in the user's mailbox and if we do not find one, we create it. We now walk through the items in the Inbox looking for `MailItem` messages that with a `SenderName` of Tom. Any that we find are moved to the `"WROX"` folder. We have now managed to write our very own Rules Wizard for the Inbox. It does not have all the functionality of the Rules Wizard, but it does show how we can build up macros to make our own rules, and because we decide for ourselves what these rules are to do, we can write macros that are better suited to our needs than the more general Rules Wizard.

PrintOut Method

The `PrintOut` method provides a way of printing out the `MailItem` and creating a hard copy.

```
MailItem.PrintOut
```

Remember that because this method takes no parameters, the item is always sent to the default printer with the default settings. The only properties that get printed by default are the properties which have values and which are displayed on the mail's GUI.

Reply Method

The `Reply` method creates a new `MailItem` addressed to the creator of the original mail and also to any of the recipients included in the `ReplyRecipients` property.

```
Set MailItem = MailItem.Reply
```

Example:
```
Dim onMAPI As NameSpace
Dim ofMyFolders As MAPIFolder
Dim ofInbox As MAPIFolder
Dim omMail As MailItem
Dim omReply As MailItem
Dim sBody As String
Dim iFor As Integer

Set onMAPI = Application.GetNameSpace("MAPI")
Set ofMyFolders = onMAPI.Folders("Mailbox - Dwayne Gifford")
Set ofInbox = ofMyFolders.Folders("Inbox")

For iFor = 1 To ofInbox.Items.Count
    If ofInbox.Items(iFor).Class = olMail Then
        If ofInbox.Items(iFor).SenderName = "Tom" _
        And InStr(ofInbox.Items(iFor).Subject, "Chapter") Then
            Set omMail = ofInbox.Items(iFor)
            Set omReply = omMail.Reply
            sBody = "I will give you a call on this one." & vbCrLf
            sBody = sBody & & vbCrLf & vbTab & "Dwayne"
            sBody = sBody & vbCrLf & vbCrLf & "-------------"
            omReply.Body = sBody & vbCrLf & omMail.Body
            omReply.Send
        End If
    End If
Next iFor
```

This example walks through the items in the Inbox. If it finds any mail items with the word "Chapter" in the subject sent by Tom, it creates a new mail with the `Reply` method, adds some text in the body, and sends the reply.

ReplyAll Method

The `ReplyAll` method creates an email reply addressed back to the sender, and also to all the recipients in the `BCC`, `CC` and `To` properties.

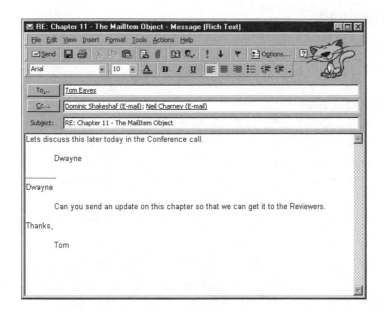

Example:

```
Dim onMAPI As NameSpace
Dim ofInbox As MAPIFolder
Dim omMail As MailItem
Dim omReply As MailItem
Dim sBody As String
Dim iFor As Integer

Set onMAPI = Application.GetNameSpace("MAPI")
Set ofInbox = onMAPI.GetDefaultFolder(olFolderInbox)

For iFor = 1 To ofInbox.Items.Count
    If ofInbox.Items(ifor).Class = olMail Then
        If ofInbox.Items(ifor).SenderName = "Tom" And _
                   InStr(ofInbox.Items(iFor).Subject, "Chapter") Then
            Set omMail = ofInbox.Items(iFor)
            Set omReply = omMail.ReplyAll
            sBody = "Lets discuss this later today in the Conference call."
            sBody  = sBody & vbCrLf & vbCrLf & vbTab & "Dwayne"
            sBody  = sBody & vbCrLf & vbCrLf & "-------------" & vbCrLf
            omReply.Body = sBody & omMail.Body
            omReply.Send
        End If
    End If
Next ifor
```

In the example above, we first get a reference to the Inbox. We then walk through the
items in the Inbox to find `MailItem` objects with the word "Chapter" in the subject
which were sent by Tom. If any items are found that match these criteria, we call the
`Reply` method, add some text to the body, and send the new mail.

Save Method

The Save method saves the mail to the current MAPIFolder or, if this is a newly created mail message, to the default MAPIFolder (for new mail items, this is the Drafts folder).

```
MailItem.Save
```

SaveAs Method

The SaveAs method provides a means of writing the MailItem object to the hard disk.

```
MailItem.SaveAs(Path [, Type])
```

Name	Data type	Description
Path	String	Required, a valid path and filename for the new file.
Type	Long	Optional, one of the OlSaveAsType constants below. The default if omitted is olMSG.

Type can be one of the following OlSaveAsType constants:

Constant	Value	Description
olTXT	0	Save as a .txt (Text) file.
olRTF	1	Save as an .rtf (Rich Text Format) file.
olTemplate	2	Save as an Outlook Template.
olMSG	3	Save in Outlook message (.msg) format.
olDoc	4	Save as a Word document.
olHTML	5	Save as an HTML page.
olVCard	6	Save as a vCard (.vcf) file.
olVCal	7	Save as a virtual calendar (.vcs) file.

Note that these OlSaveAsConstants are not all valid for all mail items. For example, if you try to save a mail as an olHTML type but the HTMLBody property is not set, an error will be raised.

Send Method

Sends the MailItem to the recipients included in the To, CC and BCC properties.

```
MailItem.Send
```

No surprises here — the mail is sent and the recipients will receive it. If the To, CC and BCC properties are all empty, this method will be ignored. If any of the recipients cannot be reached, a ReportItem is returned which explains the problem. For more information on the ReportItem object, see the section below entitled "The ReportItem Object".

MailItem Properties

Actions Property

The Actions property returns the collection of Actions available for the MailItem object. These are the special actions that can be executed on the mail, and which appear on the toolbar and/or the Actions menu of the GUI. The default actions available for the MailItem are "Forward", "Reply", "Reply to Folder" and "Reply to All". For more information on the Actions collection, see Chapter 11.

```
Set ActionsCollection = MailItem.Actions
```

AlternateRecipientAllowed Property

The AlternateRecipientAllowed property indicates you whether the mail item can be forwarded or not.

```
MailItem.AlternateRecipientAllowed = Boolean
Boolean = MailItem.AlternateRecipientAllowed
```

Application Property

The Application property returns the Application object for this session. This property does not appear on the GUI.

```
Set ApplicationObject = MailItem.Application
```

Attachments Property

The Attachments property returns a reference to the Attachments collection of the item, which contains the files and objects linked to or embedded in the body of the mail message. For more information on the Attachments collection, refer to Chapter 11.

```
Set AttachmentsCollection = MailItem.Attachments
```

AutoForwarded Property

The AutoForwarded property indicates whether this mail message was sent as an auto forward.

```
MailItem.AutoForwarded = Boolean
Boolean = MailItem.AutoForwarded
```

BCC Property

The BCC property contains a semicolon-delimited list of display names for all the recipients that will receive this mail item as a Blind Carbon Copy. Although this is a read/write property, it contains only the display names of the recipients; it is not a reference to a Recipients collection. This list can be altered by adding recipients with the Type property set to olBCC to the mail's Recipients collection. For more information on the Recipients collection, see Chapter 10.

```
MailItem.BCC = String
String = MailItem.BCC
```

BillingInformation Property

The `BillingInformation` property can be used to set or view the billing information for the `MailItem`. This property is a free-form string and can hold any text value. This property is not available on the GUI supplied by Outlook.

```
MailItem.BillingInformation = String
String = MailItem.BillingInformation
```

Body Property

The `Body` property is used to set or return the body of the `MailItem`. This is the meat of the mail — where the message itself is held. You can enter any text value you wish into the body. The body can also contain HTML tags, but in this case it must be set with the `HTMLBody` property. This is also where any attachments appear in the GUI.

```
MailItem.Body = String
String = MailItem.Body
```

Categories Property

The `Categories` property specifies the categories assigned to the `MailItem`, which can be used to select related items.

```
MailItem.Categories = String
String = MailItem.Categories
```

To add multiple categories at once, place a comma between each category:

```
Dim omMail As MailItem
...
omMail.Catergories = "VIP,Business,Me"
```

This assigns the categories "VIP", "Business" and "Me" to the `MailItem`. The `Restrict` method of the `Items` collection can be used to find the items which have these properties. For more information on the `Items` collection and its `Restrict` method, see Chapter 11.

CC Property

The `CC` property contains a semicolon-delimited list of display names for all the recipients who will receive this mail item as a Carbon Copy. Although this is a read/write property, it contains only the display names of the recipients; it is not a reference to a `Recipients` collection. This list can be altered by adding recipients with the `Type` property set to `olCC` to the mail's `Recipients` collection. For more information on the `Recipients` collection, see Chapter 10.

```
MailItem.CC = String
String = MailItem.CC
```

Class Property

This contains one of the `OlObjectClass` constants which identifies the type of the object in question. For a mail item, the value is `olMail` or 43.

```
Long = MailItem.Class
```

Companies Property

The `Companies` property contains the names of companies that are associated with the mail. The `Companies` property is a free-form string, and in reality you can enter any text value here. There is no validation done on this property and you cannot set this from the GUI.

```
MailItem.Companies = String
String = MailItem.Companies
```

ConversationIndex Property

The `ConversationIndex` property returns the index of the conversation thread. This is a string value which indicates what level the item is at in the current conversation. The first item has a `ConversationIndex` with an ASCII value of 22, and this increases by five for each message in the conversation (i.e. every time that a user replies to or forwards the item).

```
String = MailItem.ConversationIndex
```

ConversationTopic Property

The `ConversationTopic` property returns the topic of the conversation. This is set to the original subject of the message.

```
String = MailItem.ConversationTopic
```

CreationTime Property

The `CreationTime` property returns the date and time when the `MailItem` was created.

```
Date = MailItem.CreationTime
```

DeferredDeliveryTime Property

The `DeferredDeliveryTime` property specifies the date and time when the mail item is to be sent. If this value is set then the mail is held in the Outbox until the deferred time arrives.

```
MailItem.DeferredDeliveryTime = Date
Date = MailItem.DeferredDeliveryTime
```

DeleteAfterSubmit Property

The `DeleteAfterSubmit` property specifies whether a copy of this item is to be saved after the mail has been sent.

```
MailItem.DeleteAfterSubmit = Boolean
Boolean = MailItem.DeleteAfterSubmit
```

EntryID Property

The `EntryID` property returns a unique identifier for the MailItem which is generated when the `MailItem` is sent or saved. This property is not displayed in the GUI.

```
String = MailItem.EntryID
```

ExpiryTime Property

The `ExpiryTime` property specifies the date and time when the mail item becomes invalid and can be deleted. Setting this property causes the mail to be flagged as expired when the date has passed.

```
MailItem.ExpiryTime = Date
Date = MailItem.ExpiryTime
```

FlagDueBy Property

The `FlagDueBy` property specifies the date and time by which the mail needs to be followed up. This property will be ignored if the `FlagStatus` property is subsequently set to `olNoFlag`. When this time has passed, this item will appear colored red in the explorer, indicating that the due time has been missed. If the item is then marked as complete or unflagged, the item returns to its normal color.

```
MailItem.FlagDueBy = Date
Date = MailItem.FlagDueBy
```

FlagRequest Property

The `FlagRequest` property is a text field which can hold any string value. This message is displayed to the recipient of the mail above the body. This property is ignored if `FlagStatus` is subsequently set to `olNoFlag`.

```
MailItem.FlagRequest = String
String = MailItem.FlagRequest
```

FlagStatus Property

The `FlagStatus` property indicates whether the recipient is requires to follow up the message in the `MailItem`.

```
MailItem.FlagStatus = Long
Long = MailItem.FlagStatus
```

The value of `FlagStatus` can be any of the `olFlagStatus` constants:

Constant	Value	Description
olNoFlag	0	No follow up is required; no flag is shown next to the item in the explorer.
olFlagComplete	1	Flagged as completed; in the explorer the item will have a gray flag.
olFlagMarked	2	Flagged for follow up; in the explorer the item will have a red flag.

The current setting of `FlagStatus` will be overridden if `FlagRequest` or `FlagDueBy` are set afterwards.

FormDescription Property

The `FormDescription` property allows you to get a reference to the `FormDescription` object that is associated with the mail message. For more information on this object, see Chapter 11.

```
Set FormDescriptionObject = MailItem.FormDescription
```

GetInspector Property

The `GetInspector` property returns a reference to the `Inspector` object used to display the `MailItem`. For more information on the `Inspector` object, refer to Chapter 7.

```
Set InspectorObject = MailItem.GetInspector
```

HTMLBody Property

The `HTMLBody` property contains the body of the message in HTML format. This must be in HTML syntax, so you have to supply the appropriate HTML tags.

```
MailItem.HTMLBody = String
String = MailItem.HTMLBody
```

The following very simple example only begins to suggest the potential formatting and scripting power that this property makes available.

```
Dim omMail As MailItem

Set omMail = Application.CreateItem(olMailItem)
omMail.HTMLBody = "<HTML><STYLE TYPE=text/css>{font-size:16pt;color:red;" & _
                  "background:black}</STYLE><B><SPAN ID=mySpan>" & _
                  "This illustrates the formatting possibilities " & _
                  "with the HTMLBody property.</SPAN><P>" & _
                  "<BUTTON ONCLICK=fnClick()>Click here</BUTTON></B>" & _
                  "<SCRIPT LANGUAGE=JavaScript>function fnClick()" & _
                  "{ mySpan.innerHTML='<I>And this demonstrates " & _
                  "the scripting potential.</I>' }</SCRIPT></HTML>"
omMail.Recipients.Add "Dwayne Gifford"
omMail.Recipients.ResolveAll
omMail.Send
```

This example just creates a new `MailItem`, sets the `HTMLBody`, including some formatting and a button which activates a very simple script. It then adds a recipient and sends the mail.

At the time of writing, if the `HTMLBody` property is set, the `Body` is set to the same value. However, setting the `HTMLBody` does not cause the `Body` property to be set. Note also that setting this property will cause the `EditorType` of the `Inspector` for this item to be set to `olEditorHTML`.

Importance Property

The `Importance` property allows you to view or change the current importance setting for the mail.

```
MailItem.Importance = Long
Long = MailItem.Importance
```

The `Importance` property can be set to any of the `olImportance` constants.

Constant	Value	Description
olImportanceLow	0	The item is of low importance.
olImportanceNormal	1	The item is of normal importance.
olImportanceHigh	2	The item is of high importance.

This property cannot be found on the mail's GUI; you must open the Properties dialog to change or update this property.

LastModificationTime Property

The `LastModificationTime` property returns the time and date when the mail was last changed. This property is not available on the GUI.

```
Date = MailItem.LastModificationTime
```

Links Property

The `Links` property provides access to the `Links` collection. This is a grouping of items that are related to the `MailItem` (although, at the moment, it can only contain contacts). For more information of the `Links` collection, see Chapter 11.

```
Set LinksCollection = MailItem.Links
```

MessageClass Property

The `MessageClass` property returns a string identifying the type of item currently in use. This property links us to the form associated with the item. Unless this is a user-defined form, `MessageClass` will always return `"IPM.Note"` for a `MailItem`. If this property is changed to a valid string, saved and the item re-opened, you will find that it has changed its class to become an item of the new type.

```
MailItem.MessageClass = String
String = MailItem.MessageClass
```

Mileage Property

The `Mileage` property allows the user to enter a free-form string. This can be used to hold the mileage associated with the mail. This property is not available anywhere at all on the GUI supplied by Outlook.

```
MailItem.Mileage = String
String = MailItem.Mileage
```

NoAging Property

The NoAging property allows you to specify whether the MailItem can be archived or not. When Outlook auto-archives, the mail will not be archived if its NoAging property is set to True. This means that the item will be available online indefinitely.

```
MailItem.NoAging = Boolean
Boolean = MailItem.NoAging
```

OriginatorDeliveryReportRequested Property

The OriginatorDeliveryReportRequested property allows you to specify whether you wish to receive a delivery report for each recipient of the MailItem. This simply means that as soon as the MailItem is delivered, a ReportItem is returned to the originator for recipients who received the message, and another for recipients to whom the mail could not be delivered.

```
MailItem.OriginatorDeliveryReportRequested = Boolean
Boolean = MailItem.OriginatorDeliveryReportRequested
```

OutlookInternalVersion Property

The OutlookInternalVersion property returns the version number for the build of Outlook in which the item was created. Unlike OutlookVersion, which indicates only the version, this allows the exact build of Outlook in use to be determined. If the mail was not sent from Outlook, this will return nothing.

```
Long = MailItem.OutlookInternalVersion
```

OutlookVersion Property

This property returns the release number for the version of Outlook in which the item was created. For Outlook 2000, this is "9.0". If the mail was not sent from Outlook, this will return nothing. This property could be used to decide what format to send an email in. For example, if we want to send an HTML-format reply to a mail we received, we could check the OutlookVersion property of this mail to see whether the sender is using a version of Outlook that supports HTML mails.

```
String = MailItem.OutlookVersion
```

Parent Property

Returns a reference to the parent object for the current MailItem. This property always returns the MAPIFolder to which the MailItem belongs.

```
Set Object = MailItem.Parent
```

ReadReceiptRequested Property

The ReadReceiptRequested property allows you to specify whether you wish to receive a read receipt report for each recipient of the MailItem. If this is set to True, a ReportItem is returned to the originator when each recipient reads the mail.

```
MailItem.ReadReceiptRequested = Boolean
Boolean = MailItem.ReadReceiptRequested
```

ReceivedByEntryID Property

The `ReceivedByEntryID` property returns the `EntryID` for the recipient of the `MailItem`. All objects created by Outlook have an `EntryID` generated for them. So this property is set to the `EntryID` of the recipient which received the mail message.

```
String = MailItem.ReceivedByEntryID
```

ReceivedByName Property

The `ReceivedByName` property returns the display name of the original recipient of the message.

```
String = MailItem.ReceivedByName
```

ReceivedOnBehalfOfEntryID Property

The `ReceivedOnBehalfOfEntryID` property returns the `EntryID` for the recipient that has been delegated by the addressee to receive their mail messages.

```
String = MailItem.ReceivedOnBehalfOfEntryID
```

ReceivedOnBehalfOfName Property

The `ReceivedOnBehalfOfName` property returns the display name of the recipient that has been delegated by the addressee to receive their mail messages.

```
String = MailItem.ReceivedOnBehalfOfName
```

ReceivedTime Property

The `ReceivedTime` property returns the date and time when the mail was sent.

```
Date = MailItem.ReceivedTime
```

RecipientReassignmentProhibited Property

The `RecipientReassignmentProhibited` property specifies whether it is permitted (`False`) or prohibited (`True`) for the recipient to forward the mail message (`True`).

```
MailItem.RecipientReassignmentProhibited = Boolean
Boolean = MailItem.RecipientReassignmentProhibited
```

Recipients Property

The `Recipients` property returns a reference to the collection of recipients for the mail item. We can use the `Type` property of the `Recipient` object to specify whether a given recipient will appear in the To, CC or BCC field. To learn more about the `Recipients` collection and the `Recipient` object, see Chapter 10.

```
Set RecipientsCollection = MailItem.Recipients
```

ReminderOverrideDefault Property

The `ReminderOverrideDefault` property provides a way of overriding the default sound that has been set for Outlook. Setting this to `True` will cause Outlook to validate the `ReminderPlaySound` and `ReminderSoundFile` properties.

```
MailItem.ReminderOverrideDefault = Boolean
Boolean = MailItem.ReminderOverrideDefault
```

ReminderPlaySound Property

The `ReminderPlaySound` property tells Outlook to play the sound file that is set in the `ReminderSoundFile` property. When you create a new `MailItem` object this property is `True`.

```
MailItem.ReminderPlaySound = Boolean
Boolean = MailItem.ReminderPlaySound
```

ReminderSet Property

The `ReminderSet` property is a Boolean value, and if set to `True` will cause a reminder of this mail to occur on the date and time set for the `ReminderTime` property. Beware that this might annoy the recipient of the mail if you do this without a good reason!

```
MailItem.ReminderSet = Boolean
Boolean = MailItem.ReminderSet
```

ReminderSoundFile Property

The `ReminderSoundFile` property allows you to set the pathname and filename for the soundfile which you want Outlook to play when a `Reminder` is opened. No validation is carried out on this property, so no error will be raised if the pathname and filename are not valid.

```
MailItem.ReminderSet = String
String = MailItem.ReminderSet
```

ReminderTime Property

The `ReminderTime` property specifies the date and time when the reminder should occur.

```
MailItem.ReminderTime = Date
Date = MailItem.ReminderTime
```

RemoteStatus Property

The `RemoteStatus` property indicates what action will be carried out on this item the next time the remote connection is made. It can be set to any of the `OlRemoteStatus` constants.

```
MailItem.RemoteStatus = Long
Long = MailItem.RemoteStatus
```

The `OlRemoteStatus` constants are as follows:

Constant	Value	Description
olRemoteStatusNone	0	There is no remote status for this item.
olUnMarked	1	The item has not been marked.
olMarkedForDownload	2	Marked to be downloaded when retrieved by Outlook.
olMarkedForCopy	3	Marked to be copied from the server.
olMarkedForDelete	4	Marked to be deleted from the server.

Setting this property to olMarkedForCopy or olMarkedForDownload will cause the message to be downloaded to the client. Setting it to olMarkedForDelete will cause the message to be deleted from the server.

ReplyRecipientNames Property

The ReplyRecipientNames property returns a semicolon-delimited string of all the display names of the recipients who will receive a reply to this mail. This property is read-only, but the reply recipients can be modified through the collection returned by the ReplyRecipients property.

```
String = MailItem.ReplyRecipientNames
```

ReplyRecipients Property

The ReplyRecipients property returns a Recipients collection of all the recipients who will receive a mail should the recipient reply to the MailItem. For more information on the Recipients collection, see Chapter 10.

```
Set RecipientsCollection = MailItem.Recipients
```

Saved Property

The Saved property indicates whether the MailItem has been saved since it was last changed. This enables us to determine whether the user has made any changes to the item, and if they have, they can now be prompted to save these changes.

```
Boolean = MailItem.Saved
```

Example:

```
Dim omMail As MailItem
Dim iResponse As Integer
...
If Not omMail.Saved Then
    iResponse = MsgBox("Would you like to save changes?", _
            vbYesNo + vbQuestion)
    If iResponse = vbYes Then
        omMail.Save
    End If
End If
```

The example above first checks whether the `MailItem` has changed (i.e. `Saved` is `False`). If it has, the user is prompted to save these changes. If the response is **Yes**, we execute the `Save` method.

SaveSentMessageFolder Property

The `SaveSentMessageFolder` specifies the `MAPIFolder` to which the `MailItem` is to be saved after it has been sent.

```
Set MailItem.SaveSentMessageFolder = MAPIFolder
Set MAPIFolder = MailItem.SaveSentMessageFolder
```

SenderName Property

The `SenderName` property returns the name of the originator of the `MailItem`. This property is set when the `MailItem` is sent to the recipients.

```
String = MailItem.SenderName
```

Sensitivity Property

The `Sensitivity` property indicates the level of sensitivity for the `MailItem`.

```
MailItem.Sensitivity = Long
Long = MailItem.Sensitivity
```

This property can hold any of the `OlSensitivity` constants:

Constant	Value	Description
olNormal	0	The item contains no sensitive information.
olPersonal	1	The item is personal in nature.
olPrivate	2	The item is private in nature.
olConfidential	3	The item is confidential in nature.

This property is not displayed in the GUI for the mail; this property can only be viewed or updated by opening the **Properties** dialog. Note that setting this property to a value other than `olNormal` prevents the recipient from altering the mail's properties.

Sent Property

The `Sent` property indicates whether the mail item has already been mailed to the recipients. If the mail has already been sent, it will return `True`; if not, it will be `False`.

```
Boolean = MailItem.Sent
```

SentOn Property

The `SentOn` property returns the date and time when the `MailItem` was sent. This property is set to the current date and time when the `Send` method is executed. If the item has not been sent, this property will return `01/01/4501`.

```
Date = MailItem.SentOn
```

SentOnBehalfOfName Property

The `SentOnBehalfOfName` property sets or returns the display name for the person on behalf of whom the mail was sent — that is, who delegated the actual sender to send the `MailItem`.

```
MailItem.SentOnBehalfOfName = String
String = MailItem.SentOnBehalfOfName
```

Session Property

The `Session` property returns a reference to the `NameSpace` object for the current session.

```
Set NameSpaceObject = MailItem.Session
```

Size Property

The `Size` property returns the size of the `MailItem` in bytes.

```
Long = MailItem.Size
```

Subject Property

The `Subject` property specifies the subject of the mail. This appears on the GUI immediately above the body.

```
MailItem.Subject = String
```

Because this is the default property for the `MailItem`, it can be accessed directly through the `Items` collection, and thus provides the most convenient way of retrieving a specific item:

```
Dim ofFolder As MAPIFolder
Dim omMail As MailItem
...
Set omMail = ofFolder.Items("Copy Method - Mail Item")
```

This avoids the necessity of walking through the `Items` collection to find the item we want — we can just access it directly using its `Subject` property.

Submitted Property

The `Submitted` property indicates whether the mail item has been sent to the Outbox for sending. This will return `True` if the item has been submitted, otherwise `False`.

```
Boolean = MailItem.Submitted
```

To Property

The `To` property returns a semicolon-delimited list of display names for the recipients in the To field that will receive this mail item. The recipients in this list can be altered by modifying the collection returned by the `Recipients` property.

```
MailItem.To = String
String = MailItem.To
```

UnRead Property

The UnRead property indicates whether the MailItem has been opened yet (or, more accurately, whether it is *marked* as un-read, because this property can be set as well as read).

```
MailItem.UnRead = Boolean
Boolean = MailItem.UnRead
```

UserProperties Property

The UserProperties property provides a means of accessing the UserProperties collection for the mail. This contains properties which can be added to the item and which are defined by the user, rather than pre-defined. For more information on the UserProperties collection and the UserProperty object refer to Chapter 11.

```
Set UserPropertiesCollection = MailItem.UserProperties
```

VotingOptions Property

The VotingOptions property is a semicolon-delimited string containing the voting options for the mail.

```
MailItem.VotingResponse = String
String = MailItem.VotingResponse
```

These options appear on the toolbar of the mail, and allow the recipient to respond to a question in the body of the mail simply by pressing one of the buttons. A mail indicating the response is then returned to the originator.

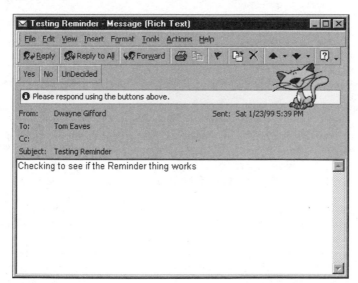

Notice how the voting options appear across the top of the mail item.

VotingResponse Property

The `VotingResponse` property specifies the response of the recipient to the voting options in the mail item. This will always be set to one of the values in the `VotingOptions` property if the recipient responds through the GUI, so I would suggest that you do the same if you automate with `VotingResponse`.

```
MailItem.VotingResponse = String
String = MailItem.VotingResponse
```

The ReportItem Object

The `ReportItem` object represents a report that the system generates if an item cannot be sent to a recipient or if a read receipt or originator delivery report was requested. These items cannot be created by the user; only the system can generate them.

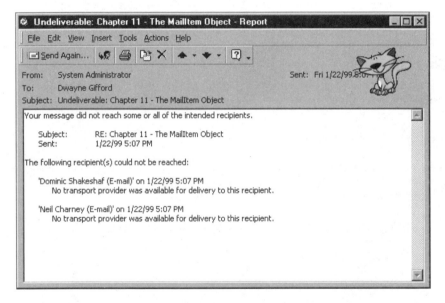

You can see from the figure above that the report outlines the message that caused the report to be sent and a list of the recipients who did not receive the message. It also indicates at what time the item was sent. As well as reporting undelivered items, a `ReportItem` can be used to confirm delivery of a mail or to inform the originator when a mail was opened by setting the `OriginatorDeliveryReportRequested` or the `ReadReceiptRequested` properties of the `MailItem`.

I imagine that you are reading this book because you want to use Outlook to write an automated system of some kind. If this is the case, you will have to understand and be able to use this item. This is because if you send out a mail message and get a report back, your application needs to be able to react to the report. This could involve logging the item, backing the item up, trying to send the item again just in case it was a system failure, on either the recipient's or the originator's side, or even removing the recipient from future mails.

ReportItem Methods

Close Method

The `Close` method provides a way of shutting down the `Inspector` object that is currently displaying the report.

```
ReportItem.Close(SaveMode)
```

Name	Data type	Description
SaveMode	Long	Required, one of the `OlInspectorClose` constants.

The `OlInspectorClose` constants are as follows:

Constant	Value	Description
olSave	0	Save the report without prompting the user.
olDiscard	1	Discard all changes to the item and close without prompting.
olPromptForSave	2	Prompt the user to save or discard the item.

The changes will be saved or discarded according to the `SaveMode` parameter even if the post has not explicitly been opened in an inspector.

Copy Method

The `Copy` method creates a new `ReportItem` that is identical to the current one.

```
Set ReportItem = ReportItem.Copy
```

Delete Method

The `Delete` method removes the current `ReportItem` from the `Items` collection of the folder to which it belongs.

```
ReportItem.Delete
```

Display Method

The `Display` method activates the `Inspector` object for the current `ReportItem`.

```
ReportItem.Display([Modal])
```

Name	Data type	Description
Modal	Boolean	`True` to display the `Inspector` window modally; `False` for modeless display.

Move Method

The Move method allows us to take the current ReportItem and move it to any new MAPIFolder which supports ReportItem objects.

```
ReportItem.Move DestFldr
```

Name	Data type	Description
DestFldr	MAPIFolder object	Required, equates to an existing MAPIFolder object.

PrintOut Method

The PrintOut method provides a way of printing out the MailItem and creating a hard copy.

```
MailItem.PrintOut
```

Remember that because this method takes no parameters, the item is always sent to the default printer with the default settings. The only properties that get printed are the properties which have values and which are displayed on the mail's GUI.

Save Method

The Save method saves the report to the current MAPIFolder.

```
ReportItem.Save
```

SaveAs Method

The SaveAs method provides a means of writing the ReportItem object to the hard disk.

```
ReportItem.SaveAs(Path [, Type])
```

Name	Data type	Description
Path	String	Required, a valid path and filename for the new file.
Type	Long	Optional, any of the OlSaveAsType constants below. The default if omitted is olMSG.

Type can be any of the following OlSaveAsType constants:

Constant	Value	Description
olTXT	0	Save as a .txt (Text) file.
olRTF	1	Save as an .rtf (Rich Text Format) file.
olTemplate	2	Save as an Outlook Template.
olMSG	3	Save in Outlook message (.msg) format.

If you try to use any of the `OlSaveAsConstants` not listed above, an error will be raised.

ReportItem Properties

Actions Property

The `Actions` property returns the collection of `Actions` available for the `ReportItem` object. These are the special actions that can be executed on the report, and which appear on the toolbar and/or the Actions menu of the GUI. The default actions available for the `ReportItem` are `"Forward"`, `"Reply"`, `"Reply to All"` and `"Reply to Folder"`, although only the first of these appears on the GUI. For more information on the `Actions` collection, see Chapter 11.

```
Set ActionsCollection = ReportItem.Actions
```

Application Property

The `Application` property returns the `Application` object for this session. This property does not appear on the GUI.

```
Set ApplicationObject = ReportItem.Application
```

Attachments Property

The `Attachments` property returns a reference to the `Attachments` collection of the item, which contains the files and objects linked to or embedded in the report. The report item is unlike other items in that attachments are not displayed in the body, and are only accessible through code or if the item is viewed in the Preview Pane. For more information on the `Attachments` collection, refer to Chapter 11.

```
Set AttachmentsCollection = ReportItem.Attachments
```

BillingInformation Property

The `BillingInformation` property can be used to set or view the billing information for the `ReportItem`. This property is a free-form string and can hold any text value. This property is not available on the GUI supplied by Outlook.

```
ReportItem.BillingInformation = String
String = ReportItem.BillingInformation
```

Body Property

The `Body` property contains the body of the report, which is where the information about the delivery status of the original message appears. You can enter anything you wish into the body. The difference between the GUI for the `ReportItem` and all the other GUIs is that the attachments are not shown in it (although attachments do appear when the item is viewed in the Preview Pane).

```
ReportItem.Body = String
String = ReportItem.Body
```

Categories Property

The `Categories` property specifies the categories which can be used to find the report item.

```
ReportItem.Categories = String
String = ReportItem.Categories
```

 To add multiple categories with a single property call, the categories must be placed in a comma-delimited string. For example, to assign the categories `"VIP"`, `"Business"` and `"Me"` to a report, we would write:

```
Dim orpReport As ReportItem
...
orpReport.Catergories = "VIP,Business,Me"
```

Class Property

This returns a unique identifier for the object type. This identifier is always one of the `OlObjectClass` constants, in the case of the `ReportItem olReport` or 46.

```
Long = ReportItem.Class
```

Companies Property

The `Companies` property contains the names of the companies that are associated with the report. This is a free-form string property and in reality you can enter whatever you wish here. There is no validation done on this property.

```
ReportItem.Companies = String
String = ReportItem.Companies
```

ConversationIndex Property

The `ConversationIndex` property will return the index of the conversation thread.

```
String = ReportItem.ConversationIndex
```

ConversationTopic Property

The `ConversationTopic` property returns the topic of the conversation. This is the subject of the original message to which the report refers.

```
String = ReportItem.ConversationTopic
```

CreationTime Property

The `CreationTime` property returns the date and time when the report was created.

```
Date = ReportItem.CreationTime
```

EntryID Property

The `EntryID` property returns the unique identifier for the specific `ReportItem`. This ID is generated when the report is created; it is not displayed in the GUI.

```
String = ReportItem.EntryID
```

FormDescription Property

The `FormDescription` property allows you to get a reference to the `FormDescription` object that is associated with the report. For more information on this object, see Chapter 11.

```
Set FormDescriptionObject = ReportItem.FormDescription
```

GetInspector Property

The `GetInspector` property returns a reference to the `Inspector` object used to display the `ReportItem`. For more information on the `Inspector` object, refer to Chapter 7.

```
Set InspectorObject = ReportItem.GetInspector
```

Importance Property

The `Importance` property allows you to view or change the current level of importance assigned to the report.

```
ReportItem.Importance = Long
Long = ReportItem.Importance
```

The `Importance` property can be set to any of the `OlImportance` constants:

Constant	Value	Description
olImportanceLow	0	The item is of low importance.
olImportanceNormal	1	The item is of normal importance.
olImportanceHigh	2	The item is of high importance.

This property cannot be found on the GUI for the report; instead, you must open the Properties dialog if you want to change or update this property.

LastModificationTime Property

The `LastModificationTime` property returns the time and date when the `ReportItem` was last changed. This property is not available through the GUI.

```
Date = ReportItem.LastModificationTime
```

Links Property

The `Links` property provides access to the `Links` collection. This is a grouping of items that are related to the `ReportItem` (although, at the moment, it can only contain contacts). For more information of the `Links` collection, see Chapter 11.

```
Set LinksCollection = ReportItem.Links
```

MessageClass Property

The `MessageClass` property returns a string identifying the type of item currently in use. This property links us to the form associated with the item. This will be `"REPORT.IPM.Note.DR"` for a delivery report, `"REPORT.IPM.Note.NDR"` for a non-delivery report, or `"REPORT.IPM.Note.IPNRN"` for a read report.

```
ReportItem.MessageClass = String
String = ReportItem.MessageClass
```

Mileage Property

The `Mileage` property allows the user to enter a free-form string. This can be used to hold the mileage associated with the report. This property is not available anywhere at all on the GUI supplied by Outlook.

```
ReportItem.Mileage = String
String = ReportItem.Mileage
```

NoAging Property

The `NoAging` property allows you to specify whether the `ReportItem` can be archived or not. When Outlook auto-archives, the report will not be archived if its `NoAging` property is set to `True`. This means that the item will be available online indefinitely.

```
ReportItem.NoAging = Boolean
Boolean = ReportItem.NoAging
```

OutlookInternalVersion Property

The `OutlookInternalVersion` property returns the version number for the build of Outlook in which the item was created. Unlike `OutlookVersion`, which indicates only the version, this allows the exact build of Outlook in use to be determined. If the report was not sent from Outlook, this will return nothing.

```
Long = ReportItem.OutlookInternalVersion
```

OutlookVersion Property

This property returns the release number for the version of Outlook in which the item was created. For Outlook 2000, this is `"9.0"`. If the report was not sent from Outlook, this will return nothing.

```
String = ReportItem.OutlookVersion
```

Parent Property

Returns a reference to the parent object of the current `ReportItem`. This property will always return the `MAPIFolder` in which the report resides.

```
Set Object = ReportItem.Parent
```

Saved Property

The Saved property indicates whether the ReportItem has been saved since it last changed. This allows us to check whether anything has been changed and if it has, we can save the changes. However, it is doubtful that it is advisable to save any changes made to a ReportItem. The reason I say this is that the report item is an information message indicating that something has gone wrong. So if this item has changed, should we save these changes? I think we should not, as we should keep this original information intact.

```
Boolean = ReportItem.Saved
```

Sensitivity Property

The Sensitivity property indicates the level of sensitivity for the ReportItem.

```
Long = ReportItem.Sensitivity
```

This property can hold any of the OlSensitivity constants:

Constant	Value	Description
olNormal	0	The item contains no sensitive information.
olPersonal	1	The item is personal in nature.
olPrivate	2	The item is private in nature.
olConfidential	3	The item is confidential in nature.

This property is not displayed in the GUI for the report; this property can only be viewed or updated by opening the Properties dialog.

Session Property

The Session property returns a reference to the NameSpace object.

```
Set NameSpaceObject = ReportItem.Session
```

Size Property

The Size property returns the size of the ReportItem in bytes.

```
Long = ReportItem.Size
```

Subject Property

The Subject of a ReportItem consists by default of a string indicating the type of report ("Delivered: ", "Undeliverable: " or "Read: ") concatenated with the subject of the mail item to which it refers.

```
ReportItem.Subject = String
String = ReportItem.Subject
```

UnRead Property

The UnRead property indicates whether the ReportItem has been opened yet (or, more accurately, whether it is *marked* as un-read, because this property can be set as well as read).

```
ReportItem.UnRead = Boolean
Boolean = ReportItem.UnRead
```

UserProperties Property

The UserProperties property provides a means of accessing the UserProperties collection for the report. This contains properties which can be added to the item and which are defined by the user, rather than pre-defined. For more information on the UserProperties collection and the UserProperty object, refer to Chapter 11.

```
Set UserPropertiesCollection = ReportItem.UserProperties
```

The RemoteItem Object

The RemoteItem object is a lightweight object that represents an Outlook item in an online profile. These objects are automatically generated by the server when a remote connection is made. The RemoteItem has the same subject, received date and time, and sender information as the original item which it represents. To download the message from the server, you need to update the RemoteStatus property of the message and reconnect again.

> The RemoteItem includes some methods and properties which are exposed by all items, but which are not applicable to the RemoteItem, since it is merely a representation of a remote item on the server.

RemoteItem Methods

Close Method

The Close method shuts down the Inspector object that is currently showing the RemoteItem.

```
RemoteItem.Close(SaveMode)
```

Name	Data type	Description
SaveMode	Long	Required, one of the OlInspectorClose constants.

The OlInspectorClose constants are as follows:

Constant	Value	Description
olSave	0	Save the item without prompting the user.
olDiscard	1	Discard all changes to the item without prompting.
olPromptForSave	2	Prompt the user to save or discard the item.

Even if the Inspector object for the RemoteItem has not been opened, any changes made to the item will be saved if SaveMode is set to olSave, or the user will be prompted if it is set to olPromptForSave. If SaveMode is set to olDiscard, note that any changes will not be lost until the object is uninstantiated (e.g. when the macro comes to an end).

Copy Method

This method does not work for the RemoteItem.

Delete Method

The Delete method deletes the RemoteItem object from the Items collection. Note that this does not delete the item on the server which the RemoteItem represents.

```
RemoteItem.Delete
```

Display Method

This method causes a dialog box to be opened, prompting the user to mark the item on the server to be retrieved from the server, copied to the client, deleted, or to unmark the item.

```
RemoteItem.Display([Modal])
```

The dialog box is always displayed modally, and the Modal parameter is ignored.

Move Method

This method does not work for the RemoteItem.

PrintOut Method

The PrintOut method prints out the RemoteItem, creating a hard copy of the information it contains on the item it represents.

```
RemoteItem.PrintOut
```

Remember that this always sends the item to the default printer using the default settings for that printer. The only properties that are printed by default are those that have values and are located on the GUI for the item.

Save Method

The Save method saves the RemoteItem to the current MAPIFolder.

```
RemoteItem.Save
```

SaveAs Method

The SaveAs method provides a means of writing the RemoteItem object to the hard disk.

```
RemoteItem.SaveAs(Path [, Type])
```

Name	Data type	Description
Path	String	Required, a valid path and filename for the new file.
Type	Long	Optional, any of the OlSaveAsType constants below. The default if omitted is olMSG.

Type can be any of the following OlSaveAsType constants:

Constant	Value	Description
olTXT	0	Save as a .txt (Text) file.
olRTF	1	Save as an .rtf (Rich Text Format) file.
olTemplate	2	Save as an Outlook Template.
olMSG	3	Save in Outlook message (.msg) format.

If you try to use any of the OlSaveAsConstants not listed above, an error will be raised. In addition, trying to open an Outlook message file or a template file will cause an error and fail.

RemoteItem Properties

Actions Property

The Actions property returns the collection of Actions available for the RemoteItem object. These are the special actions that can be executed on the item. The default actions available for the RemoteItem are "Forward", "Reply", "Reply to Folder" and "Reply to All". For more information on the Actions collection, see Chapter 11.

```
Set ActionsCollection = RemoteItem.Actions
```

Application Property

The Application property returns the Application object for this session.

```
Set ApplicationObject = RemoteItem.Application
```

Attachments Property

The Attachments property returns a reference to the Attachments collection of the item. For more information on the Attachments collection, refer to Chapter 11.

```
Set AttachmentsCollection = RemoteItem.Attachments
```

BillingInformation Property

The BillingInformation property can be used to set or view the billing information for the RemoteItem. However, it does not return the BillingInformation of the remote item on the server.

```
RemoteItem.BillingInformation = String
String = RemoteItem.BillingInformation
```

Body Property

The Body property is used to set or return the body of the RemoteItem. Although the Help Files state that this returns the first 256 characters of the body of the original item on the server, at the time of writing it returned an empty string.

```
RemoteItem.Body = String
String = RemoteItem.Body
```

Categories Property

The Categories property specifies the categories assigned to the RemoteItem. These are not inherited from the item on the server.

```
RemoteItem.Categories = String
String = RemoteItem.Categories
```

Class Property

This contains one of the OlObjectClass constants which identifies the type of the object in question. For a RemoteItem, the value is olRemote or 47.

```
Long = RemoteItem.Class
```

Companies Property

The Companies property contains the names of companies that are associated with the RemoteItem. This property is not inherited from the original item on the server.

```
RemoteItem.Companies = String
String = RemoteItem.Companies
```

ConversationIndex Property

For a RemoteItem, this returns an empty string.

```
String = RemoteItem.ConversationIndex
```

ConversationTopic Property

For a RemoteItem, this returns an empty string.

```
String = RemoteItem.ConversationTopic
```

CreationTime Property

The CreationTime property returns the date and time when the remote item on the server was created.

```
Date = RemoteItem.CreationTime
```

FormDescription Property

This property does not work for the RemoteItem.

GetInspector Property

This property does not work for the RemoteItem.

HasAttchment Property

The HasAttachment property informs you if the message item on the server has any attachments associated with it or not.

```
Boolean = RemoteItem.HasAttachment
```

Importance Property

The Importance property specifies the importance setting for the RemoteItem. This is inherited from the item on the server, but can be set to a different level.

```
RemoteItem.Importance = Long
Long = RemoteItem.Importance
```

The Importance property can be set to any of the olImportance constants.

Constant	Value	Description
olImportanceLow	0	The item is of low importance.
olImportanceNorm al	1	The item is of normal importance.
olImportanceHigh	2	The item is of high importance.

LastModificationTime

The LastModificationTime property returns the time and date when the remote item on the server was last changed.

```
Date = RemoteItem.LastModificationTime
```

Links Property

The Links property provides access to the Links collection for the RemoteItem. For more information of the Links collection, see Chapter 11.

```
Set LinksCollection = RemoteItem.Links
```

MessageClass Property

The MessageClass property returns a string identifying the type of item currently in use. This property links us to the form associated with the item. For a RemoteItem, this will return "IPM.Remote".

```
RemoteItem.MessageClass = String
String = RemoteItem.MessageClass
```

Mileage Property

The Mileage property allows the user to enter the mileage associated with the mail. This property is not inherited from that of the original item on the server.

```
RemoteItem.Mileage = String
String = RemoteItem.Mileage
```

NoAging Property

The NoAging property allows you to specify whether the RemoteItem can be archived or not.

```
RemoteItem.NoAging = Boolean
Boolean = RemoteItem.NoAging
```

OutlookInternalVersion Property

For a RemoteItem, this property always returns 0, regardless of the build of Outlook in which the original item was created.

```
Long = RemoteItem.OutlookInternalVersion
```

OutlookVersion Property

For a RemoteItem, this property always returns an empty string.

```
String = RemoteItem.OutlookVersion
```

Parent Property

Returns a reference to the parent object for the RemoteItem. This will always be a MAPIFolder object.

```
Set Object = RemoteItem.Parent
```

RemoteMessageClass Property

The RemoteMessageClass property returns the message class of the original remote item on the server.

```
String = RemoteItem.RemoteMessageClass
```

Saved Property

The Saved property indicates whether the RemoteItem has been saved since it was last changed.

```
Boolean = RemoteItem.Saved
```

Sensitivity Property

The Sensitivity property indicates the level of sensitivity for the RemoteItem. This is inherited from the original item on the server.

```
Long = RemoteItem.Sensitivity
```

This property can hold any of the OlSensitivity constants:

Constant	Value	Description
olNormal	0	The item contains no sensitive information.
olPersonal	1	The item is personal in nature.
olPrivate	2	The item is private in nature.
olConfidential	3	The item is confidential in nature.

Session Property

The Session property returns a reference to the NameSpace object.

```
Set NameSpaceObject = RemoteItem.Session
```

Size Property

The Size property returns the size of the RemoteItem in bytes.

```
Long = RemoteItem.Size
```

Subject Property

Contains the Subject of the RemoteItem. This is inherited from that of the item on the server which the RemoteItem represents, but can be changed by the user.

```
RemoteItem.Subject = String
String = RemoteItem.Subject
```

TransferSize Property

The `TransferSize` property returns the size of the item on the server in bytes.

```
Long = RemoteItem.TransferSize
```

TransferTime Property

The `TransferTime` property returns the estimated time it will take to retrieve the item from the server (in seconds).

```
Long = RemoteItem.TransferTime
```

UnRead Property

The `UnRead` property indicates whether the `RemoteItem` is marked as un-read. Executing the `Display` method sets `UnRead` to `False`, even though the item is not actually displayed.

```
RemoteItem.UnRead = Boolean
Boolean = RemoteItem.UnRead
```

UserProperties Property

The `UserProperties` property returns the `UserProperties` collection for the `RemoteItem`. For more information on the `UserProperties` collection and the `UserProperty` object refer to Chapter 11.

```
Set UserPropertiesCollection = RemoteItem.UserProperties
```

Post Items

The best way to think of a PostItem is to imagine a bulletin board such as you might have at your office. We can put various notes on this board for everyone to read. The email equivalent of this bulletin board is a public folder which is accessible to anyone in the company (or at least, anyone with the requisite permissions). And the email equivalent of a note on one of these boards is a PostItem. Actually, the analogy isn't exact, because a public folder will usually contain MailItem objects as well as PostItem objects, and a PostItem object can be posted to a personal as well as to a public folder.

So, a PostItem is essentially a message which is posted to a specific folder rather than to a specific user. As we saw, the advantage of this is that we can make a single message available to many people. On these post items we will usually give the name of the sender, a title for the note, and the description. The title is the subject and the description is the body of the post.

Existing post items can be accessed by getting a reference to a MAPIFolder that holds post items and then retrieving the specific post in that folder through its Subject property or through its index in the collection:

```
Dim opPost As PostItem
...
Set opPost = ofFolder.Items _
            ("Copy Method - Chapter 14 Post Item Object")
```

To create a new PostItem, we can use either the Add method exposed by the Items collection of the MAPIFolder in which it is to reside or the CreateItem method of the Application object:

```
Dim opPost As PostItem
...
Set opPost = ofFolder.Items.Add(olPostItem)
```

Or:

```
Dim opPost As PostItem
...
Set opPost = Application.CreateItem(olPostItem)
```

PostItem Methods

ClearConversationIndex Method

The `ClearConversationIndex` method provides us a way of clearing the conversation index. This string value indicates how many times the post has been forwarded: each time the post is forwarded, the ASCII value of the conversation index increases by 5. The `ClearConversationIndex` method resets the conversation index to the character with an ASCII value of 22, as if this were a new conversation.

```
PostItem.ClearConversationIndex
```

Close Method

The `Close` method shuts down the `Inspector` object that is currently displaying the post. The method also allows us to specify whether the changes to the post should be saved or discarded.

```
PostItem.Close(SaveMode)
```

Name	Data type	Description
SaveMode	Long	Required, indicates whether changes should be changed or discarded, or the user should be prompted.

`SaveMode` can be any of the `OlInspectorClose` constants:

Constant	Value	Description
olSave	0	Save the item without prompting the user.
olDiscard	1	Discard all changes to the item and without prompting.
olPromptForSave	2	Prompt the user to **Save** or **Discard** the item.

The changes will be saved or discarded according to the `SaveMode` parameter even if the post has not explicitly been opened in an inspector.

Copy Method

The `Copy` method creates a new `PostItem` that is identical to the current one.

```
Set PostItem = PostItem.Copy
```

This could be used, for example, to archive important items:

```
Dim opPost As PostItem
Dim opNewPost As PostItem
```

```
Dim ofFolder As MAPIFolder
Dim onMAPI As NameSpace
Dim ofNewFolder As MAPIFolder
Dim ofInbox As MAPIFolder
Dim iFor As Integer

Set onMAPI = Application.GetNamespace("MAPI")
MsgBox "Please select a folder to check for important post items."
Set ofFolder = onMAPI.PickFolder
Set ofInbox = onMAPI.GetDefaultFolder(olFolderInbox)

For iFor = 1 To ofInbox.Folders.Count
   If ofInbox.Folders(iFor).Name = "Important Items" Then
      Set ofNewFolder = ofInbox.Folders(ifor)
      Exit For
   End If
Next

If ofNewFolder Is Nothing Then
   Set ofNewFolder = ofInbox.Folders.Add("Important Items")
End If

For Each opPost In ofFolder.Items
  If opPost.Importance = olImportanceHigh Then
    Set opNewPost = opPost.Copy
    opNewPost.Subject = "Copy of Important Item: " & _
                      opNewPost.Subject
    opNewPost.Move ofNewFolder
    opNewPost.ClearConversationIndex
  End If
Next
```

This code sample first searches for a folder entitled `"Important Items"`; if it fails to find one, it creates a new folder of that name. It then prompts the user to select a folder that they want us to check for important post items to copy. Once the user has selected the folder, we iterate through the `PostItem` objects that it contains. If we find any items of high importance (i.e., with the `Importance` property set to `olImportanceHigh`), we copy this into a new `PostItem`. We then change the `Subject` property of the new entry to indicate to the user that it is a copy, and move the post into the `"Important Items"` folder. We also do one more thing here, which is to execute the `ClearConversationIndex` method. The reason for this is that the `ConversationIndex` is carried over to the new `PostItem` when the `Copy` method is used.

Delete Method

The `Delete` method removes the current `PostItem` from the `Items` collection of the folder to which it belongs.

```
PostItem.Delete
```

Display Method

The `Display` method activates the `Inspector` object for the current `PostItem`.

```
PostItem.Display([Modal])
```

Name	Data type	Description
Modal	Boolean	Optional, True to display the inspector window modally; False for modeless display.

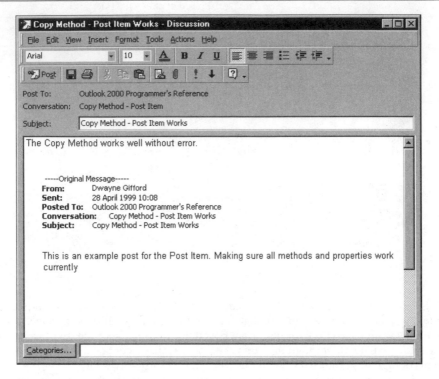

This opens the PostItem without allowing any properties to be changed before it is displayed. If you want to set a property before the item is shown, you must use the GetInspector property, which is explained later in the chapter.

Move Method

The Move method allows us to move the current post to a new MAPIFolder that supports PostItem objects.

```
PostItem.Move DestFldr
```

Name	Data type	Description
DestFldr	MAPIFolder object	Required, equates to an existing MAPIFolder object.

This method could be used to move all related post items which need to be archived to a specific public folder:

```
Dim onMAPI As NameSpace
Dim ofPublicFolder As MAPIFolder
Dim ofNewFolder As MAPIFolder
Dim ofFolder As MAPIFolder
Dim opPost As PostItem
Dim ifor As Integer

Set onMAPI = Application.GetNameSpace("MAPI")
Set ofPublicFolder = onMAPI.Folders("Public Folders").Folders _
                  ("All Public Folders")

For ifor = 1 To ofPublicFolder.Folders.Count
    If ofPublicFolder.Folders(ifor).Name = "WROX" Then
        Set ofNewFolder = ofPublicFolder.Folders(ifor)
        Exit For
    End If
Next

If ofNewFolder Is Nothing Then
    Set ofNewFolder = ofPublicFolder.Folders.Add("WROX")
End If

Set ofFolder = ofPublicFolder.Folders _
            ("Outlook 2000 Programmer's Reference")

For Each opPost In ofFolder.Items
    If InStr(opPost.Subject, "Outlook") Then
        opPost.Move ofNewFolder
    End If
Next
```

The example above selects the topmost public folder and then checks to see whether that has a child folder called `"WROX"`. We get a reference to this if it exists; otherwise, we create it (this will only work, of course, if we have the permissions needed to create public folders). We then get a reference to the folder called `"Outlook 2000 Programmer's Reference"`, which is where the post items that we want to move are. Finally, we walk through all the post items in this folder to see whether they have the keyword Outlook in their `Subject`. If they do, we move them to the `"WROX"` folder.

Post Method

The `Post` method submits the `PostItem` to the current folder. This method is comparable to the `Send` method of the `MailItem`, except that it sends the message to the specific folder rather than to a recipient.

```
PostItem.Post
```

Once a `PostItem` has been posted, other users can either post a reply to the same folder, or send a mail message to its creator. However, it is impossible to do this before the item has been posted.

PrintOut Method

The `PrintOut` method provides a way of printing out the `PostItem` and creating a hard copy of it.

```
PostItem.PrintOut
```

Remember that this always sends the item to the default printer using the default settings for that printer. The only properties that are printed are those that have values and are located on the GUI for the item; in the case of the `PostItem`, there are not many of these.

Reply Method

The `Reply` method creates a new `MailItem` addressed to the creator of the post. The body text of the post will appear in the body of the mail message.

```
PostItem.Reply
```

Example:

```
Set opPost = ofFolder.Items("Copy Method - Post Item Works")

Set omMail = opPost.Reply

omMail.Display
omMail.Body = "It looks ok to me, thanks for the update Tom." &_
              omMail.Body

omMail.Send
```

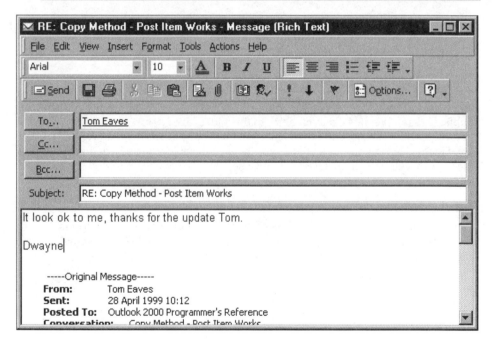

In the example above, we get a reference to an existing `PostItem`, and then execute the `Reply` method. This in turn gives us a `MailItem`. The code then adds more text to the body, keeping the existing text of the body (by concatenating the new message with the original `Body` property). The message is then sent to the recipients.

Save Method

The Save method saves the PostItem to the current folder or, if this is a newly created post, to the default MAPIFolder (which, for a PostItem, is the Inbox).

```
PostItem.Save
```

> At the time of writing, the Save method is identical to the Post method.

SaveAs Method

The SaveAs method allows you to write the PostItem object to the local hard drive.

```
PostItem.SaveAs Path [, Type]
```

Name	Data type	Description
Path	String	Required, a valid path and filename for the new file.
Type	Long	Optional, any of the OlSaveAsType constants below. The default if omitted is olMSG.

Type can be any of the following OlSaveAsType constants:

Constant	Value	Description
olTXT	0	Save as a .txt (Text) file.
olRTF	1	Save as an .rtf (Rich Text Format) file.
olTemplate	2	Save as an Outlook template.
olMSG	3	Save in Outlook Message (.msg) format.

If you try to use any of the OlSaveAsConstants not listed above, an error will be raised.

PostItem Properties

Actions Property

The Actions property returns the collection of Actions available for the PostItem object. These are the special actions that can be executed on the post, and which appear on the toolbar and/or the **A**ctions menu of the GUI. The default actions available for the PostItem are "Forward", "Reply to Folder" and "Reply to All". For more information on the Actions collection, see Chapter 11.

```
Set ActionsCollection = PostItem.Actions
```

Application Property

The `Application` property returns a reference to the `Application` object for this session. This property does not appear on the GUI.

```
Set ApplicationObject = PostItem.Application
```

Attachments Property

The `Attachments` property returns a reference to the `Attachments` collection of the item, which contains the files and objects linked to or embedded in the body of the post. For more information on the `Attachments` collection, refer to Chapter 11.

```
Set AttachmentsCollection = PostItem.Attachments
```

BillingInformation Property

The `BillingInformation` property can be used to set or return the billing information for the `PostItem`. This property is a free-form string, which can hold any text value. It is not available from the GUI.

```
PostItem.BillingInformation = String
String = PostItem.BillingInformation
```

Body Property

The `Body` property contains the body of the post. This is where we enter the information which the post contains. You can enter anything you wish into the body. This is also where any attachments are shown in the GUI. Note that the body can also be in HTML format; in this case, however, we use the `HTMLBody` property.

```
PostItem.Body = String
String = PostItem.Body
```

Categories Property

The `Categories` property specifies the categories which can be used to find the post item.

```
PostItem.Categories = String
String = PostItem.Categories
```

To add multiple categories with a single property call, the categories must be placed in a comma-delimited string. For an example of how to retrieve a collection of items belonging to the same categories, see the section on the `Restrict` method of the `Items` collection in Chapter 11.

Class Property

This property contains an `OlObjectClass` constant identifying the type of object in question. For the `PostItem`, this is `olPost` or 45.

```
Long = PostItem.Class
```

Companies Property

The Companies property contains the names of the companies that are associated with the post. This is a free-form string property and in reality you can enter whatever you wish here. There is no validation done on this property.

```
PostItem.Companies = String
String = PostItem.Companies
```

ConversationIndex Property

The ConversationIndex property will return the index of the conversation thread. This is a string value which indicates what level the item is at in the current conversation. The first item has a ConversationIndex with an ASCII value of 22, and this increases by five for each message in the conversation (i.e. every time that a user replies to or forwards the item).

```
String = PostItem.ConversationIndex
```

ConversationTopic Property

The ConversationTopic property returns the topic of the conversation. This is set to the original subject of the message.

```
String = PostItem.ConversationTopic
```

CreationTime Property

The CreationTime property returns the date and time when the post was created.

```
Date = PostItem.CreationTime
```

EntryID Property

The EntryID property returns the unique identifier for the specific PostItem. This ID is generated when the post is created; it is not displayed in the GUI.

```
String = PostItem.EntryID
```

ExpiryTime Property

The ExpiryTime property contains the date and time when the post becomes invalid and can be deleted.

```
PostItem.ExpiryTime = Date
Date = PostItem.ExpiryTime
```

FormDescription Property

The FormDescription property allows you to get a reference to the FormDescription object that is associated with the post. For more information on this object, see Chapter 11.

```
Set FormDescriptionObject = PostItem.FormDescription
```

GetInspector Property

The GetInspector property returns a reference to the Inspector object used to display the PostItem. For more information on the Inspector object, refer to Chapter 7.

```
Set InspectorObject = PostItem.GetInspector
```

HTMLBody Property

The HTMLBody contains the body of the post in HTML format. This must be in HTML syntax, so you have to supply the HTML tags.

```
PostItem.HTMLBody = String
String = PostItem.HTMLBody
```

As this simple example demonstrates, we can even include script code within this HTML:

```
Dim opPost As PostItem
Dim ofFolder As MAPIFolder
Dim onMAPI As NameSpace
Dim oaOutlook As Application
Dim sBody As String

Set oaOutlook = Outlook.Application
Set onMAPI = oaOutlook.GetNamespace("MAPI")
Set ofFolder = onMAPI.GetDefaultFolder(olFolderInbox)

Set opPost = ofFolder.Items.Add(olPostItem)
opPost.Subject = "A brain teaser"

sBody = "<HTML><B><P>A man rides into town on Friday, " & _
        "stays three days, and rides out again on Friday. How?" & _
        "</P></B><HR>Click   <BUTTON onclick=fnAnswer()>" & _
        "</BUTTON>  for the answer.<SCRIPT LANGUAGE" & _
        "=JavaScript>function fnAnswer() { alert('His " & _
        "horse is called Friday!'); } </SCRIPT></HTML>"

opPost.HTMLBody = sBody
opPost.ClearConversationIndex
opPost.Save
```

At the time of writing, if the HTMLBody property is set, the Body is set to the same value. However, setting the HTMLBody does not cause the Body property to be set. Note also that setting this property will cause the EditorType of the Inspector for this item to be set to olEditorHTML.

Importance Property

The Importance property allows you to view or change the current level of importance assigned to the post.

```
PostItem.Importance = Long
Long = PostItem.Importance
```

The Importance property can be set to any of the OlImportance constants:

Constant	Value	Description
olImportanceLow	0	The item is of low importance.
olImportanceNormal	1	The item is of normal importance.
olImportanceHigh	2	The item is of high importance.

This property cannot be found on the GUI for the post; instead, you must open the Properties dialog if you want to change or update this property.

LastModificationTime Property

The LastModificationTime property returns the time and date when the PostItem was last changed. This property is not available through the GUI.

```
Date = PostItem.LastModificationTime
```

Links Property

The Links property provides access to the Links collection. This is a grouping of items that are related to the PostItem (although, at the moment, it can only contain contacts). For more information of the Links collection, see Chapter 11.

```
Set LinksCollection = PostItem.Links
```

MessageClass Property

The MessageClass property returns a string identifying the type of item currently in use. This property links us to the form associated with the item. Unless this is a user-defined form, MessageClass will always return "IPM.Post" for a PostItem. Setting this property to another valid string value will cause this item to become an item of a different type if it is then saved and re-opened.

```
PostItem.MessageClass = String
String = PostItem.MessageClass
```

Mileage Property

The Mileage property allows the user to enter a free-form string. This can be used to hold the mileage associated with the post. This property is not available anywhere at all on the GUI supplied by Outlook.

```
PostItem.Mileage = String
String = PostItem.Mileage
```

NoAging Property

The NoAging property allows you to specify whether the PostItem can be archived or not. When Outlook auto-archives, the post will not be archived if its NoAging property is set to True. This means that the item will be available online indefinitely.

```
PostItem.NoAging = Boolean
Boolean = PostItem.NoAging
```

OutlookInternalVersion Property

The OutlookInternalVersion property returns the version number for the build of Outlook in which the item was created. Unlike OutlookVersion, which indicates only the version, this allows the exact build of Outlook in use to be determined. If the post was not posted from Outlook, this will return nothing.

```
Long = PostItem.OutlookInternalVersion
```

OutlookVersion Property

This property returns the release number for the version of Outlook in which the item was created. For Outlook 2000, this is "9.0". If the post was not posted from Outlook, this will return nothing.

```
String = PostItem.OutlookVersion
```

Parent Property

This property returns a reference to the parent object of the current PostItem. This property always returns the MAPIFolder object in which the post resides.

```
Set Object = PostItem.Parent
```

ReceivedTime Property

The ReceivedTime property returns the date and time when the post was posted to the folder.

```
Date = PostItem.ReceivedTime
```

Saved Property

The Saved property indicates whether the PostItem has been saved since it was last changed. This enables us to determine whether the user has made any changes to the post, and if they have, they can now be prompted to save these changes.

```
Boolean = PostItem.Saved
```

Example:

```
Dim opPost As PostItem
Dim iResponse As Integer
...
If Not opPost.Saved Then
    iResponse = MsgBox("Would you like to save changes", _
                                  vbYesNo + vbQuestion)
    If iResponse = vbYes Then
        opPost.Save
    End If
End If
```

The example above first checks whether the PostItem has changed (i.e. Saved is False). If it has, the user is prompted to save these changes. If the response is Yes, we execute the Save method.

SenderName Property

The SenderName property returns the display name of the creator of the post. This property is set when the post is saved or posted. Until then, this property returns an empty string.

```
String = PostItem.SenderName
```

Sensitivity Property

The Sensitivity property indicates the level of sensitivity for the PostItem.

```
PostItem.Sensitivity = Long
Long = PostItem.Sensitivity
```

This property can hold any of the OlSensitivity constants:

Constant	Value	Description
olNormal	0	The item contains no sensitive information.
olPersonal	1	The item is personal in nature.
olPrivate	2	The item is private in nature.
olConfidential	3	The item is confidential in nature.

This property is not displayed in the GUI for the post; this property can only be viewed or updated by opening the Properties dialog.

SentOn Property

The SentOn property returns the date and time when the PostItem was posted. This property is set when the Save method or the Post method is executed. If the item has not yet been posted, this property will return 01/01/4501.

```
Date = PostItem.SentOn
```

Session Property

The Session property returns a reference to the NameSpace object.

```
Set NameSpaceObject = PostItem.Session
```

Size Property

The Size property returns the size of the PostItem in bytes.

```
Long = PostItem.Size
```

Subject Property

The Subject property specifies the subject of the post. This appears on the GUI immediately above the body.

```
PostItem.Subject = String
String = PostItem.Subject
```

Because this is the default property for the PostItem, it can be accessed directly through the Items collection, and thus provides the most convenient way of retrieving a specific item:

```
Dim opPost As PostItem
...
Set opPost = ofFolder.Items("Copy Method - Post Item")
```

This avoids the necessity of walking through the Items collection to find the item we want — we can just access it directly using its Subject property.

UnRead Property

The UnRead property indicates whether the PostItem has been opened or read yet (or, more accurately, whether it is marked as un-read, since we can actually set this property through code or through the GUI).

```
PostItem.UnRead = Boolean
Boolean = PostItem.UnRead
```

UserProperties Property

The UserProperties property provides a means of accessing the UserProperties collection for the post. This contains properties which can be added to the item and which are defined by the user, rather than pre-defined. For more information on the UserProperties collection and the UserProperty object refer to Chapter 11.

```
Set UserPropertiesCollection = PostItem.UserProperties
```

15

Notes

In this busy day and age, we are always trying to remember things that we have to do. And almost every monitor in every office that I've been in has these little yellow paper squares stuck to it, reminding the owner of the monitor of something he has to do. This could be to find out the answer to a question for a partner, or to go to get the doughnuts for the meeting tomorrow. So Microsoft decided to help us out by giving us electronic versions of these little yellow sticky things. These are represented in Outlook by `NoteItem` objects.

The `NoteItem` allows you to enter any string value that you want and then save it. By default they closely resemble in size and color the yellow sticky notes that we are already familiar with.

There are two ways to create a new `NoteItem`, and one way to get a reference to an existing note. To achieve the latter, we first need to get a reference to a `MAPIFolder` that holds note items. We can then access the note through the folder's `Items` method, referencing it either by its `Subject` property or by its position in the collection.

As an example, this line will obtain a reference to the note with its `Subject` set to `"Chapter 15 - The NoteItem Object"`:

```
Dim onoNote As NoteItem
...
Set onoNote = ofFolder.Items("Chapter 15 - The NoteItem Object")
```

To create a new `NoteItem`, we can use the `Add` method that is exposed by the `Items` collection of the `MAPIFolder` object in which we want to place the note:

```
Dim onoNote As NoteItem
...
Set onoNote = ofFolder.Items.Add(olNoteItem)
```

Alternatively, we can use the `CreateItem` method that is exposed by the `Application` object. In this case,

```
Dim onoNote As NoteItem
...
Set onoNote = Application.CreateItem(olNoteItem)
```

NoteItem Methods

Close Method

The Close method provides a way of shutting down the Inspector object that is currently displaying the note.

> *NoteItem*.Close(*SaveMode*)

Name	Data type	Description
SaveMode	Long	Required, one of the OlInspectorClose constants.

The OlInspectorClose constants are as follows:

Constant	Value	Description
olSave	0	Save the note without prompting the user.
olDiscard	1	Discard all changes to the item and close without prompting.
olPromptForSave	2	Prompt the user to save or discard the item.

If this method is run on a note which is not currently displayed in an inspector, changes will still be saved if SaveMode is set to olSave or olPromptForSave. However, in the latter case, the user will not be prompted — the changes will just be saved.

Copy Method

The Copy method creates a new note that is identical to the current one.

> Set *NoteItem* = *NoteItem*.Copy

Example:

```
Dim onMAPI As NameSpace
Dim ofFolder As MAPIFolder
Dim onoNote As NoteItem
Dim onoNewNote As NoteItem

Set onMAPI = GetNameSpace("MAPI")
Set ofFolder = onMAPI.GetDefaultFolder(olFolderNotes)

Set onoNote = ofFolder.Items("Chapter 15 - The NoteItem Object")
Set onoNewNote = onoNote.Copy
onoNewNote.Body = "Chapter 14 - The PostItem Object. " & _
                  "Start working on this Item ASAP…"
onoNewNote.Save
```

In the example above, we select first the default **Notes** folder, and then the `NoteItem` that we want to copy. In this case, I know that this `NoteItem` exists, so I do not have any error handling in place. Once we have a reference to the note we want, we set the new note as equal to the copy of the original. When we have the new item, we change its properties to distinguish it from the original item: in this case, we update the `Body` property. We then `Save` the new `NoteItem`.

Delete Method

The `Delete` method removes the current `NoteItem` from the `Items` collection.

```
NoteItem.Delete
```

Executing this method causes the note to be deleted from the folder that it resided in.

Display Method

The `Display` method activates the `Inspector` object for the current `NoteItem`.

```
NoteItem.Display([Modal])
```

Name	Data type	Description
`Modal`	Boolean	Optional, `True` for the inspector to be displayed modally; `False` for modeless display. Default is `False`.

This opens the `NoteItem` without allowing the user to set or change any of its properties before it is displayed. If you have to set or change a property before the note is shown, you can use the `GetInspector` property, which is explained later in the chapter.

Move

The `Move` method allows us to move the current note to a new `MAPIFolder`, providing it supports `NoteItem` objects.

```
NoteItem.Move DestFldr
```

Name	Data type	Description
`DestFldr`	`MAPIFolder` object	Required, equates to an existing `MAPIFolder` object.

One possible use for this method is to move all note items that are similar to a common folder. This allows you to keep all notes that belong together in the same place.

Example:

```
Dim onMAPI As NameSpace
Dim ofNoteFolder As MAPIFolder
Dim ofNewNoteFolder As MAPIFolder
Dim onoNote As NoteItem
Dim ifor As Integer

Set onMAPI = Application.GetNameSpace("MAPI")
Set ofNoteFolder = onMAPI.PickFolder

If ofNoteFolder Is Nothing Then
   Exit Sub
End Sub

For ifor = 1 To ofNoteFolder.Folders.Count
   If ofNoteFolder.Folders(ifor).Name = "Note WROX" Then
      Set ofNewNoteFolder = ofNoteFolder.Folders(ifor)
      Exit For
   End If
Next

If ofNewNoteFolder Is Nothing Then
   Set ofNewNoteFolder = ofNoteFolder.Folders.Add("Note WROX")
End If

For Each onoNote In ofNoteFolder.Items
   If InStr(onoNote.Subject, "Chapter") Then
      onoNote.Move ofNewNoteFolder
   End If
Next
```

In the example above, the user is prompted to select a folder with the `PickFolder` method of the `NameSpace` object. The code then checks to see whether a `MAPIFolder` already exists with the name `"Note WROX"`. If it does, we get a reference to it; otherwise we create one. We then walk through the selected folder looking for notes with the keyword "Chapter" in their subject. To do this we use the `InStr` method that is exposed by VBA. Any that do match this criterion are moved to the `"Note WROX"` folder.

PrintOut Method

The `PrintOut` method provides a way of printing the note out, creating a hard copy of the item.

```
NoteItem.PrintOut
```

Notice that this always sends the entry to the default printer using the default settings. The only properties that get printed are those that have values and are located on the note's GUI.

Save Method

The `Save` method saves the note to the current `MAPIFolder` or, if this is a new `NoteItem`, to the default `MAPIFolder`.

```
NoteItem.Save
```

The important point to remember here is which is the default `MAPIFolder` object for the `NoteItem`; that is of course the **Notes** folder.

SaveAs Method

The `SaveAs` method allows the `NoteItem` object to be written to the local hard drive.

```
NoteItem.SaveAs Path [, Type]
```

Name	Data type	Description
Path	String	Required, a valid path and filename for the new file.
Type	Long	Optional, any of the `OlSaveAsType` constants below. The default if omitted is `olMSG`.

`Type` can be one of the following `OlSaveAsType` constants:

Name	Value	Description
olTXT	0	Save as a `.txt` (Text) file.
olRTF	1	Save as an `.rtf` (Rich Text Format) file.
olTemplate	2	Save as an Outlook template.
olMSG	3	Save in Outlook message (`.msg`) format.

If you try to use any of the `OlSaveAsType` constants not listed above, an error will be raised.

NoteItem Properties

Application Property

The `Application` property returns the `Application` object for this session. This property does not appear on the GUI.

```
Set ApplicationObject = NoteItem.Application
```

Body Property

The `Body` property sets or returns the string value for the body of the `NoteItem`; this is the essential content of the note (equivalent to whatever you write on a PostIt note). This can contain any string value you want.

```
String = NoteItem.Body
NoteItem.Body = String
```

Categories Property

The `Categories` property is a string value that sets or returns the categories to which the note is assigned.

```
String = NoteItem.Categories
NoteItem.Categories = String
```

If multiple categories are added in one call of this property, they should be separated by commas. For an example of how to filter items based on these categories, see the section on the `Restrict` method of the `Items` collection in Chapter 11.

Class Property

A unique value that identifies the type of object, this will always be one of the `OlObjectClass` constants. For a `NoteItem`, this is `olNote` or 44.

```
Long = NoteItem.Class
```

Color Property

The `Color` property is used to set or return the color of the note when it is displayed.

```
Long = NoteItem.Color
NoteItem.Color = Long
```

This can be set to any one of the `OlNoteColor` constants:

Constant	Value	Description
olBlue	0	The note has a blue background.
olGreen	1	The note has a green background.
olPink	2	The note has a pink background.
olYellow	3	The note has a yellow background.
olWhite	4	The note has a white background.

The default for this property is `OlYellow`.

CreationTime Property

The `CreationTime` property returns the date and time when the note was created.

```
Date = NoteItem.CreationTime
```

EntryID Property

The EntryID property returns the unique string identifier for the note. This ID is generated when the note is created. This property is not displayed in the GUI.

```
String = NoteItem.EntryID
```

GetInspector Property

The GetInspector property returns a reference to the note's Inspector object. For the more information on the Inspector object, refer to Chapter 7.

```
Set InspectorObject = NoteItem.GetInspector
```

Height Property

The Height property sets or returns the height for the Inspector object of the current NoteItem in pixels. This property specifies how high the inspector is to be when it is displayed. For an example of its use, see the Left property.

```
Long = NoteItem.Height
NoteItem.Height = Long
```

LastModificationTime Property

The LastModificationTime property returns the time and date when the NoteItem was last changed. This property is not displayed on the GUI.

```
Date = NoteItem.LastModificationTime
```

Left Property

The Left property specifies how far (in pixels) the left edge of the note's Inspector window is to be from the left-hand side of the screen.

```
Long = NoteItem.Left
NoteItem.Left = Long
```

Example:

```
Dim ofFolder As MAPIFolder
Dim onoNote As NoteItem

Set ofFolder = GetNameSpace("MAPI").GetDefaultFolder(olFolderNotes)
Set onoNote = ofFolder.Items.Add(olNoteItem)
With onoNote
    .Body = "Chapter 15 - The NoteItem object"
    .Color = olPink
    .Left = 300
    .Height = 200
    .Width = 300
    .Top = 200
    .Display
End With
```

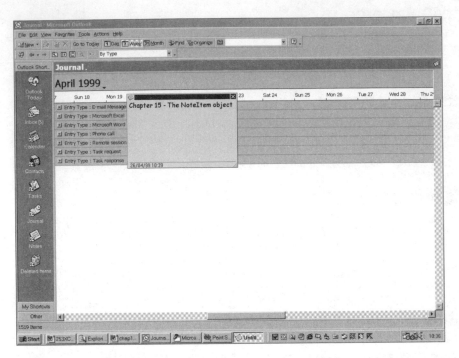

In this example, we use the `Left`, `Width` and `Height` properties to set the position and size of the note before it is displayed. The screenshot above is the result when the `Display` method is called.

Links Property

The `Links` property provides a reference to the `Links` collection for the note. The `Links` collection contains a group of `ContactItem` objects that are related to the note. For more information on the `Links` collection, see Chapter 11.

```
Set LinksCollection = NoteItem.Links
```

MessageClass Property

The `MessageClass` property returns a string indicating the type of item in question. This property also links us to the form that is associated with the `NoteItem`. Unless a customized form has been created, this property will return `"IPM.StickyNote"`. Setting this property to another valid string will cause the note to become an item of a different class if it is saved, closed and re-opened.

```
String = NoteItem.MessageClass
NoteItem.MessageClass = String
```

Parent Property

This property eturns the parent object of the current `NoteItem` object. This property will always return the `MAPIFolder` to which the item belongs. If it has been created through code and not assigned to a particular folder, this will be the default Notes folder.

```
Set Object = NoteItem.Parent
```

Saved Property

The Saved property indicates whether the NoteItem has been saved since any changes were made.

```
Boolean = NoteItem.Saved
```

This allows you to see whether any changes have been made to the note. If there have, the user can be prompted to save these changes.

Example:

```
If Not onoNote.Saved Then
    iResponse = MsgBox("Would you like to save changes?", vbYesNo + _
                                                        vbQuestion)
    If iResponse = vbYes Then
        onoNote.Save
    End If
End If
```

In the above example, we first check to see whether the note has changed. If it has, we prompt the user to save the changes. If the user selects **"Yes"**, we execute the Save method.

Session Property

The Session property returns a reference to the current NameSpace object.

```
Set NameSpaceObject = NoteItem.Session
```

Size Property

The Size property returns the size of the NoteItem in bytes.

```
Long = NoteItem.Size
```

Subject Property

The Subject property returns the subject of the note. This is extracted from the Body property, and contains the text of the body up to the first carriage return. As soon as the NoteItem is saved, the Subject property is set to the beginning of the Body text. Note that this property is read-only, and cannot be set.

```
String = NoteItem.Subject
```

Top Property

The Top property specifies the number of pixels between the top edge of the note's Inspector window and the top of the screen. For an example of its use, see the Left property.

```
Long = NoteItem.Top
NoteItem.Top = Long
```

Width Property

The Width property specifies the width in pixels of the Inspector object for the NoteItem. For an example of its use, see the Left property.

```
Long = NoteItem.Width
NoteItem.Width = Long
```

16

Journal Entries

The `JournalItem` object represents a journal entry in a Journal folder. This object works in a similar fashion to a non-electronic journal, except that you can tell it to automatically log certain things for you. These options though can only be set in the Outlook GUI; they cannot be set through code. This object also allows you to group journal entries according to type. This enables you to see easily which items belong together, and how they are related, without having to look through the entire Journal folder.

So, why would you be interested in how long a Word document has been opened or when was the last time a certain Excel file was opened? Well, let's say I have five technical editors working on this book and I want to keep track of certain statistics such as how long it takes a specific technical editor to review a book, or whether the editor even bothered to look at it in the first place. Tracking files in this way will give me an idea of when I must have each chapter to the technical editor for review when I start the planning of a new book, and so make sure that I get the book to the publisher on time.

There are two ways to create a new journal entry, and one way to get a reference to an existing `JournalItem` object. We can access an existing entry through the `Items` collection of a `MAPIFolder` that supports journal entries. We can specify the particular entry through its `Subject` property or through its index in the collection:

```
Dim ojJournal As JournalItem
...
Set ojJournal = ofFolder.Items("Chapter 16 - The JournalItem
Object")
```

To create a new journal entry, we can use either the `Add` method exposed by the `Items` collection of the `MAPIFolder` object in which it is to reside, or the `CreateItem` method of the `Application` object. In the latter case, the entry will be added to the default Journal folder.

```
Dim ojJournal As JournalItem
...
Set ojJournal = ofFolder.Items.Add(olJournalItem)
```

Or:

```
Dim ojJournal As JournalItem
...
Set ojJournal = Application.CreateItem(olJournalItem)
```

JournalItem Methods

Close Method

The `Close` method shuts down the `Inspector` object that is currently showing the `JournalItem`.

> *JournalItem*.Close(*SaveMode*)

Name	Data type	Description
SaveMode	Long	Required, one of the `OlInspectorClose` constants.

The `OlInspectorClose` constants are as follows:

Constant	Value	Description
olSave	0	Save the item without prompting the user.
olDiscard	1	Discard all changes to the item without prompting.
olPromptForSave	2	Prompt the user to save or discard the item.

Even if the `Inspector` object for the `JournalItem` has not been opened, any changes made to the item will be saved if `SaveMode` is set to `olSave`, or the user will be prompted if it is set to `olPromptForSave`. If `SaveMode` is set to `olDiscard`, note that any changes will not be lost until the object is uninstantiated (e.g. when the macro comes to an end).

Copy Method

The `Copy` method creates a new journal entry that is identical to the current `JournalItem`.

> Set *JournalItem* = *JournalItem*.Copy

Example:

```
Dim onMAPI As NameSpace
Dim ofFolder As MAPIFolder
Dim ojJournal As JournalItem
Dim ojNewJournal As JournalItem
```

```
Set onMAPI = GetNamespace("MAPI")
Set ofFolder = onMAPI.PickFolder

Set ojJournal = ofFolder.Items_
              ("Chapter 16 - The JournalItem Object")
Set ojCopyJournal = ojJournal.Copy
ojCopyJournal.Subject = "Chapter 17 - The MeetingItem Object"
ojCopyJournal.Start = #1/5/1999#
ojCopyJournal.End = #1/7/1999#
ojiCopyJournal.Save
```

In the example above, we first let the user select the folder they want to check. We then select the journal entry that we want to copy. Once we have a reference to the relevant journal entry, we set a new journal entry equal to the copy of the original. We then change the properties of this new entry to make it different from the original. In this case, we update the `Subject`, `Start` and `End` properties. Finally, we save the new journal entry.

Delete Method

The `Delete` method does just that — it removes the current `JournalItem` from the journal.

```
JournalItem.Delete
```

Display Method

The `Display` method activates the `Inspector` object for the current `JournalItem`.

```
JournalItem.Display([Modal])
```

Name	Data type	Description
Modal	Boolean	Optional, True to display the Inspector window modally; False for modeless display.

375

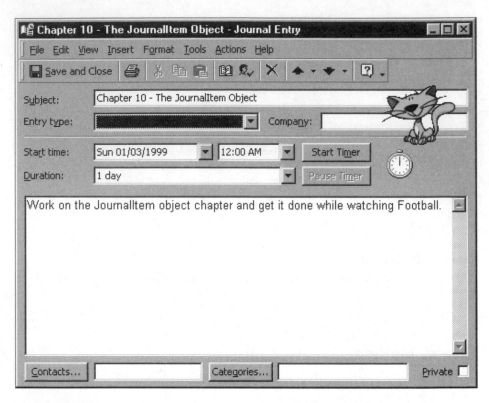

Remember that this opens the `JournalItem` without first letting you change any of the properties. If you have to set or change a property for the `Inspector` before the item is shown you can use the `GetInspector` property, which is explained later in the chapter.

Forward Method

The `Forward` method allows us to send the `JournalItem` as an attachment to a `MailItem` object. The new mail message is created when the `Forward` method is called.

```
Set MailItem = JournalItem.Forward
```

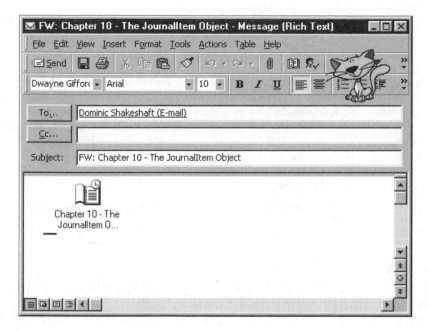

Example:

```
Dim onMAPI As NameSpace
Dim ofFolder As MAPIFolder
Dim ojJournal As JournalItem
Dim omMail As MailItem
Dim oaAttachment As Attachment
Dim owdcWord As Word.Documents
Dim oaWord As Word.Application

Set onMAPI = Application.GetNamespace("MAPI")
Set ofFolder = onMAPI.GetDefaultFolder(olFolderJournal)
'Get a Reference to the Journal Item.
For Each ojJournal In ofFolder.Items
   If ojJournal.Subject = "F:\WROX\Programmers Reference Outlook" & _
                      "\Chapter 16 - The JournalItem Object.doc"
Then
      ojJournal.StartTimer
      'Create the new Mail Item.
      ojJournal.Save
      Set omMail = ojJournal.Forward
      'Add the Recipient
      omMail.Recipients.Add "John Doe"
      omMail.Recipients.ResolveAll
      omMail.Body = "Starting the work on The Journal Item"

      'Send the Mail to the Recipients
      omMail.Send

      Set oaAttachment = ojJournal.Attachments(1)
      Set oaWord = New Word.Application
      Set owdcWord = oaWord.Documents
```

```
        oaWord.Visible = True
        owdcWord.Open oaAttachment.PathName, Visible:=True
  End If
Next
```

The code above works by getting a reference to the journal entry that is to be forwarded. When we have the reference, we start the timer on the item to record that we have started work on this document. Then we create a new `MailItem` by executing the `JournalItem`'s `Forward` method. We then add the recipients that are to receive this `MailItem` and call the `ResolveAll` method to make sure that they are valid. Once we have resolved the recipients, we update the `Body` to inform the recipient that we are working on the chapter, and send the mail. Finally, we open the attached Word document through code.

> For more information on the Word object model, check out "Word 2000 VBA Programmer's Reference", ISBN 1-861002-556.

Move Method

The `Move` method allows us to take the current journal entry and move it to a new `MAPIFolder` that supports `JournalItem` objects.

```
JournalItem.Move DestFldr
```

Name	Data type	Description
DestFldr	MAPIFolder object	Required, equates to an existing MAPIFolder object.

One possible use for this method is to move all journal entries which are related or which we want to be archived to a specific journal folder.

Example:

```
Dim onMAPI As NameSpace
Dim ofFolder As MAPIFolder
Dim ofJournalFolder As MAPIFolder
Dim ojJournal As JournalItem
Dim iFor As Integer

Set onMAPI = Application.GetNameSpace("MAPI")
Set ofFolder = onMapi.PickFolder

'Check to see if the WROX archive folder exists
For iFor = 1 To ofFolder.Folders.Count
   If ofFolder.Folders(iFor).Name = "Journal WROX" Then
      'Get a reference to the existing WROX folder
      Set ofJournalFolder = ofFolder.Folders(iFor)
      Exit For
   End If
Next
'If the Folder was not found then create it.
If ofJournalFolder Is Nothing Then
   Set ofJournalFolder = ofFolder.Folders.Add("Journal WROX")
End If
```

```
'Walk through the Journal items looking for Items with Companies
'set to WROX.
For Each ojJournal In ofFolder.Items
    If ojJournal.Companies = "WROX" Then
        ojJournal.Move ofJournalFolder
    End If
Next
```

The example above prompts the user to select the Journal folder to archive and then checks whether the MAPIFolder entitled "Journal WROX" already exists. If it does, we get a reference to it; otherwise we create it. We then walk through the selected folder looking for journal entries with the Companies property set to "WROX". Any entries that match this criterion are moved to the "Journal WROX" folder.

PrintOut Method

The PrintOut method provides a way to print out the JournalItem, creating a hard copy of it.

```
JournalItem.PrintOut
```

Remember that this method takes no parameters, so it always sends the entry to the default printer using the default settings for that printer. The only properties that get printed by default are the properties that have values and are located on GUI for the journal entry.

Reply Method

The Reply method creates a new MailItem for the originator of the JournalItem.

```
Set MailItem = JournalItem.Reply
```

The problem here is that there is no way to send a JournalItem. There is a Forward method, but this attaches the journal entry to a MailItem as an attachment. So at the time of writing, there is no way to send a JournalItem object. If you attempt to execute this method with the current version, you will receive the error message "Could not send the message".

ReplyAll Method

The ReplyAll method creates a new MailItem for the originator and all original recipients of the JournalItem.

```
Set MailItem = JournalItem.ReplyAll
```

This method has the same limitation as the Reply method.

Save Method

The Save method saves the journal entry to the current MAPIFolder object or, if this is a newly created JournalItem, to the default MAPIFolder (the Journal folder).

```
JournalItem.Save
```

SaveAs Method

The SaveAs method allows you to write the JournalItem to the hard disk.

```
JournalItem.SaveAs(Path [, Type])
```

Name	Data type	Description
Path	String	Required, a valid path and filename for the new file.
Type	Long	Optional, any of the OlSaveAsType constants below. The default if omitted is olMSG.

Type can be any of the following OlSaveAsType constants:

Constant	Value	Description
olTXT	0	Save as a .txt (Text) file.
olRTF	1	Save as an .rtf (Rich Text Format) file.
olTemplate	2	Save as an Outlook template.
olMSG	3	Save in Outlook message (.msg) format.

If you try to use any of the OlSaveAsConstants not listed above, an error will be raised.

StartTimer Method

The StartTimer method starts the timer counting on the journal entry. This timer allows us to keep track of how long it takes to complete work on a journal entry.

```
JournalItem.StartTimer
```

For this method to take effect, you must first save the journal entry. For an example of how to use this method, see the code sample under the Forward method.

StopTimer Method

The StopTimer method stops the timer once it has started. This will set the Duration property for a final time and also update the End property.

```
JournalItem.StopTimer
```

As with the StartTimer method, we have to save the journal entry for the StopTimer method to take effect.

Example:

```
Dim onMAPI As NameSpace
Dim ofFolder As MAPIFolder
Dim ojJournal As JournalItem
Dim omMail As MailItem

Set onMAPI = Application.GetNamespace("MAPI")
Set ofFolder = onMAPI.GetDefaultFolder(olFolderJournal)
'Get a Reference to the Journal Item.
For Each ojJournal In ofFolder.Items
 If ojJournal.Subject = "F:\WROX\Programmers Reference Outlook\" & _
                        "Chapter 16 - The JournalItem Object.doc"
Then
      ojJournal.StopTimer
      'Create the new Mail Item.
      ojJournal.Save
      Set omMail = ojJournal.Forward
      'Add the Recipient
      omMail.Recipients.Add "John Doe"
      omMail.Recipients.ResolveAll
      omMail.Body = "Done the work on the Journal Item. " & _
      "Finished the work in " & ojJournal.Duration & " minutes."

      'Send the Mail to the Recipients
      omMail.Send
 End If
Next
```

In the example above, we stop the timer that we started when we ran the code for the
Forward method. We also send a mail message to tell the editor that we have finished
the work on the chapter, and indicating how long it took.

If you execute this method without first calling StartTimer, nothing will happen.

JournalItem Properties

Actions Property

The Actions property returns the collection of Actions available for the
JournalItem object. These are the special actions that can be executed on the item,
and which appear on the toolbar and/or the **Actions** menu of the GUI. The default
actions available for the JournalItem are "Forward" and "Reply to Folder"
(although the latter does not appear on the GUI). For more information on the
Actions collection and the Action object, refer to Chapter 11.

```
Set ActionsCollection = JournalItem.Actions
```

Application Property

The Application property returns the Application object for this session. This
property does not appear on the GUI.

```
Set ApplicationObject = JournalItem.Application
```

Attachments Property

The Attachments property returns a reference to the Attachments collection of the item, which contains the files and objects linked to or embedded in the body of the journal entry. For more information on the Attachments collection, refer to Chapter 11.

```
Set AttachmentsCollection = JournalItem.Attachments
```

BillingInformation Property

The BillingInformation property can be used to set or view the billing information for the MailItem. This property is a free-form string and can hold any text value. This property is not available on the GUI supplied by Outlook.

```
JournalItem.BillingInformation = String
String = JournalItem.BillingInformation
```

Body Property

The Body of the JournalItem is where any attachments are shown in the GUI; it can also contain any text value that the user enters here.

```
JournalItem.Body = String
String = JournalItem.Body
```

Categories Property

The Categories property is a comma-delimited string specifying the categories assigned to the JournalItem, which can be used to select related items.

```
JournalItem.Categories = String
String = JournalItem.Categories
```

Class Property

This contains one of the OlObjectClass constants which identifies the type of the object in question. For a journal entry, the value is olJournal or 42.

```
Long = JournalItem.Class
```

Companies Property

The Companies property contains the names of companies that are associated with the item. The Companies property is a free-form string, and in reality you can enter any text value here. There is no validation done on this property.

```
JournalItem.Companies = String
String = JournalItem.Companies
```

ContactNames Property

The ContactNames property returns the display names of the recipients associated with the journal entry. To update this property you need to modify the Recipients collection. It is also important to understand that this is not the Contacts field shown at the bottom of the GUI, which represents the Links property documented later in this chapter.

The ContactNames property was the old way of associating items with a contact. However, in Outlook 2000, the Links collection was introduced as a new way of doing this.

```
String = JournalItem.ContactNames
```

ConversationIndex Property

The ConversationIndex property returns the index of the conversation thread. It is unclear what the purpose of this property is, since there is no way to reply to or even to send a journal entry.

```
String = JournalItem.ConversationIndex
```

ConversationTopic Property

The ConversationTopic property returns the topic of the conversation, which is set to the original subject of the message. Again, the question arises as to what the purpose of this property is, since a JournalItem can only be sent as an attachment. In this case, the conversation would relate to the mail message holding the journal entry, rather than the journal entry itself.

```
String = JournalItem.ConversationTopic
```

CreationTime Property

The CreationTime property returns the date and time when the journal entry was created.

```
Date = JournalItem.CreationTime
```

DocPosted Property

The DocPosted property indicates whether the document was posted as part of the journalized session. This returns True if the item referred to by the journal entry was posted to a folder during the session when the item was being tracked.

```
Boolean = JournalItem.DocPosted
```

DocPrinted Property

The DocPrinted property indicates whether the document was printed out as part of the journalized session. This returns True if the item referred to by the journal entry was printed out during the session when the item was being tracked.

```
Boolean = JournalItem.DocPrinted
```

DocRouted Property

The DocRouted property will be True if the document was routed as part of the journalized session. This is supposed to return True if the item referred to by the journal entry was auto-forwarded during the session when the item was being tracked; however, we were unable to get this property to return True during testing.

```
Boolean = JournalItem.DocRouted
```

DocSaved Property

The DocSaved property specifies whether the document was saved as part of the journalized session. This returns True if the item referred to by the journal entry was saved during the session when the item was being tracked.

```
Boolean = JournalItem.DocSaved
```

Duration Property

The Duration property specifies the length of the journalized session in minutes. This is the period for which the item was tracked by the journal.

```
JournalItem.Duration = Date
Date = JournalItem.Duration
```

End Property

The End property indicates the end date and time for the journal session.

```
JournalItem.End = Date
Date = JournalItem.End
```

Example:

```
Dim ojJournal As JournalItem
...
ojJournal.End = #1/1/99 2:00 pm#
```

The example above sets the end date of the journal to be 1/1/99 and the end time to be 2:00 pm. Changing the Duration property causes this property to be updated to correspond to the Start property plus the Duration property. Notice also that setting this property to a date/time prior to the Start property will cause an error.

EntryID Property

The EntryID property returns a unique identifier for the JournalItem which is generated when the journal entry is created. This property is not displayed in the GUI.

```
String = JournalItem.EntryID
```

FormDescription Property

The FormDescription property allows you to get a reference to the FormDescription object that is associated with the journal entry. For more information on this object, see Chapter 11.

```
Set FormDescriptionObject = JournalItem.FormDescription
```

GetInspector Property

The `GetInspector` property returns a reference to the `Inspector` object used to display the `JournalItem`. For more information on the `Inspector` object, refer to Chapter 7.

```
Set InspectorObject = JournalItem.GetInspector
```

Importance Property

The `Importance` property allows you to view or change the current importance setting for the journal entry.

```
JournalItem.Importance = Long
Long = JournalItem.Importance
```

The `Importance` property can be set to any of the `OlImportance` constants.

Constant	Value	Description
olImportanceLow	0	The item is of low importance.
olImportanceNormal	1	The item is of normal importance.
olImportanceHigh	2	The item is of high importance.

This property cannot be found on the mail's GUI; you must open the Properties dialog to change or update this property.

LastModificationTime Property

The `LastModificationTime` property returns the time and date when the entry was last changed. This property is not available on the GUI.

```
Date = JournalItem.LastModificationTime
```

Links Property

The `Links` property provides access to the `Links` collection. This is a grouping of items that are related to the `JournalItem` (although, at the moment, it can only contain contacts). For more information of the `Links` collection, see Chapter 11.

```
Set LinksCollection = JournalItem.Links
```

MessageClass Property

The `MessageClass` property returns a string identifying the type of item currently in use. This property links us to the form associated with the item. Unless this is a user-defined form, `MessageClass` will always return `"IPM.Activity"` for a `JournalItem`. Changing this to a valid string will alter the type of item that this entry is (e.g. changing it to `"IPM.StickyNote"` will cause the journal entry to become a `NoteItem`).

```
JournalItem.MessageClass = String
String = JournalItem.MessageClass
```

Mileage Property

The `Mileage` property allows the user to enter a free-form string. This can be used to hold the mileage associated with the entry. This property is not available anywhere at all on the GUI supplied by Outlook.

```
JournalItem.Mileage = String
String = JournalItem.Mileage
```

NoAging Property

The `NoAging` property allows you to specify whether the `JournalItem` can be archived or not. When Outlook auto-archives, the entry will not be archived if its `NoAging` property is set to `True`. This means that the item will be available online indefinitely.

```
JournalItem.NoAging = Boolean
Boolean = JournalItem.NoAging
```

OutlookInternalVersion Property

The `OutlookInternalVersion` property returns the version number for the build of Outlook in which the item was created. Unlike `OutlookVersion`, which indicates only the version, this allows the exact build of Outlook in use to be determined.

```
Long = JournalItem.OutlookInternalVersion
```

OutlookVersion Property

This property returns the release number for the version of Outlook in which the item was created. For Outlook 2000, this is `"9.0"`.

```
String = JournalItem.OutlookVersion
```

Parent Property

This property returns a reference to the parent object for the current `JournalItem` object. This will always be a `MAPIFolder` object.

```
Set Object = JournalItem.Parent
```

Recipients Property

The `Recipients` property returns a reference to the collection of recipients for the journal entry. To learn more about the `Recipients` collection and the `Recipient` object, see Chapter 10.

```
Set RecipientsCollection = JournalItem.Recipients
```

Saved Property

The `Saved` property indicates whether the `JournalItem` has been saved since it was last changed. This enables us to determine whether the user has made any changes to the item, and if they have, they can now be prompted to save these changes.

```
Boolean = JournalItem.Saved
```

Sensitivity Property

The Sensitivity property indicates the level of sensitivity for the JournalItem.

```
Long = JournalItem.Sensitivity
JournalItem.Sensitivity = Long
```

This property can hold any of the OlSensitivity constants:

Constant	Value	Description
olNormal	0	The item contains no sensitive information.
olPersonal	1	The item is personal in nature.
olPrivate	2	The item is private in nature.
olConfidential	3	The item is confidential in nature.

This property is not displayed in the GUI for the journal entry; this property can only be viewed or updated by opening the Properties dialog.

Session Property

The Session property returns a reference to the NameSpace object for the current session.

```
Set NameSpaceObject = JournalItem.Session
```

Size Property

The Size property returns the size of the JournalItem in bytes.

```
Long = JournalItem.Size
```

Start Property

The Start property specifies the starting date and time for the journal entry. In the GUI for the JournalItem that comes with Outlook, this property is separated into two fields (that is, a date field and a time field).

```
JournalItem.Start = Date
Date = JournalItem.Start
```

> Even when the start date and time arrive, the timer is not automatically started. To start the timer for this journal entry, it is necessary to execute the StartTimer method.

Subject Property

The Subject property specifies the subject of the journal entry. This appears on the GUI immediately underneath the toolbars.

```
JournalItem.Subject = String
String = JournalItem.Subject
```

Because this is the default property for the `JournalItem`, it can be accessed directly through the `Items` collection, and thus provides the most convenient way of retrieving a specific item:

```
Dim ojJournal As JournalItem
...
Set ojJournal = ofFolder.Items("Chapter 16 - Journal Item")
```

This avoids the necessity of walking through the `Items` collection to find the item we want — we can just access it directly using its `Subject` property.

Type Property

The `Type` property specifies the type of journal entry we are working with, such as an email message, a Microsoft Word document or an Excel spreadsheet. It is important to be aware that this is a free-form string property, which means that this can be set to any value and the journal entry will appear in Outlook under this grouping.

```
JournalItem.Type = String
String = JournalItem.Type
```

This code shows how we can change the `Type` property to any value we like:

```
Dim onMAPI As NameSpace
Dim ofFolder As MAPIFolder
Dim ojJournal As JournalItem

Set onMAPI = Application.GetNamespace("MAPI")
Set ofFolder = onMAPI.GetDefaultFolder(olFolderJournal)
Set ojJournal = ofFolder.Items.Add(olJournalItem)
With ojiJournal
    .Subject = "Chapter 16 - The JournalItem Object"
    .Start = #1/3/1999#
    .End = #1/4/1999#
    .Body = "Work on the JournalItem object"
    .Type = "Outlook 2000 Programmer's Reference"
    .Save
End With
```

This code sample creates a new journal entry and assigns it to the `Type` entitled `"Outlook 2000 Programmer's Reference"`.

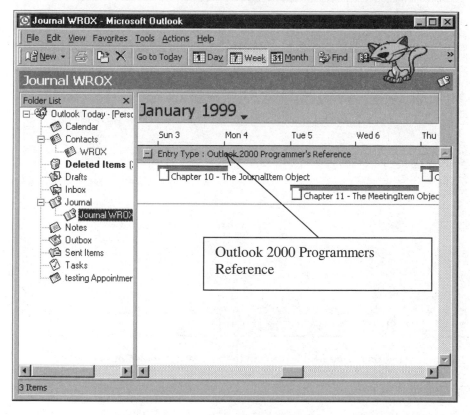

Notice that if you do not assign a `Type` to a journal entry then it will be assigned to the `"Phone Call"` Type (i.e. `"Phone Call"` is the default for the `Type` property). Another thing to remember is that this new `Type` does not appear in the GUI supplied by Outlook.

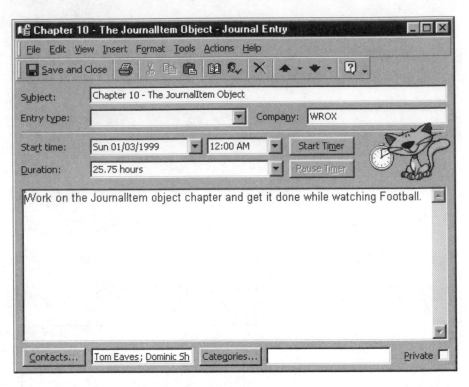

Notice that the **Entry type** field is blank in the screenshot above. But in the code where this entry was added, the `Type` was set to `"Outlook 2000 Programmer's Reference"`.

It is important to notice that even though the GUI does not show the `Type` we assigned to the entry, this type is still saved and shown when printed (as can be seen from the **Print Preview** screenshot below). However, if you open this journal entry through code, the `Type` property will be set to the type that you assigned it to.

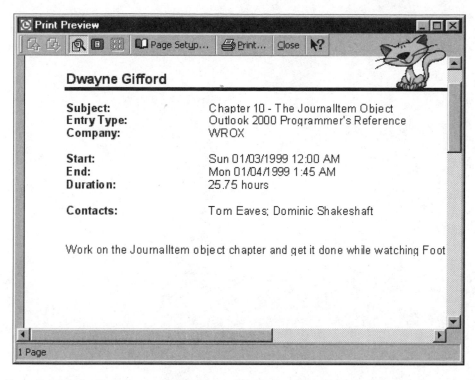

One slightly puzzling aspect of this is that the GUI supplied by Outlook restricts you to the pre-defined list of types, although the Type property can be set through code to any string value. In other cases where a property can be set to any value, Outlook would present a combo box in the GUI rather than a listbox.

UnRead Property

The UnRead property specifies whether the JournalItem is marked as un-read. This property is a bit strange because a JournalItem object cannot be mailed to another user (except as an attachment). This property will therefore only be False if it has been created through code and not yet displayed, or if the property has been changed back from True.

```
JournalItem.UnRead = Boolean
Boolean = JournalItem.UnRead
```

UserProperties Property

The UserProperties property returns the UserProperties collection for the JournalItem. For more information on the UserProperties collection and the UserProperty object refer to Chapter 11.

```
Set UserPropertiesCollection = JournalItem.UserProperties
```

17

Appointments and Meetings

In the modern business age, it is extremely important to be able to keep track of your time. In earlier mail programs, this was always handled by using a calendar or a day timer. Outlook adds to these by exposing to us the `AppointmentItem` object. This object allows us create individual appointments, recurring appointments, and if you have access to a network, you have the ability to invite others to appointments.

The `AppointmentItem` object represents a single entry in the Calendar folder. If you invite others to an appointment, Outlook will create a `MeetingItem` object, which gets sent to the invitees. It is important to realize that the `MeetingItem` can only represent a request for a meeting, or the response to that request. When a meeting request has been accepted, an `AppointmentItem` is created in the Calendar folder, so the meeting itself is represented by an `AppointmentItem`, not a `MeetingItem`.

The `RecurrencePattern` object holds the information on how either an `AppointmentItem` or a `TaskItem` recurs. If any of the recurring items differ in any way from this pattern, this information will be contained in an `Exception` object.

There are two ways to create a new `AppointmentItem` and one way to get a reference to an existing `AppointmentItem`. To get a reference to an existing entry, we must first get a reference to a `MAPIFolder` that holds appointment entries. For example:

```
Dim ofFolder As MAPIFolder
Dim oapAppointment As AppointmentItem
...
Set oapAppointment = ofFolder.Items("AppointmentItem Object")
```

To create a new `AppointmentItem`, we can use either the `Add` method that is exposed by the `MAPIFolder` object or the `CreateItem` method that is exposed by the `Application` object. For example:

```
Dim ofFolder As MAPIFolder
Dim oapAppointment As AppointmentItem
...
Set oapAppointment = ofFolder.Items.Add(olAppointmentItem)
```

Or:

```
Dim oapAppointment As AppointmentItem
...
Set oapAppointment = Application.CreateItem(olAppointmentItem)
```

There is no way to create a `MeetingItem` or a `RecurrencePattern` object directly.
These items are created for you as you work on the `AppointmentItem` itself. The
`AppointmentItem` and the `MeetingItem` both have events exposed by them and
these are fully covered in Chapter 11.

The AppointmentItem Object

The `AppointmentItem` object gives us ways to create and edit information about the
meetings and appointments that we want to keep track of in our Outlook calendar.

The figure below illustrates the default GUI for the `AppointmentItem`.

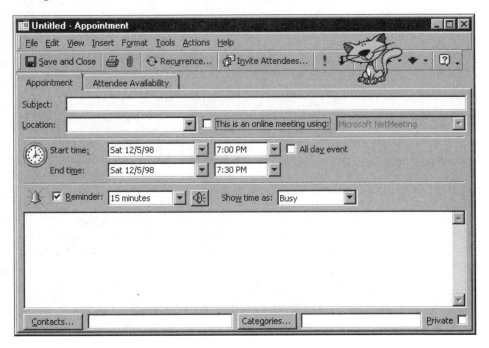

You can see from the screenshot above of the `AppointmentItem` GUI the sort of
information that you need to supply in order to set up an appointment. In the
following section, we are going to show you how to do the same thing but through
code, using the properties and methods of the `AppointmentItem` object. The
`MeetingItem` object section below shows how this default GUI changes so that you
can set up a meeting instead of an appointment.

AppointmentItem Methods

ClearRecurrencePattern Method

The `ClearRecurrencePattern` method sets a recurring meeting or appointment to back to a single occurence.

```
AppointmentItem.ClearRecurrencePattern
```

This method removes the reference to the `RecurrencePattern` object and sets the `IsRecurring` property from `True` to `False`. To make an appointment or meeting recurring, you must use the `RecurrencePattern` object described later in the chapter.

Close Method

The `Close` method allows you to shut down the `Inspector` object of a displayed `AppointmentItem`.

```
AppointmentItem.Close(SaveMode)
```

Name	Data type	Description
SaveMode	Long	Required, specifies whether any changes to the item will be saved or discarded.

`SaveMode` is a long integer value that can be made up any of the `OlInspectorClose` constants:

Constant	Value	Description
olSave	0	Save the item without prompting the user.
olDiscard	1	Discard all changes to the item without prompting the user.
olPromptFor Save	2	Prompt the user to save or discard the changes to the item.

Even if the `Inspector` object for the `AppointmentItem` has not been opened, any changes made to the item will be saved if `SaveMode` is set to `olSave`, or the user will be prompted if it is set to `olPromptForSave`. If `SaveMode` is set to `olDiscard`, note that any changes will not be lost until the object is uninstantiated (e.g. when the macro comes to an end).

Copy Method

The `Copy` method creates a new appointment that is an identical copy of the current `AppointmentItem`.

```
Set AppointmentItem = AppointmentItem.Copy
```

We can use this method, for example, to archive old appointments:

```
Dim ofAppointment As MAPIFolder
Dim oapAppointment As AppointmentItem
Dim oapCopy As AppointmentItem
Dim onNameSpace As NameSpace
Dim ofArchive As MAPIFolder
Dim ofApptArchive As MAPIFolder
Dim ofcPersonals As Folders
Dim iFor As Integer

Set onNameSpace = GetNamespace("MAPI")
Set ofcPersonals = onNameSpace.Folders _
  ("Mailbox - Dwayne Gifford").Folders
For iFor = 1 To ofcPersonals.Count
    If ofcPersonals(iFor).Name = "Archive" Then
        Set ofArchive = ofcPersonals(iFor)
        Exit For
    End If
Next

If ofArchive Is Nothing Then
    Set ofArchive = ofcPersonals.Add("Archive", olFolderInbox)
End If
For iFor = 1 To ofArchive.Folders.Count
    If ofArchive.Folders(iFor).Name = "Appointment" Then
        Set ofApptArchive = ofArchive.Folders(iFor)
        Exit For
    End If
Next

If ofApptArchive Is Nothing Then
    Set ofApptArchive = ofArchive.Folders.Add("Appointment", _
    olFolderCalendar)
End If
Set ofAppointment = onNameSpace.GetDefaultFolder(olFolderCalendar)
For Each oapAppointment In ofAppointment.Items
    If oapAppointment.End < Now Then
        Set oapCopy = oapAppointment.Copy
        oapCopy.Move ofApptArchive
    End If
Next
```

In the example above, we get a reference to the user's Personal Folders (Mailbox). We then check whether they have an `"Archive"` folder below this, and if not we create one. Within this folder, we look for an `"Appointment"` folder and again, if this does not exist, we create it. The next step is to walk through the default Calendar folder looking for `AppointmentItem` objects with an `End` property set to a time before the current date and time. If any items match this criterion, we make a copy of it and move the copy to the `"Archive"` folder.

Delete Method

The `Delete` method does just what you would expect — it removes the current `AppointmentItem` from the `Items` collection.

```
AppointmentItem.Delete
```

We could use this method to iterate through the Calendar removing old items.

```
Dim ofAppointment As MAPIFolder
Dim oaiAppointment As AppointmentItem
Dim onNameSpace As NameSpace
Dim iFor As Integer
Dim oicItems As Items

Set onNameSpace = GetNamespace("MAPI")
Set ofAppointment = onNameSpace.GetDefaultFolder(olFolderCalendar)
Set oicItems = ofAppointment.Items

For iFor = oicItems.Count To 1 Step -1
  If DatePart("yyyy", oicItems(iFor).End) <= DatePart("yyyy", Now) _
                                                           - 1 Then
      oicItems(iFor).Delete
  End If
Next
```

This code simply iterates through the default Calendar Folder searching for items that end before the current year. Any that are found are deleted.

Display Method

The `Display` method activates the `Inspector` object for the current `AppointmentItem`.

AppointmentItem.Display([*Modal*])

Name	Data type	Description
Modal	Boolean	Optional, specifies whether the inspector window will be opened modally (True) or modelessly (False).

There is a slight variation in the form that the GUI takes for an `AppointmentItem`, depending on whether the item represents a meeting or an appointment. If the item is an appointment, with no other invitees, the GUI will be as it appears below:

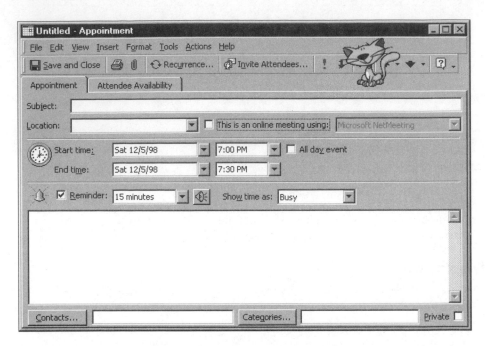

However, this form undergoes a slight change if other people have been invited, and consequently the item represents a meeting rather than an appointment:

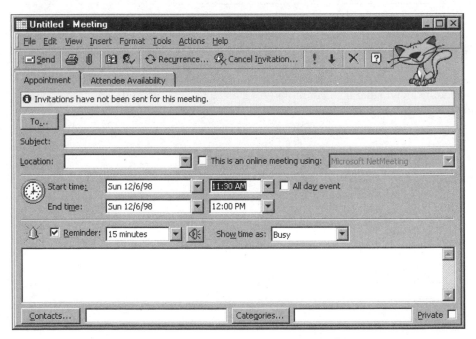

If you look closely at the two diagrams, you will notice a small change. In the first, there is an Invite Attendees... button to add recipients for the meeting; in the second this has been replaced by a button to cancel the invitations. By clicking on this, the item will revert to being an appointment instead of a meeting.

Remember that this method opens the `AppointmentItem` without letting you make any changes to the item before it is displayed.

ForwardAsVcal Method

The `ForwardAsVcal` method returns a `MailItem` that has a `vCal` (virtual calendar) file as an attachment. This file contains most of the appointment information, but lists only the recipient as an attendee. This method does not cause the appointment to become a meeting. (In other words, the recipient is not invited as an attendee.)

```
Set MailItem = AppointmentItem.ForwardAsVcal
```

Example:

```
Dim oapAppointment As AppointmentItem
Dim omMailItem As MailItem
...
Set omMailItem = oapAppointment.ForwardAsVcal
omMailItem.To = "Dwayne Gifford"
omMailItem.Send
```

The above example creates a new `MailItem` with the `AppointmentItem` as a virtual calendar attachment. Then it sets the `To` property to `"Dwayne Gifford"`. Finally, we call the `Send` method to send the `MailItem`.

GetRecurrencePattern Method

The `GetRecurrencePattern` method returns the `RecurrencePattern` object for the current item.

```
Set RecurrencePatternObject = AppointmentItem.GetRecurrencePattern
```

This method is used to get a reference to the `RecurrencePattern` object which defines the pattern in which a series of appointments recurs (e.g. whether the appointment recurs every other day, every week, or on the third Tuesday of every March). For more information on the `RecurrencePattern` object, refer to the section later in this chapter.

Move Method

The `Move` method allows us to move the current `AppointmentItem` to a new `MAPIFolder` that supports `AppointmentItem` objects.

```
AppointmentItem.Move DestFldr
```

Name	Data Type	Description
DestFldr	MAPIFolder object	Required, equates to an existing MAPIFolder object.

PrintOut Method

The `PrintOut` method provides a way to print the `AppointmentItem`, creating a hard copy of it.

```
AppointmentItem.PrintOut
```

Remember that this always sends the item to the default printer using the default settings for that printer.

Respond Method

The `Respond` method allows you to send a response to the originator of the meeting. This can only be called for `AppointmentItem` objects that represent meetings; if this is called for an item that represents an appointment, an error will be raised.

```
Set MeetingItem = AppointmentItem.Respond (IResponse _
[, fNoUI [, AdditionalText]])
```

Name	Data Type	Description
IResponse	Long	Required, can be any one of the `OlMeetingResponse` constants.
fNoUI	Boolean	Optional, can be `True` or `False`. Causes the reply message to be displayed for editing. The default value for this parameter is `True`, specifying that no GUI will be shown.
AdditionalText	Boolean	Optional. The default is `False` and this parameter is ignored unless `fNoUI` is set to `False`. In this case, setting `AdditionalText` to `True` causes a dialog box to be displayed, giving the user the option to send the response immediately, to edit the response before sending it, to or close without sending the response. In the latter case, no object will be returned, and an error will be raised if a `MeetingItem` is set to the result of the method call.

`IResponse` can be made up any of the `OlMeetingResponse` constants:

Constant	Value	Description
olMeeting Tentative	2	The meeting request has been tentatively accepted.

Constant	Value	Description
olMeeting Accepted	3	The meeting request has been accepted.
olMeeting Declined	4	The meeting request has been declined.

So what do all these options mean? When you try to respond to a meeting request through the GUI, you are presented with a dialog asking you whether you would like to edit the response, just send the response or cancel without sending a response.

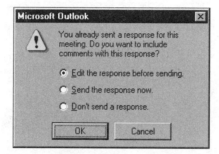

To get the above dialog to appear for the user when you are responding through code, you must set the fNoUI parameter to False and AdditionalText to True. If the user selects the **Edit the response before sending** option, or if fNoUI is set to False and AdditionalText left as False, you will get a Response message presented for editing.

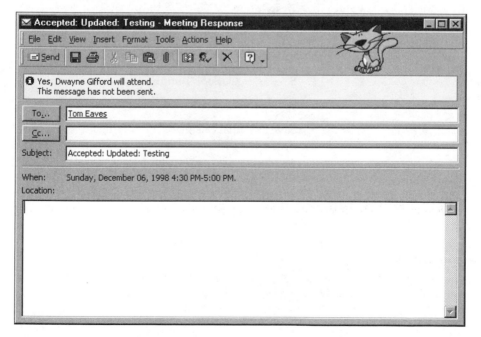

Here you can add any text or attachments that you would like to be included with your response to the originator of the meeting.

Save Method

The Save method saves the item to the current MAPIFolder object or, if this is a new AppointmentItem, to the default MAPIFolder object. The default folder for the AppointmentItem and is the Calendar folder.

```
AppointmentItem.Save
```

SaveAs Method

The SaveAs method provides a way to write the AppointmentItem object to the hard disk.

```
oapAppointmentItem.SaveAs(Path [, Type])
```

Name	Data Type	Description
Path	String	Required, a valid path and filename for the new file.
Type	Long	Optional, any of the OlSaveAsType constants listed below. The default if omitted is olMSG.

Type can be any of the following OlSaveAsType constants:

Constant	Value	Description
olTXT	0	Save as a .txt (Text) file.
olRTF	1	Save as an .rtf (Rich Text Format) file.
olTemplate	2	Save as an Outlook Template.
olMSG	3	Save in Outlook message (.msg) format.
olVCal	7	Save in virtual calendar (.vcs) format.

Attempting to use any of the OlSaveAsType constants not listed above will cause an error to be raised. At the time of writing, there is another option listed on the GUI that is not available through code. This is the iCalendar type, which creates an .ics file. This file is in a format similar to a meeting request, and opens in Outlook without error.

Send Method

Sends the AppointmentItem to the recipients in the item's Recipients collection. If the AppointmentItem is not a meeting, this method will do nothing.

```
AppointmentItem.Send
```

Remember that even if you add a recipient to the `Recipients` object for the item, the item will still not be mailed. This issue is covered in more detail under the `Recipients` property below.

AppointmentItem Properties

Actions Property

The `Actions` property returns the `Actions` collection available for the `AppointmentItem` object. The default actions available for an `AppointmentItem` are `"Forward"`, `"Reply"`, `"Reply to All"` and `"Reply to Folder"`. Note that "Forward" creates a `MeetingItem` rather than a `MailItem`. For more information on the `Actions` collection and the `Action` object, refer to Chapter 11.

```
Set ActionsCollection = AppointmentItem.Actions
```

AllDayEvent Property

The `AllDayEvent` property is a Boolean value that indicates whether the appointment is due to last all day or not. If you set this property to `True`, the times set for the `Start` and `End` properties are ignored. Setting the `Start` or `End` property causes the `AllDayEvent` property to be set to `False`.

```
AppointmentItem.AllDayEvent = Boolean
Boolean = AppointmentItem.AllDayEvent
```

Application Property

This property returns the `Application` object for the current session.

```
Set ApplicationObject = AppointmentItem.Application
```

Attachments Property

The `Attachments` property returns a reference to the `Attachments` collection for the `AppointmentItem` object. For more information on the `Attachments` collection and the `Attachment` object refer to chapter 11.

```
Set AttachmentsCollection = AppointmentItem.Attachments
```

BillingInformation Property

The `BillingInformation` property is a string value that can be used to set or return the billing information for the item. This is a free-form string — there is no mask or pattern to the format of the text that can be added to this field, so it can hold any text value. This field does not appear on the `AppointmentItem` GUI that comes with Outlook, but with the Forms Designer you could easily add it to your own form.

```
AppointmentItem.BillingInformation = String
String = AppointmentItem.BillingInformation
```

Body Property

The Body property allows you to read or update the body of the AppointmentItem. This is where the essential information about the appointment or meeting is held — where you might explain what the appointment or meeting is all about. This is the body of the message you see in the GUI.

```
AppointmentItem.Body = String
String = AppointmentItem.Body
```

BusyStatus Property

The BusyStatus property contains a long integer value that indicates how the time slot taken up by this appointment will be marked for the attendees.

```
AppointmentItem.BusyStatus = Long
Long = AppointmentItem.BusyStatus
```

It can hold any one of the OlBusyStatus constants.

Constant	Value	Description
olFree	0	The recipient is available for the time slot.
olTentative	1	The recipient may be available for the time slot.
olBusy	2	The attendee is busy for that time slot.
olOutOfOffice	3	The recipient will be out of the office for the time slot.

Categories Property

The Categories property specifies the categories to which the AppointmentItem is assigned.

```
AppointmentItem.Categories = String
String = AppointmentItem.Categories
```

Multiple Categories are added using commas as separators.

```
Dim oapAppointment As AppointmentItem
...
oapAppointment.Catergories = "VIP,Business,Me"
```

In the above example, we assign the categories of "VIP", "Business" and "Me" to our appointment. This property allows you to group similar items together. This property can be used with the Restrict method of the Items collection to select all items belonging to the same category, giving you a way to return a particular set of items that meet certain criteria. For more information on the Restrict method refer to Chapter 11.

Class Property

This returns a unique value that holds one of the OlObjectClass constants which identifies the type of object. For an AppointmentItem, this will be olAppointment or 26.

```
Long = AppointmentItem.Class
```

Companies Property

The Companies property allowa us to retrieve or update the names of companies associated with the AppointmentItem. This is a free-form string like BillingInformation, and can be set to any string value. This property does not appear on the GUI for the AppointmentItem.

```
AppointmentItem.Companies = String
String = AppointmentItem.Companies
```

ConferenceServerAllowExternal Property

A Boolean value that has been reserved for future use.

```
AppointmentItem.ConferenceServerAllowExternal = Boolean
Boolean = AppointmentItem.ConferenceServerAllowExternal
```

ConferenceServerPassword Property

A string value that has been reserved for future use.

```
AppointmentItem.ConferenceServerPassword = String
String = AppointmentItem.ConferenceServerPassword
```

ConservationIndex Property

The ConversationIndex property returns the index of the conversation thread. The ASCII value of this string indicates how many times this item has been forwarded or replied to. Every time that a new message is sent in this conversation, the ASCII value of the ConversationIndex increases by 5. The value of the first item is 22.

```
String = AppointmentItem.ConversationIndex
```

ConversationTopic Property

The ConversationTopic property returns the topic for the conversation, which is set to the Subject of the original AppointmentItem.

```
String = AppointmentItem.ConversationTopic
```

CreationTime Property

The CreationTime property returns a date value that represents the date and time that the AppointmentItem object was created.

```
Date = AppointmentItem.CreationTime
```

Duration Property

The `Duration` property holds a long integer that sets or returns the length of the `AppointmentItem`. This is in minutes, so if you want a meeting to last for an hour, you will have to set this property to 60.

```
AppointmentItem.Duration = Long
Long = AppointmentItem.Duration
```

Setting this property to any value after the `AllDayEvent` property has been set to `True` will cause that property to be set to `False`. If `AllDayEvent` is set to `True`, this property has a value of 1440. Similarly, this property interacts with the `Start` and `End` properties, so changing this sets the `End` property to be equal to the `Start` time plus the `Duration`; and setting the `Start` and `End` properties causes `Duration` to be set to the difference between them.

End Property

The `End` property allows you to update or retrieve the end date and time for the appointment object.

```
ApppointmentItem.End = Date
Date = ApppointmentItem.End
```

Example:

```
Dim oapAppointment As AppointmentItem
...
oapAppointment.End = #1/1/99 2:00 pm#
```

The example above sets the end date of the appointment to 1/1/99 and the end time to 2:00 pm. Setting this property causes `AllDayEvent` to be set to `True` and `Duration` to be set to the difference between this and the `Start` date. Similarly, setting `AllDayEvent` to `True` causes the time part of this property to be ignored, and setting `Duration` sets this to a time that number of minutes after the `Start` time.

EntryID Property

The `EntryID` property contains a unique string value that is generated when the `AppointmentItem` is created. This value does not change between sessions and the only way to change the `EntryID` is to move the `AppointmentItem` to a new `MAPIFolder`.

```
String = AppointmentItem.EntryID
```

FormDescription Property

The `FormDescription` property returns a reference to the `FormDescription` object associated with the `AppointmentItem` object; this object represents the form on which the `AppointmentItem` is based. For more information on the `FormDescription` object, refer to chapter 11.

```
Set FormDescriptionObject = AppointmentItem.FormDescription
```

GetInspector Property

The GetInspector property returns a reference to the Inspector object for the AppointmentItem object. The Inspector object represents the GUI (Graphical User Interface) in which the item is displayed, and is treated in more detail in Chapter 7.

```
Set InspectorObject = AppointmentItem.GetInspector
```

Importance Property

The Importance property holds a long integer value that specifies the level of importance attached to the AppointmentItem.

```
AppointmentItem.Importance = Long
Long = AppointmentItem.Importance
```

The Importance property can be set to any of the OlImportance constants.

Constant	Value	Description
olImportanceLow	0	The item is of low importance.
olImportanceNormal	1	The item is of normal importance.
olImportanceHigh	2	The item is of high importance.

This is the same as the Importance listbox that appears on the Properties dialog of the AppointmentItem GUI.

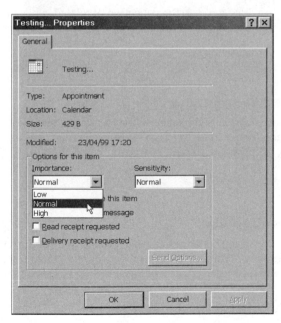

IsOnlineMeeting Property

The IsOnlineMeeting property indicates whether this is an online meeting or not. This property corresponds to the This is an online meeting field on the Outlook form. If this property is set to True, this will cause the other NetMeeting properties to be used; otherwise they are ignored, even if set.

```
AppointmentItem.IsOnlineMeeting = Boolean
Boolean = AppointmentItem.IsOnlineMeeting
```

IsRecurring Property

The IsRecurring property indicates whether the AppointmentItem is a recurring appointment or not. This is a read-only property and is set to True when the GetRecurrencePattern method is called. For more information on the RecurrencePattern object, refer to the RecurrencePattern object section below.

```
Boolean = AppointmentItem.IsRecurring
```

LastModificationTime Property

The LastModificationTime property returns the date and time when the AppointmentItem was last modified. For a newly created AppointmentItem, this returns the date 01/01/4501.

```
Date = AppointmentItem.LastModificationTime
```

Links Property

The Links property provides access to the collection of related contact items for the appointment. The Links collection and the Link object are fully covered in Chapter 11.

```
Set LinksCollection = AppointmentItem.Links
```

Location Property

The Location property can be used to specify the location where the appointment or meeting will take place, for example "Dr. Tillo's Office". This appears as the Location field on the GUI. The property can contain any string value of up to 255 characters.

```
AppointmentItem.Location = String
String = AppointmentItem.Location
```

MeetingStatus Property

The MeetingStatus property holds a long integer value that specifies the current status for the appointment — whether the item is an appointment or meeting, whether the meeting request has been received, or whether meeting has been canceled.

```
AppointmentItem.MeetingStatus = Long
Long = AppointmentItem.MeetingStatus
```

MeetingStatus can be set to any of the OlMeetingStatus constants.

Constant	Value	Description
olNonMeeting	0	The item is an appointment rather than a meeting, with only the organizer due to attend.
olMeeting	1	The current appointment is a meeting, with other attendees.
olMeetingReceived	3	The meeting request has been received.
olMeetingCanceled	5	The meeting has been canceled.

MessageClass Property

The MessageClass property specifies the type of item in use and links us to the form that is associated with the AppointmentItem. Unless you have created you own form, this property will return "IPM.Appointment". If you have created your own Calendar form based on the default Calendar that is shipped then the MessageClass will be "IPM.Appointment.Name of Form". Name of Form is the name under which the new form was saved. Changing this property to a valid string value and saving the item will cause the item to become an item of the new type after the original item has been closed.

```
AppointmentItem.MessageClass = String
String = AppointmentItem.MessageClass
```

Mileage Property

The Mileage property is a free-form string field that allows you to read and save the mileage involved with the AppointmentItem. This could be used to record the distance driven to an appointment in order to claim back expenses. However, since this is a free-form string, Outlook permits any value to be entered here, and you would have to put a mask on the property to make sure that the values entered are consistent. This property does not appear on the default Outlook form

```
AppointmentItem.Mileage = String
String = AppointmentItem.Mileage
```

NetMeetingAutoStart Property

The NetMeetingAutoStart property is a Boolean value which returns or sets whether Outlook is to start the Net Meeting automatically. If set to True, Outlook will instantiate the Net Meeting automatically. By default this occurs 15 minutes before the scheduled start of the meeting, unless the ReminderTime has been changed. The property corresponds to the **Automatically start NetMeeting with Reminder** field on the GUI.

```
AppointmentItem.NetMeetingAutoStart = Boolean
Boolean = AppointmentItem.NetMeetingAutoStart
```

NetMeetingDocPathName Property

The `NetMeetingDocPathName` property contains the path and filename to the document which will be used for the online meeting.

```
AppointmentItem.NetMeetingDocPathName = String
String = AppointmentItem.NetMeetingDocPathName
```

This property is shown on the Outlook form when you select This is an online meeting and specify a type of Microsoft NetMeeting. This causes a NetMeeting section on the GUI to become available, where you will find an Office document field which corresponds to the `NetMeetingDocPathName` property.

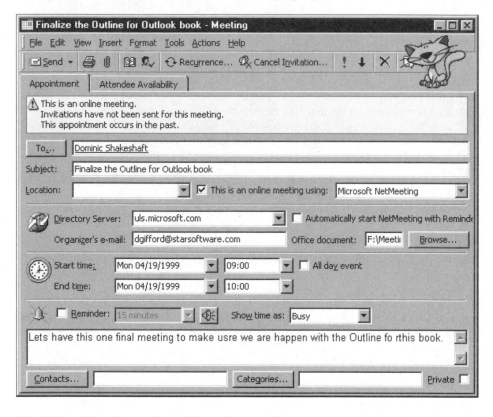

NetMeetingOrganizerAlias Property

The `NetMeetingOrganizerAlias` property is a string value that sets or returns the email address for the organizer of a net meeting. The default for this property is the current user's SMTP address.

```
AppointmentItem.NetMeetingOrganizerAlias = String
String = AppointmentItem.NetMeetingOrganizerAlias
```

NetMeetingServer Property

The NetMeetingServer property specifies the name of the server that will host the online NetMeeting. No validation will take place on this property: you can enter anything here, but if it is not the correct server name, the online meeting will cause an error when it is started. This property corresponds to the **Directory Server** listbox on the GUI for a meeting of type olNetMeeting.

```
AppointmentItem.NetMeetingServer = String
String = AppointmentItem.NetMeetingServer
```

NetMeetingType Property

The NetMeetingType property is a long integer value that sets or returns the type of the net meeting. This value is one of the OlNetMeetingType constants.

```
AppointmentItem.NetMeetingType = Long
Long = AppointmentItem.NetMeetingType
```

The OlNetMeetingType constants are as follows:

Constant	Value	Description
olNetMeeting	0	The appointment is a NetMeeting.
olNetShow	1	The appointment is a NetShow meeting.
olChat	2	The appointment is a Chat Meeting; this option was not available at the time of writing.

NetShowURL Property

The NetShowURL property is a string value that returns or sets the URL for an online meeting of type olNetShow. This property corresponds to the **Event Address** field on the Outlook form.

```
AppointmentItem.NetShowURL = String
String = AppointmentItem.NetShowURL
```

NoAging Property

The NoAging property is a Boolean value that specifies whether the AppointmentItem object will be archived or not. If the folder is auto-archived and this AppointmentItem is checked, it will not be archived if the NoAging property is set to True.

```
AppointmentItem.NoAging = Boolean
Boolean = AppointmentItem.NoAging
```

OptionalAttendees Property

The `OptionalAttendees` property allows you to add a number of optional attendees in one go. These attendees are automatically added to the `AppointmentItem`'s `Recipients` collection. For more information on the `Recipients` collection and the `Recipient` object, see Chapter 10.

```
AppointmentItem.OptionalAttendees = String
String = AppointmentItem.OptionalAttendees
```

The following code demonstrates that the names added in the `OptionalAttendees` property are added to the `Recipients` collection with a `Type` value of `olOptional` (or 2):

```
Dim oapAppointment As AppointmentItem
Dim orRecipient As Recipient
...
oapAppointment.OptionalAttendees = "Testing; Dwayne Gifford; "& _
                                   "John Doe"
For Each orRecipient In oapAppointment.Recipients
   MsgBox orRecipient.Type & " - " & orRecipient.Name
Next
```

The code adds three optional attendees to the `AppointmentItem` represented by `oapAppoinment`. It then walks through the `Recipients` collection to show you that the attendees have been added and gives the value of each recipient's `Type` property.

Organizer Property

The `Organizer` property returns a string value which equates to the name of the originator — the person who organized the meeting. When the `AppointmentItem` is created, the originator is set to the current user at that time. You cannot change this property.

```
String = AppointmentItem.Organizer
```

OutlookInternalVersion Property

The `OutlookInternalVersion` returns a long integer value that equates to the build number for the version of Outlook in which the item was created.

```
Long = AppointmentItem.OutlookInternalVersion
```

OutlookVersion Property

The `OutlookVersion` property returns a string value that equates to the version of Outlook in which the item was created. For Outlook 2000, this is `"9.0"`.

```
String = AppointmentItem.OutlookVersion
```

Parent Property

This property returns the parent object for the current `AppointmentItem` object. This property always returns the `MAPIFolder` object to which the item belongs.

```
Set Object = AppointmentItem.Parent
```

Recipients Property

The `Recipients` property returns the `Recipients` collection for the `AppointmentItem`. To learn more about the `Recipients` collection and the `Recipient` object, see Chapter 10.

```
Set RecipientsCollection = AppointmentItem.Recipients
```

RecurrenceState Property

The `RecurrenceState` property returns a long integer value that indicates whether the appointment is recurring and if so, whether it is the master appointment and whether it is an exception to the recurrence pattern. This value will be one of the `OlRecurrenceState` constants.

```
Long = Appointment.RecurrenceState
```

Constant	Value	Description
`olApptNotRecurring`	0	The appointment is a one-off appointment.
`olApptMaster`	1	The current appointment is the master.
`olApptOccurence`	2	The appointment is one of the recurring instances.
`olApptException`	3	The appointment is an exception to the normal recurring pattern.

ReminderMinutesBeforeStart Property

The `ReminderMinutesBeforeStart` property holds a long integer value that will specifies the number of minutes that the reminder should occur before the appointment.

```
AppointmentItem.ReminderMinutesBeforeStart = Long
Long = AppointmentItem.ReminderMinutesBeforeStart
```

ReminderOverrideDefault Property

The `ReminderOverrideDefault` property allows you to override the default sound file that has been set for Outlook. Setting this property to `True` causes Outlook to set the `ReminderPlaySound` and `ReminderSoundFile` to be valid properties.

```
AppointmentItem.ReminderOverrideDefault = Boolean
Boolean = AppointmentItem.ReminderOverrideDefault
```

ReminderPlaySound Property

The `ReminderPlaySound` property is a Boolean value that if set to `True` causes Outlook to play the sound file that is set in the `ReminderSoundFile` property. The default for a new `AppointmentItem` object is `True`.

```
AppointmentItem.ReminderPlaySound = Boolean
Boolean = AppointmentItem.ReminderPlaySound
```

ReminderSet Property

The `ReminderSet` property is a Boolean value indicating whether Outlook is to display a reminder before the start of the appointment.

```
AppointmentItem.ReminderSet = Boolean
Boolean = AppointmentItem.ReminderSet
```

By default this property is `False`; setting it to `True` causes Outlook to remind you of this appointment the number of minutes before the start set in the `ReminderMinutesBeforeStart` property.

For example:

```
Dim oapAppointment As AppointmentItem
...
oapAppointment.ReminderMinutesBeforeStart = 5
oapAppointment.ReminderSoundFile = < Appropriate Sound File >
oapAppointment.ReminderPlaySound = True
oapAppointment.ReminderOverrideDefault = True
oapAppointment.ReminderSet = True
```

In the example above, we set the reminder for the appointment to fire off five minutes before the appointment starts. Then we use the `ReminderSoundFile` property and the `ReminderPlaySound` property to indicate what sound to play when the reminder is fired off. Finally, we set the `ReminderSet` property to `True` to ensure that the reminder is fired.

ReminderSoundFile Property

The `ReminderSoundFile` property is a string value that specifies the pathname and filename for the file that you want Outlook to play when the reminder is fired. There is no validation done on this property, so no error will be raised if the pathname and filename are not valid. See the `ReminderSet` property for an example of how this property works.

```
AppointmentItem.ReminderSoundFile = Boolean
Boolean = AppointmentItem.ReminderSoundFile
```

ReplyTime Property

The `ReplyTime` property returns the time and date when a reply to the `AppointmentItem` was sent. A value of 01/01/4501 indicates that the `AppointmentItem` has not yet been replied to. However, note that you can override this property with any valid date you wish to set. This value will only be changed when a recipient replies to the `AppointmentItem` or it is changed through code.

```
AppointmentItem.ReplyTime = Date
Date = AppointmentItem.ReplyTime
```

RequiredAttendees Property

The `RequiredAttendees` property is a semicolon-delimited string value that can be used to set or return the required attendees for the meeting in one go. This string consists of the display names for the attendees.

Attendees added through this property are automatically added to the Recipients collection with an olRequired type. For more information on the Recipients collection and the Recipient object, see Chapter 10.

```
AppointmentItem.RequiredAttendees = String
String = AppointmentItem.RequiredAttendees
```

The following code demonstrates how the Recipients collection is updated when recipients are added through the RequiredAttendees property:

```
Dim oapAppointment As AppointmentItem
Dim orRecipient As Recipient
...
oapAppointment.RequiredAttendees = "Testing; Dwayne Gifford; John
Doe"
For Each orRecipient In oapAppointment.Recipients
    MsgBox orRecipient.Type & " - " & orRecipient.Name
Next
```

The above example adds three required attendees to the AppointmentItem represented by oapAppointment. It then walks through the Recipients collection to demonstrate that the attendees have been added, giving the Type property for each recipient. However, I would recommend that you use the Recipients collection and add the attendees one at a time. This allows you to resolve the recipients as they are added.

Resources Property

The Resources property allows you to add resources all at once. These resources are automatically added to the Recipients collection as an olResource type. For more information on the Recipients collection and the Recipient object, see Chapter 10.

```
AppointmentItem.Resources = String
String = AppointmentItem.Resources
```

Example:

```
Dim oapAppointment As Appointment
Dim orRecipient As Recipient
...
oapAppointment.Resources = "My Office"
For Each orRecipient In oapAppointment.Recipients
    MsgBox orRecipient.Type & " - " & orRecipient.Name
Next
```

This example adds "My Office" as a resource to the AppointmentItem represented by oapAppointment. It then walks through the Recipients collection to demonstrate that the attendee has been added, and of what Type it is.

ResponseRequested Property

The ResponseRequested property is a Boolean value that indicates whether the sender of the meeting request requires a response.

```
AppointmentItem.ResponseRequested = Boolean
Boolean = AppointmentItem.ResponseRequested
```

ResponseStatus Property

The `ResponseStatus` property is a long integer value that specifies how or whether the current user has responded to the meeting request. This property is only valid when you are working with an `AppointmentItem` object that represents a meeting.

```
AppointmentItem.ResponseStatus = Long
Long = AppointmentItem.ResponseStatus
```

The `ResponseStatus` property can be one of the following `OlResponseStatus` constants:

Constant	Name	Description
olResponseNone	0	No invitations to the meeting have been sent.
olResponseOrganized	1	Invitations to the meeting have been sent.
olResponseTentative	2	The recipient has tentatively accepted the meeting request.
olResponseAccepted	3	The recipient has accepted the meeting request.
olResponseDeclined	4	The recipient has declined the meeting request.
olResponseNotResponded	5	No response to the meeting request has yet been received.

Saved Property

The `Saved` property indicates whether the `AppointmentItem` has been saved since it was last changed.

```
Boolean = AppointmentItem.Saved
```

This allows you to check whether the user has made any changes to the appointment and if they have, you can now prompt them to save these changes.

```
Dim oapAppointment As AppointmentItem
Dim iResponse As Integer
...
If Not oapAppointment.Saved Then
   iResponse = MsgBox("Would you like to save changes?", _
                  vbYesNo + vbQuestion)
   If iResponse = vbYes Then
      oapAppointment.Save
   End If
End If
```

In the above example, we check to see whether the `AppointmentItem` has changed since it was last saved, and if it has, we prompt the user to save the changes. If the user selects **Yes**, we execute the `Save` method.

Sensitivity Property

The Sensitivity property holds a long integer value that returns or sets the level of sensitivity for the AppointmentItem.

```
AppointmentItem.Sensitivity = Long
Long = AppointmentItem.Sensitivity
```

This property can be set to any of the OlSensitivity constants.

Constant	Value	Description
olNormal	0	The item contains no sensitive information.
olPersonal	1	The item is personal in nature.
olPrivate	2	The item is private in nature.
olConfidential	3	The item is confidential in nature.

Session Property

This property returns a reference to the NameSpace object for the current session.

```
Set NameSpaceObject = AppointmentItem.Session
```

Size Property

The Size property returns the size of the AppointmentItem in bytes.

```
Long = AppointmentItem.Size
```

Start Property

The Start property returns or sets the starting date and time for the AppointmentItem. On the GUI supplied with Outlook, this property is separated into two fields for the time and date respectively. However, both of these fields are represented by this single property in code.

```
AppointmentItem.Start = Date
Date = AppointmentItem.Start
```

Subject Property

The Subject property is a string value that will return or set the default property for the appointment. This property can be thought of as the name for the appointment (e.g. "Doctor's Appointment"), since appointments are usually referred to by their Subject. Because this is the default property, it can be used instead of the index in the Items collection to find a specific appointment.

```
AppointmentItem.Subject = String
String = AppointmentItem.Subject
```

UnRead Property

The UnRead property is a Boolean value that updates or sets whether the appointment is marked as un-read. This will return False unless the appointment was created through code or the property has been changed through code or by the user.

```
AppointmentItem.UnRead = Boolean
Boolean = AppointmentItem.UnRead
```

UserProperties Property

The UserProperties property provides a way to interface with the user-defined custom properties for the AppointmentItem. For more information on the UserProperties collection and the UserProperty object, see Chapter 11.

```
Set UserPropertiesCollection = AppointmentItem.UserProperties
```

MeetingItem Object

The MeetingItem object represents a meeting request or the response to a meeting request. It is similar to a MailItem, except that the user is given the options Accept, Decline and Tentative as possible responses to the request. An AppointmentItem associated with this meeting request is automatically created in the user's Calendar when the request is received; this is destroyed if the user declines the request. Note that a MeetingItem does not represent a meeting — that is represented by an AppointmentItem. Bear in mind also that a meeting cannot be created through code: the AppointmentItem has a Send method, but, as we saw above, this only has an effect if the appointment is already a meeting.

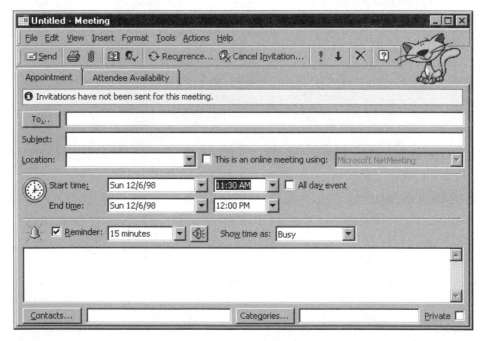

The figure above shows the form that you see when you click on the Invite Attendees... button on the `AppointmentItem` form. To generate a `MeetingItem` through the GUI, you must see this form opened as it is shown above. This indicates that there will be a `MeetingItem` object sent to each recipient associated with the `AppointmentItem`. The difference between this `AppointmentItem` and the one you saw at the start of the chapter is that you can now add attendees to be invited and send a request to these recipients.

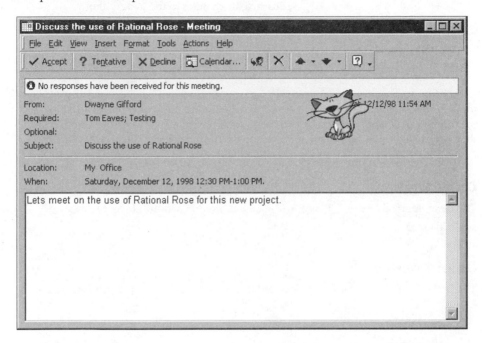

Once the request has been sent, the recipient will receive a `MeetingItem` similar to that shown above in their Inbox. They can see from this what the meeting is about and who are the required and optional attendees for the meeting. It also shows where the meeting will be held and when the meeting will occur. Finally, we can also see the `Subject` of the meeting and its `Body` — which could contain any information that the originator wanted attendees to read before the start of the meeting.

MeetingItem Methods

Close Method

The `Close` method allows you to shut down the `Inspector` object of a displayed `MeetingItem`.

> `MeetingItem.Close(SaveMode)`

Name	Data type	Description
SaveMode	Long	Required, specifies whether any changes to the item will be saved or discarded.

SaveMode is a long integer value that can be made up any of the `OlInspectorClose` constants:

Constant	Value	Description
olSave	0	Save the item without prompting the user.
olDiscard	1	Discard all changes to the item without prompting the user.
olPrompt ForSave	2	Prompt the user to save or discard the changes to the item.

Even if the Inspector object for the MeetingItem has not been opened, any changes made to the item will be saved if SaveMode is set to olSave, or the user will be prompted if it is set to olPromptForSave. If SaveMode is set to olDiscard, note that any changes will not be lost until the object is uninstantiated (e.g. when the macro comes to an end).

Copy Method

The Copy method creates a new MeetingItem identical to the current one.

```
Set MeetingItem = MeetingItem.Copy
```

Delete Method

The Delete method removes the current MeetingItem from the Items collection.

```
MeetingItem.Delete
```

Display Method

The Display method opens the Inspector object for the MeetingItem for the user to view. For an example that uses this method, see under the Body property below.

```
MeetingItem.Display([Modal])
```

Name	Data type	Description
Modal	Boolean	Optional, specifies whether the inspector window will be opened modally (True) or modelessly (False).

Forward Method

The Forward method gives invitees to the meeting a way to invite other recipients that they feel should be part of the meeting. Of course, this might make the originator unhappy, because this recipient was deliberately left off in the first place! This method returns a new MeetingItem.

```
Set MeetingItem = MeetingItem.Forward
```

Note that for the item actually to be sent, we must add recipients and call the `Send` method of the new `MeetingItem`.

```
Dim omeMeeting As MeetingItem
Dim omeNewMeeting As MeetingItem
...
Set omeNewMeeting = omeMeeting.Forward
omeNewMeeting.Recipients.Add("Dwayne Gifford")
omeNewMeeting.Recipients.ResolveAll
omeNewMeeting.Send
```

This code calls the `Forward` method of an existing `MeetingItem` to get a new item. Then a new recipient is added and resolved by calling the `ResolveAll` method of the `Recipients` collection. Lastly, this `MeetingItem` is sent to the added recipient.

GetAssociatedAppointment Method

The `GetAssociatedAppointment` method returns a reference to the `AppointmentItem` that is associated with this `MeetingItem`. An associated `AppointmentItem` is automatically created for every `MeetingItem` you receive, and to avoid the necessity of searching through the `Calendar` folder for this `AppointmentItem`, Microsoft was kind enough to give you a method to do this.

```
Set AppointmentItem =
          MeetingItem.GetAssociatedAppointment(AddToCalendar)
```

Name	Data Type	Description
AddTo Calendar	Boolean	Required, specifies whether the item is to be created in the default calendar folder (`True`). If this parameter is set to `False`, no associated `AppointmentItem` will be created if one does not already exist, and the method will return `Nothing`.

Example:

```
Dim omeMeeting As MeetingItem
Dim oapAppointment As AppointmentItem
...
Set oapAppointment = omeMeeting.GetAssociatedAppointment(False)
MsgBox omeMeeting.Body & " - " & oapAppointment.Body
oapAppointment.Respond olMeetingAccepted, False, True
```

The above example uses the `GetAssociatedAppointment` method of an existing `MeetingItem` to get a reference to the related `AppointmentItem`. Then it calls the `Respond` method for the `AppointmentItem` to accept the meeting request.

Move Method

The `Move` method is similar to that for the `AppointmentItem`, except that here we must move the item to another `MAPIFolder` that supports mail items, whereas an `AppointmentItem` has to be moved to another Calendar folder.

```
MeetingItem.Move DestFldr
```

Name	Data Type	Description
DestFldr	MAPIFolder object	Required, an existing MAPIFolder object.

PrintOut Method

The `PrintOut` method is the only way to print out a `MeetingItem`.

```
MeetingItem.PrintOut
```

Dwayne Gifford

Subject:	Discuss the use of Rational Rose
Location:	My Office
Start:	Sat 12/12/98 12:30 PM
End:	Sat 12/12/98 1:00 PM
Show time As:	Tentative
Recurrence:	(none)
Meeting Status:	Not yet responded
Required Attendees:	Tom Eaves; Testing

Lets meet on the use of Rational Rose for this new project

The printout above shows you a sample `MeetingItem` when it is printed out.

Reply Method

The `Reply` method gives us a way to send back a message about the meeting without actually accepting or declining the meeting. The method will return to us a new `MailItem` object with the originator of the meeting as a recipient. To learn more about the `MailItem`, see Chapter 13.

```
Set MailItem = MeetingItem.Reply
```

As an example, this code sends a reply to all meeting requests in the Inbox:

```
Dim ofFolder As MAPIFolder
Dim omeMeeting As MeetingItem
Dim omMail As MailItem
Dim sMessage As String
Dim iFor As Integer

Set ofFolder = Application.GetNamespace("mapi").GetDefaultFolder _
               (olFolderInbox)
For iFor = 1 To ofFolder.Items.Count
    If ofFolder.Items.Item(iFor).MessageClass = _
        "IPM.Schedule.Meeting.Request" Then
      Set omeMeeting = ofFolder.Items.Item(iFor)
      Set omMail = omeMeeting.Reply
```

```
        'Now add the message to the Body
        sMessage = "Should we invite Dominic " & _
                  "as well to this meeting Tom?"
        sMessage = sMessage & vbCrLf & vbCrLf
        'Now add a dividing line between your message and the original
        'message
        sMessage = sMessage & "--------------------------------"
        sMessage = sMessage & vbCrLf & vbCrLf
        omMail.Body = sMessage & omMail.Body
        'Now send the message
        omMail.Send
    End If
Next
```

This code checks each item in the Inbox to see if it is a meeting request. For each request, we call the `Reply` method to send a message back to the organizer. We compose a new `Body` for the mail message thus created and append to it the original `Body`. Finally, we send the mail:

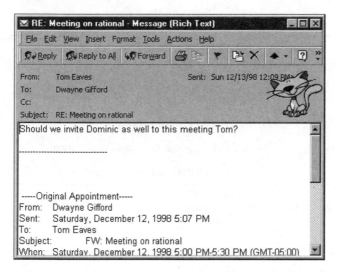

The figure above shows the `MailItem` which is received by the originator.

ReplyAll Method

The `ReplyAll` method is similar to the `Reply` method, except that it adds all the original recipients to the new `MailItem`. Again, to find out more about the `MailItem` object, see Chapter 13.

```
Set MailItem = MeetingItem.ReplyAll
```

Save Method

Since there is no way to create a `MeetingItem` through code, this method always saves the `MeetingItem` to the current `MAPIFolder`. This will usually be the Inbox.

```
MeetingItem.Save
```

SaveAs Method

The SaveAs method provides a way to write the MeetingItem object to the hard drive.

```
MeetingItem.SaveAs(Path [, Type])
```

Name	Data type	Description
Path	String	Required, a valid path and filename for the new file.
Type	Long	Optional, any of the OlSaveAsType constants below. The default if omitted is olMSG.

Type can be any of the following OlSaveAsType constants:

Constant	Value	Description
olTXT	0	Save as a .txt (Text) file.
olRTF	1	Save as an .rtf (Rich Text Format) file.
olTemplate	2	Save as an Outlook Template.
olMSG	3	Save in Outlook message (.msg) format.
olVCal	7	Save in virtual calendar (.vcs) format.

Attempting to use any of the OlSaveAsType constants not listed above will cause an error to be raised.

Send Method

The Send method submits the item to the messaging queue to be sent to the recipients. Beware that if you try to modify any of the properties for an item that has just been sent, an error will be raised.

```
MeetingItem.Send
```

MeetingItem Properties

The following properties are identical to those of the AppointmentItem; we will only be covering in detail those that are different.

Actions	Application	Attachments	Billing Information
Categories	Class	Companies	Conversation Index

Conversation Topic	CreationTime	EntryID	Form Description
Get Inspector	Importance	Last Modification Time	Links
MessageClass	Mileage	NoAging	Outlook Internal Version
Outlook Version	Parent	Recipients	ReminderSet
Reminder Time	Saved	Sensitivity	Session
Size	Subject	UnRead	User Properties

AutoForwarded Property

This property returns True if the MeetingItem was sent as an auto-forward; otherwise False.

```
MeetingItem.AutoForwarded = Boolean
Boolean = MeetingItem.AutoForwarded
```

Body Property

The Body property is a string value that sets or returns the body of the MeetingItem.

```
MeetingItem.Body = String
String = MeetingItem.Body
```

The screenshot below reprints the one given at the beginning of the MeetingItem section. Looking at this, you would expect the Body of the MeetingItem to be "Lets meet on the use of Rational Rose for this new project". But this text in the Body of the MeetingItem is in fact preceded by information on the time and location of the meeting. The other text is the body of the associated AppointmentItem.

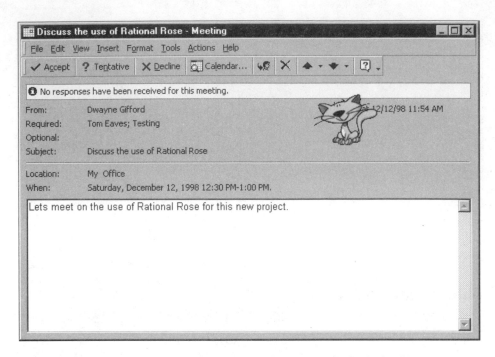

The following screenshot shows a message box containing the body for this `MeetingItem`:

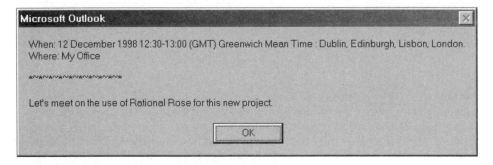

DeferredDeliveryTime Property

The `DeferredDeliveryTime` property is used to view or set the time when you wish the `MeetingItem` to be sent. It is important to realize that this property can only be used with the `Forward` method. That is because this is the only way to get a new `MeetingItem` without creating an `AppointmentItem`.

```
MeetingItem.DeferredDeliveryTime = Date
Date = MeetingItem.DeferredDeliveryTime
```

The following code shows an example of how we might use this:

```
Dim omeMeeting As MeetingItem
Dim omeNewMeeting As MeetingItem
```

```
Set omeNewMeeting = omeMeeting.Forward
omeNewMeeting.Recipients.Add "Dwayne Gifford"
omeNewMeeting.Recipients.ResolveAll
omeNewMeeting.DeferredDeliveryTime = #12/13/98 3:00:00 PM#
omeNewMeeting.Send
```

In this example, we create a new `MeetingItem` object by calling the `Forward` method of an existing `MeetingItem`. We then add the new recipient, set the `DeferredDeliveryTime` property and then fire off the `Send` method. The item will now sit in the Outbox until the correct time, when it will automatically be sent.

DeleteAfterSubmit Property

The `DeleteAfterSubmit` property specifies whether to delete the item once it has been sent (`True`) or to save a copy of the sent item. This property is set by default to the value specified in the Outlook options. If this is set to `True`, no copy of the item will be saved; setting it to `False` causes a copy to be saved in the folder specified for sent items in the Outlook options.

```
MeetingItem.DeleteAfterSubmit = Boolean
Boolean = MeetingItem.DeleteAfterSubmit
```

ExpiryTime Property

The `ExpiryTime` property returns or sets the date and time at which the `MeetingItem` becomes invalid and can be deleted. If the item is not viewed by the recipient before the `ExpiryTime`, it will be deleted. However, if the item was opened before it expired, it will remain available, but it will be colored gray and appear with a line struck through it.

```
MeetingItem.ExpiryTime = Date
Date = MeetingItem.ExpiryTime
```

FlagDueBy Property

The `FlagDueBy` property specifies the date and time by which the meeting request needs to be followed up. This property will be ignored if the `FlagStatus` property is subsequently set to `olNoFlag`. When this time has passed, this item will appear colored red in the explorer, indicating that the due time has been missed. If the item is then marked as complete or unflagged, the item returns to its normal color.

```
MeetingItem.FlagDueBy = Date
Date = MeetingItem.FlagDueBy
```

FlagRequest Property

The `FlagRequest` property is a text field which can hold any string value. This message is displayed to the recipient of the `MeetingItem` above the body. This property is ignored if `FlagStatus` is subsequently set to `olNoFlag`.

```
MeetingItem.FlagRequest = String
String = MeetingItem.FlagRequest
```

FlagStatus Property

The `FlagStatus` property indicates whether the recipient is required to follow up the meeting request.

```
MeetingItem.FlagStatus = Long
Long = MeetingItem.FlagStatus
```

The value of `FlagStatus` can be any of the `OlFlagStatus` constants:

Constant	Value	Description
olNoFlag	0	No follow up is required; no flag is shown next to the item in the explorer.
olFlagComplete	1	Flagged as completed; in the explorer the item will have a gray flag.
olFlagMarked	2	Flagged for follow up; in the explorer the item will have a red flag.

The current setting of `FlagStatus` will be overridden if `FlagRequest` or `FlagDueBy` are set afterwards.

OriginatorDeliveryReportRequested Property

The `OriginatorDeliveryReportRequested` property is a Boolean value that indicates whether the sender wishes to receive a delivery report for each recipient of the meeting. A `ReportItem` indicating whether the meeting request was delivered will be sent to the originator if this property is set to `True`.

```
MeetingItem.OriginatorDeliveryReportRequested = Boolean
Boolean = MeetingItem.OriginatorDeliveryReportRequested
```

ReceivedTime Property

The `ReceivedTime` property returns the date and time when the `MeetingItem` object was received.

```
Date = MeetingItem.ReceivedTime
```

ReplyRecipients Property

The `ReplyRecipients` property returns a reference to the collection of recipients who will receive a copy of any reply to the `MeetingItem`.

```
Set RecipientsCollection = MeetingItem.ReplyRecipients
```

This allows you to have the replies to this original message sent to multiple recipients. When a recipient clicks on the **Reply** button for this message, all of the `Recipient` objects in this collection will be added to the To field automatically.

> When you use this collection, make sure you add the current user, or the originator of the `MeetingItem` will not receive a reply from the User.

Example:

```
Dim onMAPI As NameSpace
Dim omeMeeting As MeetingItem
Dim omeNewMeeting As MeetingItem
...
Set omeNewMeeting = omeMeeting.Forward
With omeNewMeeting
    .ReplyRecipients.Add "Dwayne Gifford"
    .ReplyRecipients.Add onMAPI.CurrentUser
    .Recipients.Add "Tom"
    .Recipients.ResolveAll
    .Send
End With
```

In this example, we create a new `MeetingItem` by executing the `Forward` method of an existing `MeetingItem`. Then we add two `ReplyRecipients` to the item, one of these being the `CurrentUser` and a recipient for the meeting request. Lastly, we send the message to the recipients.

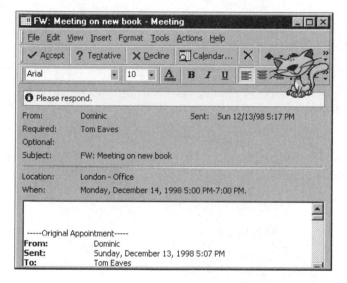

The above figure shows us how the message appears to the recipient. Notice that only Dominic and Tom appear on the message.

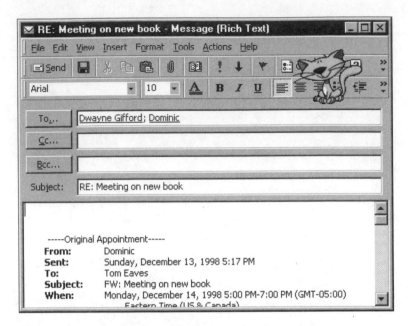

The above figure shows the GUI that will be opened when a recipient replies to the message. Notice that Dominic and Dwayne Gifford appear automatically in the To field.

SaveSentMessageFolder Property

The SaveSentMessageFolder property specifies the MAPIFolder object where the MeetingItem is to be saved after the message has been sent. This only applies if the DeleteAfterSubmit property is not set to True.

```
Set MeetingItem.SaveSentMessageFolder = MAPIFolderObject
Set MAPIFolderObject = MeetingItem.SaveSentMessageFolder
```

SenderName Property

The SenderName property returns the display name for the sender of the MeetingItem object.

```
String = MeetingItem.SenderName
```

Sent Property

The Sent property is a Boolean value that indicates whether the MeetingItem has been sent to the recipients or not. The property returns True if the item has already been sent; otherwise false.

```
Boolean = MeetingItem.Sent
```

SentOn Property

The SentOn property returns the date and time when the MeetingItem was sent.

```
Date = MeetingItem.SentOn
```

Submitted Property

The Submitted property is a Boolean value that indicates whether the MeetingItem has been submitted for mailing or not. The property returns True if the MeetingItem has already been submitted; otherwise False.

```
Boolean = MeetingItem.Submitted
```

RecurrencePattern Object

The RecurrencePattern object represents the pattern which defines the way in which an appointment or task recurs. If you open a recurring item in Outlook, it will ask you if you want to open the series or just the current item — the entire collection of appointments or tasks, or a single instance of the recurring appointment or task. In the former case, we will be working on the RecurrencePattern object itself; in the latter, on a single occurrence of the item. If an instance of the RecurrencePattern is updated, so that it no longer fits the general pattern, this occurrence becomes an Exception object and will be placed in the Exceptions collection.

To get a reference to this object you will need to use the GetReccurencePattern method that is exposed by the AppointmentItem and the TaskItem.

The Exceptions collection and the Exception object are covered in the final sections of this chapter.

RecurrencePattern Method

GetOccurence Method

The GetOccurence method returns the associated AppointmentItem for the current RecurrencePattern object.

```
Set AppointmentItem = _
RecurrencePatternObject.GetOccurrence(Date_Time)
```

Name	Data type	Description
Date_Time	Date	Required, the start date and time for the AppointmentItem to be retrieved.

The following code demonstrates how we can use this method to get a specific instance of a recurring appointment; it incidentally also demonstrates how the Exceptions collection works:

```
Dim oapAppointment As AppointmentItem
Dim orpRecurrence As RecurrencePattern
Dim oapOccurence As AppointmentItem
Dim ofCalendar As MAPIFolder
Dim onNamespace As NameSpace

Set onNamespace = GetNamespace("MAPI")
Set ofCalendar = onNamespace.GetDefaultFolder(olFolderCalendar)
Set oapAppointment = ofCalendar.Items("Chapter 17")
If oapAppointment.IsRecurring Then
   Set orpRecurrence = oapAppointment.GetRecurrencePattern
   MsgBox orpRecurrence.Exceptions.Count
   If orpRecurrence.Occurrences <> 0 Then
      Set oapOccurence = orpRecurrence.GetOccurrence _
                        (#4/20/1999 9:00:00 AM#)
      oapOccurence.Start = #4/21/1999 9:00:00 AM#
      oapOccurence.Save
      MsgBox orpRecurrence.Exceptions.Count
   End If
End If
```

We iterate through the Calendar folder looking for the AppointmentItem object
named "Chapter 17" and ensure that it is a recurring appointment (by checking its
IsRecurring property). We then get a reference to its RecurrencePattern and
display a message box with the number of exceptions to the pattern. We then use the
GetOccurrence method to obtain a reference to the specific instance of the
appointment which starts on the 20th April 1999 at 9 o'clock AM. We then change the
start time of this appointment, and set the appointment to start at the same time the
following day. We save this change, and redisplay the number of exceptions to the
RecurrencePattern. We should find that it has increased by one.

RecurrencePattern Properties

Application Property

This property returns the Application object for the current session.

```
Set ApplicationObject = RecurrencepatternObject.Application
```

Class Property

This returns a unique value that returns one of the OlObjectClass constants which
identifies the type of object. For a Recurrencepattern, this will be
olRecurrencePattern or 28.

```
Long = RecurrencePatternObject.Class
```

DayOfMonth Property

The DayOfMonth property sets or returns the day of the month on which the
appointment or task is to recur.

```
RecurrencePatternObject.DayOfMonth = Long
Long = RecurrencePatternObject.DayOfMonth
```

Used in conjunction with the `Interval` property and a `RecurrenceType` of `olRecursMonthly`, this specifies that the appointment or task will recur on the *n*th day of every month. Used with `MonthOfYear` and a `RecurrenceType` of `olRecursYearly`, it will specify that the appointment or task occurs on the *n*th day of a given month every year.

DayOfWeekMask Property

The `DayOfWeekMask` property returns or sets the days of the week on which the appointment or task occurs. Items recurring on a monthly or yearly basis can only be on a single day, but those occurring on a weekly or daily basis can be on any combination of days. To find out whether an instance of the appointment or task occurs on a specific day, you must look at the sum of the values.

```
RecurrencePatternObject.DayOfWeekMask = Long
Long = RecurrencePatternObject.DayOfWeekMask
```

`DayOfWeekMask` can contain any combination of the `OlDaysOfWeek` constants:

Constant	Value	Description
olSunday	1	Recurs on a Sunday.
olMonday	2	Recurs on a Monday.
olTuesday	4	Recurs on a Tuesday.
olWednesday	8	Recurs on a Wednesday.
olThursday	16	Recurs on a Thursday.
olFriday	32	Recurs on a Friday.
olSaturday	64	Recurs on a Saturday.

For example, an appointment or task recurring on Friday and Saturday would have a `DayOfWeekMask` value of 96, or `olFriday + olSaturday`. If the `RecurrenceType` is set to `olRecursDaily`, this appointment or task will occur every Friday and Saturday.

Duration Property

The `Duration` property is a long integer value that will set or return in minutes how long the appointment is to last. Setting this will cause the `EndTime` property to be set if `StartTime` is also set, and `Duration` will be updated if the `StartTime` and `EndTime` properties are set.

```
RecurrencePatternObject.Duration = Long
Long = RecurrencePatternObject.Duration
```

EndTime Property

The EndTime property sets or returns the time at which the meeting or appointment is to end. Note that this property affects all the recurring items, so if you change this, the end time of all the meetings or appointments in the series will be changed. If you wish to change the end time of just one, you must use the GetOccurence method and update the End property for that AppointmentItem. This will cause that one instance to be placed in the Exceptions collection.

```
RecurrencePatternObject.EndTime = Date
Date = RecurrencePatternObject.EndTime
```

Exceptions Property

The Exceptions property returns the Exceptions collection for the RecurrencePatttern object. This collection contains information on appointments which do not fit into the recurrence pattern. For more information on this collection, see the section on the Exceptions collection below.

```
Set ExceptionsCollection = RecurrencePatternObject.Exceptions
```

Instance Property

The Instance property can be used to specify that an appointment or task is to recur on the nth day of the week in a given month every year (e.g. the 3rd Tuesday in March) or on the nth day of the week every month (e.g. the 2nd Wednesday of every month). This property is only valid for RecurrencePattern objects with a RecurrenceType of olRecursMonthNth or olRecursYearNth. Setting this to a value higher than five will cause an error.

```
RecurrencePatternObject.Instance = Long
Long = RecurrencePatternObject.Instance
```

Interval Property

The Interval property specifies how often a task or appointment will recur. The units in which this interval is measured are determined by the RecurrenceType property. For example, setting RecurrenceType to olRecursMonthly and Interval to 2 causes the task or appointment to recur every other month.

```
RecurrencePatternObject.Interval = Long
Long = RecurrencePatternObject.Interval
```

MonthOfYear Property

The MonthOfYear property sets or returns the month in which the appointment or task is to recur. This is only valid for RecurrencePattern objects with a RecurrenceType of olRecursYearly or olRecursYearNth. The value can be from 1 (January) to 12 (December).

```
RecurrencePatternObject.MonthOfYear = Long
Long = RecurrencePatternObject.MonthOfYear
```

NoEndDate Property

The `NoEndDate` property is a Boolean value that indicates whether there is an end date for the `RecurrencePattern`. Setting this property to `True` specifies that the series of appointments or tasks will recur indefinitely.

```
RecurrencePatternObject.NoEndDate = Boolean
Boolean = RecurrencePatternObject.NoEndDate
```

Occurrences Property

The `Occurences` property indicates how many occurrences there are for this `RecurrencePattern`. It is important to ensure that this property does not conflict with `PatternEndDate` and `NoEndDate`. Setting these to incompatible values will cause `Occurrences` to be updated.

```
RecurrencePatternObject.Occurrences = Long
Long = RecurrencePatternObject.Occurrences
```

Parent Property

This property returns the parent object for the current `RecurrencePattern` object. This property returns the `AppointmentItem` or `TaskItem` object to which the `RecurrencePattern` belongs.

```
Set Object = RecurrencePatternObject.Parent
```

PatternEndDate Property

The `PatternEndDate` property returns or sets the date on which the series of appointments or tasks is due to end.

```
RecurrencePatternObject.PatternEndDate = Date
Date = RecurrencePatternObject.PatternEndDate
```

PatternStartDate Property

The `PatternStartDate` property returns or sets date on which the series of appointments or tasks is due to start.

```
RecurrencePatternObject.PatternStartDate = Date
Date = RecurrencePatternObject.PatternStartDate
```

RecurrenceType Property

The `RecurrenceType` property is a long integer value which returns or sets the type of pattern.

```
RecurrencePatternObject.RecurrenceType = Long
Long = RecurrencePatternObject.RecurrenceType
```

The `RecurrenceType` property can be any of the `OlRecurrenceType` constants:

Constant	Value	Description
olRecursDaily	0	The appointment/task recurs every n days.
olRecursWeekly	1	The appointment/task recurs every n weeks.
olRecursMonthly	2	The appointment/task recurs every n months.
olRecursMonthNth	3	The appointment/task recurs on the nth day of the week every month.
olRecursYearly	5	The appointment/task recurs every n years.
olRecursYearNth	6	The appointment/task recurs on the nth day of the week of a given month of the year.

Example:

```
Dim oapAppointment As AppointmentItem
Dim orpRecurrence As RecurrencePattern
Dim orcRecipients As Recipients
Dim oapOccurence As AppointmentItem

Set oapAppointment = CreateItem(olAppointmentItem)
oapAppointment.Subject = _
            "Outlook 2000 Programmers Reference Weekly meeting"
oapAppointment.Body = "Weekly Meeting to make sure " & _
                    "we are on schedule with the book."
oapAppointment.MeetingStatus = olMeeting
Set orcRecipients = oapAppointment.Recipients
orcRecipients.Add "Dwayne Gifford"
orcRecipients.ResolveAll
Set orpRecurrence = oapAppointment.GetRecurrencePattern
With orpRecurrence
   .StartTime = #9/7/1998 9:00:00 AM#
   .Duration = 60
   .RecurrenceType = olRecursWeekly
End With
oapAppointment.Send
```

The example above creates a new AppointmentItem which is set to be a recurring appointment, recurring on every Monday from the second Monday in September 1998. We could make this a fortnightly appointment by setting the RecurrencePattern object's Interval property to two. We then send the appointment to the recipients.

Regenerate Property

The Regenerate property is a Boolean value that specifies whether Outlook should recreate and update all the recurring items when the Save method is called for the appointment or task. This will happen if Regenerate is set to True, but if set to False, any changes will not be made to the other occurrences until Outlook decides to do it.

It is always wise to ensure that `Regenerate` is set to `True` every time you make a change to the `RecurrencePattern`.

```
RecurrencePatternObject.Regenerate = Boolean
Boolean = RecurrencePatternObject.Regenerate
```

Session Property

This property returns a reference to the `NameSpace` object for the current session.

```
Set NameSpaceObject = RecurrencePatternObject.Session
```

StartTime Property

The `StartTime` property returns or sets the time when the appointment or meeting is due to start for each occurrence.

```
RecurrencePatternObject.StartDate = Date
Date = RecurrencePatternObject.StartDate
```

Exceptions Collection

The `Exceptions` collection contains the `Exception` objects for a recurrence pattern. These objects contain information about exceptions to the rules defined by the `RecurrencePattern` object; that is, those instances of an appointment which do not fit into the pattern for the rest of the series of recurring appointments.

In order to get a reference to the `Exceptions` collection, we must use the `Exceptions` property of a `RecurrencePattern` object:

```
Dim orpRecur As RecurrencePattern
Dim oeccExceptions As Exceptions
...
Set oeccExceptions = orpRecur.Exceptions
```

Exceptions Method

Item Method

The `Item` method provides a way to access a particular `Exception` object within the collection.

```
Set ExceptionObject = ExceptionsCollection.Item(Index)
```

Name	Data type	Description
Index	Long	Required, the index number representing the position of the exception within the collection.

Exceptions Properties

Application Property

This property returns the `Application` object for the current session.

```
Set ApplicationObject = ExceptionsCollection.Application
```

Class Property

This returns a unique value that holds one of the `OlObjectClass` constants which identifies the type of object. For an `Exceptions` collection, this will be `olExceptions` or 29.

```
Long = ExceptionsCollection.Class
```

Count Property

This returns the number of `Exception` objects in the collection.

```
Long = ExceptionsCollection.Count
```

Parent Property

This property returns the parent object for the current `Exceptions` collection. This property always returns the `RecurrencePattern` object for the series of appointments to which it belongs.

```
Set Object = ExceptionsCollection.Parent
```

Session Property

This returns a reference to the `NameSpace` object for the current session.

```
Set NameSpaceObject = ExceptionsCollection.Session
```

Exception Object

The `Exception` object represents a change to the normal pattern of a recurring `AppointmentItem`. For example, suppose you have an appointment with you boss every Monday at 8:30 am. But one Friday he says that he is going golfing the following Monday and will be late getting in to the office, so the appointment will be postponed till 12:30. So, being a good employee, you update that one appointment in the Calendar. Outlook adds this changed appointment to the `Exceptions` collection as an `Exception` object. The `Exception` object is a "read-only" object — you cannot create one directly (it can only be created by changing an occurrence of a recurring appointment), and it has only read-only properties.

The `Exception` object has no methods and seven properties. Four of these are identical to those of the `Exceptions` collection and therefore are not covered here: `Application`, `Class`, `Parent` and `Session`.

AppointmentItem Property

The AppointmentItem property returns the associated AppointmentItem object for this exception — the specific instance of the series of appointments which breaks the rules defined by the RecurrencePattern.

```
Set AppointmentItem = ExceptionObject.AppointmentItem
```

This works in a similar way to the GetOccurence method of the RecurrencePattern. This returns Nothing if the AppointmentItem has been deleted, so it is a good idea to put a check around this call:

```
Dim oecException As Exception
Dim oapAppointment As AppointmentItem
...
If Not oecException.Deleted Then
    Set oapAppointment = oecException.AppointmentItem
End If
```

Deleted Property

The Deleted property indicates whether the item became an exception because it was deleted. This returns True if the appointment is an exception to the RecurrencePattern because it has been canceled; False if it is an exception for any other reason.

```
Boolean = ExceptionObject.Deleted
```

OriginalDate Property

The OriginalDate property returns the original date and time when the meeting or appointment was to occur. This will be set even if the exception was due to the deletion of the appointment.

```
Date = ExceptionObject.OriginalDate
```

Tasks

The `TaskItem` object allows us to keep track of jobs that we have to do (we can compare tasks to the items on a shopping list). Not only does it allow us to keep track of our tasks, but it also allows us to delegate tasks to other users. So, if you are the manager of a project, you can use the `TaskItem` to delegate and keep track of tasks that need to be accomplished on that project.

If we do delegate a `TaskItem`, then a `TaskRequestItem` object is sent to the recipients who have been assigned to the task. With this item, they can **Accept** or **Decline** the task. If they accept the task, a `TaskRequestAcceptItem` is sent to the originator of the task (that is, the person who sent the task in the first place). If the recipient declines the task, a `TaskRequestDeclineItem` will be sent to the originator. If the recipient changes the `Status` or `DueDate` of the task at any time, a `TaskRequestUpdateItem` will be sent out to the originator.

There are two ways to create a new `Task` and one way to get a reference to an existing `Task`. To get a reference to an existing entry, we first need a reference to a `MAPIFolder` that holds task entries. For example:

```
Dim ofFolder As MAPIFolder
Dim otTask As TaskItem
...
Set otTask = ofFolder.Items("Copy Method - TaskItem Object")
```

To create a new `TaskItem` we can either use the `Add` method that is exposed by the `MAPIFolder` object or the `CreateItem` method that is exposed by the `Application` object. For example:

```
Dim ofFolder As MAPIFolder
Dim otTask As TaskItem
...
Set otTask = ofFolder.Items.Add(olTaskItem)
```

Or:

```
Dim otTask As TaskItem
...
Set otTask = Application.CreateItem(olTaskItem)
```

There is no way to create a `TaskRequestItem`, `TaskRequestUpdateItem`, `TaskRequestDeclineItem` or `TaskRequestAcceptItem` object. These items are created for you as you work on the task itself.

The TaskItem Object

The `TaskItem` object represents a task that needs to be done. For example, I have to write this chapter and get it to Dominic at Wrox by a certain day or you, the customer, would not have been able to buy this book when you did. So to help me manage this, I created a `TaskItem` in my Tasks folder and assigned a due date to it. As I completed the tasks for this book, I updated the corresponding `TaskItem`.

TaskItem Methods

Assign Method

The `Assign` method is used to delegate a task to another `Recipient`. Note that assigning the task does not in itself cause a task request to be sent (we must still call the `Send` method), and that the recipient of course has the opportunity to decline the request.

```
TaskItem.Assign
```

Notice how the GUI changes when this method is called. The first figure below shows us the GUI for the `TaskItem`.

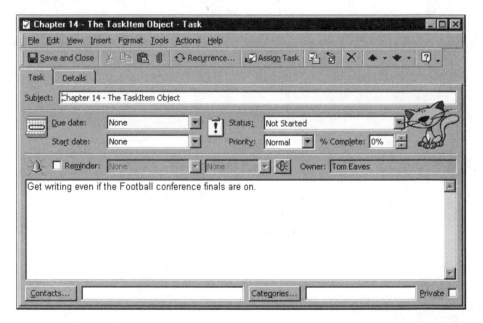

The second screenshot shows the changes to the GUI once the `Assign` method has been executed.

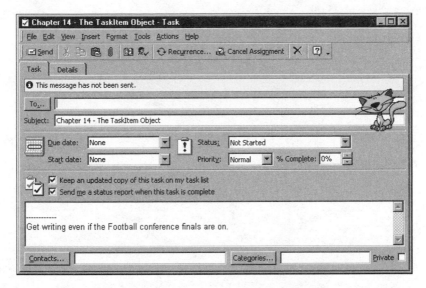

Notice how the **To...** field has been added to the task. There is also an additional section below the **Due date** and **Start date** drop-down boxes. Here we can tell Outlook whether or not we want to keep a copy of the task once sent and whether we want the recipient to send us a status report.

This code shows how we can assign recipients to a task and then send the task requests:

```
Dim otTask As TaskItem
Dim omNewMail As MailItem
Dim ofcPersonal As Folders
Dim ofInbox As MAPIFolder
Dim onNameSpace As NameSpace
Dim oicItems As Items
Dim orAcquisition As Recipient
Dim ofArchive As MAPIFolder
Dim iFor As Integer

Set onNameSpace = GetNamespace("MAPI")
Set ofcPersonal = onNameSpace.Folders("Mailbox - Wrox Help").Folders
Set ofInbox = ofcPersonal("Inbox")
Set oicItems = ofInbox.Items.Restrict("[Unread] = True")
For iFor = oicItems.Count To 1 Step -1
   If oicItems(iFor).Class = olMail Then
      Set omNewMail = oicItems(iFor)
      With omNewMail
         Set otTask = CreateItem(olTaskItem)
         otTask.Subject = .Subject
         otTask.Body = .Body
         Select Case otTask.Subject
         Case "Outlook 2000 Programmers Reference"
            otTask.Recipients.Add "Dwayne Gifford"

            'Status Reports
```

```
                    Set orAcquisition = otTask.Recipients.Add _
                                ("Acquisition Outlook")
                    orAcquisition.Type = olCC
                    'Completion Report
                    Set orAcquisition = otTask.Recipients.Add _
                                ("Acquisition Outlook")
                    orAcquisition.Type = olBCC
                    Set ofArchive = ofcPersonal("Outlook")
                Case "Excel 2000 Programmers Reference"
                    otTask.Recipients.Add "Excel Author"
                    'Status Reports
                    Set orAcquisition = otTask.Recipients.Add _
                                ("Acquisition Excel")
                    orAcquisition.Type = olCC
                    'Completion Report
                    Set orAcquisition = otTask.Recipients.Add _
                                ("Acquisition Excel")
                    orAcquisition.Type = olBCC
                    Set ofArchive = ofcPersonal("Excel")
                Case "Word 2000 Programmers Reference"
                    otTask.Recipients.Add "Word Author"
                    'Status Reports
                    Set orAcquisition = otTask.Recipients.Add _
                                ("Acquisition Word")
                    orAcquisition.Type = olCC
                    'Completion Report
                    Set orAcquisition = otTask.Recipients.Add _
                                ("Acquisition Word")
                    orAcquisition.Type = olBCC
                    Set ofArchive = ofcPersonal("Word")
                End Select
                otTask.Assign
                otTask.Recipients.ResolveAll
                otTask.Send
                omNewMail.Move ofArchive
            End With
        End If
    Next
```

The code above checks the "Wrox Help" mailbox. This is a Help desk mailbox that will receive all questions from a web site. This web site allows readers to submit questions to the different Programmer's Reference authors. In this example we are looking for Outlook, Excel and Word only. The first step is to get a reference to the Inbox for the "Wrox Help" Mailbox. We then use the `Restrict` method of its `Items` collection to select only those items that are marked as un-read. Now we walk backwards through the items — this ensures that we do not miss any items when we move them later to be archived. For each of these items that are `MailItem` objects, we then create a new `TaskItem` object, giving the task the same `Subject` and `Body` as the `MailItem`. Because these mails came from the web site, we know that they all have a pre-determined `Subject` allocated when the email was generated, so we can use this to find out to whom the task has to be delegated. When we assign the `Recipient` who will work on the task, we also assign the acquisition editors for the book to receive any Status reports when the task is updated and a completion report. This ensures that they will know that the author has answered the different questions. After we have set up the appropriate recipients for the task, the `ResolveAll` method of the `Recipients` collection is executed. This method attempts to validate each `Recipient` against the Address Book to see if we have enough information to send the task. We then call the `Assign` method, which assigns the task to the recipients. Finally, we send the task and move the original `MailItem` to the appropriate archive folder. This gives us a backup of the original mail message from the reader.

CancelResponseState Method

The `CancelResponseState` method allows you to change a task back from a delegated task to a non-delegated task. This method will only work if the task has not yet been sent.

> `TaskItem.CancelResponseState`

ClearRecurrencePattern Method

The `ClearRecurrencePattern` method will set a recurring `Task` to be a non-recurring one.

> `TaskItem.ClearRecurrencePattern`

This method removes the reference to the `RecurrencePattern` object and sets the `IsRecurring` flag from `True` to `False`. To make a task recurring, you have to use the `GetRecurrencePattern` method. The `RecurrencePattern` object is treated in Chapter 17.

Close Method

The `Close` method allows you to shut down a displayed `TaskItem` and specify whether changes should be saved or discarded.

> `TaskItem.Close(SaveMode)`

Name	Data type	Description
SaveMode	Long	Required, specifies whether any changes to the task will be saved or discarded.

The value of `SaveMode` can be any of the `OlInspectorClose` constants:

Constant	Value	Description
olSave	0	Save the item without prompting the user.
olDiscard	1	Discard all changes to the item without prompting the user.
olPromptForSave	2	Prompt the user to save or discard the item.

Even if the `Inspector` object for the `TaskItem` has not been opened, any changes made to the item will be saved if `SaveMode` is set to `olSave`, or the user will be prompted if it is set to `olPromptForSave`. If `SaveMode` is set to `olDiscard`, note that any changes will not be lost until the object is uninstantiated (e.g. when the macro comes to an end).

Copy Method

The `Copy` method creates a new task that is an identical copy of the current `TaskItem`.

```
Set TaskItem = TaskItem.Copy
```

Delete Method

The `Delete` method does just that — it removes the current `TaskItem` from the `Items` collection.

```
TaskItem.Delete
```

No surprises here — if you execute this method, the item is deleted from the folder that it belonged to.

Display Method

The `Display` method activates the `Inspector` object for the current `TaskItem`. This will be as shown in one of the two figures towards the start of the chapter.

```
TaskItem.Display([Modal])
```

Name	Data type	Description
`Modal`	Boolean	Optional, specifies whether the inspector window will be opened modally (`True`) or modelessly (`False`).

Note that this will open the `TaskItem` without letting you set any properties or do anything to the item first. If you want to make any changes before the item is shown, you can use the `GetInspector` property that is explained later in the chapter.

GetRecurrencePattern Method

The `GetRecurrencePattern` method returns the `RecurrencePattern` object for the current object.

```
TaskItem.GetRecurrencePattern
```

The `RecurrencePattern` object holds the information about the pattern in which instances of this task will recur. For more information on how to use the `RecurrencePattern` object, see Chapter 17.

The following code illustrates how to set up a recurring task:

```
Dim otTask As TaskItem
Dim ofFolder As MAPIFolder
Dim onNamespace As NameSpace
Dim ofInbox As MAPIFolder
Dim oicItems As Items
Dim omMail As MailItem
Dim orpRecurrence As RecurrencePattern
```

```
Set onNamespace = GetNamespace("MAPI")
Set ofInbox = onNamespace.GetDefaultFolder(olFolderInbox)
Set ofFolder = onNamespace.GetDefaultFolder(olFolderTasks)
Set otTask = ofFolder.Items.Add
otTask.Subject = "Grocery Shopping"
otTask.Body = "Give the grocery list to your spouse. " _
              & "This way he will get the right groceries."

otTask.ReminderSet = True
otTask.ReminderTime = Date & " " & Format(Time + 1/24, "hh:mm:ss")
otTask.ReminderOverrideDefault = True
otTask.ReminderSoundFile = < Appropriate Sound File >
otTask.ReminderPlaySound = True
otTask.Sensitivity = olConfidential
otTask.Assign
otTask.Recipients.Add "Iris Gifford"
otTask.Recipients.ResolveAll
Set orpRecurrence = otTask.GetRecurrencePattern
orpRecurrence.PatternStartDate = Date + 1
orpRecurrence.PatternEndDate = Date + 14
orpRecurrence.RecurrenceType = olRecursDaily
otTask.Send
```

In the example above, we set up a recurring task for my wife to give me the grocery list for every day for the next two weeks. To achieve this, we set the `PatternStartDate` to the day after the current day, the `PatternEndDate` to the current date plus fourteen days, and `RecurrenceType` to `olRecursDaily`. By setting these three properties, we have set up a task which will recur daily for the next two weeks.

MarkComplete Method

The `MarkComplete` method will cause the task to be marked as completed.

> `TaskItem`.MarkComplete

Marking the task as complete is comparable to when I get back from the grocery store and my spouse confirms that I bought everything on the shopping list. At this point I can say that I have completed this task. Completed tasks are displayed in the exploirer in gray and with a line through the name. When this method is executed, it will set the `PercentComplete` property to 100, `Complete` to `True`, `Status` to `olTaskComplete` and `DateCompleted` to the current date. However, setting any of the properties individually to these values will cause all the others to be reset too.

Move Method

The `Move` method allows us to take the current `TaskItem` and move it to a new `MAPIFolder` that supports `TaskItem` objects.

> `TaskItem`.Move DestFldr

There is one parameter for this method:

Name	Data type	Description
DestFldr	MAPIFolder object	Required, equates to an existing MAPIFolder object.

You could use this method to create your own rule (similar to those created by the Rules Wizard), but instead of operating on the Inbox, this new rule could go through the `MAPIFolder` which your task is in. It could check for tasks that have been completed and archive them into your personal `MAPIFolder`. The following code gives an idea of just how this rule could be written.

```
Dim otTask As TaskItem
Dim ofFolder As MAPIFolder
Dim iFor As Integer
Dim onNamespace As NameSpace
Dim ofArchive As MAPIFolder

Set onNamespace = GetNamespace("MAPI")
Set ofFolder = onNamespace.PickFolder

For Each ofArchive In ofFolder.Folders
    If ofArchive.Name = "Archive" Then
        Exit For
    End If
Next

If ofArchive Is Nothing Then
    offolder.Folders.Add "Archive"
    Set ofArchive = offolder.Folders("Archive")
End If

For iFor = ofFolder.Items.Count To 1 Step -1
    If ofFolder.Items(iFor).Class = olTask Then
        Set otTask = offolder.Items(iFor)
        If otTask.Complete Then
            If MsgBox("The task '" & otTask.Subject & _
                        "' has been completed." _
            & "Would you like to archive it?", vbQuestion _
            + vbYesNo) = vbYes Then
                otTask.Move ofArchive
            End If
        End If
    End If
Next
```

PrintOut Method

The `PrintOut` method allows you to print the task, creating a hard copy of it.

```
TaskItem.PrintOut
```

Remember that this will always send the task to the default printer, using the default settings for that printer. Also, you cannot change the information that will be printed. What you see on the GUI for the `TaskItem` is what you will see on the print out.

Respond Method

The `Respond` method allows you to send a response to the originator of the task.

```
TaskItem.Respond(IResponse, fNoUI, AdditionalText)
```

This method has three properties:

Name	Data type	Description
IResponse	Long	Required, can be any one of the OlTaskResponse constants.
fNoUI	Boolean	Required, can be True or False. If True, no dialog box will be displayed and the response will be sent automatically; if False, the user will be prompted before the response is sent.
AdditionalText	Boolean	Required, can be set to True or False. If True, the user is prompted to send the response, with or without comments; otherwise the user is not prompted for input but the response is displayed in the inspector. If fNoUI is True, this parameter is ignored. The default is False.

IResponse can be any of the OlTaskResponse constants:

Constant	Value	Description
olTaskSimple	0	Specifies that the task has not been delegated.
olTaskAssign	1	Specifies that the assigned recipient has not responded to the task.
olTaskAccept	2	Specifies that the task has been accepted.
olTaskDecline	3	Specifies that the task has been declined.

So what do all these options mean? Think about a task that you have received: when you try to respond to the task using the GUI, you are presented with a dialog box asking whether you would like to Edit the Response, just Send the response or cancel.

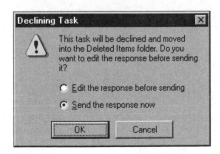

For the above dialog to appear to the user, you must set fNoUI to False and the AdditionalText to True. By selecting the Edit the response before sending option or setting fNoUI to False and setting AdditionalText to False you will get the response message presented for editing.

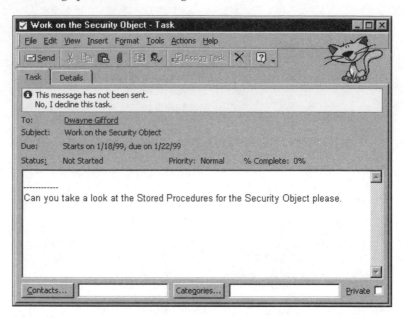

Here you can add any text or attachments that you would like to be included with your response to the originator of the meeting.

Save Method

The Save method saves your task information to the current MAPIFolder object or, if this is a new TaskItem, to the default MAPIFolder object.

```
TaskItem.Save
```

The trick with this method is to know which is the default MAPIFolder object. For the TaskItem, this is the Tasks folder.

SaveAs Method

The SaveAs method allows you to save the TaskItem object to your local hard drive.

```
TaskItem.SaveAs(Path [, Type])
```

The parameters for this method are:

Name	Data type	Description
Path	String	Required, a valid path and filename for the new file.
Type	Long	Optional, any of the olSaveAsType constants listed below. If omitted, the default is olMSG.

Type can be any of the following OlSaveAsType constants:

Constant	Value	Description
olTXT	0	Save as a .txt (Text) file.
olRTF	1	Save as an .rtf (Rich Text Format) file.
olTemplate	2	Save as an Outlook Template.
olMSG	3	Save in Outlook message (.msg) format.

If you try to use any of the olSaveAsType constants not listed above, an error will be raised.

Send Method

This method sends the TaskRequestItem and TaskItem to the item's recipients.

```
TaskItem.Send
```

It is important to realize that even if you have added a Recipient to the Recipients collection of the TaskItem, but you have not executed the Assign method, the task will not get mailed.

SkipRecurrence Method

The SkipRecurrence method tells Outlook to set the recurrence of this task to the next one in the RecurrencePattern. This is only valid for the current instance, and if you need to skip more than one recurrence, you must run this method on each instance in turn.

```
TaskItem.SkipRecurrence
```

StatusReport Method

The StatusReport method returns a MailItem outlining the current status of the task addressed to all the recipients that are on the CC list (that is, those named in the StatusUpdateRecipients property).

```
Set MailItem = TaskItem.StatusReport
```

TaskItem Properties

Actions Property

The Actions property returns the Actions collection for the TaskItem object. The default actions available for a task are "Forward", "Reply", "Reply to All" and "Reply to Folder". For more information on the Actions collection and the Action object, refer to Chapter 11.

```
Set ActionsCollection = TaskItem.Actions
```

ActualWork Property

The ActualWork property can be used to set or return the amount of work that has been done on the task in minutes. You can find this property on the Details tab of the GUI.

```
TaskItem.ActualWork = Long
Long = TaskItem.ActualWork
```

Application Property

The Application property returns the Application object for this session. This property does not appear on the GUI.

```
Set ApplicationObject = TaskItem.Application
```

Attachments Property

The Attachments property returns a reference to the Attachments collection for the TaskItem object. For more information on the Attachments collection and Attachment object, refer to Chapter 11.

```
Set AttachmentsCollection = TaskItem.Attachments
```

BillingInformation Property

The BillingInformation property sets or returns the billing information for the task. This property is a free-form string, and can hold anything you wish to enter. It is available on the Details tab of the GUI supplied by Outlook.

```
TaskItem.BillingInformation = String
String = TaskItem.BillingInformation
```

Body Property

The Body property can be used to set or return the body of the TaskItem. This is the meat of the task information — where the actual instructions for the task are usually placed. However, any text value you like can be entered into the body. This is also where the Attachments are shown in the GUI.

```
TaskItem.Body = String
String = TaskItem.Body
```

CardData Property

The `CardData` property returns or sets the card data for the task. This property does not appear on the GUI, and you can set it to anything that you might require.

```
TaskItem.CardData = String
String = TaskItem.CardData
```

As with many of the properties for all of the different Outlook items, it is not shown on the GUI, so it is hidden from the normal user's view. This allows you to use these properties in any way that you need. For example, if we are using the `TaskItem` with MS Project and want to keep the ID that MS Project has assigned to the task somewhere in the `TaskItem`, we could use this `CardData` property to do this. But note that it is important to remember to document this well within the company, so that no one gets the same idea and uses this property for something else.

Categories Property

The `Categories` property returns or sets the categories for the task.

```
TaskItem.Categories = String
String = TaskItem.Categories
```

To add multiple categories in one go, place a comma between each category:

```
otTask.Catergories = "VIP,Business,Me"
```

In this example, we are assigning the categories of `"VIP"`, `"Business"` and `"Me"` to the task. We can then use the `Restrict` method of the `Items` collection to select only tasks belonging to a given category. For more information on the `Items` collection and its `Restrict` method, see Chapter 11.

Class Property

This returns a unique value that identifies the type of the object. This value is one of the `olObjectClass` constants. For tasks, the value returned is `olTask` (or 48).

```
Long = TaskItem.Class
```

Companies Property

The `Companies` property is used to set or return the names of the companies that are associated with the task. The `Companies` property is a free-form string property, and in reality you can set it to whatever you like. There is no validation performed on this property.

```
TaskItem.Companies = String
String = TaskItem.Companies
```

Complete Property

The `Complete` property specifies whether the task has been completed or not. It returns `True` if the task is done, otherwise `False`. Setting this property to `True` also causes the `Status` property to be set to `olTaskComplete` (or 2), `PercentComplete` to 100 and `DateCompleted` to the current date.

```
TaskItem.Complete = Boolean
Boolean = TaskItem.Complete
```

ContactNames Property

The `ContactNames` property returns a comma-delimited string that represents the display names of the contacts associated with the task as `Link` objects. To update this property, you have to modify the `Links` collection.

```
String = TaskItem.ContactNames
```

Contacts Property

The `Contacts` property is documented as returning the display names of the recipients associated with the task. However, at the time of writing, this property was not working as documented.

```
String = TaskItem.Contacts
```

ConversationIndex Property

The `ConversationIndex` property returns the index of the conversation thread. The ASCII value of this string indicates how many times this item has been forwarded or replied to. Every time that a new message is sent in this conversation, the ASCII value of the `ConversationIndex` increases by 5. The value of the first item is 22.

```
String = TaskItem.ConversationIndex
```

ConversationTopic Property

The `ConversationTopic` property returns the topic of the conversation. This is the original subject of the message.

```
String = TaskItem.ConversationTopic
```

CreationTime Property

The `CreationTime` property returns the date on which and time at which the task was created.

```
Date = TaskItem.CreationTime
```

DateCompleted Property

The `DateComplted` property can be used to set or return the date and time that the task was completed. This appears on the Details tab of the GUI. Setting this to any value other than the default also causes `Status` to be set to `olTaskComplete`, `PercentComplete` to 100 and `Complete` to `True`, even if it is set to a date after the current date.

The default value is 01/01/4501, and setting the DateCompleted of a task whic
had previously been marked as complete to this value will cause Status to be set to
olTaskNotStarted (0), PercentComplete to zero, and Complete to False.

```
TaskItem.DateCompleted = Date
Date = TaskItem.DateCompleted
```

DelegationState Property

The DelegationState property returns one of the olTaskDelegationState
constants indicating whether a task has been delegated, and if so, whether the assigned
recipient has accepted, declined or not responded to the request.

```
Long = TaskItem.DelegationState
```

DelegationState can return any of the following OlTaskDelegationState
constants:

Constant	Value	Description
olTaskNotDelegated	0	Indicates that the task has not been delegated.
olTaskDelegationUnknown	1	Indicates that the assigned recipient has not responded to the request.
olTaskDelegationAccepted	2	Indicates that the assigned recipient has accepted the request.
olTaskDelegationDeclined	3	Indicates that the assigned recipient has declined the request.

Delegator Property

The Delegator property returns the display name of the Delegator for the task. If
you are the Delegator of the task, you will find that this property is empty.

```
String = TaskItem.Delegator
```

DueDate Property

The DueDate property is used to set or return the date and time that the task is due to
be completed by. This property appears on the Details tab of the GUI.

```
TaskItem.DueDate = Date
Date = TaskItem.DueDate
```

EntryID Property

The `EntryID` property returns a unique identifier for the `TaskItem` which is generated when the task is created. You will not find this property displayed on the GUI.

```
String = TaskItem.EntryID
```

FormDescription Property

The `FormDescription` property allows you to get a reference to the `FormDescription` that is associated with the `TaskItem` object. Once you have this reference you can use the `PublishForm` method to create a copy of this form for your own use. To make changes to a form, you must use the **Tools | Forms | Design a Form...** option in the GUI.

```
Set FormDescriptionObject = TaskItem.FormDescription
```

I would actually suggest that you design your forms in the Forms Designer that comes with the GUI. This allows you create your own look and feel for the original forms that come with Outlook. You can also write your own scripts for the form. However, you should be warned that the development environment is extremely basic, and scripting is consequently very difficult. The `FormDescription` object is discussed in greater detail in Chapter 11.

GetInspector Property

The `GetInspector` property returns a reference to the `Inspector` object for the `TaskItem`. For more information on the `Inspector` object, refer to Chapter 7.

```
Set InspectorObject = TaskItem.GetInspector
```

Importance Property

The `Importance` property allows you to view or change the current importance for the `TaskItem`.

```
TaskItem.Importance = Long
Long = TaskItem.Importance
```

The `Importance` property can contain any one of the `OlImportance` constants:

Constant	Value	Description
olImportanceLow	0	The item is of low importance.
olImportanceNormal	1	The item is of normal importance.
olImportanceHigh	2	The item is of high importance.

This property is not displayed on the `TaskItem` GUI — you must open the properties dialog to change or update this property.

IsRecurring Property

The `IsRecurring` property returns a Boolean value that indicates whether this task is a recurring `TaskItem` (`True`) or not (`False`).

```
Boolean = TaskItem.IsRecurring
```

LastModificationTime Property

The `LastModificationTime` property returns the time and date that the `TaskItem` was last changed. This property is not available on the GUI.

```
Date = TaskItem.LastModificationTime
```

Links Property

The `Links` property gives you access to the collection of contact items which are associated with the task. The `Links` collection and the `Link` object are fully covered in Chapter 11. The `Links` property is new to Outlook 2000 — earlier versions had the `Contacts` property which is still offered for backward compatibility, but which was not working at the time of writing.

```
Set LinksCollection = TaskItem.Links
```

MessageClass Property

The `MessageClass` property indicates the type of item we are looking at by mapping us to the form that is associated with the `TaskItem`. Unless you have created your own form, this property will return `"IPM.Task"`. Changing this to a different valid value will cause the task to become another type of item (e.g. setting the MessageClass as `"IPM.StickyNote"` causes the task to become a `NoteItem`).

```
TaskItem.MessageClass = String
String = TaskItem.MessageClass
```

Mileage Property

The `Mileage` property is a free-form string, which you could use to enter or view the mileage associated with this task (although it can store any value). This property is displayed on the Details tab of the Outlook GUI.

```
TaskItem.Mileage = String
String = TaskItem.Mileage
```

NoAging Property

The `NoAging` property allows you to specify whether the `TaskItem` object can be archived or not. When the folder is auto-archived, this task will not be archived if `NoAging` is set to `True`.

```
TaskItem.NoAging = Boolean
Boolean = TaskItem.NoAging
```

Ordinal Property

The `Ordinal` property contains a long integer value that represents its current position for the view in the `Explorer` object.

```
TaskItem.Ordinal = Long
Long = TaskItem.Ordinal
```

OutlookInternalVersion Property

The `OutlookInternalVersion` property returns the version number for the build of Outlook in which the item was created. Unlike `OutlookVersion`, which indicates only the version, this allows the exact build of Outlook in use to be determined. If the task was not sent from Outlook, this will return nothing.

```
Long = TaskItem.OutlookInternalVersion
```

OutlookVersion Property

This property returns the release number for the version of Outlook in which the item was created. For Outlook 2000, this is `"9.0"`. If the task was not sent from Outlook, this will return nothing.

```
String = TaskItem.OutlookVersion
```

Owner Property

The `Owner` property sets or returns the owner of the task — the person who is responsible for completing the task. This is a free-form string field and changing it does not affect the actual owner of the task (in other words, setting this property does not cause the task to be re-assigned to the named recipient).

```
TaskItem.Owner = String
String = TaskItem.Owner
```

Ownership Property

The `Ownership` property returns one of the `OlTaskOwnership` constants indicating the relationship between the user and the owner the task.

```
Long = TaskItem.Ownership
```

`Ownership` can contain any of the following `OlTaskOwnership` constants:

Constant	Value	Description
olNewTask	0	The task is a newly created one.
olDelegatedTask	1	The task has been delegated to another user.
olOwnTask	2	The user is the owner of the task.

Parent Property

The property returns the `Parent` object for the current `TaskItem` object. This property will always return the `MAPIFolder` object that the `TaskItem` belongs to.

```
Set Object = TaskItem.Parent
```

PercentComplete Property

The `PercentComplete` property can be used to set or return the percentage of the task which has been completed. Setting this to 100 also causes the `Status` property to be set to `olTaskComplete`, `Complete` to `True`, and `DateCompleted` to the current date. However, setting this to a value less than 100 will cause `Complete` to be set to `False` and `DateCompleted` to the default (`01/01/4501`). The `Status` property will be set to `olTaskNotStarted` (0) if `PercentComplete` is set to zero, or `olTaskInProgress` (1) if `PercentComplete` is set to a value between 0 and 100.

```
TaskItem.PercentComplete = Long
Long = TaskItem.PercentComplete
```

Recipients Property

The `Recipients` property returns a reference to the `Recipients` collection of the task. This contains the recipients who are to receive update and final status reports on the task. To learn more about the `Recipients` collection and the `Recipient` object, see Chapter 10.

```
Set RecipientsCollection = TaskItem.Recipients
```

ReminderOverrideDefault Property

The `ReminderOverrideDefault` property allows you to override the default sound that has been set for Outlook. By setting this to `True` you cause Outlook to set `ReminderPlaySound` and `ReminderSoundFile` to be valid properties.

```
TaskItem.ReminderOverrideDefault = Boolean
Boolean = TaskItem.ReminderOverrideDefault
```

ReminderPlaySound Property

The `ReminderPlaySound` property indicates whether Outlook is to play the sound file that is set in the `ReminderSoundFile` property. For a newly created `TaskItem` object, this property will be set to `True` (to play the sound).

```
TaskItem.ReminderPlaySound = Boolean
Boolean = TaskItem.ReminderPlaySound
```

ReminderSet Property

The `ReminderSet` property is a `True` or `False` value, and if it is set to `True`, Outlook will remind you of this task at the date and time to which the `ReminderTime` property is set.

```
TaskItem.ReminderSet = Boolean
Boolean = TaskItem.ReminderSet
```

Example:

```
Dim otTask As TaskItem
Dim ofFolder As MAPIFolder
Dim onNamespace As NameSpace
Dim ofInbox As MAPIFolder
Dim oicItems As Items
Dim omMail As MailItem

Set onNamespace = GetNamespace("MAPI")
Set ofInbox = onNamespace.GetDefaultFolder(olFolderInbox)
Set ofFolder = onNamespace.GetDefaultFolder(olFolderTasks)
Set oicItems = ofInbox.Items.Restrict _
                ("[Categories] = ""Outlook 2000 Programmers Reference""")

For Each omMail In oicItems
    Set otTask = ofFolder.Items.Add
    otTask.Subject = omMail.Subject
    otTask.Body = omMail.Body

    otTask.ReminderSet = True
    otTask.ReminderTime = Date & " " & Format(Time + (1/24), "hh:mm:ss")
    otTask.ReminderOverrideDefault = True
    otTask.ReminderSoundFile = < Appropriate Sound File >
    otTask.ReminderPlaySound = True
    otTask.Save
Next
```

The code above iterates through the Inbox looking for `MailItem` objects that have a `Category` value set to `"Outlook 2000 Programmers Reference"`. If such an item is found, a new `TaskItem` is created with the same `Body` and `Subject` as the `MailItem`, but we also set up a reminder for one hour from the current time. So if I get tied up doing something else, Outlook will notify me of any messages that have been sent to me from Wrox about this book. This reminds me to follow the message up with the originator of the message before they have gone home for the day.

ReminderSoundFile Property

The `ReminderSoundFile` property allows you to set the pathname and filename for the sound file you want Outlook to play when the `Reminder` is opened. No validation is carried out on this property. This means that no error will be raised if the pathname or the filename is not valid. See the `ReminderSet` property for an example of how this property works.

```
TaskItem.ReminderSoundFile = String
String = TaskItem.ReminderSoundFile
```

ReminderTime Property

The `ReminderTime` property can be used to set or return the date and time when the owner of the task should be reminded. For the reminder to occur, the `ReminderSet` property must be set to `True`.

```
TaskItem.ReminderTime = Date
Date = TaskItem.ReminderTime
```

ResponseState Property

The ReponseState property returns one of the OlTaskResponse constants, indicating whether the task has been accepted or declined, or whether the task has not been delegated or a response to the delegation request has not yet been received.

```
Long = TaskItem.ResponseState
```

ReponseState can have one of the following OlTaskReponse values:

Constant	Value	Description
olTaskSimple	0	The task has not been delegated.
olTaskAssign	1	The assigned recipient has not responded to the task.
olTaskAccept	2	The task has been accepted.
olTaskDecline	3	The task has been declined.

Role Property

The Role property will return or set the role for the task. This is a free-from string that can be set to any text value. This property does not appear on the GUI for the task.

```
TaskItem.Role = String
String = TaskItem.Role
```

Saved Property

The Saved property indicates whether the TaskItem has changed since it was last saved, returning True if the item is exactly as it was when it was last saved.

```
Boolean = TaskItem.Saved
```

You can use this property to check whether the user has made any changes to the task, and if they have, you can now prompt them to save these changes:

```
If Not otTask.Saved Then
    iResponse = MsgBox("Would you like to save changes?", _
                       vbYesNo + vbQuestion)
    If iResponse = vbYes Then
        otTask.Save
    End If
End If
```

The code above uses the Saved property to check whether the TaskItem has changed, and if it has, we prompt the user to ask whether the changes should be saved. If they want to save the changes, we execute the Save method.

SchedulePlusPriority Property

The `SchedulePlusPriority` property will return or set the priority for the Schedule+ task. It can take any of the following values: 1-9, A-Z and A1 – Z9. The value `"1"` indicates the highest priority, `"Z9"` the lowest. This is a legacy property.

```
TaskItem.SchedulePlusPriority = String
String = TaskItem.SchedulePlusPriority
```

Sensitivity Property

The `Sensitivity` property will return or set the level of sensitivity for the `TaskItem`.

```
TaskItem.Sensitivity = Long
Long = TaskItem.Sensitivity
```

The value can be any of the `OlSensitivity` constants:

Constant	Value	Description
olNormal	0	Treat the item as normal (it contains no sensitive information).
olPersonal	1	Treat the item as personal in nature
olPrivate	2	Treat the item as private in nature
olConfidential	3	Treat the item as confidential in nature.

This property is not displayed on the task's GUI: you must open the **Properties** dialog to set or view this property.

Session Property

The `Session` property returns a reference to the `NameSpace` object to which the task belongs.

```
Set NameSpaceObject = TaskItem.Session
```

Size Property

The `Size` property returns the size of the `TaskItem` in bytes.

```
Long = TaskItem.Size
```

StartDate Property

The `StartDate` property can be used to set or return the date and time when the task is to be started.

```
TaskItem.StartDate = Date
Date = TaskItem.StartDate
```

Status Property

The Status property returns or sets the progress status for the task.

```
TaskItem.Status = Long
Long = TaskItem.Status
```

This property appears on the main tab of the GUI. It can be set to any of the
OlTaskStatus constants:

Constant	Value	Description
olTaskNotStarted	0	Indicates that the task has not yet been started.
olTaskInProgress	1	Indicates that the task is being worked on.
olTaskComplete	2	Indicates that the task has been completed.
olTaskWaiting	3	Indicates that the task has been put on hold until you receive more information from a third party.
olTaskDeferred	4	Indicates that the task has been deferred until a future time.

Setting this property also affects the other properties that relate to the progress of the
task. Setting it to olTaskComplete causes the PercentComplete property to be set
to 100, Complete to True, and DateCompleted to the current date. Setting Status
to any of the other values will also set Complete to False and DateCompleted to
01/01/4501. A value of olTaskNotStarted will cause PercentComplete to be
set to zero; the other values will cause this to be set to zero if the previous value is 100;
otherwise it will be unaffected.

StatusOnCompletionRecipients Property

The StatusOnCompletionRecipients property returns a delimited string of
display names of all the recipients that are to receive a status report when the task is
marked as completed. This property is derived from the Recipients collection and
returns the display names of all the recipients that have a type of olFinalStatus.

```
String = TaskItem.StatusOnCompletionRecipients
```

StatusUpdateRecipients Property

The StatusUpdateRecipients property returns a delimited string of display
names of all the recipients that are to receive a status report whenever the task status is
updated. This property is derived from the Recipients collection and returns the
display names of all the recipients that have a type of olUpdate.

```
String = TaskItem.StatusUpdateRecipients
```

Subject Property

The `Subject` property sets or returns the subject of the task.

```
TaskItem.Subject = String
String = TaskItem.Subject
```

This is the default property for the `TaskItem`, so it can be accessed without being explicitly stated. Tasks can be identified through the items collection with this property, so it provides an easy way of accessing the task. For example, we can get a reference to a task with the `Subject` set to `"Chapter 18 - The TaskItem Object"` with the following line:

```
Set otTask = ofFolder.Items("Chapter 18 - The TaskItem Object")
```

This enables us to avoid walking through the whole of the `Items` collection to find this item — we can just access it directly through its `Subject`.

TeamTask Property

The `TeamTask` property specifies whether the task is to be a team effort. If this is set to `True`, then this is regarded as a team task. However, there is no difference in the way that Outlook treats team tasks, so this property serves merely as a tool for the programmer.

```
TaskItem.TeamTask = Boolean
Boolean = TaskItem.TeamTask
```

TotalWork Property

The `TotalWork` property can be used to set or return the length of time (in minutes) that it took to complete the `Task`. This property can be found on the **Details** Tab of the GUI. Note that setting this property does not cause the task to be marked as completed.

```
TaskItem.TotalWork = Long
Long = TaskItem.TotalWork
```

UnRead Property

The `UnRead` property returns `True` if the `TaskItem` has not yet been opened (or has been marked as un-read), otherwise `False`.

```
TaskItem.UnRead = Boolean
Boolean = TaskItem.UnRead
```

UserProperties Property

The `UserProperties` property gives us a way of accessing the `UserProperties` collection of the task. For more information on the `UserProperties` collection and the `UserProperty` object, refer to Chapter 11.

```
Set UserPropertiesCollection = TaskItem.UserProperties
```

The TaskRequestItem Object

A `TaskRequestItem` can be thought of as the `MailItem` that is created when the `TaskItem` is sent. The `TaskItem` creates a `TaskRequestItem` when the originator of the task executes the `Send` method. This could be through clicking on the **Send** button on the `TaskItem`'s GUI, or by executing the `Send` method exposed by the `TaskItem`. Once this item has been closed, it is permanently deleted from the Inbox.

If the requests and responses are not automatically processed on arrival, the `TaskRequestItem` must be displayed before you can process the tasks. This means that if you receive a `TaskRequestItem` and try to decline it before the message is displayed, an error will occur.

TaskRequestItem Methods

Close Method

The `Close` method shuts down the `Inspector` object that is displaying the task request.

```
TaskRequestItem.Close(SaveMode)
```

Name	Data type	Description
SaveMode	Long	Required, specifies whether any changes to the task request will be saved or discarded.

The value of `SaveMode` can be any of the `OlInspectorClose` constants:

Constant	Value	Description
olSave	0	Save the item without prompting the user.
olDiscard	1	Discard all changes to the item without prompting the user.
olPromptForSave	2	Prompt the user to save or discard the item.

Even if the `Inspector` object for the `TaskRequestItem` has not been opened, any changes made to the item will be saved if `SaveMode` is set to `olSave`, or the user will be prompted if it is set to `olPromptForSave`. If `SaveMode` is set to `olDiscard`, note that any changes will not be lost until the object is uninstantiated (e.g. when the macro comes to an end).

Copy Method

The `Copy` method creates a new request that is identical to the current `TaskRequestItem`.

```
Set TaskRequestItem = TaskRequestItem.Copy
```

It is important to understand that a copied `TaskRequestItem` still points at the same task, and this cannot be changed.

Delete Method

The `Delete` method does just that — it removes the current `TaskRequestItem` from the `Items` collection.

```
TaskRequestItem.Delete
```

No surprises here — if you execute this method, the item is deleted from the Folder which the item belonged to.

Display Method

The `Display` method activates the `Inspector` object for the current `TaskRequestItem`.

```
TaskRequestItem.Display([Modal])
```

Name	Data type	Description
Modal	Boolean	Optional, specifies whether the inspector window will be opened modally (`True`) or modelessly (`False`).

Here you can either accept or decline the task.

GetAssociatedTask Method

The `GetAssociatedTask` method returns a reference to the task with which the request is associated.

```
Set TaskItem = TaskRequestItem.GetAssociatedTask(AddToTaskList)
```

Name	Data type	Description
AddToTaskList	Boolean	Required, a Boolean value that indicates whether the task is to be added to the default Tasks folder.

For example:

```
Dim otrTaskRequest As TaskRequestItem
Dim otTask As TaskItem
Dim onNamespace As NameSpace
Dim ofInbox As MAPIFolder
Dim iFor as Integer

Set onNamespace = GetNamespace("MAPI")

Set ofInbox = onNameSpace.GetDefaultFolder(olFolderInbox)

For iFor = ofInbox.Items.Count To 1 Step -1
   If ofInbox.Items(iFor).Class = olTaskRequest Then
      Set otrTaskRequest = ofInbox.Items(iFor)

      If otrTaskRequest.Sensitivity = olConfidential Then
         otrTaskRequest.Display

         Set otTask = otrTaskRequest.GetAssociatedTask(True)
         otTask.Respond olTaskAccept, True, False
         otTask.ReminderSet = True
         otTask.ReminderTime = Date & " " & Format(Time, "hh") + 1 _
                              & ":" & Format(Time, "mm:ss")
         otTask.ReminderOverrideDefault = True
         otTask.ReminderSoundFile = < Appropriate Sound File >
         otTask.ReminderPlaySound = True
         otTask.Send
      End If
   End If
Next
```

In this code, we get a reference to the Inbox and enumerate through the items in it to check for any `TaskRequestItem` objects. If any are found, we then check for any items that are confidential. If we find any, then we accept the request and set a reminder to be one hour from the current time. Notice that the request has to be displayed before the `GetAssociatedTask` method can be used.

Move Method

The `Move` method allows us to take the current `TaskRequestItem` and move it to a new `MAPIFolder` that supports `TaskRequestItem` objects.

```
TaskRequestItem.Move DestFldr
```

The single parameter for this method is:

Name	Data type	Description
DestFldr	MAPIFolder object	Required, equates to an existing MAPIFolder object.

This method could be used to move all `TaskRequestItem` objects that are related or that need to be archived to a specific folder:

```
Dim ofTaskFolder As Object
Dim onNamespace As NameSpace
Dim iFor As Integer
Dim ofNewFolder As MAPIFolder
Dim ofInbox As MAPIFolder
```

Continued on Following Page

```
Dim iCount As Integer
Dim otrRequest As TaskRequestItem

Set onNamespace = GetNamespace("MAPI")
Set ofTaskFolder = onNamespace.GetDefaultFolder(olFolderTasks)

For iFor = 1 To ofTaskFolder.Folders.Count
   If ofTaskFolder.Folders(iFor).Name = "WROX" Then
      Set ofNewFolder = ofTaskFolder.Folders(iFor)
      Exit For
   End If
Next

If ofNewFolder Is Nothing Then
   Set ofNewFolder = ofTaskFolder.Folders.Add("WROX", olFolderInbox)
End If

Set ofInbox = onNamespace.GetDefaultFolder(olFolderInbox)

iFor = 1
iCount = ofInbox.Items.Count

Do While iFor <= iCount
   If InStr(ofInbox.Items(iFor).Subject, "Request") Then
      Set otrRequest = ofInbox.Items(iFor)
      otrRequest.Move ofNewFolder
      iFor = iFor - 1
      iCount = ofInbox.Items.Count
   End If
   iFor = iFor + 1
Loop
```

This example selects the user's default task folder, then checks to see whether there is already a `"WROX"` folder underneath this folder. If there is, we carry on; otherwise we create it. Notice also that if we create this folder for the user, we make it an Inbox folder rather than a task folder. The reason for this is that `TaskRequestItem` objects are really mail items rather than `TaskItem` objects. Once we have the `"WROX"` folder set up, we get a reference to the Inbox. We then walk through all of the items in the folder checking for `TaskRequestItems` by looking for the word `"Request"` in the `Subject` field. If we find one, we move it to the `"WROX"` folder and reset the `iCount` variable to the new number of items in the Inbox.

PrintOut Method

The `PrintOut` method provides a means to print the `TaskRequest` out and create a hard copy.

```
TaskRequestItem.PrintOut
```

This always sends the task request to the default printer with the default settings. The only properties that get printed by default are the properties that have values and are located on GUI for the `TaskRequest`.

Save Method

The `Save` method saves the `TaskRequestItem` to the current `MAPIFolder` object or, if this is a new `TaskRequestItem`, to the default `MAPIFolder`.

```
TaskRequestItem.Save
```

The trick with this method is to know which is the default `MAPIfolder` object. For the `TaskRequestItem`, that is the `Inbox` folder.

SaveAs Method

The `SaveAs` method allows you to write the `TaskRequestItem` object to your local hard drive.

```
TaskRequestItem.SaveAs(Path [, Type])
```

This method can take two parameters:

Name	Data type	Description
Path	String	Required, a valid path and filename for the new file.
Type	Long	Optional, one of the `OlSaveAsType` constants below. If omitted, the default is `olMSG`.

`Type` can be any of the following `OlSaveAsType` constants:

Constant	Value	Description
olTXT	0	Save as a `.txt` (Text) file.
olRTF	1	Save as an `.rtf` (Rich Text Format) file.
olTemplate	2	Save as an Outlook Template.
olMSG	3	Save in Outlook message (`.msg`) format.

An error will be raised if you try to use any of the `olSaveAsConstants` not listed above.

TaskRequestItem Properties

Actions Property

The `Actions` property returns the `Actions` collection for the `TaskRequestItem` object. The default actions available for the `TaskRequestItem` are `"Forward"`, `"Reply"`, `"Reply to All"` and `"Reply to Folder"`. For more information on the `Actions` collection and the `Action` object, refer to Chapter 11.

```
Set ActionsCollection = TaskRequestItem.Actions
```

Application Property

The `Application` property returns the `Application` object for this session. This property does not appear on the GUI.

```
Set ApplicationObject = TaskRequestItem.Application
```

Attachments Property

The `Attachments` property is a reference to the `Attachments` collection for the `TaskRequestItem` object. For more information on the `Attachments` collection and the `Attachment` object, refer to chapter 11.

```
Set AttachmentsCollection = TaskRequestItem.Attachments
```

BillingInformation Property

The `BillingInformation` property can be used to set and return the billing information for the `TaskRequestItem`. This property is a free-form string which can hold any value, but is not available from the GUI.

```
TaskRequestItem.BillingInformation = String
String = TaskRequestItem.BillingInformation
```

Body Property

The `Body` property returns or sets the body of the `TaskRequestItem`. This is where the main task request information is stored, and you can enter anything you like here.

```
TaskRequestItem.Body = String
String = TaskRequestItem.Body
```

Categories Property

The `Categories` property sets or returns the categories for the `TaskRequestItem`.

```
TaskRequestItem.Categories = String
String = TaskRequestItem.Categories
```

To add multiple categories in one go, a comma must be placed between each category. For example:

```
oTaskRequest.Catergories = "VIP,Business,Me"
```

This line assigns the categories of `"VIP"`, `"Business"` and `"Me"` to the task request. So what does this do? This enables you to find entries with these categories using the `Restrict` method of the `Items` collection.

Class Property

This returns a unique value that identifies the type of the object. This value is one of the `olObjectClass` constants. For tasks, the value returned is `olTaskRequest` (or 49).

```
Long = TaskRequestItem.Class
```

Companies Property

The `Companies` property is used to set or return the names of the companies that are associated with the task request. The `Companies` property is a free-form string property, and in reality you can set it to whatever you like. There is no validation performed on this property.

```
TaskRequestItem.Companies = String
String = TaskRequestItem.Companies
```

ConversationIndex Property

The `ConversationIndex` property returns the index of the conversation thread. This string ASCII value indicates how many times this item has been forwarded or replied to.

```
String = TaskRequestItem.ConversationIndex
```

ConversationTopic Property

The `ConversationTopic` property returns the topic of the conversation. This is the original subject of the message.

```
String = TaskRequestItem.ConversationTopic
```

CreationTime Property

The `CreationTime` property returns the date and time when the task request was created.

```
Date = TaskRequestItem.CreationTime
```

EntryID Property

The `EntryID` property returns the unique identifier for the task request. This ID is generated when the task request is created. This property is not displayed in the GUI.

```
String = TaskRequestItem.EntryID
```

FormDescription Property

The `FormDescription` property allows you to get a reference to the `FormDescription` that is associated with the `TaskItem` object. Once you have this reference you can use the `PublishForm` method to create a copy of this form for your own use. To make changes to a form, you must use the **Tools | Forms | Design a Form...** option in the GUI.

```
Set FormDescriptionObject = TaskRequestItem.FormDescription
```

I would actually suggest that you design your forms in the Forms Designer that comes with the GUI. This allows you create your own look and feel for the original forms that come with Outlook. You can also write your own scripts for the form. However, you should be warned that the development environment is extremely basic, and scripting is consequently very difficult.

GetInspector Property

The `GetInspector` property returns a reference to the `Inspector` object for the `TaskRequestItem`. For more information on the `Inspector` object, refer to Chapter 7.

```
Set InspectorObject = TaskRequestItem.GetInspector
```

Importance Property

The Importance property allows you to view or change the current importance for the TaskRequestItem.

```
TaskRequestItem.Importance = Long
Long = TaskRequestItem.Importance
```

The Importance property can contain any one of the OlImportance constants:

Constant	Value	Description
olImportanceLow	0	The item is of low importance.
olImportanceNormal	1	The item is of normal importance.
olImportanceHigh	2	The item is of high importance.

This property cannot be accessed through the task request's GUI — you must open the Properties dialog to change or view this property.

LastModificationTime Property

The LastModificationTime property returns the time and date when the TaskRequestItem was last changed. This property is not available on the GUI.

```
Date = TaskRequestItem.LastModificationTime
```

Links Property

The Links property gives you access to the Links collection for the item. The Links collection and the Link object are fully covered in the Chapter 11. The Links property is new to Outlook 2000; before this version of Outlook, there was the Contacts property that is still offered for backward compatibility.

```
Set LinksCollection = TaskRequestItem.Links
```

MessageClass Property

The MessageClass property returns a string identifying the type of item we are looking at. It also links us to the form that is associated with the item. Unless you have created you own form, this property always returns "IPM.TaskRequest".

```
TaskRequestItem.MessageClass = String
String = TaskRequestItem.MessageClass
```

Mileage Property

The Mileage property allows you to enter the mileage (or any other string value) associated with this task request. This property is displayed on the Details tab of the GUI supplied by Outlook.

```
TaskRequestItem.Mileage = String
String = TaskRequestItem.Mileage
```

NoAging Property

The NoAging property allows you to specify whether the TaskRequestItem object can be archived or not. When the folder is auto-archived, this task request will not be archived if NoAging is set to True.

```
TaskRequestItem.NoAging = Boolean
Boolean = TaskRequestItem.NoAging
```

OutlookInternalVersion Property

The OutlookInternalVersion returns the build number of the version of Outlook in use.

```
Long = TaskRequestItem.OutlookInternalVersion
```

OutlookVersion Property

The OutlookVersion property returns the number of the Outlook version in use (for Outlook 2000, this is "9.0").

```
String = TaskRequestItem.OutlookVersion
```

Parent Property

This property returns the parent object for the current TaskRequestItem object. This will always be the MAPIFolder object in which the task request resides.

```
Set Object = TaskRequestItem.Parent
```

Saved Property

The Saved property indicates whether the TaskRequestItem has been saved since it was last changed.

```
Boolean = TaskRequestItem.Saved
```

Sensitivity Property

The Sensitivity property returns or sets the level of sensitivity for the TaskRequestItem.

```
TaskRequestItem.Sensitive = Long
Long = TaskRequestItem.Sensitivity
```

The property's value can be any of the OlSensitivity constants:

Constant	Value	Description
olNormal	0	Treat the item as normal (it contains no sensitive information).
olPersonal	1	Treat the item as personal in nature.
olPrivate	2	Treat the item as private in nature.
olConfidential	3	Treat the item as confidential in nature.

This property cannot be accessed through the `TaskRequestItem` GUI — you must open the Properties dialog to change or view this property.

Session Property

The `Session` property returns a reference to the `Namespace` object to which the `TaskRequestItem` belongs.

```
Set NameSpaceObject = TaskRequestItem.Session
```

Size Property

The `Size` property returns the size of the `TaskRequestItem` in bytes.

```
Long = TaskRequestItem.Size
```

Subject Property

The `Subject` property sets or returns the subject field of the task request.

```
TaskRequestItem.Subject = String
String = TaskRequestItem.Subject
```

This is the default property for the `TaskRequestItem` and provides the most convenient way of accessing a task request through the `Items` collection:

```
Dim otTaskRequest As TaskRequestItem
Dim ofFolder As MAPIFolder
...
Set otTaskRequest = ofFolder.Items _
                    ("Task Request: Copy Method - TaskRequestItem")
```

This allows us to avoid walking through the `Items` collection to find this item — we can just access it directly using its `Subject` property.

UnRead Property

The `UnRead` property indicates whether the `TaskRequestItem` has been opened yet (or at least, whether it is marked as un-read).

```
TaskRequestItem.UnRead = Boolean
Boolean = TaskRequestItem.UnRead
```

UserProperties Property

The `UserProperties` property allows us to access the `UserProperties` collection of the task request. For more information on the `UserProperties` collection and the `UserProperty` object, refer to Chapter 11.

```
Set UserPropertiesCollection = TaskRequestItem.UserProperties
```

The TaskRequestUpdateItem Object

The TaskRequestUpdateItem is generated when the recipient changes the Status or DueDate of the TaskItem. This object is created automatically and there is no way you can create your own. Once a TaskRequestUpdateItem has been received, the GetAssociatedTask method can be used to access the corresponding TaskItem.

The methods and properties exposed by this object are the same as those of the TaskRequestItem object, so we will not be repeating them.

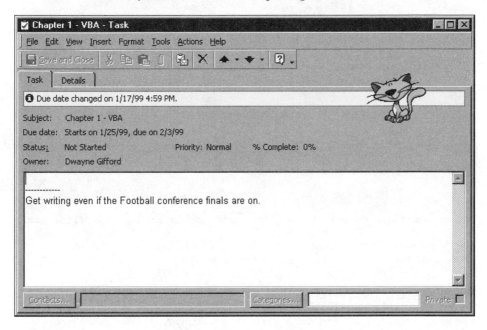

The figure above shows an open TaskRequestUpdateItem. Note that once the item has been displayed and closed, it is permanently deleted. So, curiously, the only way actually to update the task is to display and then close the task request.

The TaskRequestAcceptItem Object

The TaskRequestAcceptItem object is automatically created when the recipient of the TaskRequestItem accepts the request. Again, there is no way that you can create your own. Once this item has been received, the TaskItem can be accessed through the GetAssociatedTask method. The ResponseState of the task will automatically be set to olTaskAccept.

This object has the same methods and properties as the TaskRequestItem Object, so we will not repeat them here.

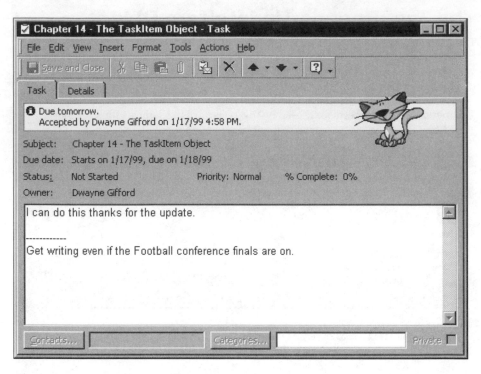

The figure above depicts an open `TaskRequestAcceptItem`. This object too is permanently deleted once it has been displayed and closed.

The TaskRequestDeclineItem Object

The `TaskRequestDeclineItem` object is automatically created when the recipient of the `TaskRequestItem` declines the request. There is no way you can create your own. Once this item has been received, the `GetAssociatedTask` method can be used to access the `TaskItem`. The `ResponseState` of the task will automatically be set to `olTaskDecline`.

The methods and properties for this object are the same as those for the `TaskRequestItem` object, so we will not be repeating them here.

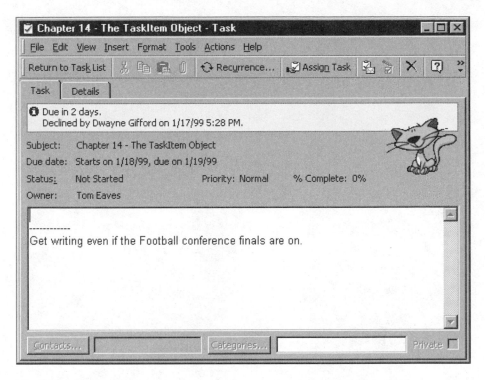

The figure above depicts an open `TaskRequestDeclineItem`. As with the `TaskRequestUpdateItem`, once it has been displayed and closed, the item is deleted permanently.

19

Office Documents in Outlook

The DocumentItem object is a non-Outlook document held in an Outlook folder. In most cases this will be another Office document but it can be any type of document or executable. Presently there is no way to create a DocumentItem object through code. To create a new document item it is necessary to use the File | New menu shown in the figure below. At the time of creation the user is asked whether they wish to send the document or to post it to a folder.

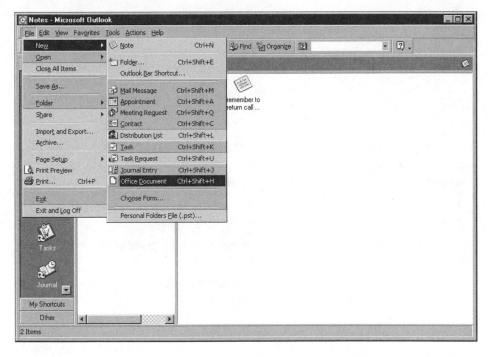

You can, however, set a reference to an existing DocumentItem object through code. This is achieved through the MAPIFolder that holds the document item.

Example:

```
Dim onMAPI As NameSpace
Dim ofDocFolder As MAPIFolder
Dim odWordDoc As DocumentItem


Set onMAPI = Application.GetNamespace("MAPI")
Set ofDocFolder = onMAPI.GetDefaultFolder(olFolderInbox). _
                Folders.Item("DocFolder")
Set odWordDoc = ofDocFolder.Items.Item(1)
```

The statement above returns the first item in the folder named DocFolder, which is a level one folder in the Inbox folder.

DocumentItem Object Methods

Close Method

The Close method shuts down a displayed DocumentItem object.

DocumentItemObject.Close(*SaveMode*)

Name	Data type	Description
SaveMode	Long	Required, determines whether any changes to the DocumentItem are saved or discarded when the item closes and whether the user is asked if they wish to save any changes.

It must be one of the OlInspectorClose constants given below.

Constant	Value	Description
olDiscard	1	Discard all changes to the item and without prompting.
olPromptForSave	2	Prompt the user to Save or Discard the item.
olSave	0	Save the changes without prompting the user.

Note that this method will take effect even if no Inspector object is open for this item. However, if SaveMode is set to olDiscard, changes will not be lost until the item is uninstantiated (e.g. when the macro comes to an end).

Copy Method

The Copy method creates and returns a new DocumentItem object that is identical to the current DocumentItem.

```
Set DocumentItemObject = DocumentItemObject.Copy
```

Delete Method

The Delete method removes the referenced DocumentItem object from the Items collection.

```
DocumentItemObject.Delete
```

Display Method

The Display method opens an Inspector object to hold the document item. If the DocumentItem object is already displayed this method will activate the appropriate Inspector object by bringing it to the front of the screen.

```
DocumentItemObject.Display([Modal])
```

Name	Data type	Description
Modal	Boolean	Optional, determines whether the Inspector is shown modally, True, or in a modeless state, False.

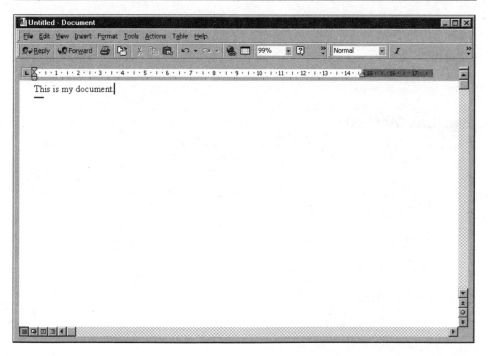

In the figure above we are showing a DocumentItem object that has a Word document embedded in it.

Move Method

The Move method moves the current DocumentItem object to a new MAPIFolder.

> *DocumentItemObject*.Move *NewFolder*

Name	Data type	Description
NewFolder	MAPIFolder	Required, an existing MAPIFolder object into which the DocumentItem is moved.

Example:

```
Dim odiDocument As DocumentItem
Dim ofFolder As MAPIFolder
Dim onMAPI As NameSpace
Dim iFor As Integer
Dim ofArchive As MAPIFolder

Set onMAPI = GetNamespace("MAPI")
Set ofFolder = onMAPI.GetDefaultFolder(olFolderInbox)
Set ofArchive = ofFolder.Folders("Archive")
For iFor = ofFolder.Items.count To 1 Step -1
    If ofFolder.Items(iFor).Class = olDocument Then
        Set odiDocument = ofFolder.Items(iFor)
        odiDocument.Move ofArchive
    End If
Next
```

In the example above we move through the Inbox looking for DocumentItem objects. If any are found they are moved to an existing archive folder.

PrintOut Method

The PrintOut method provides a way to print the document, creating a hard copy of the Document. Default printer settings will be used.

> *DocumentItemObject*.PrintOut

Save Method

The Save method saves the document item information to the current MAPIFolder.

> *DocumentItemObject*.Save

SaveAs Method

The SaveAs method provides a way to write the DocumentItem to disk.

> *DocumentItemObject*.SaveAs(*Path* [, *Type*])

Name	Data type	Description
Path	String	Required, a valid path and filename for the new file.
Type	Variant	Optional, determines in what format the item is saved.

Type can be made up of the following OlSaveAsType constants. If left blank then olMSG is used.

Name	Value	Description
olMSG	3	Outlook message format
olRTF	1	Rich Text Format
olTemplate	2	Outlook Template
olTXT	0	Text file

Although it is possible to save the document item as a .txt file, all information in the document itself, which is held as an attachment, is lost. So really there are only three meaningful ways to save a DocumentItem object.

DocumentItem Object Properties

Actions Property

The Actions property returns the Actions collection available for the DocumentItem object. The Actions collection holds all the action objects for the item. These objects represent specialized actions that can be performed on an item. For more information on the Actions collection and Action object refer to chapter 11.

```
Set ActionsCollection = DocumentItemObject.Actions
```

Application Property

The Application property returns the Application object for this session. This will be the Outlook Application object.

```
Set ApplicationObject = DocumentItemObject.Application
```

Attachments Property

The Attachments property returns a reference to the Attachments collection for the DocumentItem object. Attachments are documents or links to documents added to an Outlook item. For more information on the Attachments collection and Attachment object refer to chapter 11.

```
Set AttachmentsCollection = DocumentItemObject.Attachments
```

To run the code below you will need to set references to the Microsoft Word and Excel Object Libraries available under the Tools | References menu of the VBE.

Example:

```
Dim odiDocument As DocumentItem
Dim ofFolder As MAPIFolder
Dim onMAPI As NameSpace
Dim iFor As Integer
Dim oatAttachment As Attachment
Dim oaExcel As Excel.Application
Dim oWord As Word.Documents
Dim oaWord As Word.Application

Set onMAPI = GetNamespace("MAPI")
Set ofFolder = onMAPI.GetDefaultFolder(olFolderInbox)
For iFor = ofFolder.Items.count To 1 Step -1
    If ofFolder.Items(iFor).Class = olDocument Then
'Get a Reference to the Document Item
        Set odiDocument = ofFolder.Items(iFor)
'Get a Reference to the first Attachment of the Item
        Set oatAttachment = odiDocument.Attachments(1)
        With oatAttachment
'Find if we have a Word or Excel Document
        Select Case Mid$(.FileName, InStr(.FileName, ".") + 1)
        Case "xls"
'If it is an Excel document then check to see if we already have an
'instance of Excel
            If oaExcel Is Nothing Then
                Set oaExcel = New Excel.Application
                oaExcel.Visible = True
            End If
'Save the Attachment and then open it in Excel
            .SaveAsFile "C:\My Documents\" & .FileName
            oaExcel.Workbooks.Open "C:\My Documents\" & .FileName
        Case "doc"
'If it is a Word document then check to see if we already have an
'instance of Word
            If oaWord Is Nothing Then
                Set oaWord = New Word.Application
                oaWord.Visible = True
            End If
            Set oWord = oaWord.Documents
'Save the Attachment and then open it in Word
            .SaveAsFile "C:\My Documents\" & .FileName
            oWord.Open "C:\My Documents\" & .FileName, Visible:=True
        End Select
        End With
    End If
Next
```

In the example above we move through the Inbox folder looking for any items that are `DocumentItem` objects. If we find any document items we set a reference to the item and a reference to the first item in its `Attachments` collection. This will be the document itself as this is the only attachment that the `DocumentItem` object has. Once we have this attachment we then check to see if it is a Word or an Excel document. Finally we instantiate the appropriate application and show the document.

To learn more about the Excel and Word object models refer to the "Word 2000 VBA Programmers Reference" and the "Excel 2000 VBA Programmers Reference" also available from Wrox Press.

BillingInformation Property

The `BillingInformation` property is a string value that returns or sets the billing information. This is a free form string.

```
String = DocumentItemObject.BillingInformation
DocumentItemObject.BillingInformation = String
```

Body Property

The `Body` property is supposed to allow you to read or update the body of the DocumentItem. This is where you could give some brief notes about the document. However, if you try to set this property Outlook returns an error informing you that the property does not exist.

Categories Property

The `Categories` property returns or sets the categories for the `DocumentItem` object. If more than one category is associated with the document item, they should be separated by commas. Categories are used to group items that are related to one another in some way.

```
DocumentItemObject.Categories = "CategoryA, CategoryB, …"
"CategoryA, CategoryB, …" = DocumentItemObject.Categories
```

The one benefit I found of using this property is that you can group similar items together with this property, e.g. associate all Word documents with a category called "Word". This property can be used in conjunction with the `Restrict` method of the `Items` collection, which provides a means to return a certain subset of items that meet particular criteria. So by using this property to group specific types of document together you can employ the `Restrict` method to quickly return all `DocumentItem` objects of this type. For more information on the `Restrict` method refer to chapter 11.

Class Property

The `Class` property returns a long integer value that identifies the object's type. This will be one of the `OlObjectClass` constants and for the `DocumentItem` object is `olDocument` or 41.

```
Long = DocumentItemObject.Class
```

Companies Property

The `Companies` property allows you to retrieve or update a list of companies associated with the `DocumentItem` object. This information takes the form of a free-form string.

```
String = DocumentItemObject.Companies
DocumentItemObject.Companies = String
```

ConversationIndex Property

The `ConversationIndex` property returns the index of the conversation thread. The ASCII value of this string indicates how many times this item has been forwarded or replied to. Every time that a new message is sent in this conversation, the ASCII value of the `ConversationIndex` increases by 5. The value of the first item is 22.

> *String = DocumentItemObject*.ConversationIndex

ConversationTopic Property

The `ConversationTopic` property returns the topic of the conversation. For a document item this is the title of the document.

> *String = DocumentItemObject*.ConversationTopic

CreationTime Property

The `CreationTime` property return a date value that represents the date and time that the `DocumentItem` object was created.

> *Date = DocumentItemObject*.CreationTime

EntryID Property

The `EntryID` property holds a unique string value that is generated when the `DocumentItem` object is created. This value will not change between sessions and the only way to get a new `EntryID` is to move the document item to a new `MAPIFolder`.

> *String = DocumentItemObject*.EntryID

This property can be used in conjunction with the `GetItemFromID` property of the `NameSpace` object.

FormDescription Property

The `FormDescription` property allows you to get a reference to the `FormDescription` object that is associated with the `DocumentItem` object.

> Set *FormDescriptionObject = DocumentItemObject*.FormDescription

The `FormDescription` object holds the properties of the form that makes up the GUI in which the item is displayed. For more information on the `FormDescription` object refer to chapter 11.

GetInspector Property

The `GetInspector` property returns a reference to an `Inspector` object holding the `DocumentItem` object. If the `DocumentItem` object is not open this property will not display it. You would need to use the `Activate` method of the `Inspector` object itself. The `Inspector` object represents the GUI in which you view the item.

> Set *InspectorObject = DocumentItemObject*.GetInspector

Importance Property

The `Importance` property is a long integer value that returns or sets the importance for the `DocumentItem`. The `Importance` property holds one of the `OlImportance` constants and indicates the relative importance of the item.

```
Long = DocumentItemObject.Importance
DocumentItemObject.Importance = Long
```

Name	Value	Description
olImportanceHigh	2	The item is of high importance
olImportanceLow	0	The item is of low importance
olImportanceNormal	1	The item is of normal importance

LastModificationTime Property

The `LastModificationTime` property returns the date and time that the `DocumentItem` object was last modified.

```
Date = DocumentItemObject.LastModificationTime
```

Links Property

The `Links` property provides access to the `Links` collection. The `Link` object is used to link Outlook items together. The `Links` collection and the `Link` object are fully covered in the chapter 11.

```
Set LinksCollection = DocumentItemObject.Links
```

MessageClass Property

The `MessageClass` property returns or sets the type of the item being referenced. This property will return the string IPM.Document appended with the type of document it holds. If you change this property through code the `DocumentItem` object is transformed into an appropriate Outlook item.

```
String = DocumentItemObject.MessageClass
DocumentItemObject.MessageClass = String
```

Example:

```
Dim onMAPI As NameSpace
Dim ofDocFolder As MAPIFolder
Dim odWordDoc As DocumentItem

Set onMAPI = Application.GetNamespace("MAPI")
Set ofDocFolder =
onMAPI.GetDefaultFolder(olFolderInbox).Folders.Item("Archive")
Set odWordDoc = ofDocFolder.Items.Item(1)

odWordDoc.MessageClass = "IPM.Note"
odWordDoc.Save
```

The code above takes the first `DocumentItem` object in a folder called Archive and transforms it into a `MailItem` object. The Word document then appears as a normal attachment.

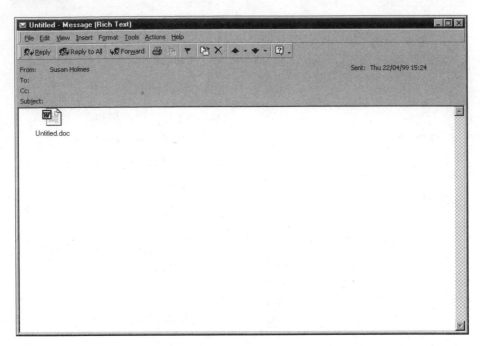

Mileage Property

The `Mileage` property is a free form string that allows you to read and save the mileage associated with the document item.

```
String = DocumentItemObject.Mileage
DocumentItemObject.Mileage = String
```

NoAging Property

The `NoAging` property holds a Boolean value that determines whether the `DocumentItem` object will be archived. This means that if AutoArchive is attempted on this `DocumentItem` it will only be archived if this property is set to False.

```
Boolean = DocumentItemObject.NoAging
DocumentItemObject.NoAging = Boolean
```

OutlookInternalVersion Property

The `OutlookInternalVersion` property returns a long integer value that equates to the Build number for the version of Outlook that the item was created in.

```
Long = DocumentItemObject.OutlookInternalVersion
```

OutlookVersion Property

The OutlookVersion property returns a long integer value indicating the version of Outlook that the item was created in.

```
Long = DocumentItemObject.OutlookVersion
```

Parent Property

The Parent property returns the parent object for the current DocumentItem object. Since a document item is accessed via the folder in which it is held, this property will hold the relevant MAPIFolder object.

```
Set MAPIFolderObject - DocumentItemObject.Parent
```

Saved Property

The Saved property tells you whether the document item has changed since it was last saved. If it holds **False** then changes have been made. Based on the information held in this property you can prompt the user to save their changes.

```
Boolean = DocumentItemObject.Saved
```

Sensitivity Property

The Sensitivity property is a long integer value that will return or set the level of sensitivity for the document item. This is the property that you can set through the Options... GUI for an Outlook item.

```
Long - DocumentItemObject.Sensitivity
DocumentItemObject.Sensitivity = Long
```

This property can be any of the OlSensitivity constants:

Constant	Value	Description
olConfidential	3	Treat the item as being confidential in nature
olNormal	0	Treat the item as normal, i.e. there is nothing sensitive about it
olPersonal	1	Treat the item as being personal in nature
olPrivate	2	Treat the item as being private in nature

Session Property

The Session property returns a reference to the Namespace object for the current session. Since at present there is only one type of NameSpace object available, this will be the messaging application programming interface or MAPI.

```
Set NameSpaceObject = DocumentItemObject.Session
```

Size Property

The `Size` property holds a long integer value that represents the size of the document item in bytes.

```
Long = DocumentItemObject.Size
```

Subject Property

The `Subject` property is a string value that will return or set the default property for the document. This is the title of the document and is also the subject of the `DocumentItem` object shown in the Explorer window.

```
String = DocumentItemObject.Subject
DocumentItemObject.Subject = String
```

Example:

```
Dim onMAPI As NameSpace
Dim ofArchive As MAPIFolder
Dim odTestDoc As DocumentItem

Set onMAPI = GetNamespace("MAPI")
Set ofArchive = onMAPI.GetDefaultFolder(olFolderInbox). _
Folders("Archive")
Set odDocument = ofArchive.Items(1)
odDocument.Subject = "This my new subject"
odDocument.Save
```

This example references the first item in a folder called "Archive". I have set up this folder to hold my document items, so if you want to try this code you will need to make changes to the code appropriate to your folder system. Then the `Subject` property is set and the `DocumentItem` object saved. The results are shown below. Both the subject of the **Outlook** item and the title of the document are set to this property.

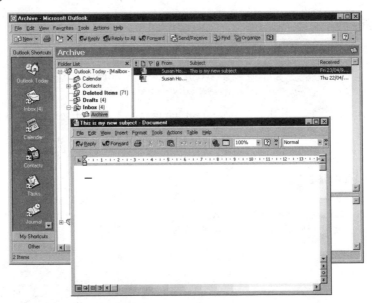

UnRead Property

The UnRead property is a Boolean value that indicates whether the item has been read yet. If set to True the item has not been read. This is a read/write property. Setting this property is equivalent to using clicking on the Mark As Read or Mark As Unread options in the menu for the item.

```
Boolean = DocumentItemObject.Unread
DocumentItemObject.Unread = Boolean
```

UserProperties Property

The UserProperties property provides a way to interface with the user properties of the DocumentItem object. It returns a reference to the UserProperties collection, detailed in chapter 11.

```
Set UserPropertiesCollection = DocumentItemObject.UserProperties
```

Outlook 2000 Object Summary

Collections

Name	Description
Actions	A collection of actions that can be executed on an item, and which can appear on the toolbar and the Actions menu of the item's GUI.
AddressEntries	This collection holds all the names and the information about a group of contacts that is contained in the address book.
AddressLists	The holder of the AddressList objects. This can be thought of as the email equivalent of a bookshelf for phone books.
Attachments	A collection of the files inserted into the body of an item.
Exceptions	This collection contains objects which hold information about any exceptions to the RecurrencePattern of an AppointmentItem.
Explorers	The collection of Explorer objects currently open.
Folders	A collection of MAPIFolder objects.
Inspectors	The collection of Inspector objects currently open.
Items	A collection of Outlook items.
Links	A collection of items linked to an Outlook item. In Outlook 2000, only ContactItem objects can be linked to other items.
OutlookBarGroups	The collection of groups on the Outlook Bar.
OutlookBar Shortcuts	The collection of shortcuts in an Outlook Bar group.

Name	Description
Pages	The collection of pages for an Inspector object.
Panes	The collection of panes displayed by an Explorer object.
PropertyPages	The collection of custom pages which have been added to the Options or Properties dialog.
Recipients	A collection containing all of the Recipient objects for an Outlook item.
Selection	The collection of the Outlook items which are currently selected in the Explorer.
SyncObjects	A collection of synchronization profiles.
UserProperties	A collection of the user-defined properties for an Outlook item.

Collection Properties

The same five properties are shared by all the collection objects. These are:

Name	Returns	Description
Application	Application object	Returns the parent application of the collection. Read-only.
Class	OlObject Class constant	Returns a numeric value specifying the class the collection object belongs to. Read-only.
Count	Long	Returns the number of objects in the collection. Read-only.
Parent	Object	Returns the parent object of the collection. Read-only.
Session	NameSpace	Returns the NameSpace object. Read only

Actions Collection

Methods

Name	Returns	Description
Add	Action object	Adds a new Action object to the collection.

Name	Returns	Description
Item(Index)	Action object	Returns the Action object specified by the Index parameter.
Remove(Index)		Removes from the collection the object specified by the Index parameter.

AddressEntries Collection

Methods

Name	Returns	Description
Add(Type, [Name], [Address])	Address Entry object	Returns a newly created AddressEntry object which is added to the collection.
GetFirst()	Address Entry object	Returns the first object in the collection.
GetLast()	Address Entry object	Returns the last object in the collection.
GetNext()	Address Entry object	Returns the next object in the collection.
GetPrevious()	Address Entry object	Returns the previous object in the collection.
Item(Index)	Address Entry object	Returns the AddressEntry object specified by the Index parameter.
Sort ([Property], [Descending])		Sorts the collection. Property specifies the property to sort by. Descending is one of the OlSortOrder constants and specifies whether the sort order will be descending or ascending.

AddressLists Collection

Methods

Name	Returns	Description
Item(Index)	Address List object	Returns the AddressList object specified by the Index parameter.

Attachments Collection

Methods

Name	Returns	Description
Add(*Source*, [*Type*], [*Position*], [*Display Name*])	Attachment object	Creates and returns a new Attachment object. The parameter Source specifies the path and file name or the item for the attachment; Type is one of the OlAttachmentType constants and DisplayName specifies the display name for an attachment of type olByValue.
Item(Index)	Attachment object	Returns the Attachment object specified by the Index parameter.
Remove(Index)		Removes from the collection the object specified by the Index parameter.

Exceptions Collection

Methods

Name	Returns	Description
Item(Index)	Exception object	Returns the Exception object specified by the Index parameter.

Explorers Collection

Methods

Name	Returns	Description
Add(Folder, [Display Mode])	Explorer object	Returns a newly created Explorer object. The parameters specify the MAPIFolder to be displayed in the explorer and one of the OlFolderDisplayMode constants to indicate the display mode for the explorer.
Item(Index)	Explorer object	Returns the Explorer object specified by the Index parameter.

Events

Name	Description
NewExplorer	Occurs after a new explorer has been created, but before it is displayed.

Folders Collection

Methods

Name	Returns	Description
Add(Name, [Type])	MAPIFolder object	Creates a new MAPIFolder object.
GetFirst()	MAPIFolder object	Returns the first object in the collection.
GetLast()	MAPIFolder object	Returns the last object in the collection.
GetNext()	MAPIFolder object	Returns the next object in the collection.
GetPrevious()	MAPIFolder object	Returns the previous object in the collection.
Item(Index)	MAPIFolder object	Returns the MAPIFolder object specified by the Index parameter.
Remove(Index)		Removes from the collection the object specified by the Index parameter.

Events

Name	Description
FolderAdd	Raised when a new MAPIFolder is added.
FolderChange	Raised when a MAPIFolder changes.
FolderRemove	Raised when a MAPIFolder is deleted.

Inspectors Collection

Methods

Name	Returns	Description
Add(Item)	Inspector	Returns a newly created Inspector object for the object Item.

Table Continued on Following Page

Name	Returns	Description
Item(Index)	Inspector object	Returns the Inspector object specified by the Index parameter.

Events

Name	Description
NewInspector	Raised when a new Inspector object is opened.

Items Collection

Methods

Name	Returns	Description
Add(Type)	Item	Creates a new Outlook item of the given Type and returns it. Type may be any valid message class or one of the OlItemType constants.
Find(Filter)	Item	Applies the filter string specified in the Filter parameter and returns the first item in the collection matching the criterion. Property names included in the filter string must be placed in square brackets.
FindNext	Item	Returns the next item meeting the criterion set by the Find method.
GetFirst()	Item	Returns the first object in the collection.
GetLast()	Item	Returns the last object in the collection.
GetNext()	Item	Returns the next object in the collection.
GetPrevious()	Item	Returns the previous object in the collection.
Item(Index)	Item	Returns the Outlook item specified by the Index parameter.
Remove(Index)		Removes from the collection the object specified by the Index parameter.
ResetColumns		Resets the properties that have been cached by the SetColumns method.
Restrict(Filter)	Items collection	Returns a new collection of items which match the criterion specified in the Filter parameter.

Name	Returns	Description
SetColumns (Columns)		Sets certain properties (listed in the comma-delimited string Columns) to be cached in memory for faster access.
Sort(Property, [Descending])		Sorts the collection. Property specifies the property to sort by. Descending is a Boolean parameter which specifies whether the sort order will be descending (True) or ascending (False).

Properties

In addition to the five properties shared by all the collections and which are listed above, the Items collection has an extra property, IncludeRecurrences:

Name	Returns	Description
Include Recurrences	Boolean	Specifies whether the collection should include recurring AppointmentItem objects. Will always be False if the collection does not contain any appointment items. Read/write.

Events

Name	Description
ItemAdd	Occurs when a new item is created.
ItemChange	Occurs when anything about an item gets modified.
ItemRemove	Occurs when an item is deleted from the Items collection.

Links Collection

Methods

Name	Returns	Description
Add(Item)	Link object	Adds the specified Item to the collection. In Outlook 2000, this must be a ContactItem.
Item(Index)	Link object	Returns the Link object specified by the Index parameter.
Remove(Index)		Removes from the collection the object specified by the Index parameter.

OutlookBarGroups Collection

Methods

Name	Returns	Description
Add(Name, [Index])	OutlookBar Group object	Adds a new group to the Outlook Bar with the specified Name at the position Index on the bar (1 is the top), and returns that group.
Item(Index)	OutlookBar Group object	Returns the OutlookBarGroup object specified by the Index parameter.
Remove(Index)		Removes from the collection the object specified by the Index parameter.

Events

Name	Description
BeforeGroupAdd	Occurs before a group is added to the Outlook Bar.
BeforeGroupRemove	Occurs before a group is removed from the Outlook Bar.
GroupAdd	Occurs when a group is added to the Outlook Bar.

OutlookBarShortcuts Collection

Methods

Name	Returns	Description
Add(Target, Name, [Index])	OutlookBar Shortcut object	Adds a new shortcut to an OutlookBarGroup and returns it as an OutlookBarShortcut object. The parameters specify the Target of the shortcut, its Name and its position within the group. Index is zero-based.
Item(Index)	OutlookBar Shortcut object	Returns the OutlookBarShortcut object specified by the Index parameter.
Remove(Index)		Removes from the collection the object specified by the Index parameter.

Name	Description
BeforeShortcutAdd	Occurs before a shortcut is added to a group.
BeforeShortcut Remove	Occurs before a shortcut is removed from a group.
ShortcutAdd	Occurs when a shortcut has been added to a group.

Pages Collection

Methods

Name	Returns	Description
Add(Name)	Page	Creates a new page with the specified Name and returns it.
Item(Index)	Page	Returns the page specified by the Index parameter.
Remove(Index)		Removes from the collection the object specified by the Index parameter.

Panes Collection

Methods

Name	Returns	Description
Item(Index)	Pane	Returns the pane specified by the Index parameter.

PropertyPages Collection

Methods

Name	Returns	Description
Add(Page, [Caption])	Property Page object	Adds a new property page to the **Options** or **Properties** dialog box with the specified Caption. The parameter Page may be either a PropertyPage object or the ProgID of the ActiveX control that implements the page.
Item(Index)	Property Page object	Returns the PropertyPage object specified by the Index parameter.

Table Continued on Following Page

Name	Returns	Description
Remove(Index)		Removes from the collection the object specified by the Index parameter.

Recipients Collection

Methods

Name	Returns	Description
Add(Name)	Recipient object	Creates a new Recipient object with the specified display name and returns it.
Item(Index)	Recipient object	Returns the Recipient object specified by the Index parameter.
Remove(Index)		Removes from the collection the object specified by the Index parameter.
ResolveAll	Boolean	Resolves each Recipient object in the collection against the Address Book. Returns True if the attempt succeeds, otherwise False.

Selection Collection

Methods

Name	Returns	Description
Item(Index)	Item	Returns the item specified by the Index parameter.

SyncObjects Collection

Methods

Name	Returns	Description
Item(Index)	SyncObject object	Returns the SyncObject specified by the Index parameter.

UserProperties Collection

Methods

Name	Returns	Description
Add(Name, Type, [AddToFolder Fields], [DisplayFormat])	UserProperty object	Creates and returns a new user property with the specified Name and of the specified Type (which may be one of the OlUserPropertyType constants). AddToFolderFields is a Boolean and specifies whether the property is to be added to the folder fields; DisplayType specifies the index of the format for the Type.
Find(Name, Custom)	UserProperty object	Finds and returns a UserProperty object with the specified Name, if it exists. The Custom parameter indicates whether the property to be found is a user property (True) or a system property (False).
Item(Index)	UserProperty object	Returns the UserProperty object specified by the Index parameter.
Remove(Index)		Removes from the collection the object specified by the Index parameter.

Objects

Name	Description
Action	An action which a recipient can execute on an item. The action's name may appear on the Actions menu and on the toolbar of the item's GUI. The actions already defined are Reply, Reply to All, Forward and Reply to Folder, although not all items support all these actions.
AddressEntry	This is the information about an individual or process to which you can send messages.

Table Continued on Following Page

Name	Description
AddressList	This is the phone book in the desk draw. If you want to find a person's address or phone number, you would look it up in the phone book. So this will be the Global Address Book, Personal Address book or the Contacts Folder if this is marked as a readable AddressList object.
Application	Represents the entire Outlook 2000 application.
Appointment Item	This is an appointment that you will find in a Calendar Folder. It can consist of a single appointment or a series of recurring appointments.
Attachment	Represents an attached file or object embedded in or linked to an Outlook item.
ContactItem	Holds the contact information that you will find in MAPIFolder objects that are of Class olFolderContacts.
DistListItem	This object allows us to group common recipients and contacts together in one object. This allows us to send mail to multiple recipients using only one Recipient entry.
DocumentItem	Represents any object other than an Outlook item — usually an Office document — in an Outlook folder.
Exception	Represents an exception to a recurring series of appointments.
Explorer	Represents the window in which the folder's content is displayed.
Form Description	Represents an Outlook form.
Inspector	This is the window that an Outlook item is displayed in.
JournalItem	The JounalItem represents a single entry for a transaction tracked by Outlook. This entry covers a given period of time.
Link	The Link object represents an Outlook item linked to another item. In Outlook 2000, only ContactItem objects can be linked to other items.
MailItem	The MailItem object represents an electronic mail message which resides in any MAPIFolder of type olFolderInbox.
MAPIFolder	This is an Outlook folder that is displayed in an explorer. This can contain items or other folders.

Name	Description
MeetingItem	This is the item that is located in the Inbox of the recipients of an AppointmentItem. The MeetingItem is always associated with an AppointmentItem.
NameSpace	This is an abstract root for any data source. The only valid namespace for Outlook is "MAPI".
NoteItem	The electronic equivalent of a yellow PostIt note. These can be used to write down facts to remember, and are not sent to other users.
OutlookBar Group	A group of shortcuts on the Outlook Bar.
OutlookBar Pane	The pane containing the Outlook Bar in an Explorer window.
OutlookBar Shortcut	A shortcut on the Outlook Bar.
OutlookBar Storage	Represents the contents of the Outlook Bar pane.
PostItem	Holds information which can be posted to public and private MAPIFolders. This object is similar to an item on a bulletin board.
PropertyPage	A custom property page which can be added to the **Options** or the **Properties** dialog box.
PropertyPage Site	The container for a PropertyPage object.
Recipient	A user or resource for Outlook. In almost all cases this will be an addressee for a mail message.
Recurrence Pattern	Holds the information about the entire collection of recurring meetings or appointments.
RemoteItem	The RemoteItem object is a smaller copy of an original message located on the server. The purpose of this object is to give you information on a message without having to download the entire message, and thus to allow much faster access.
ReportItem	The ReportItem object represents a system message, which is usually sent when a problem has occurred with a mail message sent by the user. This message will outline what the problem was.
SyncObject	Represents a synchronization profile for the user.

Table Continued on Following Page

Name	Description
TaskItem	The TaskItem object represents information about a job that needs to be completed.
TaskRequest AcceptItem	The TaskRequestAcceptItem object is created when the assigned recipient accepts a TaskRequestItem object.
TaskRequest DeclineItem	The TaskRequestDeclineItem object is created when the assigned recipient declines a TaskRequestItem object.
TaskRequest Item	The TaskRequestItem object is created in the recipient's Inbox when a TaskItem is delegated and the request is received by the recipient.
TaskRequest UpdateItem	The TaskRequestUpdateItem object is created when the assigned recipient makes a change to the status or the due date of the TaskItem object.
UserProperty	Represents a user-defined custom property added to an item.

Action Object

Methods

Name	Returns	Description
Delete		Deletes the current Action from the Actions collection.
Execute	Item	Executes the current Action and returns the item which this creates.

Properties

Name	Returns	Description
Application	Application object	Returns the parent application of the object. Read-only.
Class	OlObject Class constant	Returns a numeric value specifying the class the object belongs to. Read-only.
CopyLike	OlActionCopy Like constant	Specifies the inheritance style for the properties of the item created by the action. Read/write.
Enabled	Boolean	Specifies whether the action is to be available. Read/write.

Name	Returns	Description
MessageClass	String	A string specifying the form for the item which results from the execution of the action. Only valid for default actions. Read/write.
Name	String	The name of the Action, by which it can be referenced. Read/write.
Parent	Object	Returns the object's parent object. Read-only.
Prefix	String	A string (for example "Re") which is prefixed to the subject of the Action's parent item. Read/write.
ReplyStyle	OlAction ReplyStyle constant	A long integer indicating the style for including the original text in the new item. Read/write.
Response Style	OlAction Response Style constant	A long integer indicating whether the item created by the action should be opened or sent immediately. Read/write.
Session	NameSpace object	Returns the current NameSpace object. Read-only.
ShowOn	OlActionShow On constant	Specifies whether the action will be shown on the menu and/or toolbar of the item's GUI. Read/write.

AddressEntry Object

Methods

Name	Returns	Description
Delete		Deletes the current AddressEntry from the AddressEntries collection.
Details ([HWnd])		Displays a dialog box showing the properties of the AddressEntry, allowing the user to make changes to them. The optional parameter HWnd is a long integer which specifies the parent window handle. Default is zero.

Table Continued on Following Page

Name	Returns	Description
GetFreeBusy (StartDate, Interval, [Complete Format])	String	Returns a string representing the user's schedule for the next 30 days starting at the start date passed in, with each character representing a slot of Interval minutes. If CompleteFormat is False or omitted, free time is represented by a zero, busy time by a one. If CompleteFormat is True, the intervals are each represented by the appropriate OlBusyStatus constant.
Update([makeP ermanent], [refresh Object])		Posts the changes to the AddressEntry to the messaging system.

Properties

Name	Returns	Description
Address	String	The email address of the Recipient. Read/write.
Application	Application object	Returns the parent application of the object. Read-only.
Class	OlObject Class constant	Returns a numeric value specifying the class the object belongs to. Read-only.
DisplayType	OlDisplay Type constant	Returns the type of Recipient the AddressEntry refers to. Do not confuse this with the Type property. Read-only.
ID	String	Returns a string that uniquely identifies the object. Read-only.
Manager	AddressEntry object	Returns the AddressEntry for the manager of the user represented by the current AddressEntry. Read-only.
Members	Address Entries collection	If the AddressEntry is a distribution list, this returns a collection of AddressEntry objects for its members. Otherwise, it returns Nothing. Read-only.
Name	String	The display name for the AddressEntry. Read/write.

Name	Returns	Description
Parent	Object	Returns the object's parent object. Read-only.
Session	NameSpace object	Returns the current NameSpace object. Read-only.
Type	String	The type of email address (e.g. "SMTP") that is stored in the Address property. Read/write.

AddressList Object

Properties

Name	Returns	Description
Address Entries	Address Entries collection	Returns the collection of AddressEntry objects that belong to the AddressList. Read-only.
Application	Application object	Returns the parent application of the object. Read-only.
Class	OlObject Class constant	Returns a numeric value specifying the class the object belongs to. Read-only.
ID	String	Returns a string that uniquely identifies the object. Read-only.
Index	Long	Returns the position of the AddressList in the AddressLists collection (starting from 1). Read-only.
IsReadOnly	Boolean	Specifies whether the AddressList object can be modified. Read-only.
Name	String	Returns the display name for the AddressList. Read-only.
Parent	Object	Returns the object's parent object. Read-only.
Session	NameSpace object	Returns the current NameSpace object. Read-only.

Application Object

Methods

Name	Returns	Description
ActiveExplorer	Explorer object	Returns the currently active Explorer object. If no explorer is active then Nothing is returned.
ActiveInspector	Inspector object	Returns the current Inspector object. If no inspector is active then Nothing is returned.
ActiveWindow	Explorer or Inspector object	Returns the topmost window for Outlook. This will either be an Explorer or Inspector object. If there is no active window then Nothing is returned.
CreateItem(Item Type)	Item	Generates a new item based on the value supplied in the parameter, which can be any of the OlItemType constants.
CreateItemFrom Template(Template Path, [Infolder])	Item	Will generate a new item in the Infolder folder, based on the template (.otf file) with the path and file name given in the TemplatePath parameter.
CreateObject (ObjectName)	Object	Creates a new automated object of the class specified in the ObjectName parameter.
GetNameSpace(Type)	NameSpace object	Gets a reference to the root object for any data source. The only Type supported is "MAPI" (though this is not case-sensitive).
Quit		Causes Outlook to close down and sign out of the messaging system.

Properties

Name	Returns	Description
Answer Wizard()	AnswerWizard object	Returns the AnswerWizard object for the Outlook application. Read-only.
Application	Application object	Returns another reference to the Application object itself. Read-only.
Assistant	Assistant object	Returns a reference to the Office Assistant. Read-only.
Class	OlObjectClass constant	Returns a numeric value specifying the class the object belongs to. Read-only.
COMAddIns	COMAddIns collection	Returns a collection that represents all of the COM add-ins loaded in Outlook. Read-only.
Explorers	Explorers collection	Returns the Explorers collection containing all loaded Explorer objects. Read-only.
Inspectors	Inspectors collection	Returns the Inspectors collection that contains all loaded Inspector objects. Read-only.
Language Settings()	Language Settings object	Returns a LanguageSettings object that represents all the language settings for Microsoft Office. Read-only.
Name	String	Returns the name of the application object. This will normally be "Outlook". Read-only.
Parent	Object	Returns the object which instantiated Outlook. If called from within an Outlook macro, this will return Nothing. Read-only.
ProductCode	String	Returns the GUID for Outlook.
Session	NameSpace object	Returns the current NameSpace object. Read-only.
Version	String	Returns the full version number for the application. Read-only.

Events

Name	Description
ItemSend	Occurs when an item is sent to the recipients.
NewMail	Occurs when a new item is received in the Inbox.
OptionsPagesAdd	Occurs before the Options dialog is shown.
Quit	Occurs when Outlook shuts down.
Reminder	Occurs before the Reminder dialog is shown.
Startup	Occurs after all the add-ins have been loaded when Outlook is starting up.

AppointmentItem Object

Methods

Name	Returns	Description
ClearRecurrence Pattern		Resets the item to a single occurrence.
Close(SaveMode)		Causes the Inspector object for the item to be closed. The SaveMode parameter specifies whether changes to the item will be saved or discarded, and may be one of the OlInspectorClose constants.
Copy	Appointment Item object	Creates and returns an identical AppointmentItem object.
Delete		Deletes the current item.
Display([Modal])		Causes the Inspector object for the item to be opened. The Modal parameter specifies whether the window is to be opened modally (True) or modelessly (False). The default is False.
ForwardAsVcal	MailItem object	Creates a new MailItem with the AppointmentItem attached as a virtual calendar item.
GetRecurrence Pattern	Recurrence Pattern object	Returns the RecurrencePattern object that contains the information about the recurrence of the appointment.

Name	Returns	Description
Move(Dest Fldr)		Moves the current AppointmentItem to the new MAPIFolder, DestFldr.
PrintOut		Prints the item using the printer's default settings.
Respond(IResponse, [fNoUI], [fAdditional TextDialog])	MeetingItem object	Allows the user to accept or decline the meeting. IResponse may be one of the OlMeetingResponse constants olMeetingAccepted, olMeetingDecline or olMeetingTentative. The fNoUI parameter is True if there is no User Interface, and fAdditionalDialog is True if the user is to be prompted to send or send with comments.
Save		Saves the item to the current folder for an existing item or to the default folder for a newly created item.
SaveAs(Path, [Type])		Saves the current item to the hard drive with the path and filename specified in the Path parameter. The type of file the item is to be saved as may be specified in the Type parameter, which may be one of the OlSaveAsType constants.
Send		Sends the item to the recipients defined in the Recipients property.

Properties

Name	Returns	Description
Actions	Actions collection	Returns an Actions collection of the available Action objects for the item. Read-only.
AllDayEvent	Boolean	Specifies whether the appointment is to occupy the whole day. Read/write.
Application	Application object	Returns the parent application of the object. Read-only.
Attachments	Attachments collection	Returns a collection of the attachments associated with the item. Read-only.

Table Continued on Following Page

Name	Returns	Description
Billing Information	String	Contains a free-form string that can be used to hold the billing information associated with the item. Read/write.
Body	String	A free-form string containing the body of the item. Setting this causes the EditorType of the item's Inspector object to revert to default. Read/write.
BusyStatus	OlBusyStatus constant	Indicates the busy status for the user for this appointment. Read/write.
Categories	String	Specifies the categories that are assigned to the item. Read/write.
Class	OlObject Class constant	Returns a numeric value specifying the class the object belongs to. Read-only.
Companies	String	A free form string containing the company names associated with the item. Read/write.
Conference ServerAllow External	Boolean	Reserved for future use.
Conference Server Password	String	Reserved for future use.
Conversation Index	String	Returns the index representing the current conversation thread. Read-only.
Conversation Topic	String	Returns the topic for the conversation thread. Read-only.
CreationTime	Date	Returns the date and time at which the item was created. Read-only.
Duration	Long	Specifies the length of time that the appointment is due to last, in minutes. Read/write.
End	Date	Specifies the date and time at which the appointment is due to finish. Read/write.
EntryID	String	Returns a unique string identifier for the item. Read-only.

Name	Returns	Description
Form Description	Form Description object	Returns the `FormDescription` object for the item. Read-only.
GetInspector	Inspector object	Returns the `Inspector` object for displaying the current item. Read-only.
Importance	OlImportance constant	Specifies the importance level for the item. Read/write.
IsOnline Meeting	Boolean	Specifies whether the appointment is an on-line meeting or not. Read/write.
IsRecurring	Boolean	Indicates whether this is a recurring appointment or not. Read-only.
Last Modification Time	Date	Returns the date and time that the item was last changed. Read-only.
Links	Links collection	Returns a `Links` collection that represents the contacts with which this item is associated. Read-only.
Location	String	Contains information that identifies where the appointment is to occur. Read/write.
Meeting Status	OlMeeting Status constant	Specifies the status for the meeting. Read/write.
MessageClass	String	Specifies the message class of the item. This property maps you to the form that is associated with the item. Read/write.
Mileage	String	A free-form string which can be used to hold the mileage for the item. Read/write.
NetMeeting AutoStart	Boolean	Specifies whether an online meeting should be started automatically or not. Read/write.
NetMeeting DocPathName	String	Specifies the path for the Office document that is associated with the meeting. Read/write.
NetMeeting Organizer Alias	String	Specifies the email address for the organizer of the meeting. Read/write.

Table Continued on Following Page

Name	Returns	Description
NetMeeting Server	String	Specifies the name of the net server that will host the meeting. Read/write.
NetMeeting Type	OlNetMeeting Type constant	Specifies the type of meeting. Read/write
NetShowURL	String	Specifies the URL for a NetShow meeting. Read/write.
NoAging	Boolean	Specifies whether or not the item can be archived. Read/write.
Optional Attendees	String	Returns the string of names of the optional attendees. Read-only.
Organizer	String	Returns the name of the organizer. Read-only.
Outlook Internal Version	Long	Returns the build number of the Outlook version used to create the item. Read-only.
Outlook Version	String	Returns the major and minor version number for the Outlook Application used to create the item. For Outlook 2000, this is "9.0". Read-only.
Parent	Object	Returns the object's parent object. Read-only.
Recipients	Recipients collection	Returns the collection of Recipients that have been invited to the appointment. Read-only.
Recurrence State	OlRecurrence State constant	Returns the recurrence status of the appointment. Read-only.
Reminder Minutes BeforeStart	Long	Specifies the number of minutes the reminder should occur before the start of the appointment. Read/write.
Reminder Override Default	Boolean	Specifies whether the defaults for the reminder should be ignored. Read/write.
ReminderPlay Sound	Boolean	Specifies whether the reminder should play a sound or not. Read/write.
ReminderSet	Boolean	Specifies whether a reminder should be fired for this appointment. Read/write.

Name	Returns	Description
Reminder SoundFile	String	Specifies the path and filename for the sound file for the reminder. Read/write.
ReplyTime	Date	Specifies the date and time when the reply to the meeting request was sent. Read/write.
Required Attendees	String	A semicolon-delimited string of the names of the required attendees for the appointment. Read/write.
Resources	String	A semicolon-delimited string containing the names of resources (recipients who will be blind-CC'd) for this meeting. Read/write.
Response Requested	Boolean	Specifies whether the originator wants a response to the meeting request or not. Read/write.
Response Status	OlResponse Status constant	Specifies the status for the appointment. Read/write.
Saved	Boolean	Indicates whether the item has changed since it was last saved. Read-only.
Sensitivity	OlSensitivity constant	Specifies the level of sensitivity for the item. Read/write.
Session	NameSpace object	Returns the current NameSpace object. Read-only.
Size	Long	Returns the size of the item in bytes. Read-only.
Start	Date	Specifies the start date and time for the appointment. Read/write.
Subject	String	Contains the subject of the item. Read/write.
UnRead	Boolean	Indicates whether the item is to be marked as "Unread". Read/write.
User Properties	User Properties collection	Returns the UserProperties collection for the item. Read-only.

Events

Name	Description
AttachmentAdd	Occurs when a new attachment is added to the item.
AttachmentRead	Occurs when an attachment is opened.
BeforeAttachment Save	Occurs just before the attachment is saved.
BeforeCheckNames	Occurs just before Outlook resolves the recipients for the item.
Close	Occurs when the Inspector object is shut down.
CustomAction	Occurs when a custom action is executed.
CustomProperty Change	Occurs when one of the custom properties for the item is changed.
Forward	Occurs when the item is forwarded.
Open	Occurs when the item is opened in an Inspector.
PropertyChange	Occurs when one of the non-custom properties is changed.
Read	Occurs when the item is opened for editing.
Reply	Occurs when the Reply action is executed on the item.
ReplyAll	Occurs when the ReplyAll action is executed on the item.
Send	Occurs when the item is sent.
Write	Occurs when the Save or SaveAs method is executed on the item.

Attachment Object

Methods

Name	Returns	Description
Delete		Deletes the current Attachment from the Attachments collection.
SaveAsFile(Path)		Saves the attachment with the specified path and filename.

Properties

Name	Returns	Description
Application	Application object	Returns the parent application of the object. Read-only.
Class	OlObjectClass constant	Returns a numeric value specifying the class the object belongs to. Read-only.
DisplayName	String	The name displayed below the attachment icon (this does not have to be the attachment's filename.) Read/write.
FileName	String	The attachment's filename. Read-only.
Index	Long	Returns the position of the Attachment in the Attachments collection (starting from 1). Read-only.
Parent	Object	Returns the object's parent object. Read-only.
PathName	String	The attachment's full path (for a linked attachment). Read-only.
Position	Long	Specifies the position of the attachment within the body of the item. Read/write.
Session	NameSpace object	Returns the current NameSpace object. Read-only.
Type	OlAttachmentType constant	Returns the type of the attachment. Read-only.

ContactItem Object

Methods

Name	Returns	Description
Close (SaveMode)		Causes the Inspector object for the item to be closed. The SaveMode parameter specifies whether changes to the item will be saved or discarded, and may be one of the OlInspectorClose constants.

Table Continued on Following Page

Name	Returns	Description
Copy	Contact Item object	Creates and returns an identical ContactItem object.
Delete		Deletes the current contact item.
Display ([Modal])		Causes the Inspector object for the item to be opened. The Modal parameter specifies whether the window is to be opened modally (True) or modelessly (False). The default is False.
ForwardAs Vcard	MailItem object	Forwards the contact as an attachment to the returned MailItem.
Move (DestFldr)		Moves the current ContactItem to the new MAPIFolder, DestFldr.
PrintOut		Prints the item using the printer's default settings.
Save		Saves the item to the current folder for an existing item or to the default folder for a newly created item.
SaveAs(Path, [Type])		Saves the current item to the hard drive with the path and filename specified in the Path parameter. The type of file the item is to be saved as may be specified in the Type parameter, which may be one of the OlSaveAsType constants.

Properties

Name	Returns	Description
Account	String	Specifies the account information. Read/write.
Actions	Actions collection	Returns an Actions collection of the available Action objects for the item. Read-only.
Anniversary	Date	Specifies the date of the contact's anniversary. Read/write.
Application	Application object	Returns the parent application of the object. Read-only.

Name	Returns	Description
AssistantName	String	The name of the contact's assistant. Read/write.
Assistant Telephone Number	String	The telephone number for the contact's assistant. Read/write.
Attachments	Attachments collection	Returns a collection of the attachments associated with the item. Read-only.
Billing Information	String	Contains a free-form string that can be used to hold the billing information associated with the item. Read/write.
Birthday	Date	The date of the contact's birthday. Read/write
Body	String	A free-form string containing the body of the item. Setting this causes the EditorType of the item's Inspector object to revert to default. Read/write.
Business2 Telephone Number	String	The second business telephone number for the contact. Read/write.
Business Address	String	The entire unparsed business address for the contact. Read/write.
Business AddressCity	String	The city part of the contact's business address. Read/write.
Business AddressCountry	String	The country part of the contact's business address. Read/write.
Business AddressPostal Code	String	The postal code part of the contact's business address. Read/write.
Business AddressPost OfficeBox	String	The Post Office Box of the contact's business address. Read/write.
Business AddressState	String	The state code for the contact's business address. Read/write.

Table Continued on Following Page

Name	Returns	Description
Business AddressStreet	String	The street information for the contact's business address. Read/write.
BusinessFax Number	String	The contact's business fax number. Read/write.
BusinessHome Page	String	The URL of the home web page of the business. Read/write.
Business Telephone Number	String	The contact's business telephone number. Read/write.
Callback Telephone Number	String	The telephone number at which the contact may be called back. Read/write.
CarTelephone Number	String	The contact's car telephone number. Read/write.
Categories	String	Specifies the categories that are assigned to the item. Read/write.
Children	String	The names of the contact's children. Read/write.
Class	OlObject Class constant	Returns a numeric value specifying the class the object belongs to. Read-only.
Companies	String	A free form string containing the company names associated with the item. Read/write.
CompanyAndFull Name	String	A concatenation of the CompanyName and the contact's full name. Read-only.
CompanyLast FirstNoSpace	String	The CompanyName concatenated with the contact's LastName, FirstName and MiddleName, having no spaces between and the last and first names. Read-only.
CompanyLast FirstSpaceOnly	String	The CompanyName concatenated with the LastName, FirstName and MiddleName, with a space between and the last and first name. Read-only.

Name	Returns	Description
CompanyMain Telephone Number	String	The main telephone number for the contact's company. Read/write.
CompanyName	String	The name of the company that the contact works for. Read/write.
Computer NetworkName	String	The name of the contact's computer network. Read/write.
Conversation Index	String	Returns the index representing the current conversation thread. Read-only.
Conversation Topic	String	Returns the topic for the conversation thread. Read-only.
CreationTime	Date	Returns the date and time at which the item was created. Read-only.
CustomerID	String	The customer ID for the contact. Read/write.
Department	String	The name of the department the contact works in. Read/write.
Email1Address	String	The contact's first email address. Read/write.
Email1Address Type	String	The address type (e.g. "SMTP") of the contact's first email address. Read/write.
Email1Display Name	String	The display name for the contact's first email address. This is formed from the FullName property. Read-only.
Email1EntryID	String	The entry ID of the contact's first email address. Read-only.
Email2Address	String	The contact's second email address. Read/write.
Email2Address Type	String	The address type (e.g. "SMTP") of the contact's second email address. Read/write.
Email2Display Name	String	The display name for the contact's second email address. This is formed from the FullName property. Read-only.
Email2EntryID	String	The entry ID of the contact's second email address. Read-only.

Table Continued on Following Page

Name	Returns	Description
Email3Address	String	The contact's third email address. Read/write.
Email3Address Type	String	The address type (e.g. "SMTP") of the contact's third email address. Read/write.
Email3Display Name	String	The display name for the contact's third email address. This is formed from the FullName property. Read-only.
Email3EntryID	String	The entry ID of the contact's third email address. Read-only.
EntryID	String	Returns a unique string identifier for the item. Read-only.
FileAs	String	The keyword for the contact. Read/write.
FirstName	String	The contact's first name. Read/write.
Form Description	Form Description object	Returns the FormDescription object for the item. Read-only.
FTPSite	String	The contact's FTP site entry. Read/write.
FullName	String	The whole name of the contact. Read/write.
FullNameAnd Company	String	The full name and the company name concatenated together. Read-only.
Gender	OlGender constant	The gender of the contact. Read/write.
GetInspector	Inspector object	Returns the Inspector object for displaying the current item. Read-only.
GovernmentID Number	String	The government ID number for the contact. Read/write.
Hobby	String	The contact's hobby. Read/write.
Home2Telephone Number	String	The second home telephone number for the contact. Read/write.

Name	Returns	Description
HomeAddress	String	The entire unparsed home address of the contact. Read/write.
HomeAddress City	String	The city part of the home address. Read/write.
HomeAddress Country	String	The country part of the home address. Read/write.
HomeAddress PostalCode	String	The postal code part of the home address. Read/write.
HomeAddress PostOfficeBox	String	The Post Office Box of the home address. Read/write.
HomeAddress State	String	The state code for the home address. Read/write.
HomeAddress Street	String	The street information for the home address. Read/write.
HomeFaxNumber	String	The contact's home fax number. Read/write.
HomeTelephone Number	String	The home telephone number of the contact. Read/write.
Importance	OlImportance constant	Specifies the importance of this contact. Read/write.
Initials	String	The initials of the contact. These are extracted from the FullName. Read/write (but note that any changes to this property will be overridden by the FullName property).
InternetFree BusyAddress	String	The URL for the contact's free/busy information. Read/write.
ISDNNumber	String	The contact's ISDN number. Read/write.
JobTitle	String	The contact's job title. Read/write.
Journal	Boolean	Specifies whether all transactions are to be entered into the journal. Read/write.
Language	String	Specifies the language for the contact. Read/write.

Table Continued on Following Page

Name	Returns	Description
LastFirstAnd Suffix	String	Returns the LastName, FirstName, MiddleName and Suffix with a comma between the last and first names; all the other names have a space between them. Returns nothing if there is no suffix. Read-only.
LastFirstNo Space	String	Returns the LastName, FirstName and MiddleName with no space between the last and first names. Read-only.
LastFirstNo SpaceCompany	String	Returns the LastName, FirstName and MiddleName with no space between the last and first names, followed by the company name. Read-only.
LastFirstSpace Only	String	Returns the LastName, FirstName and MiddleName with a space between them. Read-only.
LastFirstSpace OnlyCompany	String	Returns the LastName, FirstName and MiddleName with a space between them, followed by the company name. Read-only.
Last Modification Time	Date	Returns the date and time that the item was last changed. Read-only.
LastName	String	Specifies the contact's last name. Read/write.
LastNameAnd FirstName	String	Returns the LastName and FirstName, separated by a comma. Read-only.
Links	Links collection	Returns a Links collection that represents the other contacts with which this contact is associated. Read-only.
MailingAddress	String	The entire unparsed mailing address of the contact. By default this is the address specified by the SelectedMailingAddress property. Read/write.
MailingAddress City	String	The city part of the mailing address. Read/write.
MailingAddress Country	String	The country part of the mailing address. Read/write.

Name	Returns	Description
MailingAddress PostalCode	String	The postal code part of the mailing address. Read/write.
MailingAddress PostOfficeBox	String	The Post Office Box of the mailing address. Read/write.
MailingAddress State	String	The state code for the mailing address. Read/write.
MailingAddress Street	String	The street information for the mailing address. Read/write.
ManagerName	String	The name of the manager of the contact. Read/write.
MessageClass	String	Specifies the message class of the item. This property maps you to the form that is associated with the item. Read/write.
MiddleName	String	The middle name of the contact. Read/write.
Mileage	String	A free-form string which can be used to hold the mileage for the item. Read/write.
Mobile Telephone Number	String	The contact's mobile phone number. Read/write.
NetMeeting Alias	String	The contact's ID or alias for Net Meetings. Read/write.
NetMeeting Server	String	The name of the server to host the Net Meeting. Read/write.
NickName	String	The contact's nickname. Read/write.
NoAging	Boolean	Specifies whether or not the item can be archived. Read/write.
OfficeLocation	String	The office location information for the contact. Read/write.
Organizational IDNumber	String	The organizational ID number for the contact. Read/write.
OtherAddress	String	The entire, unparsed form of another address for the contact. Read/write.
OtherAddress City	String	The city part of the other address. Read/write.

Name	Returns	Description
OtherAddress Country	String	The country part of the other address. Read/write.
OtherAddress PostalCode	String	The postal code part of the other address. Read/write.
OtherAddress PostOfficeBox	String	The Post Office Box part of the other address. Read/write.
OtherAddress State	String	The state code for the other address. Read/write.
OtherAddress Street	String	The street information for the other address. Read/write.
OtherFaxNumber	String	Another fax number for the contact. Read/write.
OtherTelephone Number	String	Another telephone number for the contact. Read/write.
Outlook Internal Version	Long	Returns the build number of the Outlook version used to create the item. Read-only.
Outlook Version	String	Returns the major and minor version number for the Outlook Application used to create the item. For Outlook 2000, this is "9.0". Read-only.
PagerNumber	String	The contact's pager number. Read/write.
Parent	Object	Returns the object's parent object. Read-only.
PersonalHome Page	String	The URL for the contact's personal web page. Read/write.
Primary Telephone Number	String	The primary phone number for the contact. Read/write.
Profession	String	The profession of the contact. Read/write.
RadioTelephone Number	String	The radio telephone number of the contact. Read/write.
ReferredBy	String	The name of the person that referred this contact to you. Read/write.
Saved	Boolean	Indicates whether the item has changed since it was last saved. Read-only.

Name	Returns	Description
Selected MailingAddress	OlMailing Address constant	Specifies which address is the mailing address: none, home, business or other. Read/write.
Sensitivity	OlSensitivity constant	Specifies the level of sensitivity for the item. Read/write.
Session	NameSpace object	Returns the current NameSpace object. Read-only.
Size	Long	Returns the size of the item in bytes. Read-only.
Spouse	String	The name of the contact's spouse. Read/write.
Subject	String	Contains the subject of the item. Read/write.
Suffix	String	The contact's suffix. Read/write.
TelexNumber	String	The contact's telex number. Read/write.
Title	String	The contact's title. Read/write.
TTYTDD Telephone Number	String	The TTY/TDD telephone number of the contact. Read/write.
UnRead	Boolean	Indicates whether the item is to be marked as "Unread". Read/write.
User1	String	The first MS Schedule+ user for the contact. Read/write.
User2	String	The second MS Schedule+ user for the contact. Read/write.
User3	String	The third MS Schedule+ user. for the contact. Read/write.
User4	String	The fourth MS Schedule+ user for the contact. Read/write.
User Certificate	String	The authentication certificate for the contact. Read/write.
UserProperties	User Properties collection	Returns the UserProperties collection for the item. Read-only.

Name	Returns	Description
WebPage	String	The URL for the contact's web page. Read/write.
YomiCompanyName	String	The Japanese phonetic rendering of the company name. Read/write.
YomiFirstName	String	The Japanese phonetic rendering of the contact's first name. Read/write.
YomiLastName	String	The Japanese phonetic rendering of the contact's last name. Read/write.

Events

Name	Description
AttachmentAdd	Occurs when a new attachment is added to the item.
AttachmentRead	Occurs when an attachment is opened.
BeforeAttachment Save	Occurs just before the attachment is saved.
BeforeCheckNames	Occurs just before Outlook resolves the recipients for the item.
Close	Occurs when the Inspector object is shut down.
CustomAction	Occurs when a custom action is executed.
CustomProperty Change	Occurs when one of the custom properties for the item is changed.
Forward	Occurs when the item is forwarded.
Open	Occurs when the item is opened in an Inspector.
PropertyChange	Occurs when one of the non-custom properties is changed.
Read	Occurs when the item is opened for editing.
Reply	Occurs when the Reply action is executed on the item.
ReplyAll	Occurs when the ReplyAll action is executed on the item.
Send	Occurs when the item is sent.
Write	Occurs when the Save or SaveAs method is executed on the item.

DistListItem Object

Methods

Name	Returns	Description
AddMembers (Recipients)		Adds to the distribution list all the Recipient objects that are part of the Recipients collection passed in as a parameter.
Close(Save Mode)		Causes the Inspector object for the item to be closed. The SaveMode parameter specifies whether changes to the item will be saved or discarded, and may be one of the OlInspectorClose constants.
Copy	DistList Item object	Creates and returns an identical DistListItem object.
Delete		Deletes the current item.
Display ([Modal])		Causes the Inspector object for the item to be opened. The Modal parameter specifies whether the window is to be opened modally (True) or modelessly (False). The default is False.
GetMember (Index)	Recipient object	Returns the member of the distribution list specified in the Index parameter as a Recipient object.
Move(Dest Fldr)		Moves the current item to the new MAPIFolder, DestFldr.
PrintOut		Prints the item using the printer's default settings.
Remove Members (Recipients)		Removes from the distribution list all the Recipient objects that are part of the Recipients collection passed in as a parameter.
Save		Saves the item to the current folder for an existing item or to the default folder for a newly created item.
SaveAs(Path, [Type])		Saves the current item to the hard drive with the path and filename specified in the Path parameter. The type of file the item is to be saved as may be specified in the Type parameter, which may be one of the OlSaveAsType constants.

Properties

Name	Returns	Description
Actions	Actions collection	Returns an Actions collection of the available Action objects for the item. Read-only.
Application	Application object	Returns the parent application of the object. Read-only.
Attachments	Attachments collection	Returns a collection of the attachments associated with the item. Read-only.
Billing Information	String	Contains a free-form string that can be used to hold the billing information associated with the item. Read/write.
Body	String	A free-form string containing the body of the item. Setting this causes the EditorType of the item's Inspector object to revert to default. Read/write.
Categories	String	Specifies the categories that are assigned to the item. Read/write.
Class	OlObject Class constant	Returns a numeric value specifying the class the object belongs to. Read-only.
Companies	String	A free form string containing the company names associated with the item. Read/write.
Conversation Index	String	Returns the index representing the current conversation thread. Read-only.
Conversation Topic	String	Returns the topic for the conversation thread. Read-only.
CreationTime	Date	Returns the date and time at which the item was created. Read-only.
DLName	String	Specifies the name of the distribution list. Read/write.
EntryID	String	Returns a unique string identifier for the item. Read-only.
Form Description	Form Description object	Returns the FormDescription object for the item. Read-only.

Name	Returns	Description
GetInspector	Inspector object	Returns the `Inspector` object for displaying the current item. Read-only.
Importance	OlImportance constant	Specifies the importance level for the item. Read/write.
Last Modification Time	Date	Returns the date and time that the item was last changed. Read-only.
Links	Links collection	Returns a `Links` collection that represents the contacts with which this item is associated. Read-only.
MemberCount	Long	Returns the number of members in the distribution list. Read-only.
MessageClass	String	Specifies the message class of the item. This property maps you to the form that is associated with the item. Read/write.
Mileage	String	A free-form string which can be used to hold the mileage for the item. Read/write.
NoAging	Boolean	Specifies whether or not the item can be archived. Read/write.
Outlook Internal Version	Long	Returns the build number of the Outlook version used to create the item. Read-only.
Outlook Version	String	Returns the major and minor version number for the Outlook Application used to create the item. For Outlook 2000, this is `"9.0"`. Read-only.
Parent	Object	Returns the object's parent object. Read-only.
Saved	Boolean	Indicates whether the item has changed since it was last saved. Read-only.
Sensitivity	OlSensitivity constant	Specifies the level of sensitivity for the item. Read/write.

Table Continued on Following Page

Name	Returns	Description
Session	NameSpace object	Returns the current NameSpace object. Read-only.
Size	Long	Returns the size of the item in bytes. Read-only.
Subject	String	Contains the subject of the item. Read/write.
UnRead	Boolean	Indicates whether the item is to be marked as "Unread". Read/write.
User Properties	UserProperties collection	Returns the UserProperties collection for the item. Read-only.

Events

Name	Description
AttachmentAdd	Occurs when a new attachment is added to the item.
AttachmentRead	Occurs when an attachment is opened.
BeforeAttachment Save	Occurs just before the attachment is saved.
BeforeCheckNames	Occurs just before Outlook resolves the recipients for the item.
Close	Occurs when the Inspector object is shut down.
CustomAction	Occurs when a custom action is executed.
CustomProperty Change	Occurs when one of the custom properties for the item is changed.
Forward	Occurs when the item is forwarded.
Open	Occurs when the item is opened in an Inspector.
PropertyChange	Occurs when one of the non-custom properties is changed.
Read	Occurs when the item is opened for editing.
Reply	Occurs when the Reply action is executed on the item.
ReplyAll	Occurs when the ReplyAll action is executed on the item.
Send	Occurs when the item is sent.
Write	Occurs when the Save or SaveAs method is executed on the item.

DocumentItem Object

Methods

Name	Returns	Description
Close (SaveMode)		Causes the Inspector object for the item to be closed. The SaveMode parameter specifies whether changes to the item will be saved or discarded, and may be one of the OlInspectorClose constants.
Copy	DocumentItem object	Creates and returns an identical DocumentItem object.
Delete		Deletes the current item.
Display ([Modal])		Causes the Inspector object for the item to be opened. The Modal parameter specifies whether the window is to be opened modally (True) or modelessly (False). The default is False.
Move (DestFldr)		Moves the current item to the new MAPIFolder, DestFldr.
PrintOut		Prints the item using the printer's default settings.
Save		Saves the item to the current folder for an existing item or to the default folder for a newly created item.
SaveAs (Path, [Type])		Saves the current item to the hard drive with the path and filename specified in the Path parameter. The type of file the item is to be saved as may be specified in the Type parameter, which may be one of the OlSaveAsType constants.

Properties

Name	Returns	Description
Actions	Actions collection	Returns an Actions collection of the available Action objects for the item. Read-only.
Application	Application object	Returns the parent application of the object. Read-only.

Table Continued on Following Page

Name	Returns	Description
Attachments	Attachments collection	Returns a collection of the attachments associated with the item. Read-only.
Billing Information	String	Contains a free-form string that can be used to hold the billing information associated with the item. Read/write.
Body	String	A free-form string containing the body of the item. Setting this causes the EditorType of the item's Inspector object to revert to default. Read/write.
Categories	String	Specifies the categories that are assigned to the item. Read/write.
Class	OlObject Class constant	Returns a numeric value specifying the class the object belongs to. Read-only.
Companies	String	A free form string containing the company names associated with the item. Read/write.
Conversation Index	String	Returns the index representing the current conversation thread. Read-only.
Conversation Topic	String	Returns the topic for the conversation thread. Read-only.
CreationTime	Date	Returns the date and time at which the item was created. Read-only.
EntryID	String	Returns a unique string identifier for the item. Read-only.
Form Description	Form Description object	Returns the FormDescription object for the item. Read-only.
GetInspector	Inspector object	Returns the Inspector object for displaying the current item. Read-only.
Importance	OlImportance constant	Specifies the importance level for the item. Read/write.
Last Modification Time	Date	Returns the date and time that the item was last changed. Read-only.
Links	Links collection	Returns a Links collection that represents the contacts with which this item is associated. Read-only.

Name	Returns	Description
Message Class	String	Specifies the message class of the item. This property maps you to the form that is associated with the item. Read/write.
Mileage	String	A free-form string which can be used to hold the mileage for the item. Read/write.
NoAging	Boolean	Specifies whether or not the item can be archived. Read/write.
Outlook Internal Version	Long	Returns the build number of the Outlook version used to create the item. Read-only.
Outlook Version	String	Returns the major and minor version number for the Outlook Application used to create the item. For Outlook 2000, this is "9.0". Read-only.
Parent	Object	Returns the object's parent object. Read-only.
Saved	Boolean	Indicates whether the item has changed since it was last saved. Read-only.
Sensitivity	OlSensitivity constant	Specifies the level of sensitivity for the item. Read/write.
Session	NameSpace object	Returns the current NameSpace object. Read-only.
Size	Long	Returns the size of the item in bytes. Read-only.
Subject	String	Contains the subject of the item. Read/write.
UnRead	Boolean	Indicates whether the item is to be marked as "Unread". Read/write.
User Properties	User Properties collection	Returns the UserProperties collection for the item. Read-only.

Events

Name	Description
AttachmentAdd	Occurs when a new attachment is added to the item.
AttachmentRead	Occurs when an attachment is opened.
BeforeAttachment Save	Occurs just before the attachment is saved.
BeforeCheckNames	Occurs just before Outlook resolves the recipients for the item.
Close	Occurs when the Inspector object is shut down.
CustomAction	Occurs when a custom action is executed.
CustomProperty Change	Occurs when one of the custom properties for the item is changed.
Forward	Occurs when the item is forwarded.
Open	Occurs when the item is opened in an Inspector.
PropertyChange	Occurs when one of the non-custom properties is changed.
Read	Occurs when the item is opened for editing.
Reply	Occurs when the Reply action is executed on the item.
ReplyAll	Occurs when the ReplyAll action is executed on the item.
Send	Occurs when the item is sent.
Write	Occurs when the Save or SaveAs method is executed on the item.

Exception Object

Properties

Name	Returns	Description
Application	Application object	Returns the parent application of the object. Read-only.
AppointmentItem	Appointment Item object	Returns the instance of the AppointmentItem which is the exception to the recurrence pattern. Read-only.
Class	OlObjectClass constant	Returns a numeric value specifying the class the object belongs to. Read-only.

Name	Returns	Description
Deleted	Boolean	Indicates whether the AppointmentItem has been deleted from the recurrence pattern. Read-only.
OriginalDate	Date	Returns the original date and time of the AppointmentItem. Read-only.
Parent	Object	Returns the object's parent object. Read-only.
Session	NameSpace object	Returns the current NameSpace object. Read-only.

Explorer Object

Methods

Name	Returns	Description
Activate		Causes the Explorer window to move to the foreground.
Close		Closes the Explorer object.
Display		Opens the Explorer object (included for backward compatibility).
IsPaneVisible (Pane)	Boolean	Indicates whether a pane is visible in the explorer. The parameter Pane must be one of the OlPane constants.
ShowPane (Pane, Visible)		Displays or hides the pane specified in the Pane parameter, which should be one of the OlPane constants. Visible must be set to True to show the pane or False to hide it.

Properties

Name	Returns	Description
Application	Application object	Returns the parent application of the object. Read-only.
Caption	String	Returns the title of the explorer window. Read-only.

Table Continued on Following Page

Name	Returns	Description
Class	OlObject Class constant	Returns a numeric value specifying the class the object belongs to. Read-only.
CommandBars	CommandBars collection	Returns a collection representing all the toolbars and menus available for the explorer. Read-only.
Current Folder	MAPIFolder object	Specifies the currently displayed MAPIFolder. Read/write.
CurrentView	String	Specifies the current view for the explorer. Read/write.
Height	Long	Specifies the height of the explorer in pixels. Read/write.
Left	Long	Specifies the number of pixels the left edge of the explorer window is from the left edge of the screen. Read/write.
Panes	Panes collection	Returns the collection of panes currently displayed by the explorer. Read-only.
Parent	Object	Returns the object's parent object. Read-only.
Selection	Items collection	Returns a Selection collection of all the selected items in the Explorer object. Read-only.
Session	NameSpace object	Returns the current NameSpace object. Read-only.
Top	Long	Specifies the number of pixels the top edge of the explorer window is from the top edge of the screen. Read/write.
Width	Long	Specifies the width of the explorer window in pixels. Read/write.
WindowState	OlWindow State constant	Specifies whether the window is normal, maximized or minimized. Read/write.

Events

Name	Description
Activate	Occurs when the explorer window becomes the active window.

Name	Description
BeforeFolder Switch	Occurs before the active MAPIFolder is switched.
BeforeViewSwitch	Occurs before the active view is switched.
Deactivate	Occurs when the explorer window is deactivated and another window becomes active.
FolderSwitch	Occurs when a new MAPIFolder is activated.
SelectionChange	Occurs when the current collection of selected items is changed.
ViewSwitch	Occurs when the view is changed.

FormDescription Object

Method

Name	Description
PublishForm (Registry, [Folder])	Registers the FormDescription object in the form registry. Registry is one of the OlFormRegistry constants and defines the class of the form; Folder (used only with folder form registry) is a MAPIFolder object which specifies the folder from which the form must be accessed.

Properties

Name	Returns	Description
Application	Application object	Returns the parent application of the object. Read-only.
Category	String	The category assigned to the FormDescription. Read/write.
CategorySub	String	The sub-category assigned to the FormDescription. Read/write.
Class	OlObjectClass constant	Returns a numeric value specifying the class the object belongs to. Read-only.
Comment	String	A comment assigned to the FormDescription. Read/write.

Table Continued on Following Page

Name	Returns	Description
ContactName	String	The name of a person to contact about the `FormDescription`. Read/write.
DisplayName	String	The display name of the form. Read/write.
Hidden	Boolean	Specifies whether the form is hidden (whether it can be used only as the response from another custom form). Read/write.
Icon	String	The path and filename of the icon for the form. Read/write.
Locked	Boolean	Specifies whether the form can be modified. Read/write.
MessageClass	String	Specifies the message class of the item. This property maps you to the form that is associated with the item. Read-only.
MiniIcon	String	The path and filename of the mini-icon for the form. Read/write.
Name	String	The name of the `FormDescription` object and the caption for the form. Read/write.
Number	String	The number for the form. Read/write.
OneOff	Boolean	Specifies whether the form will be discarded after use. Read/write.
Parent	Object	Returns the object's parent object. Read-only.
Password	String	Specifies the password required to modify the form. Read/write.
ScriptText	String	A string containing all the VBScript for the form. Read-only.
Session	Name Space object	Returns the current `NameSpace` object. Read-only.
Template	String	The name of the form's template (`.dot` file). Read/write.
UseWordMail	Boolean	Specifies whether MS Word is to be used as the default editor for the form. Read/write.
Version	String	Specifies the version number. Read/write.

Inspector Object

Methods

Name	Returns	Description
Activate		Causes the Inspector move to the foreground.
Close (SaveMode)		Closes the Inspector object with the option of saving the changes (specified in the SaveMode parameter, which can be one of the OlInspectorClose constants).
Display ([Modal])		Opens the Inspector. The parameter specifies the modality of the inspector window: True for modal and False for modeless. Note that not all Inspector objects support modal display.
HideFormPage (PageName)		Causes the form page with the display name PageName to be hidden.
IsWordMail	Boolean	Specifies whether the item is actually shown in an Inspector object (False) or in Microsoft Word (True).
SetCurrent FormPage (PageName)		Displays the form page with the display name PageName and causes it to have the focus.
ShowFormPage (PageName)		Shows the form page with the display name PageName but does not set the focus to it.

Properties

Name	Returns	Description
Application	Application object	Returns the parent application of the object. Read-only.
Caption	String	Returns the title of the inspector window. Read-only.
Class	OlObject Class constant	Returns a numeric value specifying the class the object belongs to. Read-only.
CommandBars	CommandBars collection	Returns a collection representing all the toolbars and menus available for the inspector. Read-only.

Table Continued on Following Page

Name	Returns	Description
CurrentItem	Item	Returns the item being displayed by the inspector. Read-only.
EditorType	OlEditorType constant	Returns a constant that defines the type of editor that that will be used to display the item. Read-only.
Height	Long	Specifies the height of the inspector in pixels. Read/write.
HTMLEditor	HTML Document Object Model	Returns the HTML DOM of the message being displayed. Read-only.
Left	Long	Specifies the number of pixels the left edge of the inspector window is from the left edge of the screen. Read/write.
ModifiedForm Pages	Pages collection	Returns the form pages that are available in the item, which can include up to five customizable pages. Read-only.
Parent	Object	Returns the object's parent object. Read-only.
Session	NameSpace object	Returns the current NameSpace object. Read-only.
Top	Long	Specifies the number of pixels the top edge of the inspector window is from the top edge of the screen. Read/write.
Width	Long	Specifies the width of the inspector window in pixels. Read/write.
WindowState	OlWindow State constant	Specifies whether the window is normal, maximized or minimized. Read/write.
WordEditor	Word Document Object Model	Returns the Word object model for the message being displayed. Read-only.

Events

Name	Description
Activate	Occurs when the inspector is activated.
Deactivate	Occurs when the inspector is deactivated and another window is activated.

JournalItem

Methods

Name	Returns	Description
Close (SaveMode)		Causes the Inspector object for the item to be closed. The SaveMode parameter specifies whether changes to the item will be saved or discarded, and may be one of the OlInspectorClose constants.
Copy	Journal Item object	Creates and returns an identical JournalItem object.
Delete		Deletes the current item.
Display ([Modal])		Causes the Inspector object for the item to be opened. The Modal parameter specifies whether the window is to be opened modally (True) or modelessly (False). The default is False.
Forward	MailItem object	Executes the Forward action on the item and returns the resulting JournalItem.
Move (DestFldr)		Moves the current item to the new MAPIFolder, DestFldr.
PrintOut		Prints the item using the printer's default settings.
Reply	MailItem object	Creates a MailItem addressed to the originator of the item.
ReplyAll	MailItem object	Creates a new MailItem addressed to the sender and all original recipients of the item.
Save		Saves the item to the current folder for an existing item or to the default folder for a newly created item.
SaveAs (Path, [Type])		Saves the current item to the hard drive with the path and filename specified in the Path parameter. The type of file the item is to be saved as may be specified in the Type parameter, which may be one of the OlSaveAsType constants.
StartTimer		Starts the timer for the journal item.
StopTimer		Stops the timer for the journal item.

Properties

Name	Returns	Description
Actions	Actions collection	Returns an Actions collection of the available Action objects for the item. Read-only.
Application	Application object	Returns the parent application of the object. Read-only.
Attachments	Attachments collection	Returns a collection of the attachments associated with the item. Read-only.
Billing Information	String	Contains a free-form string that can be used to hold the billing information associated with the item. Read/write.
Body	String	A free-form string containing the body of the item. Setting this causes the EditorType of the item's Inspector object to revert to default. Read/write.
Categories	String	Specifies the categories that are assigned to the item. Read/write.
Class	OlObject Class constant	Returns a numeric value specifying the class the object belongs to. Read-only.
Companies	String	A free form string containing the company names associated with the item. Read/write.
ContactNames	String	Returns a string containing the display names of the contacts associated with the item. Read-only.
Conversation Index	String	Returns the index representing the current conversation thread. Read-only.
Conversation Topic	String	Returns the topic for the conversation thread. Read-only.
CreationTime	Date	Returns the date and time at which the item was created. Read-only.
DocPosted	Boolean	Returns True if the journal item was posted as part of the journalized session. Read-only.
DocPrinted	Boolean	Returns True if the journal item was printed out as part of the journalized session. Read-only.
DocRouted	Boolean	Returns True if the journal item was routed as part of the journalized session. Read-only.

Name	Returns	Description
DocSaved	Boolean	Returns True if the journal item was saved as part of the journalized session. Read-only.
Duration	Long	Specifies the length of time that the item is due to last, in minutes. Read/write.
End	Date	Specifies the date and time at which the journal entry is due to finish. Read/write.
EntryID	String	Returns a unique string identifier for the item. Read-only.
Form Description	Form Description object	Returns the FormDescription object for the item. Read-only.
GetInspector	Inspector object	Returns the Inspector object for displaying the current item. Read-only.
Importance	OlImportance constant	Specifies the importance level for the item. Read/write.
Last Modification Time	Date	Returns the date and time that the item was last changed. Read-only.
Links	Links collection	Returns a Links collection that represents the contacts with which this item is associated. Read-only.
MessageClass	String	Specifies the message class of the item. This property maps you to the form that is associated with the item. Read/write.
Mileage	String	A free-form string which can be used to hold the mileage for the item. Read/write.
NoAging	Boolean	Specifies whether or not the item can be archived. Read/write.
Outlook Internal Version	Long	Returns the build number of the Outlook version used to create the item. Read-only.
Outlook Version	String	Returns the major and minor version number for the Outlook Application used to create the item. For Outlook 2000, this is "9.0". Read-only.

Table Continued on Following Page

Name	Returns	Description
Parent	Object	Returns the object's parent object. Read-only.
Recipients	Recipients collection	Returns a collection of the Recipient objects associated with the item. Read-only.
Saved	Boolean	Indicates whether the item has changed since it was last saved. Read-only.
Sensitivity	OlSensitivity constant	Specifies the level of sensitivity for the item. Read/write.
Session	NameSpace object	Returns the current NameSpace object. Read-only.
Size	Long	Returns the size of the item in bytes. Read-only.
Start	Date	Specifies the start date and time for the journal entry. Read/write.
Subject	String	Contains the subject of the item. Read/write.
Type	String	A free-form string that can be used to identify the type of the journal entry. Read/write.
UnRead	Boolean	Indicates whether the item is to be marked as "Unread". Read/write.
User Properties	User Properties collection	Returns the UserProperties collection for the item. Read-only.

Events

Name	Description
AttachmentAdd	Occurs when a new attachment is added to the item.
AttachmentRead	Occurs when an attachment is opened.
BeforeAttachmentSave	Occurs just before the attachment is saved.
BeforeCheckNames	Occurs just before Outlook resolves the recipients for the item.
Close	Occurs when the Inspector object is shut down.

Name	Description
CustomAction	Occurs when a custom action is executed.
CustomProperty Change	Occurs when one of the custom properties for the item is changed.
Forward	Occurs when the item is forwarded.
Open	Occurs when the item is opened in an Inspector.
PropertyChange	Occurs when one of the non-custom properties is changed.
Read	Occurs when the item is opened for editing.
Reply	Occurs when the Reply action is executed on the item.
ReplyAll	Occurs when the ReplyAll action is executed on the item.
Send	Occurs when the item is sent.
Write	Occurs when the Save or SaveAs method is executed on the item.

Link Object

Properties

Name	Returns	Description
Application	Application object	Returns the parent application of the object. Read-only.
Class	OlObject Class constant	Returns a numeric value specifying the class the object belongs to. Read-only.
Item	Item	Returns the item represented by the Link. Read-only.
Name	String	Returns the display name of the item represented by the Link. Read-only.
Parent	Object	Returns the object's parent object. Read-only.
Session	NameSpace object	Returns the current NameSpace object. Read-only.
Type	Long	Returns the OlObjectClass constant for the type of item the Link represents. Since in Outlook 2000, the item must always be a ContactItem, this will always return olContact, or 40. Read-only.

MailItem Object

Methods

Name	Returns	Description
ClearConversation Index		Clears the conversation index.
Close(SaveMode)		Causes the Inspector object for the item to be closed. The SaveMode parameter specifies whether changes to the item will be saved or discarded, and may be one of the OlInspectorClose constants.
Copy	MailItem object	Creates and returns an identical MailItem object.
Delete		Deletes the current item.
Display([Modal])		Causes the Inspector object for the item to be opened. The Modal parameter specifies whether the window is to be opened modally (True) or modelessly (False). The default is False.
Forward	MailItem object	Executes the **Forward** action on the item and returns the resulting MailItem.
Move(DestFldr)		Moves the current item to the new MAPIFolder, DestFldr.
PrintOut		Prints the item using the printer's default settings.
Reply	MailItem object	Creates a MailItem addressed to the originator of the item.
ReplyAll	MailItem object	Creates a new MailItem addressed to the sender and all original recipients of the item.
Save		Saves the item to the current folder for an existing item or to the default folder for a newly created item.

Name	Returns	Description
SaveAs(Path, [Type])		Saves the current item to the hard drive with the path and filename specified in the Path parameter. The type of file the item is to be saved as may be specified in the Type parameter, which may be one of the OlSaveAsType constants.
Send		Sends the item to the recipients defined in the Recipients property.

Properties

Name	Returns	Description
Actions	Actions collection	Returns an Actions collection of the available Action objects for the item. Read-only.
Alternate Recipient Allowed	Boolean	If set to True then the Recipient can forward the message. Read/write.
Application	Application object	Returns the parent application of the object. Read-only.
Attachments	Attachments collection	Returns a collection of the attachments associated with the item. Read-only.
Auto Forwarded	Boolean	Specifies whether the MailItem was automatically forwarded. Read/write.
BCC	String	Returns a string containing the display names of the Blind Carbon Copy recipients. Read/write.
Billing Information	String	Contains a free-form string that can be used to hold the billing information associated with the item. Read/write.
Body	String	A free-form string containing the body of the item. Setting this causes the EditorType of the item's Inspector object to revert to default. Read/write.
Categories	String	Specifies the categories that are assigned to the item. Read/write.
CC	String	Returns a string containing the display names of the Carbon Copy recipients. Read/write.

Table Continued on Following Page

Name	Returns	Description
Class	OlObject Class constant	Returns a numeric value specifying the class the object belongs to. Read-only.
Companies	String	A free form string containing the company names associated with the item. Read/write.
Conversation Index	String	Returns the index representing the current conversation thread. Read-only.
Conversation Topic	String	Returns the topic for the conversation thread. Read-only.
CreationTime	Date	Returns the date and time at which the item was created. Read-only.
Deferred DeliveryTime	Date	Specifies the date and time when the message is due to be sent. Read/write.
DeleteAfter Submit	Boolean	Specifies whether the message is to be deleted after being sent. Read/write.
EntryID	String	Returns a unique string identifier for the item. Read-only.
ExpiryTime	Date	Specifies the date and time when the item is to become invalid and can be deleted. Read/write.
FlagDueBy	Date	Specifies the date and time by which the FlagRequest is due. Read/write.
FlagRequest	String	A free-form string specifying the request to be flagged to the recipient. Read/write.
FlagStatus	OlFlagStatus constant	Specifies the flag status for the message. Read/write.
Form Description	Form Description object	Returns the FormDescription object for the item. Read-only.
GetInspector	Inspector object	Returns the Inspector object for displaying the current item. Read-only.
HTMLBody	String	Specifies the body of the MailItem in HTML format. Read/write.
Importance	OlImportance constant	Specifies the importance level for the item. Read/write.

Name	Returns	Description
Last Modification Time	Date	Returns the date and time that the item was last changed. Read-only.
Links	Links collection	Returns a `Links` collection that represents the contacts with which this item is associated. Read-only.
MessageClass	String	Specifies the message class of the item. This property maps you to the form that is associated with the item. Read/write.
Mileage	String	A free-form string which can be used to hold the mileage for the item. Read/write.
NoAging	Boolean	Specifies whether or not the item can be archived. Read/write.
Originator Delivery Report Requested	Boolean	Determines whether a delivery report is returned when a message is delivered. Read/write
Outlook Internal Version	Long	Returns the build number of the Outlook version used to create the item. Read-only.
Outlook Version	String	Returns the major and minor version number for the Outlook Application used to create the item. For Outlook 2000, this is `"9.0"`. Read-only.
Parent	Object	Returns the object's parent object. Read-only.
ReadReceipt Requested	Boolean	Specifies whether a read report will be returned upon the message being read. Read/write.
ReceivedBy EntryID	String	Returns the Entry ID of the recipient who received the message. Read-only.
ReceivedBy Name	String	Returns the display name of the recipient who received the message. Read-only.
ReceivedOn BehalfOf EntryID	String	Returns the Entry ID of the delegated recipient. Read-only.
ReceivedOn BehalfOfName	String	Returns the display name of the delegated recipient. Read-only.

Table Continued on Following Page

Name	Returns	Description
ReceivedTime	Date	Returns the date and time when the MailItem was received. Read-only.
Recipient Reassignment Prohibited	Boolean	Specifies whether the recipient can forward the message. Read/write.
Recipients	Recipients collection	Returns a collection of the Recipient objects associated with the item. Read-only.
ReminderOver rideDefault	Boolean	Specifies whether the defaults for the reminder should be ignored. Read/write.
ReminderPlay Sound	Boolean	Specifies whether the reminder should play a sound or not. Read/write.
ReminderSet	Boolean	Specifies whether a reminder should be fired for this item. Read/write.
Reminder SoundFile	String	Specifies the path and filename for the sound file for the reminder. Read/write.
ReminderTime	Date	Specifies the date and time when the reminder is to be fired. Read/write.
RemoteStatus	OlRemote Status constant	Specifies the remote status of the item. Read/write.
Reply Recipient Names	String	Returns a semicolon-delimited string containing the display names of the reply recipients. Read-only.
Reply Recipients	Recipients collection	Returns a collection of the recipients to be included on the reply message if the recipient should reply to the message. Read-only.
Saved	Boolean	Indicates whether the item has changed since it was last saved. Read-only.
SaveSent Message Folder	MAPIFolder object	Specifies the MAPIFolder where the copy of the message will be saved after it has been sent. Read/write.
SenderName	String	Returns the display name of the sender. Read-only.

Name	Returns	Description
Sensitivity	OlSensitivity constant	Specifies the level of sensitivity for the item. Read/write.
Sent	Boolean	Returns True if the message has already been sent. Read-only.
SentOn	Date	Returns the date and time when the item was sent. Read-only.
SentOnBehalf OfName	String	Returns the display name of the intended sender. Read/write.
Session	NameSpace object	Returns the current NameSpace object. Read-only.
Size	Long	Returns the size of the item in bytes. Read-only.
Subject	String	Contains the subject of the item. Read/write.
Submitted	Boolean	Returns True if the item has been submitted. This informs you if the message is in the Outbox but has not yet been sent. Read-only.
To	String	Contains a semicolon-delimited string containing the display names of the recipients named in the To field. Read/write.
UnRead	Boolean	Indicates whether the item is to be marked as "Unread". Read/write.
User Properties	User Properties collection	Returns the UserProperties collection for the item. Read-only.
Voting Options	String	A semicolon-delimited string containing the options for the voter. Read/write.
Voting Response	String	A string containing the voting response of the sender. Read/write.

Events

Name	Description
AttachmentAdd	Occurs when a new attachment is added to the item.
AttachmentRead	Occurs when an attachment is opened.

Table Continued on Following Page

Name	Description
BeforeAttachment Save	Occurs just before the attachment is saved.
BeforeCheckNames	Occurs just before Outlook resolves the recipients for the item.
Close	Occurs when the Inspector object is shut down.
CustomAction	Occurs when a custom action is executed.
CustomProperty Change	Occurs when one of the custom properties for the item is changed.
Forward	Occurs when the item is forwarded.
Open	Occurs when the item is opened in an Inspector.
PropertyChange	Occurs when one of the non-custom properties is changed.
Read	Occurs when the item is opened for editing.
Reply	Occurs when the Reply action is executed on the item.
ReplyAll	Occurs when the ReplyAll action is executed on the item.
Send	Occurs when the item is sent.
Write	Occurs when the Save or SaveAs method is executed on the item.

MAPIFolder Object

Methods

Name	Returns	Description
CopyTo (DestFldr)	MAPIFolder object	Copies the current MAPIFolder object to the new folder DestFldr.
Delete		Deletes the current MAPIFolder from the Folders collection.
Display		Causes the Explorer object for the MAPIFolder to be opened.
GetExplorer	Explorer object	Returns an inactive Explorer object initialized to the current MAPIFolder.
MoveTo (DestFldr)		Moves the current MAPIFolder object to the new folder DestFldr.

Properties

Name	Returns	Description
Application	Application object	Returns the parent application of the object. Read-only.
Class	OlObject Class constant	Returns a numeric value specifying the class the object belongs to. Read-only.
Default ItemType	OlItemType constant	Returns the constant that represents the default item type for the folder. Read-only.
Default MessageClass	String	Returns the message class that represents the default item type for the folder. Read-only.
Description	String	Contains the description for the MAPIFolder. Read/write.
EntryID	String	Returns a unique string identifier for the folder. Read-only.
Folders	Folders collection	Returns a collection containing all the sub-folders of the MAPIFolder. Read-only.
Items	Items collection	Returns a collection of all the items in the MAPIFolder. Read-only.
Name	String	The display name of the MAPIfolder. Read/write.
Parent	Object	Returns the object's parent object. Read-only.
Session	NameSpace object	Returns the current NameSpace object. Read-only.
StoreID	String	A unique identifier that is generated when the MAPIFolder is created. Read-only.
Type	String	The type of folder. The only type currently supported is "MAPI". Read-only.
UnReadItem Count	Long	The number of items in the folder that have not yet been read. Read-only.
WebViewAllow Navigation	Boolean	Specifies whether the Back and Forward buttons on the toolbar are enabled. Read/write.

Table Continued on Following Page

Name	Returns	Description
WebViewOn	Boolean	Specifies whether the web paged specified by the WebViewURL property is displayed. Read/write.
WebViewURL	String	Specifies the web page to be shown if WebViewOn is set to True. Read/write.

MeetingItem Object

Methods

Name	Returns	Description
Close (SaveMode)		Causes the Inspector object for the item to be closed. The SaveMode parameter specifies whether changes to the item will be saved or discarded, and may be one of the OlInspectorClose constants.
Copy	MeetingItem object	Creates and returns an identical MeetingItem object.
Delete		Deletes the current item.
Display ([Modal])		Causes the Inspector object for the item to be opened. The Modal parameter specifies whether the window is to be opened modally (True) or modelessly (False). The default is False.
Forward	MeetingItem object	Executes the Forward action on the item and returns the resulting MeetingItem.
GetAssociate dAppointment (AddTo Calendar)	Appointment Item object	Returns the associated AppointmentItem object. The Boolean AddToCalendar parameter specifies whether the appointment should be added to the default calendar folder.
Move (DestFldr)		Moves the current item to the new MAPIFolder, DestFldr.
PrintOut		Prints the item using the printer's default settings.

Name	Returns	Description
Reply	MailItem object	Creates a MailItem addressed to the originator of the item.
ReplyAll	MailItem object	Creates a new MailItem addressed to the sender and all original recipients of the item.
Save		Saves the item to the current folder for an existing item or to the default folder for a newly created item.
SaveAs(Path, [Type])		Saves the current item to the hard drive with the path and filename specified in the Path parameter. The type of file the item is to be saved as may be specified in the Type parameter, which may be one of the OlSaveAsType constants.
Send		Sends the item to the recipients defined in the Recipients property.

Properties

Name	Returns	Description
Actions	Actions collection	Returns an Actions collection of the available Action objects for the item. Read-only.
Application	Application object	Returns the parent application of the object. Read-only.
Attachments	Attachments collection	Returns a collection of the attachments associated with the item. Read-only.
Auto Forwarded	Boolean	Specifies whether the MeetingItem was automatically forwarded. Read/write.
Billing Information	String	Contains a free-form string that can be used to hold the billing information associated with the item. Read/write.
Body	String	A free-form string containing the body of the item. Setting this causes the EditorType of the item's Inspector object to revert to default. Read/write.
Categories	String	Specifies the categories that are assigned to the item. Read/write.

Table Continued on Following Page

Name	Returns	Description
Class	OlObject Class constant	Returns a numeric value specifying the class the object belongs to. Read-only.
Companies	String	A free-form string containing the company names associated with the item. Read/write.
Conversation Index	String	Returns the index representing the current conversation thread. Read-only.
Conversation Topic	String	Returns the topic for the conversation thread. Read-only.
CreationTime	Date	Returns the date and time at which the item was created. Read-only.
Deferred DeliveryTime	Date	Specifies the date and time when the message is due to be sent. Read/write.
DeleteAfter Submit	Boolean	Specifies whether the message is to be deleted after being sent. Read/write.
EntryID	String	Returns a unique string identifier for the item. Read-only.
ExpiryTime	Date	Specifies the date and time when the item is to become invalid and can be deleted. Read/write.
FlagDueBy	Date	Specifies the date and time by which the FlagRequest is due. Read/write.
FlagRequest	String	A free-form string specifying the request to be flagged to the recipient. Read/write.
FlagStatus	OlFlagStatus constant	Specifies the flag status for the message. Read/write.
Form Description	Form Description object	Returns the FormDescription object for the item. Read-only.
GetInspector	Inspector object	Returns the Inspector object for displaying the current item. Read-only.
Importance	OlImportance constant	Specifies the importance level for the item. Read/write.
Last Modification Time	Date	Returns the date and time that the item was last changed. Read-only.

Name	Returns	Description
Links	Links collection	Returns a Links collection that represents the contacts with which this item is associated. Read-only.
MessageClass	String	Specifies the message class of the item. This property maps you to the form that is associated with the item. Read/write.
Mileage	String	A free-form string which can be used to hold the mileage for the item. Read/write.
NoAging	Boolean	Specifies whether or not the item can be archived. Read/write.
Originator Delivery Report Requested	Boolean	Specifies whether the originator of the meeting will receive a delivery report. Read/write.
Outlook Internal Version	Long	Returns the build number of the Outlook version used to create the item. Read-only.
Outlook Version	String	Returns the major and minor version number for the Outlook Application used to create the item. For Outlook 2000, this is "9.0". Read-only.
Parent	Object	Returns the object's parent object. Read-only.
ReceivedTime	Date	Returns the date and time when the MeetingItem was received. Read-only.
Recipients	Recipients collection	Returns a collection of the Recipient objects associated with the item. Read-only.
ReminderSet	Boolean	Specifies whether a reminder has been set for the MeetingItem. Read/write.
ReminderTime	Date	Specifies the date and time when the reminder is to be fired. Read/write.
Reply Recipients	Recipients collection	Returns a collection of the Recipients who will receive a message should one of the recipients reply to the message. Read-only.
Saved	Boolean	Indicates whether the item has changed since it was last saved. Read-only.

Table Continued on Following Page

Name	Returns	Description
SaveSent Message Folder	MAPIFolder object	Specifies the MAPIFolder where the copy of the item will be saved after it has been sent. Read/write.
SenderName	String	Returns the display name of the sender. Read-only.
Sensitivity	OlSensitivity constant	Specifies the level of sensitivity for the item. Read/write.
Sent	Boolean	Returns True if the item has already been sent. Read-only.
SentOn	Date	Returns the date and time when the item was sent. Read-only.
Session	NameSpace object	Returns the current NameSpace object. Read-only.
Size	Long	Returns the size of the item in bytes. Read-only.
Subject	String	Contains the subject of the item. Read/write.
Submitted	Boolean	Returns True if the item has been submitted. This informs you if the message is in the Outbox but has not yet been sent. Read-only.
UnRead	Boolean	Indicates whether the item is to be marked as "Unread". Read/write.
User Properties	User Properties collection	Returns the UserProperties collection for the item. Read-only.

Events

Name	Description
AttachmentAdd	Occurs when a new attachment is added to the item.
AttachmentRead	Occurs when an attachment is opened.
BeforeAttachment Save	Occurs just before the attachment is saved.
BeforeCheckNames	Occurs just before Outlook resolves the recipients for the item.
Close	Occurs when the Inspector object is shut down.

Name	Description
CustomAction	Occurs when a custom action is executed.
CustomProperty Change	Occurs when one of the custom properties for the item is changed.
Forward	Occurs when the item is forwarded.
Open	Occurs when the item is opened in an Inspector.
PropertyChange	Occurs when one of the non-custom properties is changed.
Read	Occurs when the item is opened for editing.
Reply	Occurs when the Reply action is executed on the item.
ReplyAll	Occurs when the ReplyAll action is executed on the item.
Send	Occurs when the item is sent.
Write	Occurs when the Save or SaveAs method is executed on the item.

NameSpace Object

Methods

Name	Returns	Description
AddStore(Store)		Creates a new personal profile folder. The Store parameter contains the path of the profile folder (.pst file).
CreateRecipient (RecipientName)	Recipient object	Used mostly with GetSharedDefaultFolder, but it can also be used to verify a name in the address book.
GetDefaultFolder (FolderTypeEnum)	MAPIFolder object	Returns the default MAPIFolder object for the item type specified in the FolderTypeEnum parameter, which can be one of the OlDefaultFolder constants.

Table Continued on Following Page

Name	Returns	Description
GetFolderFromID (EntryID, [StoreID])	MAPIFolder object	Returns the MAPIFolder object based on its Entry ID. Its Store ID may also be given as a parameter.
GetItemFromID (EntryID, [StoreID])	Item	Returns the item that is specified by the Entry ID.
GetRecipientFrom ID(EntryID)	Recipient object	Will return the Recipient based on its Entry ID.
GetSharedDefault Folder(Recipient, Object, FolderTypeEnum)	MAPIFolder object	Returns the specified default MAPIFolder for the specified recipient. FolderTypeEnum may be any of the OlDefaultFolders constants.
Logoff		Logs the user off from the current MAPI session.
Logon		Logs the user onto a MAPI session.
PickFolder	MAPIFolder object	Presents the user with a list of available folders to select from. If **Cancel** is selected instead of a folder then Nothing is returned.

Properties

Name	Returns	Description
AddressLists	Address Lists collection	Returns an AddressLists collection representing the root of the Address Book. Read-only.
Application	Application object	Returns the parent application of the object. Read-only.
Class	OlObject Class constant	Returns a numeric value specifying the class the object belongs to. Read-only.
CurrentUser	Recipient object	Returns a Recipient object representing the current user. Read-only.
Folders	Folders collection	Returns a collection containing all the MAPIFolder objects in the NameSpace. Read-only.

Name	Returns	Description
Parent	Object	Returns the object's parent object. Read-only.
Session	NameSpace object	Returns the current NameSpace object. Read-only.
SyncObjects	SyncObjects collection	Returns a collection of all the synchronization profiles. Read-only.
Type	String	The type of namespace. The only type currently supported is "MAPI". Read-only.

Events

Name	Description
OptionsPagesAdd	Occurs when a Properties dialog is opened.

NoteItem Object

Methods

Name	Returns	Description
Close(Save Mode)		Causes the Inspector object for the item to be closed. The SaveMode parameter specifies whether changes to the item will be saved or discarded, and may be one of the OlInspectorClose constants.
Copy	NoteItem object	Creates and returns an identical NoteItem object.
Delete		Deletes the current item.
Display ([Modal])		Causes the Inspector object for the item to be opened. The Modal parameter specifies whether the window is to be opened modally (True) or modelessly (False). The default is False.
Move (DestFldr)		Moves the current item to the new MAPIFolder, DestFldr.
PrintOut		Prints the item using the printer's default settings.

Table Continued on Following Page

Name	Returns	Description
Save		Saves the item to the current folder for an existing item or to the default folder for a newly created item.
SaveAs(Path, [Type])		Saves the current item to the hard drive with the path and filename specified in the Path parameter. The type of file the item is to be saved as may be specified in the Type parameter, which may be one of the OlSaveAsType constants.

Properties

Name	Returns	Description
Application	Application object	Returns the parent application of the object. Read-only.
Body	String	A free-form string containing the body of the item. Setting this causes the EditorType of the item's Inspector object to revert to default. Read/write.
Categories	String	Specifies the categories which are assigned to the item. Read/write.
Class	OlObject Class constant	Returns a numeric value specifying the class the object belongs to. Read-only.
Color	OlNote Color constant	Specifies the color in which the note is to be displayed. Read/write.
CreationTime	Date	Returns the date and time at which the item was created. Read-only.
EntryID	String	Returns a unique string identifier for the item. Read-only.
GetInspector	Inspector object	Returns the Inspector object for displaying the current item. Read-only.
Height	Long	Specifies the height of the note in pixels. Read/write.
Last Modification Time	Date	Returns the date and time that the item was last changed. Read-only.

Name	Returns	Description
Left	Long	Specifies the number of pixels the left edge of the NoteItem window is from the left edge of the screen. Read/write.
Links	Links collection	Returns a Links collection that represents the contacts with which this item is associated. Read-only.
MessageClass	String	Specifies the message class of the item. This property maps you to the form that is associated with the item. Read/write.
Parent	Object	Returns the object's parent object. Read-only.
Saved	Boolean	Indicates whether the item has changed since it was last saved. Read-only.
Session	NameSpace object	Returns the current NameSpace object. Read-only.
Size	Long	Returns the size of the item in bytes. Read-only.
Subject	String	Returns the subject of the item, calculated from the body of the note. Read-only.
Top	Long	Specifies the number of pixels the top edge of the note window is from the top edge of the screen. Read/write.
Width	Long	Specifies the width of the note window in pixels. Read/write.

OutlookBarGroup Object

Properties

Name	Returns	Description
Application	Application object	Returns the parent application of the object. Read-only.
Class	OlObject Class constant	Returns a numeric value specifying the class the object belongs to. Read-only.

Table Continued on Following Page

Name	Returns	Description
Name	String	The display name for the object. Read-only.
Parent	Object	Returns the object's parent object. Read-only.
Session	NameSpace object	Returns the current NameSpace object. Read-only.
Shortcuts	OutlookBar Shortcuts collection	Returns the collection of OutlookBarShortcut objects within the OutlookBarGroup. Read-only.
ViewType	OlOutlookBar ViewType constant	Specifies the size of the icons for the OutlookBarGroup. Read/write.

OutlookBarPane Object

Properties

Name	Returns	Description
Application	Application object	Returns the parent application of the object. Read-only.
Class	OlObject Class constant	Returns a numeric value specifying the class the object belongs to. Read-only.
Contents	OutlookBar Storage object	Returns the OutlookBarStorage object for the OutlookBarPane. Read-only.
CurrentGroup	OutlookBar Group object	Specifies the OutlookBarGroup currently open in the OutlookBarPane. Read/write.
Name	String	The display name for the object. Read-only.
Parent	Object	Returns the object's parent object. Read-only.
Session	NameSpace object	Returns the current NameSpace object. Read-only.
Visible	Boolean	Specifies whether the OutlookBarPane is currently visible (True) or hidden (False). Read/write.

Events

Name	Description
BeforeGroupSwitch	Occurs before the active group is switched and a new OutlookBarGroup is opened.
BeforeNavigate	Occurs before the user navigates to another pane.

OutlookBarShortcut Object

Properties

Name	Returns	Description
Application	Application object	Returns the parent application of the object. Read-only.
Class	OlObjectClass constant	Returns a numeric value specifying the class the object belongs to. Read-only.
Name	String	The display name for the object. Read-only.
Parent	Object	Returns the object's parent object. Read-only.
Session	NameSpace object	Returns the current NameSpace object. Read-only.
Target	Variant	Specifies the target of the shortcut. This may be a MAPIFolder, a file-system folder, a file-system path or a URL. Read-only.

OutlookBarStorage Object

Properties

Name	Returns	Description
Application	Application object	Returns the parent application of the object. Read-only.
Class	OlObjectClass constant	Returns a numeric value specifying the class the object belongs to. Read-only.
Groups	OutlookBar Groups collection	Returns a collection of the OutlookBarGroup objects in the OutlookBarStorage object. Read-only.

Table Continued on Following Page

Name	Returns	Description
Parent	Object	Returns the object's parent object. Read-only.
Session	NameSpace object	Returns the current NameSpace object. Read-only.

PostItem Object

Methods

Name	Returns	Description
Clear Conversation Index		Clears the conversation index.
Close (SaveMode)		Causes the Inspector object for the item to be closed. The SaveMode parameter specifies whether changes to the item will be saved or discarded, and may be one of the OlInspectorClose constants.
Copy	PostItem object	Creates and returns an identical PostItem object.
Delete		Deletes the current item.
Display ([Modal])		Causes the Inspector object for the item to be opened. The Modal parameter specifies whether the window is to be opened modally (True) or modelessly (False). The default is False.
Forward	PostItem object	Executes the Forward action on the item and returns the resulting PostItem.
Move (DestFldr)		Moves the current item to the new MAPIFolder, DestFldr.
Post		Submits the PostItem to the target public folder. This is equivalent to sending a MailItem.
PrintOut		Prints the item using the printer's default settings.
Reply	MailItem object	Creates a MailItem addressed to the originator of the item.

Name	Returns	Description
Save		Saves the item to the current folder for an existing item or to the default folder for a newly created item.
SaveAs(Path, [Type])		Saves the current item to the hard drive with the path and filename specified in the Path parameter. The type of file the item is to be saved as may be specified in the Type parameter, which may be one of the OlSaveAsType constants.

Properties

Name	Returns	Description
Actions	Actions collection	Returns an Actions collection of the available Action objects for the item. Read-only.
Application	Application object	Returns the parent application of the object. Read-only.
Attachments	Attachments collection	Returns a collection of the attachments associated with the item. Read-only.
Billing Information	String	Contains a free-form string that can be used to hold the billing information associated with the item. Read/write.
Body	String	A free-form string containing the body of the item. Setting this causes the EditorType of the item's Inspector object to revert to default. Read/write.
Categories	String	Specifies the categories that are assigned to the item. Read/write.
Class	OlObject Class constant	Returns a numeric value specifying the class the object belongs to. Read-only.
Companies	String	A free form string containing the company names associated with the item. Read/write.
Conversation Index	String	Returns the index representing the current conversation thread. Read-only.
Conversation Topic	String	Returns the topic for the conversation thread. Read-only.

Table Continued on Following Page

Name	Returns	Description
CreationTime	Date	Returns the date and time at which the item was created. Read-only.
EntryID	String	Returns a unique string identifier for the item. Read-only.
ExpiryTime	Date	Specifies the date and time when the item is to become invalid and can be deleted. Read/write.
Form Description	Form Description object	Returns the FormDescription object for the item. Read-only.
GetInspector	Inspector object	Returns the Inspector object for displaying the current item. Read-only.
HTMLBody	String	Specifies the body of the PostItem in HTML format. Read/write.
Importance	OlImportance constant	Specifies the importance level for the item. Read/write.
Last Modification Time	Date	Returns the date and time that the item was last changed. Read-only.
Links	Links collection	Returns a Links collection that represents the contacts with which this item is associated. Read-only.
MessageClass	String	Specifies the message class of the item. This property maps you to the form that is associated with the item. Read/write.
Mileage	String	A free-form string which can be used to hold the mileage for the item. Read/write.
NoAging	Boolean	Specifies whether or not the item can be archived. Read/write.
Outlook Internal Version	Long	Returns the build number of the Outlook version used to create the item. Read-only.
Outlook Version	String	Returns the major and minor version number for the Outlook Application used to create the item. For Outlook 2000, this is "9.0". Read-only.

Name	Returns	Description
Parent	Object	Returns the object's parent object. Read-only.
ReceivedTime	Date	Returns the date and time when the post was received. Read-only.
Saved	Boolean	Indicates whether the item has changed since it was last saved. Read-only.
SenderName	String	Returns the display name of the sender. Read-only.
Sensitivity	OlSensitivity constant	Specifies the level of sensitivity for the item. Read/write.
SentOn	Date	Returns the date and time when the item was sent. Read-only.
Session	NameSpace object	Returns the current NameSpace object. Read-only.
Size	Long	Returns the size of the item in bytes. Read-only.
Subject	String	Contains the subject of the item. Read/write.
UnRead	Boolean	Indicates whether the item is to be marked as "Unread". Read/write.
User Properties	User Properties collection	Returns the UserProperties collection for the item. Read-only.

Events

Name	Description
Attachment Add	Occurs when a new attachment is added to the item.
Attachment Read	Occurs when an attachment is opened.
Before Attachment Save	Occurs just before the attachment is saved.
BeforeCheck Names	Occurs just before Outlook resolves the recipients for the item.

Table Continued on Following Page

Name	Description
Close	Occurs when the Inspector object is shut down.
CustomAction	Occurs when a custom action is executed.
Custom Property Change	Occurs when one of the custom properties for the item is changed.
Forward	Occurs when the item is forwarded.
Open	Occurs when the item is opened in an Inspector.
Property Change	Occurs when one of the non-custom properties is changed.
Read	Occurs when the item is opened for editing.
Reply	Occurs when the Reply action is executed on the item.
ReplyAll	Occurs when the ReplyAll action is executed on the item.
Send	Occurs when the item is sent.
Write	Occurs when the Save or SaveAs method is executed on the item.

PropertyPage Object

Methods

Name	Description
Apply	Applies any changes that have been made to the PropertyPage.
GetPageInfo (HelpFile, HelpContext)	Returns information about the PropertyPage. The parameters specify the path of the help file for the page and the context ID for the help topic associated with the page.

Property

Name	Returns	Description
Dirty	Boolean	Specifies whether the contents of the PropertyPage have been modified.

PropertyPageSite Object

Method

Name	Description
OnStatus Change	Notifies Outlook that a PropertyPage has been altered.

Properties

Name	Returns	Description
Application	Application object	Returns the parent application of the object. Read-only.
Class	OlObject Class constant	Returns a numeric value specifying the class the object belongs to. Read-only.
Parent	Object	Returns the object's parent object. Read-only.
Session	NameSpace object	Returns the current NameSpace object. Read-only.

Recipient Object

Methods

Name	Returns	Description
Delete		Deletes the current Recipient from the Recipients collection.
FreeBusy (Start, MinPerChar, [Complete Format])	String	Returns a string representing the Recipient's schedule for the next 30 days starting at the start date passed in, with each character representing a slot of MinPerChar minutes. If CompleteFormat is False or omitted, free time is represented by a zero, busy time by a one. If CompleteFormat is True, the intervals are each represented by the appropriate OlBusyStatus constant.
Resolve	Boolean	Resolves the current recipient against the Address Book. Returns True if the attempt succeeds, False if it fails.

Properties

Name	Returns	Description
Address	String	Specifies the email address for the current Recipient. Read/write.
AddressEntry	AddressEntry object	Returns the AddressEntry object for the recipient. If the recipient has not yet been resolved, the Resolve method for the recipient will be called. Read-only.
Application	Application object	Returns the parent application of the object. Read-only.
AutoReponse	String	Contains the text of the automatic response for the current recipient. Read/write.
Class	OlObjectClass constant	Returns a numeric value specifying the class the object belongs to. Read-only.
DisplayType	OlDisplayType constant	Returns the type of Recipient this is. Do not confuse this with the Type property. Read-only.
EntryID	String	Returns a unique string identifier for the item. Read-only.
Index	Long	Returns the position of the Recipient in the Recipients collection (starting from 1). Read-only.
Meeting Response Status	OlResponse Status constant	Returns the status of the recipient's response to a meeting request. Read-only.
Name	String	The display name for the object. Read-only.
Parent	Object	Returns the object's parent object. Read-only.
Resolved	Boolean	Indicates whether the recipient has been validated against the address book. Read-only.
Session	NameSpace object	Returns the current NameSpace object. Read-only.
Tracking Status	OlTracking Status constant	Specifies the tracking status for the recipient. Read/write.

Name	Returns	Description
Tracking StatusTime	Date	Specifies the tracking status date and time. Read/write.
Type	OlJournal RecipientType, OlMailRecipient Type, OlMeeting RecipientType or OlTaskRecipient Type constant.	Specifies the type of the recipient depending on the type of item the recipient belongs to. Read/write.

RecurrencePattern Object

Method

Name	Returns	Description
GetOccurrence (Date_Time)	AppointmentItem object	Returns the AppointmentItem object for the specified date and time.

Properties

Name	Returns	Description
Application	Application object	Returns the parent application of the object. Read-only.
Class	OlObjectClass constant	Returns a numeric value specifying the class the object belongs to. Read-only.
DayOfMonth	Long	Specifies the day of the month on which the recurring appointment or task will occur. Read/write.
DayOfWeekMask	olDaysOfWeek constant	Specifies the mask for the day of the week on which the appointment or task occurs. Read/write.
Duration	Long	Specifies the length of time that the item is due to last, in minutes. Valid only for recurring appointments. Read/write.

Table Continued on Following Page

Name	Returns	Description
EndTime	Date	Specifies the date and time at which the appointment is due to end. Read/write.
Exceptions	Exceptions collection	Returns the collection of exceptions to the recurrence pattern. Read-only.
Instance	Long	Specifies the recurrence pattern for recurrences of the type olRecursMonthNth or olRecursYearNth. Read/write.
Interval	Long	Specifies the number of units (weeks, months etc.) between one occurrence and the next. Read/write.
MonthOfYear	Long	Specifies the month on which the recurrence pattern is to occur. Read/write.
NoEndDate	Boolean	Specifies whether the recurrence pattern recurs indefinitely or has an end date. Read/write.
Occurrences	Long	Specifies how many times the recurrence will occur. Read/write.
Parent	Object	Returns the object's parent object. Read-only.
PatternEndDate	Date	Specifies the date on which the recurrence pattern is due to end. Read/write.
PatternStart Date	Date	Specifies the date on which the recurrence pattern is to start. Read/write.
RecurrenceType	OlRecurrence Type constant	Specifies the frequency of the recurrence pattern. Read/write.
Regenerate	Boolean	Specifies whether the recurrence pattern should be regenerated after it has been passed through. Read/write.
Session	NameSpace object	Returns the current NameSpace object. Read-only.
StartTime	Date	Specifies the start date and time for this occurrence. Read/write.

RemoteItem Object

Methods

Name	Returns	Description
Close (SaveMode)		Closes the item. The `SaveMode` parameter specifies whether changes to the item will be saved or discarded, and may be one of the `OlInspectorClose` constants. However, note that a `RemoteItem` cannot be displayed.
Copy		This method does not work for the `RemoteItem` object.
Delete		Deletes the current item.
Display ([Modal])		Causes a message box to be displayed prompting the user to select what action will be carried out on the item on the server the next time a connection is made.
Move (DestFldr)		This does not work for the `RemoteItem` object.
PrintOut		Prints the item using the printer's default settings.
Save		Saves the `RemoteItem` object to the current `MAPIFolder`.
SaveAs(Path, [Type])		Saves the current item to the hard drive with the path and filename specified in the `Path` parameter. The type of file the item is to be saved as may be specified in the `Type` parameter, which may be one of the `OlSaveAsType` constants.

Properties

Name	Returns	Description
Actions	Actions collection	Returns an `Actions` collection of the available `Action` objects for the item. Read-only.
Application	Application object	Returns the parent application of the object. Read-only.
Attachments	Attachments collection	Returns a collection of the attachments associated with the item. Read-only.

Table Continued on Following Page

Name	Returns	Description
Billing Information	String	Contains a free-form string that can be used to hold the billing information associated with the item. Note that this property is not inherited from the original item. Read/write.
Body	String	Specifies the body for the RemoteItem object, although it is not displayed and is not inherited from the original item. Read/write.
Categories	String	Specifies the categories that are assigned to the item. Note that this property is not inherited from the original item. Read/write.
Class	OlObject Class constant	Returns a numeric value specifying the class the object belongs to. Read-only.
Companies	String	A free-form string containing the company names associated with the item. Note that this property is not inherited from the original item. Read/write.
Conversation Index	String	Returns the index representing the current conversation thread. Read-only.
Conversation Topic	String	Returns the topic for the conversation thread. Read-only.
CreationTime	Date	Returns the date and time at which the item was created. Read-only.
EntryID	String	Returns a unique string identifier for the item. Read-only.
Form Description	Form Description object	This does not work for the RemoteItem object.
GetInspector	Inspector object	This does not work for the RemoteItem object.
Has Attachment	Boolean	Returns True if there are attachments associated with the RemoteItem. Read-only.
Importance	OlImportance constant	Specifies the importance level for the item. Read/write.

Name	Returns	Description
Last Modification Time	Date	Returns the date and time that the item was last changed. Read-only.
Links	Links collection	Returns a Links collection that represents the contacts with which this item is associated. Read-only.
MessageClass	String	Specifies the message class of the item. This property maps you to the form that is associated with the item. Read/write.
Mileage	String	A free-form string which can be used to hold the mileage for the item. Note that this property is not inherited from the original item. Read/write.
NoAging	Boolean	Specifies whether or not the item can be archived. Read/write.
Outlook Internal Version	Long	Returns the build number of the Outlook version used to create the item. For the RemoteItem, this always returns zero. Read-only.
Outlook Version	String	Returns the major and minor version number for the Outlook Application used to create the item. For the RemoteItem, this always returns an empty string. Read-only.
Parent	Object	Returns the object's parent object. Read-only.
Remote MessageClass	String	Returns the message class of the remote item represented by the RemoteItem object. Read-only.
Saved	Boolean	Indicates whether the item has changed since it was last saved. Read-only.
Sensitivity	OlSensitivity constant	Specifies the level of sensitivity for the item. Read-only.
Session	NameSpace object	Returns the current NameSpace object. Read-only.
Size	Long	Returns the size of the item in bytes. Read-only.

Table Continued on Following Page

Name	Returns	Description
Subject	String	Contains the subject of the item. Read/write.
TransferSize	Long	Returns the transfer size of the remote item in bytes. Read-only.
TransferTime	Long	Returns the estimated transfer time in seconds for the remote item. Read-only.
UnRead	Boolean	Indicates whether the item is to be marked as "Unread". Read/write.
User Properties	User Properties collection	Returns the UserProperties collection for the item. Read-only.

Events

Name	Description
AttachmentAdd	Occurs when a new attachment is added to the item.
AttachmentRead	Occurs when an attachment is opened.
BeforeAttachment Save	Occurs just before the attachment is saved.
BeforeCheckNames	Occurs just before Outlook resolves the recipients for the item.
Close	This event does not work for the RemoteItem object.
CustomAction	Occurs when a custom action is executed.
CustomProperty Change	Occurs when one of the custom properties for the item is changed.
Forward	This event does not work for the RemoteItem object.
Open	This event does not work for the RemoteItem object.
PropertyChange	Occurs when one of the non-custom properties is changed.
Read	Occurs when the item is opened for editing.
Reply	This event does not work for the RemoteItem object.
ReplyAll	This event does not work for the RemoteItem object.
Send	This event does not work for the RemoteItem object.
Write	Occurs when the Save or SaveAs method is executed on the item.

ReportItem

Methods

Name	Returns	Description
Close (SaveMode)		Causes the Inspector object for the item to be closed. The SaveMode parameter specifies whether changes to the item will be saved or discarded, and may be one of the OlInspectorClose constants.
Copy	ReportItem object	Creates and returns an identical ReportItem object.
Delete		Deletes the current item.
Display ([Modal])		Causes the Inspector object for the item to be opened. The Modal parameter specifies whether the window is to be opened modally (True) or modelessly (False). The default is False.
Move (DestFldr)		Moves the current item to the new MAPIFolder, DestFldr.
PrintOut		Prints the item using the printer's default settings.
Save		Saves the item to the current folder for an existing item or to the default folder for a newly created item.
SaveAs(Path, [Type])		Saves the current item to the hard drive with the path and filename specified in the Path parameter. The type of file the item is to be saved as may be specified in the Type parameter, which may be one of the OlSaveAsType constants.

Properties

Name	Returns	Description
Actions	Actions collection	Returns an Actions collection of the available Action objects for the item. Read-only.
Application	Application object	Returns the parent application of the object. Read-only.

Table Continued on Following Page

Name	Returns	Description
Attachments	Attachments collection	Returns a collection of the attachments associated with the item. Read-only.
Billing Information	String	Contains a free-form string that can be used to hold the billing information associated with the item. Read/write.
Body	String	A free-form string containing the body of the item. Setting this causes the EditorType of the item's Inspector object to revert to default. Read/write.
Categories	String	Specifies the categories that are assigned to the item. Read/write.
Class	OlObject Class constant	Returns a numeric value specifying the class the object belongs to. Read-only.
Companies	String	A free-form string containing the company names associated with the item. Read/write.
Conversation Index	String	Returns the index representing the current conversation thread. Read-only.
Conversation Topic	String	Returns the topic for the conversation thread. Read-only.
CreationTime	Date	Returns the date and time at which the item was created. Read-only.
EntryID	String	Returns a unique string identifier for the item. Read-only.
Form Description	Form Description object	Returns the FormDescription object for the item. Read-only.
GetInspector	Inspector object	Returns the Inspector object for displaying the current item. Read-only.
Importance	OlImportance constant	Specifies the importance level for the item. Read/write.
Last Modification Time	Date	Returns the date and time that the item was last changed. Read-only.
Links	Links collection	Returns a Links collection that represents the contacts with which this item is associated. Read-only.

Name	Returns	Description
MessageClass	String	Specifies the message class of the item. This property maps you to the form that is associated with the item. Read/write.
Mileage	String	A free-form string which can be used to hold the mileage for the item. Read/write.
NoAging	Boolean	Specifies whether or not the item can be archived. Read/write.
Outlook Internal Version	Long	Returns the build number of the Outlook version used to create the item. Read-only.
Outlook Version	String	Returns the major and minor version number for the Outlook Application used to create the item. For Outlook 2000, this is "9.0". Read-only.
Parent	Object	Returns the object's parent object. Read-only.
Saved	Boolean	Indicates whether the item has changed since it was last saved. Read-only.
Sensitivity	OlSensitivity constant	Specifies the level of sensitivity for the item. Read-only.
Session	NameSpace object	Returns the current NameSpace object. Read-only.
Size	Long	Returns the size of the item in bytes. Read-only.
Subject	String	Contains the subject of the item. Read/write.
UnRead	Boolean	Indicates whether the item is to be marked as "Unread". Read/write.
User Properties	User Properties collection	Returns the UserProperties collection for the item. Read-only.

Events

Name	Description
AttachmentAdd	Occurs when a new attachment is added to the item.
AttachmentRead	Occurs when an attachment is opened.
BeforeAttachment Save	Occurs just before the attachment is saved.
BeforeCheckNames	Occurs just before Outlook resolves the recipients for the item.
Close	Occurs when the Inspector object is shut down.
CustomAction	Occurs when a custom action is executed.
CustomProperty Change	Occurs when one of the custom properties for the item is changed.
Forward	Occurs when the item is forwarded.
Open	Occurs when the item is opened in an Inspector.
PropertyChange	Occurs when one of the non-custom properties is changed.
Read	Occurs when the item is opened for editing.
Reply	Occurs when the Reply action is executed on the item.
ReplyAll	Occurs when the ReplyAll action is executed on the item.
Send	Occurs when the item is sent.
Write	Occurs when the Save or SaveAs method is executed on the item.

SyncObject Object

Methods

Name	Description
Start	Begins the synchronization process.
Stop	Ends the synchronization process.

Properties

Name	Returns	Description
Application	Application object	Returns the parent application of the object. Read-only.
Class	OlObjectClass constant	Returns a numeric value specifying the class the object belongs to. Read-only.
Name	String	The display name for the object. Read-only.
Parent	Object	Returns the object's parent object. Read-only.
Session	NameSpace object	Returns the current NameSpace object. Read-only.

Events

Name	Description
OnError	Raised when an error occurs during synchronization.
Progress	Raised periodically during synchronization.
SyncEnd	Raised when synchronization ends.
SyncStart	Raised when synchronization begins.

TaskItem Object

Methods

Name	Returns	Description
Assign		Prepares the TaskItem to be delegated to another recipient. This method must be run before the task can be sent.
Cancel Response State		Resets an unsent response to a task request back to its state before the response.
Clear Recurrence Pattern		Resets the item to a single occurrence.

Table Continued on Following Page

Name	Returns	Description
Close (SaveMode)		Causes the Inspector object for the item to be closed. The SaveMode parameter specifies whether changes to the item will be saved or discarded, and may be one of the OlInspectorClose constants.
Copy	TaskItem object	Creates and returns an identical TaskItem object.
Delete		Deletes the current item.
Display ([Modal])		Causes the Inspector object for the item to be opened. The Modal parameter specifies whether the window is to be opened modally (True) or modelessly (False). The default is False.
Get Recurrence Pattern	Recurrence Pattern object	Returns the RecurrencePattern object that contains the information about the recurrence of the task.
Mark Complete		Marks the task as completed.
Move (DestFldr)		Moves the current item to the new MAPIFolder, DestFldr.
PrintOut		Prints the item using the printer's default settings.
Respond (IResponse, fNoUI, fAdditional TextDialog)		Allows the user to accept or decline the task. IResponse may be one of the OlTaskResponse constants olTaskAccept or olTaskDecline. The fNoUI parameter is True if there is no User Interface, and fAdditionalDialog is True if the user is to be prompted to send or send with comments.
Save		Saves the item to the current folder for an existing item or to the default folder for a newly created item.
SaveAs(Path, [Type])		Saves the current item to the hard drive with the path and filename specified in the Path parameter. The type of file the item is to be saved as may be specified in the Type parameter, which may be one of the OlSaveAsType constants.

Name	Returns	Description
Send		Sends the item to the recipients defined in the `Recipients` property.
Skip Recurrence		Skips the current instance of the recurring task and sets you to the next instance.
StatusReport	MailItem object	Creates a status report for the task addressed to the recipients specified in the `StatusUpdateRecipients` property.

Properties

Name	Returns	Description
Actions	Actions collection	Returns an `Actions` collection of the available `Action` objects for the item. Read-only.
ActualWork	Long	Specifies the actual amount of time in minutes spent on the task. Read/write.
Application	Application object	Returns the parent application of the object. Read-only.
Attachments	Attachments collection	Returns a collection of the attachments associated with the item. Read-only.
Billing Information	String	Contains a free-form string that can be used to hold the billing information associated with the item. Read/write.
Body	String	A free-form string containing the body of the item. Setting this causes the `EditorType` of the item's `Inspector` object to revert to default. Read/write.
CardData	String	Specifies the text for the card data. Read/write.
Categories	String	Specifies the categories that are assigned to the item. Read/write.
Class	OlObject Class constant	Returns a numeric value specifying the class the object belongs to. Read-only.
Companies	String	A free-form string containing the company names associated with the item. Read/write.

Table Continued on Following Page

Name	Returns	Description
Complete	Boolean	Indicates whether the task has been completed. Read/write.
ContactNames	String	Returns a string containing the display names of the recipients associated with the item. Read-only.
Contacts	String	Returns a string containing the display names of the Link objects associated with the task. Read/write.
Conversation Index	String	Returns the index representing the current conversation thread. Read/write.
Conversation Topic	String	Returns the topic for the conversation thread. Read-only.
CreationTime	Date	Returns the date and time at which the item was created. Read-only.
Date Completed	Date	Specifies the date and time when the task was completed. Read/write.
Delegation State	OlTask Delegation Status constant	Returns the delegation state for the task. Read-only.
Delegator	String	Returns the display name of the delegator. Read-only.
DueDate	Date	Specifies the date and time by which the task is due to be completed. Read/write.
EntryID	String	Returns a unique string identifier for the item. Read-only.
Form Description	Form Description object	Returns the FormDescription object for the item. Read-only.
GetInspector	Inspector object	Returns the Inspector object for displaying the current item. Read-only.
Importance	OlImportance constant	Specifies the importance level for the item. Read/write.
IsRecurring	Boolean	Indicates whether this is a recurring task or not. Read-only.

Name	Returns	Description
Last Modification Date	Date	Returns the date and time when the item was last changed. Read-only.
Links	Links collection	Returns a `Links` collection that represents the contacts with which this item is associated. Read-only.
MessageClass	String	Specifies the message class of the item. This property maps you to the form that is associated with the item. Read/write.
Mileage	String	A free-form string which can be used to hold the mileage for the item. Read/write.
NoAging	Boolean	Specifies whether or not the item can be archived. Read/write.
Ordinal	Long	Specifies the position in the view for the task. Read/write.
Outlook Internal Version	Long	Returns the build number of the Outlook version used to create the item. Read-only.
Outlook Version	String	Returns the major and minor version number for the Outlook Application used to create the item. For Outlook 2000, this is `"9.0"`. Read-only.
Owner	String	Specifies the display name of the owner for the task. Setting this does not affect the ownership of the task. Read/write.
Ownership	OlTask Ownership constant	Indicates the ownership state of the task. Read-only.
Parent	Object	Returns the object's parent object. Read-only.
Percent Complete	Long	Indicates the percentage of the task that has been completed. Read/write.
Recipients	Recipients collection	Returns a collection of the `Recipient` objects associated with the item. Read-only.

Table Continued on Following Page

Name	Returns	Description
Reminder Override Default	Boolean	Specifies whether the defaults for the reminder should be ignored. Read/write.
ReminderPlay Sound	Boolean	Specifies whether the reminder should play a sound or not. Read/write.
ReminderSet	Boolean	Specifies whether a reminder should be fired for this task. Read/write.
Reminder SoundFile	String	Specifies the path and filename for the sound file for the reminder. Read/write.
ReminderTime	Date	Specifies the date and time when the reminder is to be fired. Read/write.
Response State	OlTask Response constant	Returns the overall status of the response for the task. Read-only.
Role	String	A free-form string which specifies the role that the owner has to the task. Read/write.
Saved	Boolean	Indicates whether the item has changed since it was last saved. Read-only.
SchedulePlus Priority	String	Indicates the Schedule+ priority for the task. Read/write.
Sensitivity	OlSensitivity constant	Specifies the level of sensitivity for the item. Read/write.
Session	NameSpace object	Returns the current NameSpace object. Read-only.
Size	Long	Returns the size of the item in bytes. Read-only.
StartDate	Date	Specifies the start date and time for the task. Read/write.
Status	OlTaskStatus constant	Indicates the progress of work on the task. Read/write.

Name	Returns	Description
StatusOn Completion Recipients	String	Returns a semicolon-delimited string of the display names of recipients which are to receive a completion report for this task. The recipients that appear here will be assigned a BCC type. Read-only.
StatusUpdate Recipients	String	Returns a semicolon-delimited string of the display names of recipients which are to receive update reports for this task. The recipients that appear here will be assigned a CC type. Read-only.
Subject	String	Contains the subject of the item. Read/write.
TeamTask	Boolean	Indicates whether this is a team task. Read/write.
TotalWork	Long	Specifies the total work for the task. Read/write.
UnRead	Boolean	Indicates whether the item is to be marked as "Unread". Read/write.
User Properties	User Properties collection	Returns the UserProperties collection for the item. Read-only.

Events

Name	Description
AttachmentAdd	Occurs when a new attachment is added to the item.
AttachmentRead	Occurs when an attachment is opened.
BeforeAttachment Save	Occurs just before the attachment is saved.
BeforeCheckNames	Occurs just before Outlook resolves the recipients for the item.
Close	Occurs when the Inspector object is shut down.
CustomAction	Occurs when a custom action is executed.
CustomProperty Change	Occurs when one of the custom properties for the item is changed.
Forward	Occurs when the item is forwarded.
Open	Occurs when the item is opened in an Inspector.

Table Continued on Following Page

Name	Description
PropertyChange	Occurs when one of the non-custom properties is changed.
Read	Occurs when the item is opened for editing.
Reply	Occurs when the Reply action is executed on the item.
ReplyAll	Occurs when the ReplyAll action is executed on the item.
Send	Occurs when the item is sent.
Write	Occurs when the Save or SaveAs method is executed on the item.

TaskRequestAcceptItem Object

Methods

Name	Returns	Description
Close (SaveMode)		Causes the Inspector object for the item to be closed. The SaveMode parameter specifies whether changes to the item will be saved or discarded, and may be one of the OlInspectorClose constants.
Copy	TaskRequest AcceptItem object	Creates and returns an identical TaskRequestAcceptItem object.
Delete		Deletes the current item.
Display ([Modal])		Causes the Inspector object for the item to be opened. The Modal parameter specifies whether the window is to be opened modally (True) or modelessly (False). The default is False.
GetAssociated Task (AddTo TaskList)	TaskItem object	Returns a reference to the associated TaskItem. The parameter indicates whether the item is to added to default tasks folder.
Move(DestFldr)		Moves the current item to the new MAPIFolder, DestFldr.

Name	Returns	Description
PrintOut		Prints the item using the printer's default settings.
Save		Saves the item to the current folder for an existing item or to the default folder for a newly created item.
SaveAs(Path, [Type])		Saves the current item to the hard drive with the path and filename specified in the Path parameter. The type of file the item is to be saved as may be specified in the Type parameter, which may be one of the OlSaveAsType constants.

Properties

Name	Returns	Description
Actions	Actions collection	Returns an Actions collection of the available Action objects for the item. Read-only.
Application	Application object	Returns the parent application of the object. Read-only.
Attachments	Attachments collection	Returns a collection of the attachments associated with the item. Read-only.
Billing Information	String	Contains a free-form string that can be used to hold the billing information associated with the item. Read/write.
Body	String	A free-form string containing the body of the item. Setting this causes the EditorType of the item's Inspector object to revert to default. Read/write.
Categories	String	Specifies the categories that are assigned to the item. Read/write.
Class	OlObject Class constant	Returns a numeric value specifying the class the object belongs to. Read-only.
Companies	String	A free form string containing the company names associated with the item. Read/write.
Conversation Index	String	Returns the index representing the current conversation thread. Read-only.

Table Continued on Following Page

597

Name	Returns	Description
Conversation Topic	String	Returns the topic for the conversation thread. Read-only.
CreationTime	Date	Returns the date and time at which the item was created. Read-only.
EntryID	String	Returns a unique string identifier for the item. Read-only.
Form Description	Form Description object	Returns the `FormDescription` object for the item. Read-only.
GetInspector	Inspector object	Returns the `Inspector` object for displaying the current item. Read-only.
Importance	OlImportance constant	Specifies the importance level for the item. Read/write.
Last Modification Time	Date	Returns the date and time that the item was last changed. Read-only.
Links	Links collection	Returns a `Links` collection that represents the contacts with which this item is associated. Read-only.
MessageClass	String	Specifies the message class of the item. This property maps you to the form that is associated with the item. Read/write.
Mileage	String	A free-form string which can be used to hold the mileage for the item. Read/write.
NoAging	Boolean	Specifies whether or not the item can be archived. Read/write.
Outlook Internal Version	Long	Returns the build number of the Outlook version used to create the item. Read-only.
Outlook Version	String	Returns the major and minor version number for the Outlook Application used to create the item. For Outlook 2000, this is `"9.0"`. Read-only.
Parent	Object	Returns the object's parent object. Read-only.

Name	Returns	Description
Saved	Boolean	Indicates whether the item has changed since it was last saved. Read-only.
Sensitivity	OlSensitivity constant	Specifies the level of sensitivity for the item. Read/write.
Session	NameSpace object	Returns the current NameSpace object. Read-only.
Size	Long	Returns the size of the item in bytes. Read-only.
Subject	String	Contains the subject of the item. Read/write.
UnRead	Boolean	Indicates whether the item is to be marked as "Unread". Read/write.
User Properties	UserProperties collection	Returns the UserProperties collection for the item. Read-only.

Events

Name	Description
AttachmentAdd	Occurs when a new attachment is added to the item.
AttachmentRead	Occurs when an attachment is opened.
BeforeAttachment Save	Occurs just before the attachment is saved.
BeforeCheckNames	Occurs just before Outlook resolves the recipients for the item.
Close	Occurs when the Inspector object is shut down.
CustomAction	Occurs when a custom action is executed.
CustomProperty Change	Occurs when one of the custom properties for the item is changed.
Forward	Occurs when the item is forwarded.
Open	Occurs when the item is opened in an Inspector.
PropertyChange	Occurs when one of the non-custom properties is changed.
Read	Occurs when the item is opened for editing.

Table Continued on Following Page

Name	Description
Reply	Occurs when the Reply action is executed on the item.
ReplyAll	Occurs when the ReplyAll action is executed on the item.
Send	Occurs when the item is sent.
Write	Occurs when the Save or SaveAs method is executed on the item.

TaskRequestDeclineItem Object

Methods

Name	Returns	Description
Close(SaveMode)		Causes the Inspector object for the item to be closed. The SaveMode parameter specifies whether changes to the item will be saved or discarded, and may be one of the OlInspectorClose constants.
Copy	TaskRequest DeclineItem object	Creates and returns an identical TaskRequestDeclineItem object.
Delete		Deletes the current item.
Display([Modal])		Causes the Inspector object for the item to be opened. The Modal parameter specifies whether the window is to be opened modally (True) or modelessly (False). The default is False.
GetAssociated Task (AddTo TaskList)	TaskItem object	Returns a reference to the associated TaskItem. The parameter indicates whether the item is to added to default tasks folder.
Move(DestFldr)		Moves the current item to the new MAPIFolder, DestFldr.
PrintOut		Prints the item using the printer's default settings.

Name	Returns	Description
Save		Saves the item to the current folder for an existing item or to the default folder for a newly created item.
SaveAs(Path, [Type])		Saves the current item to the hard drive with the path and filename specified in the Path parameter. The type of file the item is to be saved as may be specified in the Type parameter, which may be one of the OlSaveAsType constants.

Properties

Name	Returns	Description
Actions	Actions collection	Returns an Actions collection of the available Action objects for the item. Read-only.
Application	Application object	Returns the parent application of the object. Read-only.
Attachments	Attachments collection	Returns a collection of the attachments associated with the item. Read-only.
Billing Information	String	Contains a free-form string that can be used to hold the billing information associated with the item. Read/write.
Body	String	A free-form string containing the body of the item. Setting this causes the EditorType of the item's Inspector object to revert to default. Read/write.
Categories	String	Specifies the categories that are assigned to the item. Read/write.
Class	OlObject Class constant	Returns a numeric value specifying the class the object belongs to. Read-only.
Companies	String	A free form string containing the company names associated with the item. Read/write.
Conversation Index	String	Returns the index representing the current conversation thread. Read-only.

Name	Returns	Description
Conversation Topic	String	Returns the topic for the conversation thread. Read-only.
CreationTime	Date	Returns the date and time at which the item was created. Read-only.
EntryID	String	Returns a unique string identifier for the item. Read-only.
Form Description	Form Description object	Returns the `FormDescription` object for the item. Read-only.
GetInspector	Inspector object	Returns the `Inspector` object for displaying the current item. Read-only.
Importance	OlImportance constant	Specifies the importance level for the item. Read/write.
Last Modification Time	Date	Returns the date and time that the item was last changed. Read-only.
Links	Links collection	Returns a `Links` collection that represents the contacts with which this item is associated. Read-only.
MessageClass	String	Specifies the message class of the item. This property maps you to the form that is associated with the item. Read/write.
Mileage	String	A free-form string which can be used to hold the mileage for the item. Read/write.
NoAging	Boolean	Specifies whether or not the item can be archived. Read/write.
Outlook Internal Version	Long	Returns the build number of the Outlook version used to create the item. Read-only.
Outlook Version	String	Returns the major and minor version number for the Outlook Application used to create the item. For Outlook 2000, this is `"9.0"`. Read-only.
Parent	Object	Returns the object's parent object. Read-only.

Name	Returns	Description
Saved	Boolean	Indicates whether the item has changed since it was last saved. Read-only.
Sensitivity	OlSensitivity constant	Specifies the level of sensitivity for the item. Read/write.
Session	NameSpace object	Returns the current NameSpace object. Read-only.
Size	Long	Returns the size of the item in bytes. Read-only.
Subject	String	Contains the subject of the item. Read/write.
UnRead	Boolean	Indicates whether the item is to be marked as "Unread". Read/write.
User Properties	User Properties collection	Returns the UserProperties collection for the item. Read-only.

Events

Name	Description
AttachmentAdd	Occurs when a new attachment is added to the item.
AttachmentRead	Occurs when an attachment is opened.
BeforeAttachment Save	Occurs just before the attachment is saved.
BeforeCheckNames	Occurs just before Outlook resolves the recipients for the item.
Close	Occurs when the Inspector object is shut down.
CustomAction	Occurs when a custom action is executed.
CustomProperty Change	Occurs when one of the custom properties for the item is changed.
Forward	Occurs when the item is forwarded.
Open	Occurs when the item is opened in an Inspector.
PropertyChange	Occurs when one of the non-custom properties is changed.
Read	Occurs when the item is opened for editing.

Table Continued on Following Page

Name	Description
Reply	Occurs when the Reply action is executed on the item.
ReplyAll	Occurs when the ReplyAll action is executed on the item.
Send	Occurs when the item is sent.
Write	Occurs when the Save or SaveAs method is executed on the item.

TaskRequestItem Object

Methods

Name	Returns	Description
Close(SaveMode)		Causes the Inspector object for the item to be closed. The SaveMode parameter specifies whether changes to the item will be saved or discarded, and may be one of the OlInspectorClose constants.
Copy	TaskRequest Item object	Creates and returns an identical TaskRequestItem object.
Delete		Deletes the current item.
Display ([Modal])		Causes the Inspector object for the item to be opened. The Modal parameter specifies whether the window is to be opened modally (True) or modelessly (False). The default is False.
GetAssociated Task (AddTo TaskList)	TaskItem object	Returns a reference to the associated TaskItem. The parameter indicates whether the item is to added to default tasks folder.
Move(DestFldr)		Moves the current item to the new MAPIFolder, DestFldr.
PrintOut		Prints the item using the printer's default settings.
Save		Saves the item to the current folder for an existing item or to the default folder for a newly created item.

Name	Returns	Description
SaveAs(Path, [Type])		Saves the current item to the hard drive with the path and filename specified in the Path parameter. The type of file the item is to be saved as may be specified in the Type parameter, which may be one of the OlSaveAsType constants.

Properties

Name	Returns	Description
Actions	Actions collection	Returns an Actions collection of the available Action objects for the item. Read-only.
Application	Application object	Returns the parent application of the object. Read-only.
Attachments	Attachments collection	Returns a collection of the attachments associated with the item. Read-only.
Billing Information	String	Contains a free-form string that can be used to hold the billing information associated with the item. Read/write.
Body	String	A free-form string containing the body of the item. Setting this causes the EditorType of the item's Inspector object to revert to default. Read/write.
Categories	String	Specifies the categories that are assigned to the item. Read/write.
Class	OlObjectClass constant	Returns a numeric value specifying the class the object belongs to. Read-only.
Companies	String	A free form string containing the company names associated with the item. Read/write.
Conversation Index	String	Returns the index representing the current conversation thread. Read-only.

Table Continued on Following Page

Name	Returns	Description
Conversation Topic	String	Returns the topic for the conversation thread. Read-only.
CreationTime	Date	Returns the date and time at which the item was created. Read-only.
EntryID	String	Returns a unique string identifier for the item. Read-only.
Form Description	Form Description object	Returns the FormDescription object for the item. Read-only.
GetInspector	Inspector object	Returns the Inspector object for displaying the current item. Read-only.
Importance	OlImportance constant	Specifies the importance level for the item. Read/write.
Last Modification Time	Date	Returns the date and time that the item was last changed. Read-only.
Links	Links collection	Returns a Links collection that represents the contacts with which this item is associated. Read-only.
MessageClass	String	Specifies the message class of the item. This property maps you to the form that is associated with the item. Read/write.
Mileage	String	A free-form string which can be used to hold the mileage for the item. Read/write.
NoAging	Boolean	Specifies whether or not the item can be archived. Read/write.
Outlook Internal Version	Long	Returns the build number of the Outlook version used to create the item. Read-only.
Outlook Version	String	Returns the major and minor version number for the Outlook Application used to create the item. For Outlook 2000, this is "9.0". Read-only.
Parent	Object	Returns the object's parent object. Read-only.

Name	Returns	Description
Saved	Boolean	Indicates whether the item has changed since it was last saved. Read-only.
Sensitivity	OlSensitivity constant	Specifies the level of sensitivity for the item. Read/write.
Session	NameSpace object	Returns the current NameSpace object. Read-only.
Size	Long	Returns the size of the item in bytes. Read-only.
Subject	String	Contains the subject of the item. Read/write.
UnRead	Boolean	Indicates whether the item is to be marked as "Unread". Read/write.
User Properties	UserProperties collection	Returns the UserProperties collection for the item. Read-only.

Events

Name	Description
AttachmentAdd	Occurs when a new attachment is added to the item.
AttachmentRead	Occurs when an attachment is opened.
BeforeAttachment Save	Occurs just before the attachment is saved.
BeforeCheckNames	Occurs just before Outlook resolves the recipients for the item.
Close	Occurs when the Inspector object is shut down.
CustomAction	Occurs when a custom action is executed.
CustomProperty Change	Occurs when one of the custom properties for the item is changed.
Forward	Occurs when the item is forwarded.
Open	Occurs when the item is opened in an Inspector.
PropertyChange	Occurs when one of the non-custom properties is changed.
Read	Occurs when the item is opened for editing.

Table Continued on Following Page

Name	Description
Reply	Occurs when the Reply action is executed on the item.
ReplyAll	Occurs when the ReplyAll action is executed on the item.
Send	Occurs when the item is sent.
Write	Occurs when the Save or SaveAs method is executed on the item.

TaskRequestUpdateItem

Methods

Name	Returns	Description
Close(SaveMode)		Causes the Inspector object for the item to be closed. The SaveMode parameter specifies whether changes to the item will be saved or discarded, and may be one of the OlInspectorClose constants.
Copy	TaskRequest UpdateItem object	Creates and returns an identical TaskRequestUpdateItem object.
Delete		Deletes the current item.
Display ([Modal])		Causes the Inspector object for the item to be opened. The Modal parameter specifies whether the window is to be opened modally (True) or modelessly (False). The default is False.
GetAssociated Task (AddToTask List)	TaskItem object	Returns a reference to the associated TaskItem. The parameter indicates whether the item is to added to default tasks folder.
Move(DestFldr)		Moves the current item to the new MAPIFolder, DestFldr.
PrintOut		Prints the item using the printer's default settings.
Save		Saves the item to the current folder for an existing item or to the default folder for a newly created item.

Name	Returns	Description
SaveAs(Path, [Type])		Saves the current item to the hard drive with the path and filename specified in the Path parameter. The type of file the item is to be saved as may be specified in the Type parameter, which may be one of the OlSaveAsType constants.

Properties

Name	Returns	Description
Actions	Actions collection	Returns an Actions collection of the available Action objects for the item. Read-only.
Application	Application object	Returns the parent application of the object. Read-only.
Attachments	Attachments collection	Returns a collection of the attachments associated with the item. Read-only.
Billing Information	String	Contains a free-form string that can be used to hold the billing information associated with the item. Read/write.
Body	String	A free-form string containing the body of the item. Setting this causes the EditorType of the item's Inspector object to revert to default. Read/write.
Categories	String	Specifies the categories that are assigned to the item. Read/write.
Class	OlObject Class constant	Returns a numeric value specifying the class the object belongs to. Read-only.
Companies	String	A free form string containing the company names associated with the item. Read/write.
Conversation Index	String	Returns the index representing the current conversation thread. Read-only.
Conversation Topic	String	Returns the topic for the conversation thread. Read-only.
CreationTime	Date	Returns the date and time at which the item was created. Read-only.
EntryID	String	Returns a unique string identifier for the item. Read-only.

Table Continued on Following Page

Name	Returns	Description
Form Description	Form Description object	Returns the `FormDescription` object for the item. Read-only.
GetInspector	Inspector object	Returns the `Inspector` object for displaying the current item. Read-only.
Importance	OlImportance constant	Specifies the importance level for the item. Read/write.
Last Modification Time	Date	Returns the date and time that the item was last changed. Read-only.
Links	Links collection	Returns a `Links` collection that represents the contacts with which this item is associated. Read-only.
MessageClass	String	Specifies the message class of the item. This property maps you to the form that is associated with the item. Read/write.
Mileage	String	A free-form string which can be used to hold the mileage for the item. Read/write.
NoAging	Boolean	Specifies whether or not the item can be archived. Read/write.
Outlook Internal Version	Long	Returns the build number of the Outlook version used to create the item. Read-only.
Outlook Version	String	Returns the major and minor version number for the Outlook Application used to create the item. For Outlook 2000, this is `"9.0"`. Read-only.
Parent	Object	Returns the object's parent object. Read-only.
Saved	Boolean	Indicates whether the item has changed since it was last saved. Read-only.
Sensitivity	OlSensitivity constant	Specifies the level of sensitivity for the item. Read/write.
Session	NameSpace object	Returns the current `NameSpace` object. Read-only.

Name	Returns	Description
Size	Long	Returns the size of the item in bytes. Read-only.
Subject	String	Contains the subject of the item. Read/write.
UnRead	Boolean	Indicates whether the item is to be marked as "Unread". Read/write.
User Properties	UserProperties collection	Returns the UserProperties collection for the item. Read-only.

Events

Name	Description
AttachmentAdd	Occurs when a new attachment is added to the item.
AttachmentRead	Occurs when an attachment is opened.
BeforeAttachmentSave	Occurs just before the attachment is saved.
BeforeCheckNames	Occurs just before Outlook resolves the recipients for the item.
Close	Occurs when the Inspector object is shut down.
CustomAction	Occurs when a custom action is executed.
CustomPropertyChange	Occurs when one of the custom properties for the item is changed.
Forward	Occurs when the item is forwarded.
Open	Occurs when the item is opened in an Inspector.
PropertyChange	Occurs when one of the non-custom properties is changed.
Read	Occurs when the item is opened for editing.
Reply	Occurs when the Reply action is executed on the item.
ReplyAll	Occurs when the ReplyAll action is executed on the item.
Send	Occurs when the item is sent.
Write	Occurs when the Save or SaveAs method is executed on the item.

UserProperty Object

Method

Name	Returns	Description
Delete		Deletes the current UserProperty object from the UserProperties collection.

Properties

Name	Returns	Description
Application	Application object	Returns the parent application of the object. Read-only.
Class	OlObjectClass constant	Returns a numeric value specifying the class the object belongs to. Read-only.
Formula	String	Specifies the formula for the property. Read/write.
Name	String	The display name for the object. Read-only.
Parent	Object	Returns the object's parent object. Read-only.
Session	NameSpace object	Returns the current NameSpace object. Read-only.
Type	OlUser PropertyType constant	Indicates the data type that the property can hold. Read-only.
Validation Formula	String	A free-form string containing the validation formula for the property. Read/write.
ValidationText	String	The validation text for the property. Read/write.
Value	Variant	Specifies the value for the property. Read/write.

Outlook Constants Reference

OlActionCopyLike Constants

Constant	Value	Description
olReply	0	The new item is sent to the sender only.
olReplyAll	1	The new item is sent to the sender and addressees of the original, and carbon-copied to the recipients who received a CC of the original.
olForward	2	The new item is forwarded to another recipient.
olReplyFolder	3	The new item is posted to a specific folder.
olRespond	4	As olReply, but a message requesting the user to respond is added to the GUI of the original item.

OlActionReplyStyle Constants

Constant	Value	Description
olOpen	0	The item created by the action is opened for editing.
olSend	1	The item created by the action is sent immediately.
olPrompt	2	The user is prompted to open the item, send it immediately or cancel the action.

OlActionResponseStyle Constants

Constant	Value	Description
olOmitOriginalText	0	The original text is not included in the reply.
olEmbedOriginalItem	1	The original item is included in the reply as an attachment.
olIncludeOriginal Text	2	The original text is included in the reply.
olIndentOriginalText	3	The original text is included in the reply and indented.
olLinkOriginalItem	4	A shortcut to the original item is included in the text as an attachment.
olUserPreference	5	The user's default reply style is used.
olReplyTick OriginalText	1000	The original text is included with a greater than sign before each line.

OlActionShowOn Constants

Constant	Value	Description
olDontShow	0	The action appears neither on the menu nor on the toolbar.
olMenu	1	The action appears on the Actions menu only.
olMenuAndToolbar	2	The action appears on the menu and on the toolbar.

OlAttachmentType Constants

Constant	Value	Description
olByValue	1	The attachment is inserted into the item body.
olByReference	4	A shortcut to the attachment is inserted into the item body.
olEmbeddedItem	5	The attachment is an Outlook item.
olOLE	6	The attachment is an OLE object.

OlBusyStatus Constants

Constant	Value	Description
olFree	0	The appointment slot is marked as free.
olTentative	1	The user has tentatively accepted an appointment for that slot.
olBusy	2	The appointment slot is marked as busy.
olOutOfOffice	3	The user is marked as out of office for that slot.

OlDaysOfWeek Constants

Constant	Value	Description
olSunday	1	The appointment/task recurs on a Sunday.
olMonday	2	The appointment/task recurs on a Monday.
olTuesday	4	The appointment/task recurs on a Tuesday.
olWednesday	8	The appointment/task recurs on a Wednesday.
olThursday	16	The appointment/task recurs on a Thursday.
olFriday	32	The appointment/task recurs on a Friday.
olSaturday	64	The appointment/task recurs on a Saturday.

OlDefaultFolders Constants

These constants are used to define the types of MAPIfolder.

Constant	Value	Description
olFolder DeletedItems	3	Represents the **Deleted Items** folder.
olFolder Outbox	4	Represents the **Outbox** folder.
olFolderSent Mail	5	Represents the **Sent Mail** folder.
olFolderInbox	6	Represents the **Inbox** folder.
olFolder Calendar	9	Represents the **Calendar** folder.

Table Continued on Following Page

Constant	Value	Description
olFolder Contacts	10	Represents the Contacts folder.
olFolder Journal	11	Represents the Journal folder.
olFolderNotes	12	Represents the Notes folder.
olFolderTasks	13	Represents the Tasks folder.
olFolder Drafts	16	Represents the Drafts folder.

OlDisplayType Constants

Constant	Value	Description
olUser	0	The recipient is a user.
olDistList	1	The recipient is a distribution list.
olForum	2	The recipient is a forum.
olAgent	3	The recipient is an agent.
olOrganization	4	The recipient is an organization.
olPrivateDist List	5	The recipient is a private distribution list.
olRemoteUser	6	The recipient is a remote user.

OlEditorType Constants

Constant	Value	Description
olEditorText	1	Represents a text editor.
olEditorHTML	2	Represents an HTML editor.
olEditorRTF	3	Represents an RTF editor.
olEditorWord	4	Represents the Microsoft Word editor.

OlFlagStatus Constants

Constant	Value	Description
olNoFlag	0	No flag will be displayed to the recipient.
olFlagComplete	1	The flag request will be marked as completed.

Constant	Value	Description
olFlagMarked	2	The flag request will be displayed to the recipient.

OlFolderDisplayMode Constants

Constant	Value	Description
olFolder DisplayNormal	0	The default display settings will be used.
olFolderDisplay FolderOnly	1	Only the contents of the specific folder will be displayed.
olFolderDisplay NoNavigation	2	The Folder List will not be displayed.

OlFormRegistry Constants

Constant	Value	Description
olDefault Registry	0	The item is handled without regard to its form class.
olPersonal Registry	2	The form is accessible only to the current store user.
olFolder Registry	3	The form is accessible only from a specific folder.
olOrganization Registry	4	The form is accessible to everyone in the organization.

OlGender Constants

Constant	Value	Description
olUnspecified	0	The contact's gender has not been specified.
olFemale	1	The contact is a woman.
olMale	2	The contact is a man.

OlImportance Constants

Constant	Value	Description
olImportanceLow	0	The item is of low importance.

Table Continued on Following Page

Constant	Value	Description
olImportanceNormal	1	The item is of normal importance.
olImportanceHigh	2	The item is of high importance.

OlInspectorClose Constants

Constant	Value	Description
olSave	0	Save any changes unconditionally. If no changes have been made then this has no effect.
olDiscard	1	Close without prompting the user to save, discarding any changes.
olPromptForSave	2	Prompt the user to save or discard any changes.

OlItemType Constants

Constant	Value	Description
olMailItem	0	The item will be a mail message.
olAppointmentItem	1	The item will be an appointment.
olContactItem	2	The item will be a contact.
olTaskItem	3	The item will be a task.
olJournalItem	4	The item will be a journal entry.
olNoteItem	5	The item will be a note.
olPostItem	6	The item will be a post item.
olDistributionList Item	7	The item will be a distribution list.

OlJournalRecipientType Constants

Constant	Value	Description
olAssociatedContact	1	The recipient is an associated contact of a JournalItem.

OIMailingAddress Constants

Constant	Value	Description
olNone	0	The contact has no mailing address set.
olHome	1	The contact's mailing address is the same as the HomeAddress.
olBusiness	2	The contact's mailing address is the same as the BusinessAddress.
olOther	3	The contact's mailing address is the same as the OtherAddress.

OIMailRecipientType Constants

Constant	Value	Description
olOriginator	0	The recipient was the the sender of the original mail item.
olTo	1	The recipient was specified in the To field.
olCC	2	The recipient received a carbon copy of the mail item.
olBCC	3	The recipient received a blind carbon copy of the mail item.

OIMeetingRecipientType Constants

Constant	Value	Description
olOrganizer	0	The recipient is the organizer of the meeting.
olRequired	1	The recipient is a required attendee at the meeting.
olOptional	2	The recipient is an optional attendee of the meeting.
olResource	3	The recipient is a resource of the MeetingItem.

OIMeetingResponse Constants

Constant	Value	Description
olMeeting Tentative	2	The meeting has been tentatively accepted.
olMeeting Accepted	3	The meeting has been accepted.

Constant	Value	Description
olMeeting Declined	4	The meeting has been declined.

OlMeetingStatus Constants

Constant	Value	Description
olNonMeeting	0	This is an appointment only, with no associated meeting.
olMeeting	1	There is a meeting associated with the appointment.
olMeeting Received	3	The meeting request has been received.
olMeeting Canceled	5	The meeting has been canceled.

OlNetMeetingType Constants

Constant	Value	Description
olNetMeeting	0	The online meeting uses Microsoft NetMeeting.
olNetShow	1	The online meeting uses NetShow Services.
olChat	2	The online meeting is a Chat Meeting; this option is not currently supported.

OlNoteColor Constants

Constant	Value	Description
olBlue	0	Blue.
olGreen	1	Green.
olPink	2	Pink.
olWhite	4	White.
olYellow	3	Yellow.

OlObjectClass Constants

Constant	Value	Description
olApplication	0	The object is an Application object.
olNamespace	1	The object is a NameSpace object.
olFolder	2	The object is a MAPIFolder object.
olRecipient	4	The object is a Recipient object.
olAttachment	5	The object is an Attachment object.
olAddressList	7	The object is an AddressList object.
olAddressEntry	8	The object is an AddressEntry object.
olFolders	15	The object is a Folders collection.
olItems	16	The object is an Items collection.
olRecipients	17	The object is a Recipients collection.
olAttachments	18	The object is an Attachments collection.
olAddressLists	20	The object is an AddressLists collection.
olAddress Entries	21	The object is an AddressEntries collection.
olAppointment	26	The object is an AppointmentItem object.
olRecurrence Pattern	28	The object is an RecurrencePattern object.
olExceptions	29	The object is an Exceptions collection.
olException	30	The object is an Exception object.
olAction	32	The object is an Action object.
olActions	33	The object is an Actions collection.
olExplorer	34	The object is an Explorer object.
olInspector	35	The object is an Inspector object.
olPages	36	The object is a Pages collection.
olForm Description	37	The object is a FormDescription object.
olUser Properties	38	The object is a UserProperties collection.

Table Continued on Following Page

Constant	Value	Description
olUserProperty	39	The object is a UserProperty object.
olContact	40	The object is a ContactItem object.
olDocument	41	The object is a DocumentmentItem object.
olJournal	42	The object is a JournalItem object.
olMail	43	The object is a MailItem object.
olNote	44	The object is a NoteItem object.
olPost	45	The object is a PostItem object.
olReport	46	The object is a ReportItem object.
olRemote	47	The object is a RemoteItem object.
olTask	48	The object is a TaskItem object.
olTaskRequest	49	The object is a TaskRequestItem object.
olTaskRequest Update	50	The object is a TaskRequestUpdateItem object.
olTaskRequest Accept	51	The object is a TaskRequestAcceptItem object.
olTaskRequest Decline	52	The object is a TaskRequestDeclineItem object.
olMeeting Request	53	The object is a MeetingItem object which has not yet been answered.
olMeeting Cancellation	54	The object is a canceled MeetingItem object.
olMeeting Response Negative	55	The object is a MeetingItem object which has been declined.
olMeeting Response Positive	56	The object is a MeetingItem object which has been accepted.
olMeeting Response Tentative	57	The object is a MeetingItem object which has been tentatively accepted.
olExplorers	60	The object is an Explorers collection.
olInspectors	61	The object is an Inspectors collection.

Constant	Value	Description
olPanes	62	The object is a Panes collection.
olOutlookBar Pane	63	The object is an OutlookBarPane object.
olOutlookBar Storage	64	The object is an OutlookBarStorage object.
olOutlookBar Groups	65	The object is an OutlookBarGroups collection.
olOutlookBar Group	66	The object is an OutlookBarGroup object.
olOutlookBar Shortcuts	67	The object is an OutlookBarShortcuts collection.
olOutlookBar Shortcut	68	The object is an OutlookBarShortcut object.
olDistribution List	69	The object is a DistListItem object.
olOutlook PropertyPage Site	70	The object is a PropertyPageSite object.
olProperty Pages	71	The object is a PropertyPages collection.
olSyncObject	72	The object is a SyncObject object.
olSyncObjects	73	The object is a SyncObjects collection.
olSelection	74	The object is a Selection collection.
olLink	75	The object is a Link object.
olLinks	76	The object is a Links collection.

OlOutlookBarViewType Constants

Constant	Value	Description
olLargeIcon	0	Specifies large icons for the Outlook Bar.
olSmallIcon	1	Specifies small icons for the Outlook Bar.

OlPane Constants

Constant	Value	Description
olOutlookBar	1	Represents the bar that holds the command bar buttons.
olFolderList	2	Represents the list of folders available to the current session.
olPreview	3	Represents the preview pane which allows you to view the contents items without opening them.

OlRecurrenceState Constants

Constant	Value	Description
olApptNot Recurring	0	The appointment is not recurrent.
olApptMaster	1	The current instance is the original AppointmentItem.
olAppt Occurrence	2	The current instance is a recurrence of the appointment.
olAppt Exception	3	The current instance is an exception to the appointment's recurrence pattern.

OlRecurrenceType Constants

Constant	Value	Description
olRecursDaily	0	The appointment/task recurs every n days.
olRecursWeekly	1	The appointment/task recurs every n weeks.
olRecurs Monthly	2	The appointment/task recurs every n months.
olRecursMonth Nth	3	The appointment/task recurs on the nth day of the week every month.
olRecursYearly	5	The appointment/task recurs every n years.
olRecursYear Nth	6	The appointment/task recurs on the nth day of the week of a given month of the year.

OlRemoteStatus Constants

Constant	Value	Description
olRemoteStatusNone	0	There is no remote status for this item.
olUnMarked	1	The item has not been marked.
olMarkedForDownload	2	Marked to be downloaded when retrieved by Outlook.
olMarkedForCopy	3	Marked to be copied from the server.
olMarkedForDelete	4	Marked to be deleted from the server.

OlResponseStatus Constants

Constant	Value	Description
olResponseNone	0	No invitations to the meeting have been sent.
olResponseOrganized	1	Invitations to the meeting have been sent.
olResponseTentative	2	The meeting request has been tentatively accepted.
olResponseAccepted	3	The meeting request has been accepted.
olResponseDeclined	4	The meeting request has been declined.
olResponseNotResponded	5	No response to the meeting request has been sent.

OlSaveAsType Constants

Constant	Value	Description
olTXT	0	Save as a .txt (Text) file.
olRTF	1	Save as an .rtf (Rich Text Format) file.
olTemplate	2	Save as an Outlook template.
olMSG	3	Save in Outlook message format.
olDoc	4	Save as a Word document.
olHTML	5	Save as an HTML page.
olVCard	6	Save as a vCard (.vcf) file.
olVCal	7	Save as a virtual calendar (.vcs) file.

OlSensitivity Constants

Constant	Value	Description
olNormal	0	The item contains no sensitive information.
olPersonal	1	The item is personal in nature.
olPrivate	2	The item is private in nature.
olConfidential	3	The item is confidential in nature.

OlSortOrder Constants

Constant	Value	Description
olSortNone	0	The sort order is not changed.
olAscending	1	The collection will be sorted in ascending order.
olDescending	2	The collection will be sorted in descending order.

OlSyncState Constants

Constant	Value	Description
olSyncStopped	0	Synchronization has stopped.
olSyncStarted	1	Synchronization has started.

OlTaskDelegationStatus Constants

Constant	Value	Description
olTaskNot Delegated	0	The task request has not yet been delegated.
olTaskDelegation Unknown	1	The delegated recipient has yet to respond to the task request.
olTaskDelegation Accepted	2	The task request has been accepted.
olTaskDelegation Declined	3	The task request has been declined.

OlTaskOwnership Constants

Constant	Value	Description
olNewTask	0	The task is a newly created one.
olDelegatedTask	1	The task has been delegated to another user.
olOwnTask	2	The user is the owner of the task.

OlTaskRecipientType Constants

Constant	Value	Description
olUpdate	2	The recipient receives update reports of the task.
olFinalStatus	3	The recipient receives notification only of the final status of the task.

OlTaskResponse Constants

Constant	Value	Description
olTaskSimple	0	The task has not been delegated.
olTaskAssign	1	The task has been assigned, but the recipient has not yet responded.
olTaskAccept	2	The task has been accepted.
olTaskDecline	3	The task has been declined.

OlTaskStatus Constants

Constant	Value	Description
olTaskNotStarted	0	Work on the task has not yet begun.
olTaskInProgress	1	Work on the task is in progress.
olTaskComplete	2	The task has been completed.
olTaskWaiting	3	The task has been put on hold until more information has been received from a third party.
olTaskDeferred	4	The task has been deferred until a future time.

OlTrackingStatus Constants

Constant	Value	Description
olTrackingNone	0	No tracking was set.
olTracking Delivered	1	The recipient has received the item.
olTrackingNot Delivered	2	The recipient has not yet received the item.
olTrackingNot Read	3	The recipient has not yet read the item.
olTrackingRecall Failure	4	The originator is unable to retrieve the mail message back from the recipient.
olTrackingRecall Success	5	The originator was able to retrieve back from the recipient. If the message is unread and the recall was successful, no evidence of the message being sent remains in the recipient's mailbox.
olTrackingRead	6	The recipient has read the item.
olTrackingReplied	7	The recipient has replied to the item.

OlUserPropertyType Constants

Constant	Value	Description
olText	1	The user property holds text values.
olNumber	3	The user property holds numeric values.
olDateTime	5	The user property holds date/time values.
olYesNo	6	The user property holds Boolean values.
olDuration	7	The user property holds a time interval.
olKeywords	11	The user property holds keywords.
olPercent	12	The user property holds percent values.
olCurrency	14	The user property holds currency values.
olFormula	18	The user property holds formulae.
olCombination	19	The user property holds variant values.

OlWindowState Constants

Constant	Value	Description
olMaximized	0	The window is maximized.
olMinimized	1	The window is minimized.
olNormal	2	The window is neither maximized nor minimized.

Index

Index

Index

WROX PRESS INC.

Wrox writes books for you. Any suggestions, or ideas
about how you want information given in your
ideal book will be studied by our team.
Your comments are always valued at Wrox.

Free phone in USA 800-USE-WROX
Fax (312) 397 8990

UK Tel. (0121) 687 4100   Fax   (0121) 687 4101

NB. If you post the bounce back card below in the UK, please send it to:
Wrox Press Ltd., Arden House, 1102 Warwick Road, Acocks Green, Birmingham. B27 6BH. UK.

253X

Outlook 2000 Programmer's Reference

Name

Address

City   State/Region

Country   Postcode/Zip

E-mail

Occupation

How did you hear about this book?

☐ Book review (name)

☐ Advertisement (name)

☐ Recommendation

☐ Catalog

☐ Other

Where did you buy this book?

☐ Bookstore (name)   City

☐ Computer Store (name)

☐ Mail Order

☐ Other

What influenced you in the
purchase of this book?

☐ Cover Design

☐ Contents

☐ Other (please specify)

What did you find most useful about this book?

What did you find least useful about this book?

Please add any additional comments.

What other subjects will you buy a computer
book on soon?

What is the best computer book you have used this year?

How did you rate the overall
contents of this book?

☐ Excellent   ☐ Good

☐ Average   ☐ Poor

*Note: This information will only be used to keep you updated
about new Wrox Press titles and will not be used for any other
purpose or passed to any other third party.*

Check here if you DO NOT want to receive further support for this book. ■

253X

wrox
PROGRAMMER TO PROGRAMMER™